CHALLENGING BEHAVIOR

of Persons With Mental Health Disorders and Severe Developmental Disabilities

Edited by
Norman A. Wieseler, PhD
Eastern Minnesota Community Support Center
and
Ronald H. Hanson, PhD
Anoka-Metro Regional Treatment Center

Gary Siperstein, PhD
Editor

AAMR

American Association on Mental Retardation

Published by
American Association on Mental Retardation
444 North Capitol Street, NW
Suite 846
Washington, DC 20001-1512

The points of view expressed herein are those of the authors and do not neccessarily represent the official policy or opinion of the American Association on Mental Retardation. Publication does not imply endorsement by the editor, the Association, or its individuals members.

Printed in the United States of America

Library of Congress Cataloging-in-Publication Data

Challenging behavior of persons with mental health disorders and severe developmental disabilities / edited by Norman A. Wieseler and Ronald H. Hanson; Gary Siperstein, editor.

     p. cm.
   Includes bibliographical references.
   ISBN 0-940898-66-7
   1. Mentally handicapped—Mental health.   2. Mentally handicapped—Behavior modification.   3. Self-injurious behavior—Prevention.
I. Wieseler, Norman Anthony. II. Hanson, Ronald Halton. III. Siperstein, Gary N.
RC451.4.M47C486   1999
616.89—dc21   99-33488
                                                   CIP

Contributors

Carol Davis, PhD
University of Minnesota
Minneapolis, MN

Judith E. Favell, PhD
AdvoServ
Mount Dora, FL

Frederick R. Ferron, MD
Southern Cities Community Health Clinic
Faribault, MN

Rachel Freeman, PhD
University of Minnesota
Minneapolis, MN

William I. Gardner, PhD
University of Wisconsin—Madison
Madison, WI

John R. Gates, MD
Minnesota Epilepsy Group, PA, and
University of Minnesota
Minneapolis, MN

Ronald H. Hanson, PhD
Anoka-Metro Regional Treatment Center
Anoka, MN

Jessica Hellings, MD
University of Kansas
Lawrence, KS

Laura Heyser, MA
University of California at San Diego
San Diego, CA

Robert Horner, PhD
University of Oregon
Eugene, OR

Anne DesNoyers Hurley, PhD
Tufts University School of Medicine
Boston, MA

John E. Kalachnik, MEd
University of South Carolina
Columbia, SC

Cynthia A. Kern, RN, PharmD, BCPP
Southern Cities Community Health Clinic
Faribault, MN

Pippa Loupe, PhD
University of Kansas
Lawrence, KS

James F. McGimsey, PhD
AdvoServ
Mount Dora, FL

Raymond G. Miltenberger, PhD
North Dakota State University
Fargo, ND

R. Matthew Reese, PhD
University of Kansas
Lawrence, KS

Joe Reichle, PhD
University of Minnesota
Minneapolis, MN

Laura Schreibman, PhD
University of California at San Diego
San Diego, CA

Stephen R. Schroeder, PhD
University of Kansas
Lawrence, KS

Robert Sovner, MD (Deceased)
Tufts University School of Medicine
Boston, MA

Aubyn Stahmer, PhD
Children's Hospital and Health Center
University of California at San Diego
San Diego, CA

Frank J. Symons, PhD
Frank Porter Graham Child Development Center
University of North Carolina at Chapel Hill
Chapel Hill, NC

R. E. Tessel, PhD
University of Kansas
Lawrence, KS

Travis Thompson, PhD
John F. Kennedy Center
Peabody College
Vanderbilt University
Nashville, TN

Norman A. Wieseler, PhD
Eastern Minnesota Community Support Services
Faribault, MN

Penny Willmering, PhD
University of Wisconsin—Madison
Madison, WI

Contents

TABLES

FIGURES

Introduction

Norman A. Wieseler
Eastern Minnesota Community Support Services
Faribault, Minnesota

Ronald H. Hanson
Anoka-Metro Regional
Treatment Center
Anoka, Minnesota

The diagnosis and treatment of persons with severe intellectual disabilities who have mental health disorders, often manifested by challenging behavior, have been a source of frustration and great concern for many practitioners, service providers, and caregivers. One source for this feeling of inadequacy stems from a lack of current information concerning dual disorders. What is known about state of the art assessment and treatment has not been widely disseminated to direct service providers. Knowledge of effective interventions for disorders in this population is a pressing need. Comprehensive treatment to address destructive behavior and other behavioral challenges was identified by the National Institute of Health (1989) Consensus Development Conference as a critical topic for focused scientific investigation.

This edited volume helps address the pressing need by describing the current and emerging practices in the treatment and diagnosis of mental health disorders in persons with severe developmental disabilities, especially when disturbed patterns of behavior are evident. Keeping pace with the latest developments in psychiatric and behavioral disorders is an arduous task for scholars and academicians, let alone clinicians whose days are filled with unpredictable and perplexing behavioral emergencies while caring for this vulnerable population. This volume provides a valuable compendium concerning the identification of dual disorders and information about empirically tested interventions.

This book is intended for practitioners and care providers who are not extensively trained in the principles of behavioral psychology or neuropharmacology. This is an emerging subspecialty. The information contained in this text will assist interdisciplinary team members in designing comprehensive individual treatment plans. There are three parts to the book.

Part 1: Mental Health Disorders

Part 1 describes the major mental health disorders experienced by persons with severe developmental disabilities. In these first five chapters, the continuum of mental heath disturbances and their behavioral sequelae are reviewed. Specific individual chapters are devoted to mood disorders, autism, and self-injury. These topics are highlighted as they are prevalent and refractory to treatment. Traditional psychotherapeutic approaches have only limited impact in addressing these disorders.

Psychiatric diagnosis in persons with severe mental retardation is the subject of the first chapter. The authors, Frederick Ferron, Cynthia Kern, Ronald Hanson, and Norman Wieseler, begin with a succinct discussion important to the differential diagnosis of persons with mental illness and mental retardation. In the past, psychiatric involvement in the field of mental retardation has been sorely limited. The authors discuss the reasons for the absence, the importance of a therapeutic alliance, and the manner in which a psychiatric diagnosis is established or ruled-out.

In Chapter 2, William Gardner and Penny Willmering present a lucid discussion of mood disorders in persons with severe and profound mental retardation. As the authors lament, the prevailing historical attitude within the mental health community had been that mood disorders in persons with intellectual disabilities were unlikely. They present the Multimodal Contextual Behavior Analytic Model which directs the diagnostician to evaluate mood disorders as possible contributors to the nonspecific behavioral symptoms.

In Chapter 3, Laura Schreibman, Laura Heyser, and Aubyn Stahmer recount what is known about autism and the differential diagnosis criteria portrayed in the *Diagnostic and Statistical Manual of Mental Disorders* (4th ed.) (*DSM–IV*; American Psychiatric Association, 1994). The implications and options of specialized treatment for this condition enlighten those providing care for these individuals. As the authors stress, it is critically important that treatment procedures are individualized based upon the response to the complex considerations reviewed in this chapter.

In Chapter 4, Stephen Schroeder, R. Matthew Reese, Jessica Hellings, Pippa Loupe, and R. E. Tessel present their comprehensive discussion of the causes of self-injury and the clinical implications. This provocative chapter explores the question of why persons with severe developmental disabilities display severe, and at times life-threatening, self-injury. The challenge in identifying the relative contributions from biological and environmental factors is confronted. The authors conclude that recent advances in the diagnosis and treatment of self-injury have resulted in significant clinical efficacy. Although the authors note that considerably more knowledge is needed about this devastating disorder, humane and effective treatments are available for the majority of clients with severe mental retardation.

In Chapter 5, Robert Sovner and Anne DesNoyers Hurley critically dispel five mythical conceptions concerning the mental illness of clients with developmental disabilities. Many of these myths are codified in federal and state regulations and have had a profound influence on professional practice. The absence of psychiatric disorders in this population was based on past misconceptions assuming these individuals were immune to mental illness. The authors stress that state-of-the-art psychiatric care is required for individuals with intellectual disabilities.

Part 2: Pharmacotherapy

Part 2 of the text discusses pharmacotherapy which is often the first-line treatment for mental health disorders. In Chapter 6, Cynthia Kern provides a comprehensive overview of pharmacotherapy to treat the mental and behavioral disturbances of persons with severe developmental disabilities. The author confronts the difficult issue of prescribing a psychoactive agent when an accurate diagnosis is greatly complicated. Considerations of behavioral symptoms, history of the effects of previous psychotropic medications, family history of mental health disorders, and collateral information from caregivers are important points to consider when selecting a chemical agent and determining whether a medication is clinically warranted.

The topic of Chapter 7, the adverse behavioral effects of antiepileptic medications, is a prominent issue in the treatment for clients with severe developmental disabilities since many of these agents produce behavior changes mimicking mental illness symptoms. The author, John Gates, describes the behavioral effects of many of the commonly prescribed antiepileptic medications. He concludes that all of the antiepileptic medicines should be carefully considered given their possible adverse behavioral effects. Care providers must be aware of this dilemma to avoid the inappropriate administration of psychotropic drugs or the implementation of unnecessary behavior management programs.

In Chapter 8, Travis Thompson and Frank Symons deliver a thought-provoking discussion concerning destructive behavior and psychotropic medication use within the context of a functional model. Framed within a functional diagnostic approach, psychotropic medication selection is based upon the results of the functional assessment. The authors cogently argue that the pattern of consequences (i.e., reinforcement schedules) directly affects the action of medications. The understanding of the behavioral mechanisms of psychotropic agent action remains a challenge for practitioners and service providers who treat individuals with mental heath disorders and severe developmental disabilities.

In Chapter 9, John Kalachnik offers a comprehensive review of psychotropic medication monitoring. Within the deinstitutionalization movement, the author cautions that psychotropic medication misuse in small community-based residential facilities may increase. He reviews and discusses the core concepts of medication monitoring. Kalachnik advocates the "biopsychosocial model" in which the biological, psychological, and sociological aspects of care are interdependent and each is considered to ensure optimal client care. Specific monitoring methods are presented.

Part 3: Behavioral Strategies

Part 3 provides four chapters espousing behavioral strategies that have proven successful in ameliorating challenging behaviors. These disorders have historically only been mildly assisted by traditional insight-oriented psychotherapy.

In Chapter 10, Norman Wieseler and Ronald Hanson expose the false dichotomy that exists between challenging behaviors and mental health disorders. Emotional distress and mental health disorders are likely to affect both antecedent and consequent behavioral features. The identification of mental health disorders in clients functioning in the severe/profound range of intellectual disability presents a difficult challenge. The authors stress the importance of the multidisciplinary approach in serving clients with challenging behaviors and the importance of considering mental health disorders in treatment planning.

In Chapter 11, Raymond Miltenberger discusses mental health disorders in persons with severe disabilities as problem behaviors affected by reinforcement contingencies derived from a functional assessment. He articulates the components and alternative methods of conducting this assessment. An essential value of the functional assessment is to replace the challenging behavior with an alternative response possessing the same reinforcing properties as the problem behavior. The alternate behavior needs to be functionally equivalent. Information from a variety of sources results in a solid basis for hypothesizing the reinforcement contingencies that can aid the selection of meaningful treatments.

In Chapter 12, Joe Reichle, Carol Davis, Rachel Freeman, and Robert Horner generate a treatment-oriented discussion of how effective positive behavioral support is provided for persons with challenging behaviors and severe developmental disabilities. Effective behavioral support espouses a positive, antecedent-based approach to teaching functionally equivalent alternatives to the problem behaviors often displayed by clients with mental health disorders and severe mental retardation. It emphasizes the importance of a careful systematic review and modification of the physical environment in reducing the possibility of destructive behavior.

In the final chapter, Judith Favell and James McGimsey integrate the considerations in designing effective treatment for persons with severe developmental disabilities and mental health disorders. As the authors advocate, even though the behavior challenges are confounded by a mental disturbance, the application of fundamental principles of behavior remain the essential substrate for effective treatment. The design and utilization of effective treatment strategies consist of interlocking treatment options individually designed for specific clients. The basic components implemented in treatment designs are clearly described.

Summary

This text contains treatment-oriented information that will assist both clinicians and care providers. It provides topics to enable sophisticated treatment decisions. The amelioration of the challenging behavior alone is not sufficient when evaluating treatment effectiveness. Broader-based lifestyle changes such as the client's living arrangement, work, leisure activities, and relationships with others are also critical measures of treatment responsiveness. These measures of social validity are the significant outcomes. It is hoped this book will enhance the lives of persons with mental health disorders and severe intellectual disabilities.

REFERENCES

American Psychiatric Association. (1994). *Diagnostic and statistical manual of mental disorders* (4th ed.). Washington, DC: Author.

National Institutes of Health. (1989, September 11-13). *Treatment of destructive behaviors in persons with developmental disabilities* (Consensus development conference statement). Bethesda, MD: Author.

PART ONE

Mental Health Disorders

Psychiatric Diagnosis in Mental Retardation

Frederick R. Ferron
Cynthia A. Kern
Southern Cities Community Health Clinic
Faribault, Minnesota

Ronald H. Hanson
Anoka-Metro Regional Treatment Center
Anoka, Minnesota

Norman A. Wieseler
Eastern Minnesota Community Support Services
Faribault, Minnesota

Differential Diagnosis

Historically, the diagnosis of mental health disorders in people with severe mental retardation has been uncommon. There has been a perception that the effects of retardation are so devastating that these individuals would not likely experience emotional disturbances. Many of the aberrant response patterns displayed by people with severe mental retardation were perceived as typical problem behaviors unrelated to an emotional disturbance. This negation or ignoring of mental illness in individuals with developmental disabilities has been termed "diagnostic overshadowing" (Reiss, Levitan, & Szyszko, 1982). Pharmacotherapy has generally been restricted to neuroleptics, frequently in high doses (Gualtieri, 1991). Until the 1980s, psychiatric disturbances were either unrecognized or devalued in people with developmental disabilities.

Psychiatric evaluations of individuals with mental retardation have not generally occurred for a variety of reasons:

1. Traditional psychiatric methods of diagnosis have not been a significant help for individuals with mental retardation (Sovner, 1986).

2. The client with severe developmental disabilities is unable to vocally provide a useful history, often an important factor in making a psychiatric diagnosis.

3. Significant stigma has been associated with psychiatric diagnoses, and continues to be; thus, treatment teams have been and are discouraged from suggesting the need for psychiatric involvement.

4. Few psychiatrists are trained or experienced in treating individuals with severe mental retardation (Matson, 1988a).

The *Diagnostic and Statistical Manual of Mental Disorders* (4th ed.)*(DSM-IV;* American Psychiatric Association, 1994), the diagnostic nosology for the field of psychiatry, offers several descriptions of mental health disorders without suggesting treatment madalities. It does, however, acknowledge the scope of the problem: "Individuals with Mental Retardation have a prevalence of comorbid mental disorders that is estimated to be three to four times greater than in the general population" (p. 42).

Recently King and his colleagues (King, DeAntonio, McCracken, Forness, & Ackerland, 1994) reported, as others have (e.g., Costello, 1982; Menolascino, 1988; Reiss, 1993), that it is possible to make psychiatric diagnoses of individuals with severe and profound mental retardation and that psychiatric disorders are common with this population. The authors underscored the importance of psychiatric involvement in the multidisciplinary assessment and treatment of individuals with retardation.

The psychiatric evaluation can be divided into four distinct components, as shown in Table 1.1

The Importance of Therapeutic Alliance

The psychiatric examination evaluates the client's appearance, behavioral symptoms, perceptual symptoms, and cognition. It is accomplished through informal observation by the psychiatrist and includes the history provided by caregivers who accompany the client. The examination also includes formal assessment using such instruments as portions of the *Folstein "Mini-Mental State"* examination (Folstein, Folstein, & McHugh, 1975), the *Reiss Screen for Maladaptive Behavior* (Reiss, 1988), the *PIMRA (Psychopathology in Mentally Retarded Adults*; Matson, 1988b), and the DASH II (Diagnostic Assessment for the Severely Handicapped, II; Matson, Gardner, Coe, & Sovner, 1991). Recording the scores on these instruments on multiple visits may help the clinician with serial estimations of symptomatology. Not all of the instruments need be completed in the course of every psychiatric evaluation on every client. The amount of time available often precludes completing every category, and the skilled clinician will be able to structure the important elements of the mental status examination as believed necessary based on information gathered during the interview.

Individuals accompanying the client may include family or guardian, day program staff, residential program staff, friends, and advocates for the client, as well as others. The more severe the impairment, the more important collateral care-provider observations become. In caring for this client population, it is most important that input from other interdisciplinary team members be sought. Frequently, observations by those involved are of para-

TABLE 1.1

The Four Components of the Psychiatric Evaluation

I. The Psychiatric History
  A. Chief Complaint
  B. History of Present Illness
  C. Past Psychiatric History
  D. Family and Social History
  E. Past Medical History
    1. Histories of surgeries or medical illnesses
    2. Results of most recent medical examination
    3. Review of other pertinent medical information including medications the client takes

II. The Mental Status Exam
  A. Appearance
  B. Mood
  C. Thought Process
  D. Thought Content
  E. Cognition
    1. Orientation
    2. Fund of Information
    3. Memory
    4. Judgment
    5. Insight

III. Multiaxial Diagnosis Using *DSM-IV*
  Axis I.   Clinical Disorders; Other Conditions That May Be a Focus of Clinical Attention
  Axis II. Personality Disorders; Mental Retardation
  Axis III. General Medical Conditions
  Axis IV. Psychosocial and Environmental Problems
  Axis V. Global Assessment Functioning

IV. The Treatment Plan
  A. Social and Environmental Factors
  B. Psychopharmacologic Approaches
  C. Behavioral Approaches

mount importance in reaching a psychiatric diagnosis and further developing the treatment plan. One of the most important elements of the psychiatric evaluation is lost when the client cannot provide a personal history; hence, other sources of information must be sought. In this context, therapeutic alliance, the ability of the client's caregivers and the physician to work together for the best benefit to the client, becomes very important.

The Psychiatric History

Chief Complaint

It is useful to record the client's statement about why he or she is coming for a psychiatric evaluation. If the client cannot communicate vocally or through an alternative or augmentative communication system, the practitioner should look to those care providers accompanying the client to articulate the individual's chief concern. It is important for the care providers to furnish details as to the reason for the visit.

History of Present Illness

Once the reason for psychiatric evaluation has been determined, information as to when the symptoms began, how long they have lasted, and how the symptoms relate to issues that will be more fully discussed in the mental status examination are obtained. If there are related medical complications, these should be listed in the history of present illness as well.

Past Psychiatric History

It is important to determine whether the client has had past psychiatric diagnoses and treatment plans. If there have been hospitalizations, the dates and reasons for hospitalizations will provide important information. If the client has taken psychotropic medications in the past, this should be noted along with the effectiveness of these medications. It is also important to determine if the client has been in individual psychotherapy, group therapy, or other structured psychosocial programs.

Family and Social History

The psychiatrist inquires about the client's family to determine past history of psychiatric illness, substance abuse and dependence, or other medical problems experienced by the family. Relevant information should be sought concerning the client's siblings, children, parents, aunts, uncles, cousins, and grandparents.

Questions regarding the developmental history (including prenatal history), middle childhood, late childhood, and adolescence are important. The psychiatrist frequently inquires into the client's developmental sexual history and includes questions about possible sexual abuse. Asking the client or caregiver whether or not there have been traumas in the client's life—which can include physical or sexual abuse—may be a way to approach this difficult but important component of the diagnostic evaluation.

Past Medical History

This section includes the date of the client's last physical examination, including blood chemistries and whether or not significant problems were detected. A signed release of information to speak with the client's attending physician or to exchange medical records is usually necessary. Also of importance are histories of surgeries, significant medical illnesses, and reviews of other pertinent medical information including currently prescribed medications. It may be useful to evaluate the client's attitude toward his or her medical problems and the treatment provided by previous health professionals.

The etiology of mental retardation is also important. Often, no etiology can be determined; however, approximately 5% of cases are due to inborn errors of metabolism, 30% due to early alterations of embryonic development, 10% due to pregnancy and perinatal problems, 5% due to general medical conditions acquired in infancy and childhood, and 15% to 20% due to environmental influences and to other mental disorders, such as autism (DSM-IV, 1994).

Mental Status Examination

The Mental Status Exam is as essential to a psychiatrist as the physical examination is to the attending primary care physician (Scheiber, 1988). Its assessment of mental functioning aids the psychiatrist in diagnostic formulation. However, it is important to note that there are few factors in the mental status examination that provide a clear diagnosis of mental disorder in a client with severe mental retardation (Doherty & Szymanski, 1989).

An accurate mental status examination in any setting is a complicated endeavor that draws on the skills of the examiner. Given the complexities of the human brain and resulting thought processes, it is rare that one can definitively conclude what another person is thinking. Diagnoses are made based on available information, but, at the same time, are not an overstatement of the exactness of the conclusions. Making this fine distinction is the challenge.

Other complications arise when a clinician attempts to identify mood stages or the specifics of the client's thought content. For example, in this population, all that can be concluded is a hypothesis of depression present based on the information provided. Likewise, it can only be inferred that thought content disturbances, such as hallucinations or delusions, are present, given the behavioral information presented by the treatment team.

A comprehensive mental status examination (MacKinnon & Yudofsky, 1988; Scheiber, 1988) includes consideration of appearance, mood, thought process, thought content, and cognition.

Appearance

The psychiatrist summarizes the client's presentation, including a description of how alert the client appears to be, the manner in which the client is dressed, motor behavior, and speech.

Mood

Mood can best be described as an emotion that prevails over an extended period of time. Commonly noted moods are happiness, sadness, anger, apathy, and anxiousness. Other moods may include fear and guilt.

In the severely disabled population, it is generally not sufficient to focus only on the vocal report of the client. It is also necessary to obtain collateral information and to study unspoken aspects of the client's emotions. Additional inquiries are made into suicidal ideation, interests and activities, psychomotor activity, agitation, appetite and weight loss, interest in sexual desire, mood swings, compulsive symptoms, and behavior suggestive of hopelessness, helplessness, and worthlessness.

Suicidal ideation or dangerousness to others are topics necessitating significant discussion. (These issues are addressed in more detail in Chapter 2 of this volume).

Thought Process

The form of how a client thinks is scrutinized. Organization and expression of thoughts are observed. The rate of speech and continuity in the client's thoughts are considered. Tangentiality occurs when a client demonstrates irrelevant thinking emanating from the subject matter. *Loose associations* refers to the client's jumping from one subject to another without demonstrating logical connections. It is essential to determine whether the thought processes of the client represent a psychiatric disorder or the poor verbal skills often associated with a severe developmental disability.

Thought Content

This generally refers to delusional beliefs the client expresses which have no basis in reality. They are commonly expressed as persecution, jealousy, guilt, or love.

It is during this part of the Mental Status Examination that perceptual disturbances can be evaluated; that is, is there presence of a hallucination (a distortion that a client experiences for which there are no external stimuli). Hallucinations may be auditory, visual, tactile, gustatory, or olfactory. Evidence of paranoid thinking may also be observed. Paranoia is frequently expressed as suspiciousness and hostility, often with accompanying delusional beliefs of persecution.

Many of the important diagnostic formulations can be established by answers from care providers who accompany the client. This further underscores the importance of the team members attending the evaluation. One of the most difficult diagnoses to make is whether or not psychosis is present. Often the psychiatrist will inquire as to whether the client appears to respond to internal stimuli or respond to voices not present which suggests the client is not functioning within the realm of reality. This distinction is difficult to make with nonverbal clients. It is nonetheless important to inquire about psychotic behavior, as it can greatly affect treatment planning.

Cognition

A variety of elements need to be considered when assessing cognition. Orientation to time, place, person, and situation are evaluated. The level of concentration, memory, and judgment are also appraised. Information regarding the client's apparent impulse control, insight, and fund of information is also sought.

Assessing cognition needs to be accomplished with an awareness of the client's level of functioning. When testing the client's judgment or insight, it is more useful to assess why the client is being psychiatrically evaluated, what the client understands about the interview, and how the client has been performing in his or her environment.

Multiaxial Diagnosis Using *DSM-IV*

In the United States, the *DSM-IV* (1994) has become the standard for diagnostic assessment from which most treatment plans follow. The *DSM-IV* essentially establishes a multiaxial system of diagnosis described below.

Axis I—Clinical Disorders; Other Conditions That May Be a Focus of Clinical Attention: The clinical disorders in Axis I include all the psychiatric disorders except the Personality Disorders; Axis I also excludes Mental Retardation. When a client has more than one Axis I disorder, all need to be reported and the

principal diagnosis should be indicated by listing it first.

Axis II—Personality Disorders; Mental Retardation: This may also be used for noting maladaptive personality features. The level of mental retardation is noted on this axis for every client.

Axis III—General Medical Conditions: This axis pertains to current general medical conditions that may be relevant to the understanding or management of the individual's mental disorder.

Axis IV—Psychosocial and Environmental Problems: This axis is for reporting psychosocial and environmental problems that may affect diagnosis, treatment, and prognosis in mental disorders.

Axis V—Global Assessment of Functioning: This report of the clinician's judgment of the individual's overall level of functioning can be most useful in delineating successful treatment plans. However, it is noteworthy that many practitioners believe that the Social and Occupational Functioning Assessment Scale (SOFAS) may be of greater utility with clients with mental retardation *(DSM-IV,* 1994, p. 760).

To accurately diagnose and participate in treatment decisions for clients with mental retardation, the *DSM-IV* (1994) is essential. The following section reviews the diagnostic categories and offers a meaningful method of conducting diagnostic assessments.

Diagnosis

It is beyond the scope of this chapter to detail the contents of the *DSM-IV.* Nonetheless, to make use of this chapter, it is suggested that clinicians will need to familiarize themselves with the information.

It is also beyond the scope of this chapter to discuss each of the 15 major categories that comprise Axis I; however, a useful distinction can be made by determining whether psychosis is present. One reason this is important is because historically, antipsychotic medications have been frequently used with individuals with mental retardation. Conceptually, gross impairment in reality testing is considered, with or without hallucinations and delusions being present. Disorganized speech and behavior may be prominent as well. If these symptoms are observed, the most likely diagnosis will be one of the following:

1. disorder usually diagnosed in infancy, childhood, or adolescence;

2. delirium, dementia, and amnesia and other cognitive disorders;

3. mental disorders due to a general medical condition;

4. adjustment-related disorders;

5. schizophrenia and other psychotic disorders;

6. mood disorders;

7. dissociative disorders.

Chapters in Part 1 of this book cover the majority of the primary diagnoses often seen in profoundly and severely mentally retarded individuals (see Chapters 2, 3, & 4). Special consideration in this chapter is given to schizophrenia and other psychotic disorders, as well as other anxiety disorders, which are not covered in detail in the other parts of this text.

Characteristic symptoms of schizophrenia include the psychotic symptoms mentioned earlier. These can include delusions, hallucinations, disorganized speech, grossly disorganized or catatonic behavior, or negative symptoms, which include flat affect, lack of speech, and lack of interest in activities. This is a serious and persistent illness that often affects major areas of functioning. Schizophrenia generally is a chronic condition with remission and exacerbation being common, but with a steadily worsening course noted when untreated. Subtypes of schizophrenia include paranoid type, disorganized type, catatonic type, and an undifferentiated type.

The anxiety disorders include panic disorder (with and without agoraphobia), specific phobia, social phobia, obsessive-compulsive disorder, post traumatic stress disorder, acute stress disorder, and generalized anxiety disorder.

Persistent, excessive anxiety and worry are noted in a generalized anxiety disorder. Acute and post traumatic stress disorders include

reexperiencing extremely traumatic events with symptoms of increased arousal and avoidance of stimuli associated with the trauma.

Panic disorder is a common disorder leading to significant morbidity and is frequently misunderstood as a primary cardiovascular, gastrointestinal, or other medical disorder. A panic attack is experienced as a period of time with sudden, intense apprehension, fearfulness, or terror often associated with a feeling of impending doom. Whether or not agoraphobia is present depends on whether there is a significant effort to avoid situations which may bring on an attack. This can be a difficult diagnosis to make in individuals with mental retardation.

Obsessive-compulsive disorder is a combination of obsessive thoughts that cause anxiety and compulsive actions that may at times neutralize the anxiety. This diagnosis is commonly made in individuals with severe and profound mental retardation, likely due to prominent symptoms that often have an obsessive-compulsive quality. However, caution must be used when making this diagnosis. Behaviors frequently described as compulsive may not necessarily cause marked anxiety or distress for the client.

The Treatment Plan

Once a diagnosis is completed, treatment planning is initiated. Psychotropic medications, especially antipsychotic agents, may have use not only in the treatment of schizophrenia, for which they are most often prescribed, but for other disorders including psychotic conditions not otherwise specified, psychosis associated with mood disorders, compulsive disorders, or dissociative disorders. Although pharmacotherapy is very effective in the treatment of psychiatric disorders, behavioral interventions (with or without psychotropic medication) also produce significant improvement.

Psychopharmacotherapy

Significant behavioral symptoms in individuals with severe and profound mental retardation may be effectively treated with drug therapy in combination with other treatment methods.

Many psychiatric diagnoses are highly medication responsive. Treatment, nevertheless, is frequently complex due to multiple psychiatric issues combined with complicating medical conditions. Also, drug response tends to be more unpredictable in this population than in the general citizenry (Arnold, 1993).

As noted by Gabriel (1994), all classes of psychotropic medications have been shown to be useful in treating psychiatric disorders in clients with severe and profound mental retardation. Psychotropic medication classes include antidepressants, mood stabilizers, antipsychotics, anxiolytics, stimulants, and others (e.g., beta-blockers, calcium channel blockers, other antihypertensives, and opiate antagonists). The array of psychotropic medication options should not be restricted because the client has severe or profound mental retardation. The more medication options available, the more opportunities exist for successful treatment of mental disorders. In addition, the newer psychotropic agents may allow for more effective treatment and an improved side-effect profile.

Psychiatric diagnosis is the primary indication for psychotropic medication treatment. Unfortunately, as diagnosis is difficult in clients with severe or profound mental retardation, there is generally either a hypothesis of a specific psychiatric diagnosis or the treatment is based on the functional properties of the behavior disorder (see Chapter 8, for a functional diagnostic approach) which dictates the appropriateness and selection of psychotropic agents.

Treatment Based on the Principles of Behavioral Psychology

Psychological treatment for individuals with severe developmental disabilities is very different from treating clients with well-developed verbal abilities. The lack of verbal skills prevents or impairs both the accurate communication of emotional distress the person experiences and the ability to profit from insight-oriented psychotherapy. The resulting limitations to traditional psychotherapy has motivated practitioners to seek other modalities of treatment.

An empirically validated approach in treating the mental health disorders of individuals with severe mental retardation is behavior analysis. This approach relies on scientifically derived principles to modify the social and physical environment in a manner which motivates and rewards adaptive, functional behaviors and reduces dysfunctional behavior patterns.

In behavior analysis, target behaviors are clearly defined and measured to empirically evaluate individual client treatment effects. For individuals with mental health disorders and severe intellectual disabilities, the target behavior may or may not be directly related to the emotional disturbance. That is, the challenging behavior may be only an indirect indicator of the psychological disturbance and not a clear manifestation of mental illness. However, with some clients, it is directly related. In both situations, the behaviors of concern can generally be altered through changes in antecedent conditions and environmental consequences. An approach utilizing the principles of behavior analysis, regardless of the etiology of the initial disturbance, is frequently very effective in producing the desired behavior change.

The first step in designing a behavior analysis treatment plan is to conduct a functional assessment. This assessment includes an operational definition of the target behavior, the identification of situations in which the target behavior is more and less likely to occur, and a hypothesis concerning the motivational properties of the target behavior (Chapter 11, this volume; O'Neill et al., 1997). Conducting a thorough functional assessment can be a long and arduous process (Carr et al., 1994). It is critical to selecting intervention strategies with a higher likelihood of success (Mace, Lalli, Lalli, & Shea, 1991; Chapter 12, this volume). The development of augmentative and alternative communication often is a vitally important component in replacing the aberrant behavior with socially acceptable alternative responses which share equivalent functional properties (Doss & Riechle, 1991).

No matter how wisely interventions are chosen, they will result in only minimal gains unless a proper treatment environment is established (Favell & McGimsey, 1993). The supportive environment must provide staff who are caring and skilled and have other essential therapeutic attributes, as discussed by Favell and McGimsey (see Chapter 13).

As with most intervention strategies, the principle of the least restrictive alternative is followed. When crisis intervention procedures are essential to protect the client or others, they are only implemented within the context of an overall comprehensive proactive positive approach. At times, a combination of behavioral and psychopharmacologic interventions produces the optimal outcome for the individual client. As the difficult treatment decisions are made, care providers should focus on quality of life issues pertinent to the desires of the individual client.

REFERENCES

American Psychiatric Association. (1994). *Diagnostic and statistical manual of mental disorders* (4th ed.). Washington, DC: Author.

Arnold, L. E. (1993). Clinical pharmacological issues in treating psychiatric disorders of patients with mental retardation. *Annals of Clinical Psychiatry, 5,* 189-197.

Carr, E. G., Levin, L., McConnachie, G., Carlson, J. I., Kemp, D. C., & Smith, C. E. (1994). *Communication-based intervention for problem behavior: A user's guide for producing positive change.* Baltimore: Brookes.

Costello, A. (1982). Assessment and diagnosis of psychopathology. In J. L. Matson & R. P. Barrett (Eds.), *Psychopathology in the mentally retarded* (pp. 37-52). New York: Grune & Stratton.

Doherty, M. B., & Szymanski, L. S. (1989). Severely and profoundly retarded persons: A conceptual framework for assessment and treatment. In I. L. Rubin & A. C. Crocker (Eds.), *Developmental disabilities: Delivery of medical care for children and adults* (pp. 341-348). Philadelphia: Lea & Febiger.

Doss, L. S., & Reichle, J. (1991). Replacing excess behavior with an initial communicative repertoire. In J. Reichle, J. York, & J. Sigafoos (Eds.), *Implementing augmentative and alternative communication* (pp. 215-237). Baltimore: Brookes.

Favell, J. E., & McGimsey, J. F. (1993). Defining an acceptable treatment environment. In R. Van Houten & S. Axelrod (Eds.), *Behavior analysis and treatment* (pp. 25-45). New York: Plenum Press.

Folstein, M. F., Folstein, S. W., & McHugh, P. R. (1975). "Mini-Mental State," A practical method of grading the cognitive state of patients for the clinician. *Journal of Psychiatric Research, 12,* 189-198.

Gabriel, S. R. (1994). The developmentally disabled, psychiatrically impaired client. Proper treatment of dual diagnosis. *Journal of Psychosocial Nursing and Mental Health Services, 32,* 35-39.

Gualtieri, C. T. (1991). TMS: A system for prevention and control. In J. J. Ratey (Ed.), *Mental retardation: Developing pharmacotherapies* (pp. 35-50). Washington, DC: American Psychiatric Press.

King, B. H., DeAntonio, C., McCracken, J. T., Forness, S. R., & Ackerland, V. (1994). Psychiatric consultation in severe and profound mental retardation. *American Journal of Psychiatry, 151,* 1802-1808.

Mace, F. C., Lalli, J. S., Lalli, E. P., & Shea, M. C. (1991). Functional analysis and treatment of aberrant behavior. *Research in Developmental Disabilities, 12,* 155-180.

MacKinnon, R. A., & Yudofsky, S. C. (1988). Outline of the psychiatric history and mental status examination. In J. A. Talbott, R. E. Hales, & S. C. Yudofsky (Eds.), *Textbook of Psychiatry* (pp. 195-199). Washington DC: American Psychiatric Press.

Matson, J. L. (1988a). Balanced treatment and assessment approaches. In J. A. Stark, F. J. Menolascino, M. H. Albarelli, & V. C. Gray (Eds.), *Mental retardation and mental health: Classification, diagnosis, treatment, services* (pp. 197-202). New York: Springer-Verlag.

Matson, J. L. (1988b). *The PIMRA.* Orland Park, IL: International Diagnostic Systems.

Matson, J. L., Gardner, W. I., Coe, D. A., & Sovner, R. (1991). A scale for evaluating emotional disorders in severely and profoundly mentally retarded persons. *British Journal of Psychiatry, 159,* 404-409.

Menolascino, F. J. (1988). Mental illness in the mentally retarded: Diagnostic and treatment issues. In J. A. Stark, F. J. Menolascino, M. H. Albarelli, & V. C. Gray (Eds.), *Mental retardation and mental health: classification, diagnosis, treatment, services* (pp. 109-123). New York: Springer-Verlag.

O'Neill, R. E., Horner, R. H., Albin, R. W., Sprague, J. R., Storey, K., & Newton, J. S. (1997). *Functional assessment and program development for problem behavior: A practical handbook.* New York: Brooks/Cole.

Reiss, S. (1988). *Reiss Screen for Maladaptive Behavior.* Orland Park, IL: International Diagnostic Systems.

Reiss, S. (1993). Assessment of psychopathology in persons with mental retardation. In J. L. Matson & R. B. Barrett (Eds.), *Psychopathology in the mentally retarded* (2nd ed.). Boston: Allyn & Bacon.

Reiss, S., Levitan, G. W., & Szyszko, J. (1982). Emotional disturbance and mental retardation: Diagnostic overshadowing. *American Journal of Mental Deficiency, 86,* 567-574.

Scheiber, S. C. (1988). Psychiatric interview, psychiatric history, and mental status examination. In J. A. Talbott, R. E. Hales, & S. C. Yudofsky (Eds.), *Textbook of Psychiatry* (pp. 163-194). Washington DC: American Psychiatric Press.

Sovner, R. (1986). Limiting factors in the use of *DSM-III* for mentally ill/mentally retarded persons. *Psychopharmacology Bulletin, 22,* 1055-1059.

CHAPTER TWO

Mood Disorders in People With Severe Mental Retardation

William I. Gardner
Penny Willmering
University of Wisconsin
Madison, WI

As late as the 1960s within the mental health community, many believed that mood disorders among persons with significant cognitive and adaptive behavior impairments was inconsistent with explanatory models of etiology. These explanatory models suggested that the language and cognitive features of persons with severe levels of impairment reduced the risk of mood disturbances (Gardner, 1967). As Penrose (1963) explained, commenting on affective disorders among persons with mental retardation:

> In the concepts of Freud, the ego, and consequently the super-ego, is weak in people of sub-normal intelligence. Thus the conscious and unconscious feelings of guilt and unworthiness, characteristic of the affective disorders, engendered by a hypertrophic super-ego, are lessened. (p. 263)

Other writers reasoned in a similar vein that complex verbal skills and a high level of abstract intelligence were required for the development of the guilt reactions presumed to be basic to depressive reactions. Herskovitz and Plesset (1941), as illustration, hypothesized that "patients with low intelligence do not appreciate the factors (taboos, restrictions, training in habit and character formation) which in persons of higher intelligence cause mental conflict" (p. 583).

Although in a minority at that time, some writers expressed a contrary view: that the life experiences of persons with mental retardation did represent fertile grounds for development of affective disturbances. Hutt and Gibby (1958) serve as one example:

> It is likely, due to the persistent dependency needs of the mentally retarded child, a lack of understanding of his problems by the mother, and also because of her emotional reaction to the child's deficiencies, that rejection is more apt to occur in the case of a mentally retarded child than in one of more normal capacities. Because mothers of retarded children may often unconsciously reject such children (and may even separate themselves physically from their children), they may fail to provide adequate or consistent mothering. When such a situation develops, such children are more likely to become depressed. The retarded child is thus more prone to such depressive reactions. (p. 160)

Nonetheless, prevailing practice among mental health clinicians was consistent with the view that occurrence of affective disorders was incompatible with the cognitive limitations of mental retardation. This conceptual view of etiology and the diagnostic bias it engendered influenced other professional activities that contributed to previously reported low rates of mood disorders, namely (a) a lack of interest in developing appropriate diagnostic tools (Reynolds & Baker, 1988) and (b) limited concern with specific training of caregivers and professionals in detecting and diagnosing clinically significant deviations of mood among this clinical population (Menolascino, 1970; Menolascino & McCann, 1983).

Within the last two decades, coinciding with a gradual shift in provision of enlightened mental health services for persons with mental retardation, a substantial increase in interest in identification and treatment of clinically significant disturbances of mood has occurred (Sovner & Hurley, 1983). A plethora of recent reports suggest significantly higher prevalence rates of mood-related disorders than have been previously described (Dosen & Menolascino, 1990; Sovner & Pary, 1993).

This chapter provides formal definitions of depressive and manic disturbances of mood. The definitions are followed by descriptions of various behavioral and biological functioning equivalents of primary diagnostic symptoms among persons with more severe cognitive and adaptive behavior impairments.[1] Treatment models and approaches are the next topic.

Because pharmacological interventions for depression and mania are described in later chapters, attention in this chapter is restricted to a psychosocial model of etiology and treatment of depression. The chapter closes with consideration of the possible influences of features of mood disorders on occurrence of nonspecific behavioral symptoms. A multimodal contextual behavior analytic model is offered as a scheme for integrating psychiatric and psychosocial diagnoses and related interventions for these behavioral symptoms.

Categories of Mood Disorders

Mood disorders, as suggested, represent frequent mental health problems among persons with more severe impairments, especially those disorders reflecting symptoms of depression. Mood refers to a prolonged emotional state, such as depression or euphoria, that pervasively influences the person's experience. The disorders of mood are classified in the *Diagnostic and Statistical Manual of Mental Disorders* (4th ed.) (*DSM-IV*; American Psychiatric Association, 1994) as major depressive (unipolar) disorders and bipolar disorders. The *depressive disorders* are characterized by a period of depressed mood and loss of interest in activities occurring in conjunction with other cognitive, behavioral, and somatic features. The *bipolar disorders* typically involve recurrent episodes of mania, or elevated/euphoric mood, in conjunction with pervasive overactivity and major depression interspersed with periods of normal affective functioning. As the mania phase of the disorder in persons with severe to profound impairments has not been reported to be responsive in a psychotherapeutic manner to psychosocial interventions, attention to this disorder is restricted to definition and procedures of diagnosis (Reudrich, 1993b). The reader is encouraged to refer to Sovner and Pary (1993), Reudrich (1993a, 1993b), and to later chapters on pharmacological interventions in this book for a discussion of the types and usefulness of drug therapies for mania and associated clinical features.

An understanding of depressive symptoms, in contrast, is important because these are reported to occur among more severely impaired individuals; they produce considerable psychological distress, reduce an individual's overall psychosocial and physical functioning, and potentially are responsive to psychosocial interventions (Dosen & Menolascino, 1990; Sovner & Pary, 1993). Additionally, as is observed with the euphoric mood states associated with mania, a depressed or dysphoric mood state may represent a significant contributor to occurrence and severity of a range of disruptive behaviors (e.g., self-injury, physical aggression) frequently present among the more severely impaired (Charlot, Doucette, & Mezzacappa, 1993; Meins, 1995).

---

[1] The reader interested in mood disorders in people with developmental disabilities presenting less severe cognitive impairments should refer to recent works by Dosen and Menolascino (1990), Fletcher and Dosen (1993), and Sovner and Pary (1993).

Barriers to Diagnosis of Mood Disorders

Both diagnosis and related treatment of mood disorders pose unique problems for the clinician who serves persons with mental retardation, especially those who present severe impairments in cognitive and language functioning. A number of writers have expressed concern that, due to these language and cognitive limitations, affective disorders in people with mental retardation may go unidentified and untreated (Reynolds & Baker, 1988; Sovner & Hurley, 1983; Szymanski & Biederman, 1984). Others have been concerned that a person's nonspecific behavioral symptoms reflecting the effects of clinically significant mood deviations may be viewed as resulting solely from psychological or socio-environmental influences (e.g., Gardner, 1996).

Persons with severe and profound cognitive impairments have difficulty describing the affective, cognitive, and physical symptoms associated with disturbances of mood. As a result, the clinician must depend upon either direct observation or reports from informants to identify the critical symptoms reflecting mood disturbances, especially those required for formal *DSM-IV* (1994) diagnoses. For example, depressed mood, a central diagnostic marker, rather than being reported by the person with limited language skills must be inferred from observations such as increased irritability, recurrent episodes of crying, and changes in the person's responsiveness to previously enjoyed events and activities. Changes in biological functions such as appetite and resulting weight changes, sleep patterns, and quality and level of psychomotor activity, rather than being self-reported, must be recorded by others. These biological changes become especially significant markers in people with more severe cognitive impairments because they are readily observable by informants (Pawlarcyck & Beckwith, 1987; Sovner & Pary, 1993).

As noted by Sovner and colleagues, diagnostic clarity is further complicated by differences in the specific nature of the affective symptoms manifested (Sovner & Fogelman, 1996; Sovner & Hurley, 1983; Sovner & Lowry, 1990). Variations in irritability level may be more evident than either the sadness or euphoria typically expressed by people without cognitive impairment. Additionally, these writers suggest that increased irritability influences the frequency and severity of disruptive behaviors. These changes may offer further valuable diagnostic markers. These unique manifestations are described in the following sections, which present depressive and manic symptoms.

Depression: Symptom, Episode, and Disorder

The term *depression* is often used to refer to variations in mood that range from normal to problematic. The term is used at various times to describe (a) a time-limited sad or "down" feeling in response to a disappointment or loss, (b) more intense expressions of dysphoria termed depressive *symptoms*, (c) a cluster of emotional and somatic signs and symptoms labeled as a depressive *episode*, and (d) a depressive or dysthymic *disorder*.

A Time-Limited Sad or "Down" Feeling

The sad or "down" feeling typically represents a response to a disappointment or loss. Predisposing stressful situations, such as physical illness, disruption or termination of a relationship with a valued staff member, or numerous changes in schedules of daily activities, are commonly experienced by people with severe impairments, especially those who live in large congregate environments. Feeling sad, "blue," discouraged, or "down" are normal reactions to these losses and disappointments. Sadness alone or any other single response does not constitute clinical depression as defined in formal diagnostic systems (e.g., *DSM-IV*; 1994). A normal psychological response to a stressful event is characterized as proportionate to the change or loss, and adaptive to the individual in coping with the stressor. These natural responses are generally time-limited in relation to the nature of the stressful events.

Depressive Symptoms

More intense expressions of dysphoria and related changes in somatic and psychosocial functioning represent depressive symptoms.

Depressive symptoms include a broad range of feeling, cognitive, and behavioral responses. Many of these symptoms normally are experienced with such exceptionally stressful events as bereavement after the death of a parent, abrupt loss of a valued care provider through employment termination or change, or disappearance of a highly valued roommate through discharge from a residential facility. Clinical concern is warranted when the duration of the depressive symptoms is prolonged. Depressive symptoms, as defined in the *DSM-IV* (1994), include the primary features of (a) a dysphoric or irritable mood and/or (b) a markedly diminished interest or pleasure in most or almost all activities.

These dysphoric or irritable mood state features may be associated with a combination of the following:

1. significant weight loss or gain;

2. insomnia or hypersomnia;

3. psychomotor agitation or retardation;

4. fatigue or loss of energy;

5. feelings of worthlessness or excessive guilt;

6. diminished ability to become or remain involved in an activity requiring concentration;

7. recurrent thoughts of death.

Depressive Episode

A cluster of emotional and somatic signs and symptoms comprises a depressive episode. A major depressive episode is diagnosed when the individual experiences during 2 consecutive weeks at least five of the above symptoms with one of the two primary features and these symptoms represent change from previous functioning (*DSM-IV*; 1994). This diagnosis involves a collection of symptoms that are out of proportion in intensity or duration to particular stressors and thus interfere with the individual's overall functioning.

Depressive Disorder

The diagnosis of major depressive disorder is made whenever the criteria for one or more major depressive episodes are met in the absence of any of the following that could account for the symptoms or represent other

mental disorders: (a) mood disorder due to a general medical condition, (b) substance-induced mood disorder, (c) dysthymic disorder, (d) schizoaffective disorder, (e) mood features associated with schizophrenia, (f) bereavement, or (g) a previous manic or hypomanic episode (*DSM-IV*; 1994).

Dysthymic Disorder

A dysthymic disorder, in contrast to a major depressive disorder, is a chronic condition characterized by a sad, "down-in-the-dumps," or depressed mood most of the day, more days than not, for at least 2 years (irritable mood for a minimum 1-year duration for children and adolescents). The depressed mood is accompanied by at least two of the following: problems involving appetite, sleep patterns, energy level, concentration, and low self-esteem/feelings of hopelessness (*DSM-IV*, 1994).

Summary

This series of descriptors denotes the variation of individual responses along a continuum ranging from mild sadness in response to loss or disappointment to prolonged periods of dysphoric mood and significant changes in behavioral, somatic, and cognitive features. Given the presence of a negative mood state, an individual's relative position on the continuum is distinguished by factors such as the particular predisposing situation and the resulting type, range, intensity, and duration of symptoms.

Behavioral Equivalents of Depressive Symptoms

Because the presence of severe to profound mental retardation often makes it difficult to detect these classic criteria, symptoms of depression typically are detected through close attention to various behavioral equivalents. These behavioral equivalents are changes from previous levels of functioning or status and are not a result of other current biomedical or psychosocial influences. Menolascino, Levitas, and Gilson (1986), Menolascino and Weiler (1990), and Sovner and colleagues (Sovner & Hurley, 1982; Sovner & Lowry, 1990) have offered the following descriptions.

Depressed Mood, Irritability, Agitation

Rarely or never smiles; sad expression; cries easily; tearful for no apparent reason; easily annoyed, provoked, or angered with increased difficulty in tolerating usual aggravations or disruptions in routine; easily provoked to disruptive outbursts; if verbal, may repeatedly express desire to return to a previous residential setting.

Decreased Interest/Pleasure

Usual activities are refused; typical events serving as reinforcers lose their effectiveness; apathetic; social withdrawal; spends excessive time alone; minimal response to environmental stimuli; minimal eye contact; rarely initiates activity or interactions.

Self-Care Skills

Toileting and grooming skills may deteriorate; in cases of severe loss of interest and withdrawal, may soil self, become incontinent, and lose interest in grooming such as bathing and changing clothing.

Cognitive performance

Lowered performance in programs such as work activities; increased difficulty in maintaining attention to tasks, even routines; appears confused in attempts to complete routines requiring concentration, focus, and span of attention.

Sleep Patterns

Hypersomnia: sleep becomes a preferred activity; gets upset when attempts are made to awake and direct into usually preferred activities; takes excessive naps during the day. Insomnia: reduction in number of hours spent in sleep during night; difficulty falling asleep; repeatedly awakes in middle of night; awakes one or more hours before time to get up and then remains awake for rest of the day; may present new or more severe behavior problems at bedtime, during night, or early hours.

Weight/Appetite

Increase: significant weight gain (5% body weight over 1 month); if free access to food is not available, may begin, or increase in frequency of, food stealing and pica. Decrease: significant weight loss (5% weight body weight over 1 month); decreased food intake; rejects favorite food; resists prompts to attend or complete meals.

Psychomotor Retardation/Low Energy

Remains in one location with minimal motor activity for lengthy periods of time; passive; rarely initiates activity or interactions; spends excessive time lying or sitting; may actively resist activities; may present catatonic signs; extremely slow body movements; stops talking/communicating.

Feelings of Worthlessness

In person with verbal skills, uses derogatory labels to describe self, "I'm retarded," "I'm ugly," "I'm bad."

Excessive Concern for Death and Self-Harm

In person with verbal skills, excessive expression of concern over death of family or friends, funerals, or dying; in more severely impaired, suicidal ideation may take the form of increased fearfulness, clinging dependency, mimicry of a suicidal act, or drawings suggestive of death and burial; threatens or attempts to harm self.

Nonspecific Behavioral Symptoms

Occurrence/increased occurrence and severity, or occurrence in new settings, of various behavior problems such as aggression, self-injury, and tantrums out of proportion to social or environmental changes or events; repeated complaints of aches, pains, or physical ailments.

Mania: Symptom, Episode, and Disorder

Manic Symptoms

The central symptom in mania is a distinct period of abnormally and persistently elevated, expansive, or irritable mood. Related symptoms include inflated self-esteem or grandiosity, decreased need for sleep, increased talkativeness, flights of ideas or subjective experience that thoughts are racing, distractibility, psychomotor agitation or increased goal-directed activity (may be social, work, school, or sexual), and excessive involvement in pleasurable activities that have high likelihood of painful consequences.

Manic Episode

A manic episode refers to a period of persistent and abnormally elevated, expansive, or irritable mood lasting a minimum of 1 week (less if hospitalization is required). Additionally, this abnormal mood occurs in the presence of at least three of the above symptoms of mania (four symptoms if the mood is only irritable). Further, the mood disturbance must be sufficiently severe to produce marked impairment in the person's functioning (*DSM-IV*; 1994).

Hypomanic Episode

A hypomanic episode refers to a period of abnormally and persistently elevated, expansive, or irritable mood for at least a 4-day period occurring in combination with at least three of the above manic symptoms. If an irritable mood is present, at least four of the symptoms of mania must be present. The mood must be different from the person's usual demeanor, accompanied by a clear change in functioning, and not due to the direct physiological effects of a substance or a general medical condition (*DSM-IV*; 1994).

Mixed Episode

A mixed episode diagnosis is present whenever the symptom patterns for both a manic episode and a major depressive episode are present for at least 1 week. The person experiences rapidly alternating moods of sadness, irritability, and euphoria along with the symptom patterns of both conditions (*DSM-IV*; 1994).

Bipolar I Disorder

A diagnosis of bipolar I disorder is made whenever the criteria of a single manic episode are met in the absence of a history of major depressive episodes. Additionally the manic episode is not the result of a schizoaffective disorder and is not superimposed on schizophrenia, schizophreniform disorder, delusional disorder, or psychotic disorder not otherwise specified (*DSM-IV*; 1994).

Bipolar II Disorder

A diagnosis of bipolar II disorder (recurrent major depressive episodes with hypomanic episodes) is made on occurrence or history of one or more major depressive episodes accompanied by at least one (or history of) hypomanic episode. A history of a manic or mixed episode precludes the biopolar II disorder. Further, the mood symptoms are not better accounted for by a schizoaffective disorder or not superimposed on schizophrenia, schizophreniform disorder, delusional disorder, or psychotic disorder not otherwise specified (*DSM-IV*; 1994).

Rapid Cycling Bipolar Disorder

A specifier of *rapid-cycling* can be applied to either a bipolar I disorder or a bipolar II disorder whenever at least four episodes of a mood disturbance occur within a 12-month period that meet criteria for a major depressive, manic, mixed, or hypomanic episode. Additionally, episodes must be separated either by a period of full remission or by a change to an episode of opposite polarity.

Cyclothymic Disorder

Cyclothymic disorder is a chronic (2 years for adults and 1 year for children and adolescents) fluctuating mood disturbance involving periods of hypomanic symptoms and periods of depressive symptoms. The mood symptoms are of insufficient number, severity, pervasiveness, or duration to meet the criteria for either a manic or depressive episode (*DSM-IV*; 1994).

Behavioral Equivalents of Mania

Presence of these behavioral equivalents reflect changes from previous levels of functioning or status and are not a result of other current biomedical or psychosocial influences. The listed equivalents have been identified by Menolascino et al. (1986), Menolascino and Weiler (1990), and Sovner and colleagues (Sovner & Hurley, 1982; Sovner & Lowry, 1990).

Euphoric/Elated/Irritable Mood

Appears boisterous, excited; easily provoked to disruptive outbursts; periods of acute and excessive anger.

Inflated Self-Esteem/Grandiosity

Has unrealistic notions of own skill; views self as peer of staff members or bosses.

Sleep

Decrease in total sleep time; behavior problems occur at night when prompted to go to and remain in bed.

Speech

Pressured speech; increased rate of verbalizations/babbling; nonstop vocalizations/does not seem to be able to stop.

Cognitive

Flights of ideas; racing thoughts; jumps from one topic to another in a frenzied manner.

Attention Span/Focus

Distractibility; unable to stay on task when other activities are occurring.

Psychomotor Activity Level

Psychomotor agitation; seems wired; unable to stop an activity.

Interests/Pleasure

Excessive involvement in pleasurable activities; masturbates excessively or at inappropriate locations/times; sexually provocative; excessive provocative teasing; persistently requests reinforcers.

Self-Care Skills

Loss of skills; may become incontinent of urine and feces during day or night; decrease in daily living skills.

Nonspecific Behavioral Symptom

Occurrence or increased occurrence and severity or occurrence in new settings of various behavior problems such as aggression, self-injury, and tantrums that are out of proportion to social or environmental changes or events; repeated complaints of aches, pains, or physical ailments.

Diagnostic Protocols for Detection of Mood Disorders

As noted earlier, in view of the limited verbal and other cognitive skills of people with severe and profound mental retardation, the usual assessment procedures involving clinical interviews and self-report measures have limited utility. Clinical contact during which attempts are made to get the person engaged in various activities may reveal some impressions about affective responsiveness (Dosen & Gielen, 1993). However, such impressions must be supplemented with diagnostic information obtained through interviews with others who have knowledge of the person's affective, social, and problem behavioral responsiveness through frequent daily contact. This informant information may be supplemented further by direct observation of the person being assessed in selected residential, leisure, work, and related settings and conditions (Love & Matson, 1990; Reiss, 1993). Additionally, some clinicians have found value in direct measurement or frequent staff affective behavior ratings, following operational definitions, of *DSM-IV* (1994) symptoms of depression. Graphic display of these objective somatic and behavioral data has been shown to reveal relationships that become diagnostically significant (Lowry, 1993; Lowry & Sovner, 1992; Sovner & Lowry, 1990; Wieseler, Campbell, & Sonis, 1988).

Structured interviews with informants, rating scales, and checklists of potential value in identification of mood disorder symptoms include the *Aberrant Behavior Checklist* (Aman & Singh, 1987), Children's Depression Inventory (Meins, 1993), Emotional Disorders Rating Scale for Developmental Disabilities (Feinstein, Kaminer, Barrett, & Tylenda, 1988), Diagnostic Assessment for the Severely Handicapped (*DASH*; Matson, Coe, Gardner, & Sovner, 1991; Matson, Gardner, Coe, & Sovner, 1991), *Psychopathology Instrument for Mentally Retarded Adults* (Matson, Kazdin, & Senatore, 1984), *Reiss Scales for Children's Dual Diagnosis* (Reiss & Valenti-Hein, 1990), and the *Reiss Screen for Maladaptive Behavior* (Reiss, 1988). These assessment protocols may indicate the presence of various symptoms and symptom clusters, information that is of value in arriving at a formal diagnosis of a specific mood disorder.

Usefulness of Diagnostic Information

Identification of the cluster of symptoms that defines a mood disorder is useful in providing direction to treatment selection. Specific treatment evolves from two major models of etiology, generally termed the *biomedical* or *illness model* and the *psychosocial model*. The biomedical or illness model uses pharmaco-therapy as treatment for both manic and depressive symptoms under the assumption that these symptoms reflect biochemical abnormalities. A differential diagnosis of specific mood disorders is critical to the selection of medications found useful in reducing or eliminating both the somatic and psychological symptoms reflecting different psychiatric illnesses or disorders (e.g., Fletcher & Dosen, 1993; Sovner & Hurley, 1985; Sovner & Pary, 1993). This medication selection process is described in subsequent chapters on psychopharmacology.

In contrast to this biomedical approach to etiology and treatment, various versions of a psychosocial approach to understanding and modifying depressive symptoms emphasize experiential influences as critical in the onset and continuation of depressive symptoms. Psychosocial approaches to treatment, regard-less of the specific theoretical paradigm used, attempt to directly influence the person's affective, behavioral, and cognitive features by changing current experiences (Dosen & Petry, 1993; Hurley & Sovner, 1991). The psychosocial model, as noted by a number of writers (e.g., Beckham, 1990; Free & Oei, 1989; Lewinsohn, Hoberman, Teri, & Hautzinger, 1985; Young, Beck, & Weinberger, 1993), should not be viewed as a competing theory of depression. Rather, each model represents a different focus of analysis and intervention. The biomedically oriented therapist intervenes at the biochemi-cal level and the psychosocial therapist intervenes at the behavioral, affective, and cognitive levels. Just as changes in the person's biochemistry facilitate behavioral, affective, and cognitive changes, a circular process model would assume that changes in psychological features resulting from psychosocial therapy would also facilitate changes in the biochemis-try of major depression (Free & Oei, 1989).

Unequivocal support for and elucidation of the mechanism and magnitude of change, however, await further experimental clarification.

Integrative Psychosocial Model of Depression in People With Severe Mental Retardation

The following represents a modification of a general integrative theory offered by Lewinsohn et al. (1985) to account for the development of unipolar depression in the general population. The model views the occurrence of depression as a product of both environmental events and personal vulnerabil-ity features. The vulnerability features, as noted below, become highly significant for people with severe impairments because of their characteristically impoverished repertoires of language, social, motivational, and coping personal features. Modifications have been made in the Lewinsohn et al. (1985) theoretical account to reflect these impaired cognitive and related repertoires of people with severe mental retardation.

In this model, the symptom cluster defining a depressive episode represents the culmination of changes in behavior, affect, and cognition precipitated by environmental or situational events. As later illustrated in case studies, such stressors as acute or chronic physical illness, commonly observed in people with severe cognitive impairments, may serve as a risk or vulnerability factor that increases the likelihood of depressive symptoms when the stressor results in or occurs in combination with other losses of a psychological nature.

Onset Instigating Conditions

The depressogenic process begins with stressors or life events that serve as onset instigating conditions. For people with severe impairments, these stressors may represent a wide range of events or changes but may be somewhat idiosyncratic, as the personal meaning of any type of loss is specific to an individual. A stressor may be highly significant to a person but appears mundane or minor to an observer. However, due to the frequently restricted or impoverished life structure of many people with severe impairments, seemingly minor losses may have considerable psychological meaning to such a person, who may also lack alternative skills in accommodating the losses.

Although depression has not been studied systematically in people with severe cognitive impairments, Ghaziuddin, Alessi, and Greden (1995) provide some preliminary information concerning the types of losses that precede occurrence of depression in this group. These clinical researchers identified the types of life events occurring within 12 months prior to the onset of depression in children with pervasive developmental disorders. The depressive symptoms consisted of a clear history of increasing social withdrawal, loss of interest in activities, frequent crying spells, and disturbance of sleep and appetite. Unpleasant life events representing social factors and environmental stressors that preceded depression included changes in group homes, change of education programs, parental marital discord, family sickness, and bereavement. As is evident, some of these are acute stressors and others involve chronic adversity. These findings are consistent with those reported previously by Ghaziuddin (1988) and Stack, Haldipur, and Thompson (1987).

In reviewing published reports of depression in people with more severe impairments, Sovner and Pary (1993) also found illness or death of a family member implicated as a precipitating influence. Other writers have suggested that people with mental retardation respond in an exaggerated manner to apparently commonplace life experiences that in turn may result in a degree of disorganization and hopelessness (Menolascino & McCann, 1983; Sovner, 1986). Cochran, Sran, and Varano (1977) provide an example in their description of the reactions of some residents following transfer from a large residential care facility, in which they had lived for extended periods of time, to a smaller, unfamiliar regional center. Some people with severe cognitive impairment "became profoundly depressed, refused to eat, lost weight, and wept a great deal" (p. 10). As not all people showed these symptoms of depression, the writers suggested that people who had a history of some degree of emotional

instability or lability were likely to be affected most by residential relocation.

A brief case study illustrates more specifically the kinds of stressors that represent onset conditions in a person with profound mental retardation:

> *Ms. Susan G, living in a large community residential facility, was referred for mental health consultation with the following concerns: refuses to attend program, poor appetite, resists attendance at meals, isolates self in her room, displays minimal interaction with others, cries easily if staff are persistent in attempting to get her involved in program activities, refuses community outings, changes in grooming, looks sad. Each concern represented a distinct change from a previous level of functioning. During the interview, staff indicated that Ms. G had been socially outgoing, seldom missed vocational and leisure programs and seemed to enjoy them, demonstrated pride in her grooming, and had been eager to attend community outings. The depressogenic process apparently began with a chronic and serious gum and tooth infection that required prolonged hospitalization and surgery. Additionally, on return from the hospital, she found that her roommate and close friend of many years had been transferred during her absence to a community group home in another city. Staff had assumed that her initial emotional flatness and related behavior changes were reflections of her physical illness. Careful evaluation of these changes and their persistence after surgery led to the conclusion that, while the physical illness produced chronic aversive events and represented a significant vulnerability influence, the major life event initiating the depressogenic process was the traumatic loss of her roommate.*

Immediate Disruptive Effects

These antecedent life events are of significance to the extent that they "disrupt substantial important and relatively automatic behavior patterns" (Lewinsohn et al., 1985, p. 344). For Ms. G, the abrupt loss of her roommate of many years resulted in significant disruption in her daily life. Ms. G had been the dominant person in this relationship and typically assisted her physically impaired roommate in her morning grooming routine. Following this, she accompanied her companion to breakfast, sat at the same table during the meal, and then walked with her, typically arm-in-arm, as they returned to their living area. Although the program schedule during the day found them in different locations and activities, they were inseparable during unscheduled time. They were quite protective of each other and seldom interacted with other peers unless in structured program and prompted by staff to do so. Suddenly, numerous routine and scripted behavior patterns became nonfunctional. Predictable and expected valued daily patterned behaviors were no longer possible.

Reduction in Positive Reinforcers

This disruption creates a loss of meaningful reinforcers and reduction in positive affective experiences. Interactions with the environment become balanced in a negative direction. This loss of meaningful reinforcers is especially significant for people with severe impairments who have a limited number of alternative behavior patterns that consistently provide predictable and valuable positive consequences. Ms. G, for example, continued to reside in an environment containing numerous cues for following her routines (e.g., room, time, residential facility, program schedule, leisure time) that previously had resulted in emotionally valuable interactions, but now was without her significant other with whom to relate. These multitude of cues were triggers for scripted behaviors that could not be consummated. Although another roommate was moved into the room, Ms. G had neither the motivation nor the social skills to establish a relationship with her. She quickly isolated herself.

Emotional Consequences

This disruption of patterned behaviors and the loss of valued reinforcers result in an immediate negative emotional reaction, the intensity and pervasiveness of which is related to the importance of the loss to the person, the availability of alternative sources of valued reinforcement, and the person's skills in obtaining these. Loss of a roommate through community placement may be of minor significance to one person residing in a congregate facility if that individual can spend quality time with and obtain positive experiences from a range of other peers and staff. A similar loss for another person may represent a major disruption of scripted or frequently occurring positive social interactions and thus is more likely to produce significant emotional distress. Such was the case with Ms. G. She had minimal generalized social skills and showed no inclination to relate to others or to get involved in alternative activities that would foster new friends who in turn could offer positive interpersonal/emotional relationships. Her loss represented a major traumatic event with significant distressful and disruptive emotional consequences. As suggested in the later section on treatment, such skill and motivational limitations call for aggressive therapeutic intervention at this early stage in the depressogenic process to ensure timely replacement of the lost interpersonal and activity sources of emotionally meaningful reinforcers.

As noted in a prospective longitudinal study by Lewinsohn and Hoberman (1982), the mere frequency of pleasant or unpleasant events in a person's life does not predict the later occurrence of depression. Rather, the aversiveness of unpleasant events and the number of major stressors represent the best predictor of depressive onset. Again, for people with severe impairments, limited coping skills, a relatively impoverished motivational structure, and a limited number of valued personal relationships, such seemingly minor stressors as short-term hospitalization for dental surgery, separation from a roommate, or removal from a familiar environment with a structured predictable routine may represent macrostressors, especially if these occur in juxtaposition.

Turning Inward

Following limited or unsuccessful attempts to gain replacements for the losses or to reduce the stressors, the person begins to focus excessively on the current state of emotional distress produced by the loss or change. This excessive self-focus on internal distress interferes with alternative attempts to gain environmentally based experiences that will replace the loss of reinforcers. This results in intensification of the distressing dysphoric affective reactions. With increasing focus on the internal state of unpleasant emotional arousal, the person tends to become less able and less motivated to attempt to regain meaningful scripted behaviors or to develop new ones that will provide sources of valued positive experiences. The person thus increasingly withdraws from social and program participation (work, leisure, chores, activities of daily living) and exerts less effort and persistence at any endeavor. A downward cycle is perpetuated, and a more pervasive dysphoric mood state results. As the limited cognitive and associated internal speech of people with a severe cognitive impairment restrict the complexity and frequency of verbal ruminations about the loss experienced, as observed in people with higher skills, the prevailing influence of self-focus becomes the dysphoric mood state. The person's actions thus become unduly influenced by this internal state of distress.

Appearance of Multiple Depressive Symptoms

The pervasive dysphoric state and the resulting self-focus on the internal distress result in a range of behavioral, affective, somatic, cognitive, and interpersonal characteristics described earlier as defining a depressive episode. The self-focus and dysphoria reduce the person's social competency and render the person less attractive to others, further perpetuating the social isolation and dysphoria. A state of irritability or exaggerated need for emotional support evolves. As the person becomes more isolated or disruptive and demanding, even interactions with caregivers become increasingly negative. This was observed by Schloss (1982) in his study of adults residing in a large residential facility and diagnosed as displaying major depressive symptoms. More negative interactions with peers and staff were observed than among matched peers without depressive symptoms.

Excessively dysphoric or irritable mood correlates with regression in basic self-care and bodily functions, as illustrated in the following vignette:

When observed initially in a small residential facility, 14-year-old Diane was sitting in her bed crying and resisting all prompts by staff to dress and attend the noon meal. Staff reported that this severely cognitively impaired adolescent had recently begun to refuse to dress, use the toilet, go to meals, or attend her scheduled programs without staff escort. Interviews indicated that these behaviors represented distinct changes from a few weeks earlier when Diane was independent in fulfilling basic care skills on prompting from staff and routinely attended scheduled programs, even though she had no close peer friends and was quite dependent on staff for structuring her day. The depressogenic process apparently began when one of her parents had become seriously ill and required extended hospitalization while visiting relatives in Europe. This prolonged absence disrupted a long-standing pattern of weekend trips with her parents away from the residential facility. These highly valued visits were abruptly terminated. Even though she was informed of her parent's illness, she either did not understand or was emotionally unable to accept the loss. Diane was quite vulnerable to adverse emotional effects due to her major dependency on her parents and their weekly visits. She had developed only superficial relationships with peers and staff and had acquired only minimal social skills for developing and sustaining alternative ones that would serve as meaningful substitutes during this period of separation from her parents.

Vulnerability Influences

This case vignette, like the story of Ms. G, emphasizes that personal and environmental characteristics influence the type and magnitude of effects of life events as stressors. Such predisposing personal and socioenvironmental characteristics may serve as moderator variables that either increase (function as vulnerabilities) or decrease (function as immunities) the risk of a depressive episode following exposure to stressful life events (Lewinsohn et al., 1985). In both vignettes, personal characteristics reflecting previous experiences served as vulnerability influences. Other people exposed to similar life events may respond quite differently based on different personal characteristics. In fact, some personal characteristics and socioenvironmental conditions may serve as immunities and render an individual unlikely to develop a depressive response following stressful life events.

A number of personal characteristics of people with more severe cognitive impairments may serve as significant vulnerability influences for development of depression. A myriad of biomedical abnormalities increase the likelihood of aberrant emotional responsiveness (Sovner & Fogelman, 1996). Aberrant psychological histories that include such experiences as rejection, restricted opportunities, segregation, inadequate social supports, victimization, and infantilization are not uncommon in people with more severe cognitive impairments. Such personal features as learned helplessness, limited behavioral repertoires, limited skills of coping with negative emotional distress, and an aberrant motivational structure may reflect the effects of the damaging histories. Additionally, current socioenvironmental factors such as lack of or inconsistent social supports and limited access to a range of reinforcing events and associated emotionally enhancing experiences are vulnerability influences. In these settings, stressful life events can lead to intense emo-

tional consequences when individuals lack the means of gaining valuable alternatives (Dosen & Gielen, 1993; Menolascino & Weiler, 1990; Reiss, 1994; Reiss & Havercamp, 1997). Brief discussion is provided concerning a selected few of these personal features that offer possibilities for psychosocial intervention.

Learned helplessness. Learned helplessness, a term suggested by Maier and Seligman (1976) to refer to a helpless and inactive state produced whenever a person is unable to escape from or avoid punishing conditions, has been identified by Matson (1983) as a possible etiologic influence in depression among people with cognitive impairment. The experiences of many individuals with severe impairments, especially of those with lengthy placement in institutional settings, are consistent with the development of a general characteristic of learned helplessness. This depressive nonresponsiveness in the presence of aversive experiences is attributed to the person's learning that his or her behavior cannot influence the occurrence of aversive events. Failure of the person to effectively reduce the aversiveness of one set of environmental events may promote a generalized helplessness in the face of a variety of noxious conditions. Individuals with a history of uncontrollable aversive experiences may behave passively in the face of new and diverse aversive contexts even though a response is available that would alter or remove the noxious stimulus (Maier & Seligman, 1976).

Learned helplessness may be compounded by the general dependency observed in many people with severe impairments. This often is created by an oversolicitous social environment that provides excessive support when the individual tries but fails (Koegel & Koegel, 1988). These writers suggest that the person learns that responding and reinforcement are not related and future responding becomes lethargic.

Social and coping skill deficits. Limitations in the range and complexity of interpersonal and other socially related skills such as those involving leisure and work as well as skills of effectively coping with unfamiliar and emotionally laden incidents are inherent in the definition of severe and profound mental retardation. It is evident, nonetheless, that people within this group vary considerably in such skills and in their vulnerability to depressive responding. Limited social skills, excessive attachment and dependency on a small number of significant others, activities and objects, and limited leisure and work skills that restrict opportunities for obtaining significant sources of positive feedback all serve as significant psychosocial vulnerabilities.

Benson, Reiss, Smith, and Laman (1985) and Laman and Reiss (1987) found that social skill deficiencies correlated with depressed mood in people with mental retardation. Individuals with depressed moods were described both as withdrawn in their social interactions and as inappropriate and ineffective in interactions that did occur. As noted earlier, Schloss (1982) reported similar observations. Although the people included in these studies were mildly cognitively impaired, these findings do support the supposition that limited and ineffective social skills represent distinct vulnerabilities for development and persistence of a depressed mood.

Limited range of affective attachments.

Clinical observations suggest that the life experiences of people with severe and profound mental retardation are not conducive to development of affective attachments to a range of different people. All too frequently, when attachments are developed, these become excessively valuable to the person, with the result that a debilitating dependency develops. This feature places the person at high risk for depressive responding upon loss of these objects of attachment. The person has limited replacement alternatives and thus is without sources of valued emotional support. This was illustrated by the vignettes presented earlier.

Observations also suggest that some people with severe disabilities may become emotionally blunted after a series of losses involving valued peers or caregivers and excessively cautious in developing further personal attachments. Losses or changes are not experienced as aversive as the person remains emotionally detached. Although this could be viewed as a protective psychological immunity

to development of depression following loss, such generalized detachment obviously would not be viewed as a healthy coping mechanism.

Emotional lability and generalized irritability.

Emotional lability related either to a pathological psychological history (Dosen & Gielen, 1993) or to neurological and neurochemical abnormalities (Sovner & Fogelman, 1996) may represent a further vulnerability for development of depression following loss or significant change. Sovner and Fogelman (1996) suggest that a person with severe and profound impairments may present generalized irritability. Even minor sources of provocation or loss may result in exaggerated affective and behavioral reactions. One could speculate that major losses would be even more emotionally disruptive. Without skills to cope or calm, the person would be increasingly likely to be excessively influenced in daily activities by the internal distress produced by losses. This observation is consistent with that reported by Cochran et al. (1977) of a correlation between development of depressive symptoms following residential relocation and a history of emotional lability and instability.

Additional motivational limitations.

The life experiences of people with severe and profound cognitive impairments frequently result in a highly constricted motivational structure. Due to limited exposure, the person does not learn to value a variety of activities and objects. The person is prone to become excessively dependent upon a limited number of reinforcers and may appear to be insatiable relative to these (Reiss & Havercamp, 1997). When these are lost or greatly restricted, the person becomes vulnerable to depressive responding due to the lack of responsiveness to alternative sources of reinforcement.

Implications for Treatment

Treatment of depression from a psychosocial perspective entails two major objectives. Therapeutic efforts initially address the current depressive symptoms with the objective of reducing or eliminating these as a means of returning the person to the level of functioning present prior to the current episode. The second objective involves therapeutic efforts to reduce the psychosocial vulnerabilities that place the person at continued risk for future development of depressive symptoms. Prior to brief discussion of psychosocial treatment, the reader is reminded that these approaches may coexist with pharmacological interventions. As indicated earlier, the biomedical and psychosocial treatment paradigms address different factors presumed to contribute to the development, severity, and duration of depressive symptoms. It is evident, however, that drug treatment may alleviate depressive symptoms but does not change the underlying pathophysiology or psychological and environmental vulnerabilities responsible for the disorder. As psychosocial therapies are designed to teach new coping strategies and to change other critical personal and socioenvironmental vulnerability features, they offer unique opportunities for increasing a person's immunities that should mitigate the impact of future psychological losses or disappointments.

Although limited, there is a growing clinical literature on psychosocial treatment of depression in people with mental retardation (e.g., Dosen, 1990; Hurley, 1989; Hurley & Sovner, 1991; Matson, 1982, 1983; Matson, Dettling, & Senatore, 1981). These writers, with the exception of Dosen (1990), who describes approaches based on developmental and various psychodynamic theories, report on interventions derived mostly from those cognitive, cognitive-behavioral, and behavioral approaches found useful in treatment of unipolar depression in people without mental retardation (Beckham, 1990; Free & Oei, 1989). Due to the limited cognitive resources of those with severe and profound mental retardation, these language-based procedures have had only limited applicability to this group. Psychosocial treatment thus must supplement verbally based procedures with those that more directly influence new behavioral routines offering valuable emotional experiences. These will replace the dysphoric mood state and related behavioral and somatic symptoms.

Although space does not permit suitable elaboration, the integrative model would suggest the following types of treatment strategies for meeting the initial therapy objective of regaining the predepression functional status:

1. Whenever possible, prepare the person for major change or loss when these can be anticipated. Develop substitute or alternative personal relationships and routines that will be available on occurrence of the loss or change.

   If such preparation is not possible or if ineffective, intervene as early as possible in the depressogenic process. Identify the loss(es) that the person has experienced, the resulting behavioral routines that become nonfunctional, and the range and types of interpersonal and activity reinforcing experiences that are lost. Develop alternatives to these valued routines.

2. Provide frequent and consistent emotional support during this grieving and adaptation period. Remove excessive demands and minimize additional aversive experiences. Recall, however, that depressive behaviors attract positive social reinforcement (e.g., sympathy, assurance, physical presence) and may be strengthened if the focus on the depressive behaviors is prolonged. Minimize attention to dependency and helplessness.

3. Concurrently, expose the person to people, activities, and environments that offer suitable replacements. Provide a variety of social stimulation offered by a number of favored caregivers and peers. Expose to social models who predominantly demonstrate positive affective behaviors. Identify activities (e.g., eating out, dancing, bowling) and objects (e.g., pictures, jewelry, miniature cars) that are valuable to the person and make these available. Use the necessary verbal and physical assistance as needed to insure that the person does not withdraw into nonresponsiveness.

   A recent experience with an adult with severe cognitive impairment illustrates this therapeutic approach.

After the sudden death of a retired caregiver who visited him each week, Mr. J began to show a number of depressive symptoms, including sitting for long periods of time in self-imposed isolation from peers and staff. He became increasingly nonresponsive and would begin to cry if urged to interact with others. Staff reported that he enjoyed polka music and would dance with others whenever his friend had accompanied him to dances. After initially refusing to attend a dance at which a polka band was playing, he did attend with considerable physical urging. He initially sat with his head down and refused to acknowledge his peers when they asked him to dance. Eventually, after persistent requests from a favored staff member, he began to dance and smiled as the band leader acknowledged his presence. For the next hour, he actively participated in the festivities. Although on return to his residential area he again detached himself, this experience represented the beginning of a more active involvement in his daily routine. Staff provided frequent positive comments for a range of prosocial behaviors. Independence in fulfilling daily routines was prompted and reinforced even in those instances that required frequent urging and persistence. This approach was followed to encourage a sense of personal competency and worth. Additionally, relationships with a range of peers and caregivers were encouraged to broaden his scripted behaviors as a means of ensuring available replacements in the event that some of these people were no longer available.

Following resolution of a depressive episode, the range of personal and socioenvironmental vulnerabilities present with any specific person would become the focus of longer-term therapeutic endeavors. The specific approaches selected would be determined by the particular constellation of psychosocial risk factors present for that individual. As a brief illustration, the social support network may become the focus of therapeutic intervention for a person with a limited number of significant others who provide opportunities for positive emotional experiences. The negative emotional impact of loss of contact with any one person in this expanded group would be lessened by the immediate availability of others for meaningful personal interactions and support.

Affective Disorders and Disruptive Behavioral Symptoms

A number of writers have described the increased occurrence of aggression, self-injury, and other nonspecific behavioral symptoms in people presenting various mood disorders (e.g., Charlot et al., 1993; Jawed, Krishnan, Prasher, & Corbett, 1993; Meins, 1995; Reiss & Rojahn, 1993). Charlot et al. (1993) reported behavioral symptoms of aggression, self-injury, and property destruction in over two thirds of a group of adults with affective disorders who resided in a large institutional facility; 74% of this group had severe or profound mental retardation.

Jawed et al. (1993) described a clinically significant increase in pica in a young adult with severe mental retardation. Systematic observations revealed difficulties of mood and irritability, appetite changes, sleep disturbance, and an increase in other problem behaviors including self-injury. Following a diagnosis of depression and successful pharmacological treatment, pica became a minimal problem. Withdrawal of drug treatment following remission of the depressive symptoms resulted in recurrence in pica and agitation, both of which were minimized following reinstatement of medication. Meins (1995) reported aggression, self-injury, and property destruction in one third of a group of individuals identified as presenting a disorder of mood. A modified form of the *Children's Depression Inventory* and a follow-up psychiatric evaluation were used in the diagnostic process. One third of the group diagnosed with major depression presented severe mental retardation. Aggression and property destruction was found to occur more frequently in this group than in those classified with mild mental retardation.

As a final example, Reiss and Rojahn (1993) detected symptoms of depression in a large sample of children, adolescents and adults served by community-based agencies. The *Reiss Screen for Maladaptive Behavior* (Reiss, 1988) and *Reiss Scales for Children's Dual Diagnosis* (Reiss & Valenti-Hein, 1990) were used as diagnostic tools. Forty percent of individuals showing significant mood difficulties also demonstrated problems of aggression.

These rates of nonspecific behavioral symptoms are four to six times greater among individuals with clinically significant symptoms of depression than rates reported in large-scale studies of behavior problems among individuals with mental retardation without psychiatric disorders (Rojahn, Borthwick-Duffy, & Jacobson, 1993). In sum, these differential rates suggest that mood disorder symptoms place the person at increased risk for occurrence of these behavioral symptoms.

Current psychiatric or behavior analytic clinical case formulation models do not include constructs that permit the clinician to describe the specific role assumed by these mood symptoms in influencing occurrence of nonspecific behavioral symptoms (Gardner, 1996). Even though some diagnostic models (e.g., Bailey & Pyles, 1989; O'Neill, Horner, Albin, Storey, & Sprague, 1990; Pyles, Muniz, Cade, & Silva, 1997; Sturmey, 1995) identify psychiatric conditions, including mood disorders, as possible contributors to occurrence of nonspecific behavioral symptoms, neither the specific roles served by a mood disorder nor the manner in which features of the disorder may combine with those features of a psychosocial nature to produce the problem behaviors are articulated.

As a result, such questions as the following are left unanswered: In what manner do features of a mood disorder influence occurrence, severity, fluctuation in occurrence and severity, and persistence of nonspecific behavioral symptoms? Does the mood disorder represent a sufficient condition for producing the behavioral symptoms (i.e., does the mood

disorder produce the behavioral symptoms independent of any other current biomedical or psychosocial influences)? If not a sufficient condition, does the mood disorder represent a necessary contributing condition for occurrence of the behavioral symptoms (i.e., does the behavioral symptoms only occur when a mood disorder is present even though other instigating conditions must also be present)? If a contributing influence is present but is neither sufficient nor necessary, what is the nature of this facilitative relationship?

Although the empirical and clinical literatures do report instances in which features of a mood disorder may represent sufficient instigating conditions for nonspecific behavioral symptoms, this relationship is rare. In a review of studies reporting on possible factors influencing self-injurious acts, for example, psychiatric abnormalities were described in most instances as representing *contributing and facilitative,* but neither *sufficient* nor *necessary* conditions for occurrence of this nonspecific behavioral symptom (Gardner & Sovner, 1994).

A diagnostic understanding of the specific effects of various mood disorders on occurrence of nonspecific symptoms as a basis for person-specific treatment selection, as illustrated by Gardner (1998) and Gardner and Sovner (1994), is best accomplished when these symptoms are viewed in a broader *biopsychosocial* context. In the absence of such a broad case formulation model, there is danger that the mood disorder may be viewed as causing the problem behavior. As a result the only clinical intervention for the nonspecific symptom may be pharmacological in nature without consideration of other critical factors that may, in combination with features of a mood disorder, comprise an instigating and reinforcing stimulus complex influencing its occurrence and recurrence.

A diagnostic case formulation model that accounts for the occurrence as well as the persistent recurrence of nonspecific behavioral symptoms should thus consider (a) the *complete stimulus complex* that precedes and serves to instigate these symptoms, (b) the person's biopsychosocial *vulnerabilities* or risk factors for engaging in these nonspecific symptoms when confronted with this instigating stimulus complex, as well as (c) those proximate *consequences* that follow behavioral occurrences and may contribute to their *functionality and strength*. As noted below, the instigating stimulus complex may include the arousing/activating features of various components of a mood disorder. In these instances the objective of a comprehensive diagnostic assessment is "to see past" the mood disorder and to ascertain the specific role served by features of this condition in contributing to the *occurrence, severity, fluctuation,* and *chronic recurrence* of the behavioral symptom. In this manner, informed speculation can be made about the extent of reduction in critical features of the nonspecific symptom to be expected following effective treatment of the mood disorder (Gardner & Sovner, 1994).

Multimodal Contextual Behavior Analytic Model

A multimodal (*bio-, psycho-,* and *socioenvironmental* modalities of influences) contextual (contexts of *instigating, vulnerability,* and *maintaining* conditions) behavior analytic model is offered as a representation of this broader diagnostic-treatment case formulation process. It represents an elaboration of a similar model described by Gardner (1996, 1998), Gardner and Sovner (1994), and Gardner and Whalen (1996). This model directs the diagnostician to evaluate mood disorders as possible contributors to occurrence of nonspecific behavioral symptoms. It provides a means of interfacing psychiatric diagnostic insights and related diagnostically based interventions with those addressing other biomedical, psychological, and socioenvironmental influences.

Psychiatric conditions reflecting disorders of moods may contribute to the occurrence and repeated recurrence of nonspecific behavioral symptoms in three different ways. As suggested, psychological concomitants of the disorder may (a) serve an *instigating* role and (b) may render the person *vulnerable* or at *increased risk* to engage in the behavioral symptoms

when exposed to various other instigating conditions. Additionally, occurrence of a nonspecific behavioral symptom may result in changes in the stimulus states created by the mood disorder. These changes may contribute to the *strength* and *functionality* of the behavioral symptoms. As an example of the latter, a nonspecific symptom such as self-injury may represent, for different individuals or for the same person under varying conditions, (a) a functional means of modulating psychological distress resulting from a mood disorder or (b) an attempt to modulate unpleasant emotional discomfort produced by medications used to treat the disorder (Gardner & Sovner, 1994). Thus, a suitable analysis must examine nonspecific symptoms in the three different contexts of instigating, vulnerability, and maintaining conditions.

Context 1: Mood Disorder Features as Instigating Conditions

Instigating conditions represent preceding stimulus events that, when present, influence the occurrence of nonspecific behavioral symptoms. These instigating conditions may serve either (a) a *sufficient* role or (b) a *contributing* role in influencing occurrence of these symptoms.

Sufficient instigating conditions reflecting mood. In some instances, even though infrequent, the sufficient instigating condition for a nonspecific behavioral symptom may represent *internal* psychological conditions associated with a mood disorder. As an example, a person with profound mental retardation and without language skills to communicate his needs, may be provoked to autoaggressive ear slapping by a high level of distress associated with a dysphoric mood. In this example, the internal painful distress serves as a sufficient instigating stimulus condition for the autoaggression independent of any additional provocation from social or physical sources.

Whenever a person's nonspecific behavioral symptoms occur only in the presence of a critical level of discomfort produced by a dysphoric mood, a *state-dependent* relationship is present. In this instance, effective treatment

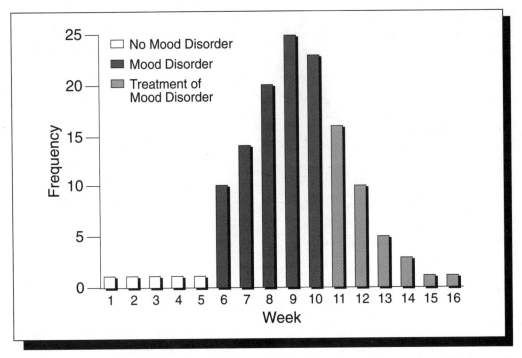

Figure 2.1. Depicting a state-dependent relationship between agitated episodes involving self-injury and features of a mood disorder. Features of the mood disorder serve as sufficient instigating conditions independent of additional sources of provocation.

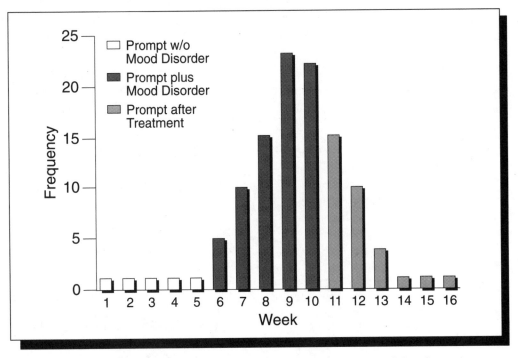

Figure 2.2. Depicting a state-dependent relationship in which features of a mood disorder serve a necessary but not sufficient instigating role. Both features of the mood disorder and social prompts must be present for the behavioral symptom to occur.

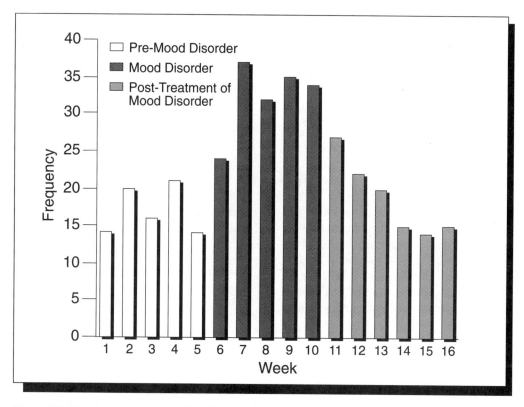

Figure 2.3. Depicting a state-exacerbated relationship between a preexisting nonspecific behavioral symptom and occurrence of a mood disorder. Features of the mood disorder increase the likelihood of occurrence of the behavioral symptom when other instigating conditions are present but are neither sufficient nor necessary conditions of instigation.

of the underlying stimulus condition (e.g., dysphoric mood) should remove or eliminate this instigating aversive internal state and the associated behavioral symptoms. This relationship is depicted in Figure 2.1.

In other instances, a person's behavioral symptoms, such as aggression or self-injury, may *also* be instigated by antecedent stimulus conditions unrelated to features of the person's depression. In this instance, as the behavioral symptoms may occur in the absence of the mood disorder, a state-dependent relationship would not be present; interventions addressing both sets of instigating conditions would be necessary.

Contributing instigating events reflecting mood disorders. In most instances aberrant affective states represent contributing stimulus conditions that, even though in isolation are not sufficient to produce a nonspecific behav-

ioral symptom, do combine with additional conditions of provocation to result in a behavioral symptom (Gardner, Cole, Davidson, & Karan, 1986). The degree of influence of these *contributing* stimulus conditions in producing specific target symptoms may vary from *minor* to *major* in their instigating effects.

Contributing stimulus conditions associated with mood difficulties may also assume a *state-dependent* role in influencing nonspecific behavioral symptoms. In this role, the stimulus features of the mood disorder represent necessary conditions, even though insufficient in isolation, to produce the nonspecific behavioral symptoms. The instigating role of such internal stimulus states as anxiety, irritability, and dysphoria associated with disorders of mood is illustrated in reports of Lowry (1994), Lowry and Sovner (1992), and Sovner, Foxx, Lowry, and Lowry (1993).

These clinicians described the co-occurrence of episodes of nonspecific behavioral symptoms of aggression and autoaggression and various affective states associated with depression or rapid cycling bipolar disorders. In individuals with mental retardation diagnosed with a rapid cycling disorder, occurrence of the behavioral symptoms was dependent on the presence of the psychological state associated with the psychiatric disorder *plus* occurrence of various staff prompts, even though different external prompts served as the instigating events during different phases (depression or mania) of the disorder. During depressive episodes, staff prompts *intended to get the person involved* in an activity produced the problem behavior. During manic episodes, prompts to slow the person down or focus attention produced the behavioral symptom.

These prompts, even though necessary conditions, were not sufficient in the absence of the mood state to instigate the nonspecific behaviors. Both the staff prompts and the mood state formed the stimulus complex that represented the necessary precursors for the nonspecific behavior symptoms. To emphasize, neither was sufficient, independent of the other, to produce the behavioral symptoms.

In this state-dependent role, interventions resulting in removal of either of these contributing and necessary components of the stimulus complex (mood states or the prompts) would effectively manage occurrence of the nonspecific behavior problem. The obvious focus of intervention, nonetheless, would be that of eliminating the aberrant mood states that rendered staff prompts as aversive conditions to be removed or avoided through use of the aggression or autoaggression. Following successful medication treatment of the bipolar disorder and removal of the associated instigating stimulus conditions (i.e., aberrant mood states), reduction or elimination of the nonspecific behavioral symptom would coincide with the concurrent reduction in the aversiveness of staff prompt. This relationship is depicted in Figure 2.2.

Stimulus features of a mood disorder may also serve a contributing role in producing behavioral symptoms in which these features are not necessary precursors. In this *state-exacerbated* relationship, the behavioral symptoms predate the mood disorder and increase in frequency and/or severity on occasion of the disorder. Instigating features of the mood disorder combine with other sources of provocation to increase the frequency and/or intensity of the behavioral symptoms but in isolation are neither necessary nor sufficient to produce these. In this instance, effective treatment of the mood disorder would result in reduction of the nonspecific behavioral symptoms related to the instigating features of the disorder. This relationship is depicted in Figure 2.3.

To summarize, mood disorder features serve various roles as instigating conditions for nonspecific behavioral symptoms. On some occasions, various aberrant stimulus components resulting from the disorder may serve as *contributing* instigating conditions (see Figure 2.3). These stimulus components may occasionally function as *necessary* conditions for occurrence of the behavioral symptoms (see Figure 2.2). However, even in these instances only infrequently can it be assumed that these mood-related stimulus features represent *sufficient* features in isolation from other psychosocial instigating conditions to produce the behavioral symptoms (see Figure 2.1).

That a mood disorder ipso facto is a sufficient condition to produce behavioral symptoms is negated by the observation that even though some people presenting mood disorders may engage in nonspecific behavioral symptoms, others with similar conditions will not. Treatment of a person's mood disorder may indeed be effective in reducing or eliminating the primary symptoms of the disorder but be ineffective in reducing the person's nonspecific behavioral symptoms unless features of these mood disorders do contribute to the stimulus complex producing these behaviors.

Context 2: Vulnerability Influences

A number of personal features associated with mood disorders render a person at risk for engaging in nonspecific behavioral symptoms. The fluctuating intensity of mood states, the mood lability, increased likelihood of physical fatigue associated with sleep disturbances, energy loss associated with eating difficulties, and the aberrant activity levels, as examples, all increase the likelihood of aversive states of psychological distress. When present, these states may either produce nonspecific behavioral symptoms or may increase the likelihood of these behaviors when the person is exposed to other sources of provocation. These combine with a broad array of psychological coping skill deficits to further increase the likelihood of occurrence of nonspecific symptoms (Gardner & Sovner, 1994).

Context 3: Mood Influences on Functionality of Nonspecific Symptoms

Occurrence of nonspecific behavioral symptoms may result in changes in the internal affective states associated with a mood disorder. These changes may contribute to the strength and functionality of the behavioral symptoms. In illustration, responding aggressively may remove a staff directive to attend a scheduled training program rendered aversive by a dysphoric mood state. As a result, aggressive responding is strengthened. Self-injurious face slapping may become functional as it results in frequent personal attention in a person who becomes excessively emotionally needy during periods of sadness. In these instances, the nonspecific behavioral symptoms become more likely under similar instigating conditions as these result in consequences valuable to the person.

Psychiatric and Psychosocial Diagnostic-Treatment Formulations

The multimodal contextual behavior analytic model offers a means of developing a set of integrated diagnostic-treatment formulations that reflect the multiple factors that potentially influence the occurrence and persistence of nonspecific behavioral symptoms. Psychosocial and biomedical interventions based on this comprehensive diagnostic assessment hold promise for addressing the multiple current influences rather than suggesting a single focus of drug treatment directed at the biochemistry of the psychiatric mood disorder (Gardner, 1998; Gardner, Graeber, & Cole, 1996; Gardner & Sovner, 1994).

Summary

Disorders of mood do occur among people with severe and profound mental retardation. A number of behavioral equivalents and diagnostic protocols have been offered by various writers to facilitate identification of these disorders. While use of pharmacological agents represents the major therapeutic intervention for mood disorders among persons with severe impairments, psychosocial interventions offer possible parallel approaches. An integrative psychosocial model of depression is described as a possible paradigm of etiology and treatment. As nonspecific behavioral symptoms such as aggression and self-injury frequently accompany mood disorders, a case formulation process based on a multimodal contextual behavior analysis is offered to account for this coexistence.

REFERENCES

Aman, M. G., & Singh, N. N. (1987). *Aberrant Behavior Checklist manual.* East Aurora, NY: Slosson Educational.

American Psychiatry Association. (1994). *Diagnostic and statistical manual of mental disorders* (4th ed.). Washington, DC: Author.

Bailey, J. S., & Pyles, D. A. (1989). Behavioral diagnostics. In E. Cipani (Ed.), *The treatment of severe behavior disorders: Behavior analysis approaches* (pp. 85–107). Washington, DC: American Association on Mental Retardation.

Beckham, E. E. (1990). Psychotherapy of depression research at a crossroads: Directions for the 1990s. *Clinical Psychology Review, 10,* 207–228.

Benson, B. A., Reiss, S., Smith, D. C., & Laman, D. S. (1985). Psychosocial correlates of depression in mentally retarded adults: II. Poor social skills and difficult life goals. *American Journal of Mental Deficiency, 89,* 657–659.

Charlot, L. R., Doucette, A. C, & Mezzacappa, E. (1993). Affective symptoms of institutionalized adults with mental retardation. *American Journal on Mental Retardation, 98,* 408–416.

Cochran, W. E., Sran, P. K., & Varano, G. A. (1977). The relocation syndrome in mentally retarded individuals. *Mental Retardation, 15,* 10–12.

Dosen, A. (1990). Psychotherapeutic approaches in the treatment of depression in mentally retarded children. In A. Dosen & F. J. Menolascino (Eds.), *Depression in mentally retarded children and adults.* Leiden: Logon.

Dosen, A., & Gielen, J. J. M. (1993). Depression in persons with mental retardation: Assessment and diagnosis. In R. Fletcher & A. Dosen (Eds.), *Mental health aspects of mental retardation* (pp. 70–97). New York: Lexington Books.

Dosen, A., & Menolascino, F. (Eds.). (1990). *Depression in mentally retarded children and adults.* Leiden: Logon.

Dosen, A., & Petry, D. (1993). Treatment of depression in persons with mental retardation. In R. Fletcher & A. Dosen (Eds.), *Mental health aspects of mental retardation* (pp. 242–261). New York: Lexington Books.

Feinstein, C., Kaminer, Y., Barrett, R. P., & Tylenda, B. (1988). The assessment of mood and affect in developmentally disabled children and adolescents: The Emotional Disorders Rating Scale. *Research in Developmental Disabilities, 9,* 109–122.

Fletcher, R., & Dosen A. (Eds.). (1993). *Mental health aspects of mental retardation.* New York: Lexington Books.

Free, M. L., & Oei, T. P. S. (1989). Biological and psychological processes in the treatment and maintenance of depression. *Clinical Psychology Review, 9,* 653–688.

Gardner, W. I. (1967). Occurrence of severe depressive reactions in the mentally retarded. *American Journal of Psychiatry, 124,* 386–388.

Gardner, W. I. (1996). Nonspecific behavioral symptoms in persons with a dual diagnosis: A psychological model for integrating biomedical and psychosocial diagnoses and interventions. *Psychology in Mental Retardation and Developmental Disabilities, 21,* 6–11.

Gardner, W. I. (1998). Initiating the case formulation process. In D. M. Griffiths, W. I. Gardner, & J. A. Nugent (Eds.), *Individual centered behavioral interventions: A multimodal functional approach* (pp. 17–65). Kingston, NY: NADD Press.

Gardner, W. I., Cole, C. L., Davidson, D., & Karan, O. (1986). Reducing aggression in individuals with developmental disabilities: An expanded stimulus control assessment and intervention model. *Education and Training of the Mentally Retarded, 21,* 3–21.

Gardner, W. I., Graeber, J. L., & Cole, C. L. (1996). Behavior therapies: A multimodal diagnostic and intervention model. In J. Jacobson, & J. Mulick (Eds.), *Manual on diagnosis and professional practice in mental retardation* (pp. 355–369). Washington, DC: American Psychological Association.

Gardner, W. I., & Sovner, R. (1994). *Self-injurious behaviors: A multimodal functional approach.* Willow Street, PA: VIDA Publishing.

Gardner, W. I., & Whalen, P. J. (1996). Discussion: A multimodal behavior analytic model for evaluating the effects of medical problems on nonspecific behavioral symptoms in persons with developmental disabilities. *Behavioral Interventions, 11,* 147–161.

Ghaziuddin, M. (1988). Behavior disorders in the mentally handicapped. The role of life events. *British Journal of Psychiatry, 152,* 683–686.

Ghaziuddin, M., Alessi, N., & Greden, J. F. (1995). Life events and depression in children with pervasive developmental disorders. *Journal of Autism and Developmental Disorders, 25,* 495–502.

Herskovitz, H. H., & Plesset, M. R. (1941). Psychoses in adult mental defectives. *Psychiatric Quarterly, 15,* 574–588.

Hurley, A. D. (1989). Behavior therapy for psychiatric disorders in mentally retarded individuals. In R. Fletcher & F. J. Menolascino (Eds.), *Mental retardation and mental illness* (pp. 127–140). Lexington, MA: Lexington Books.

Hurley, A. D., & Sovner, R. (1991). Cognitive behavioral therapy for depression in individuals with developmental disabilities. *The Habilitative Mental Healthcare Newsletter, 10,* 41–47.

Hutt, M. L., & Gibby, R. G. (1958). *The mentally retarded child.* Boston: Allyn & Bacon.

Jawed, S. H., Krishnan, V. H. R., Prasher, V. P., & Corbett, J. A. (1993). Worsening of pica as a symptom of depressive illness in a persons with severe mental handicap. *British Journal of Psychiatry, 162,* 835–837.

Koegel, R. L., & Koegel, L. K. (1988). Generalized responsivity and pivotal behaviors. In R. H. Horner, G. Dunlap, & R. L. Koegel, *Generalization and maintenance* (pp. 41–66). Baltimore: Paul H. Brookes.

Laman, D. S., & Reiss, S. (1987). Social skill deficiencies associated with depressed mood of mentally retarded adults. *American Journal of Mental Deficiency, 92,* 224–229.

Lewinsohn, P. M., & Hoberman, H. M. (1982). Depression. In A. S. Bellack, M. Hersen, & A. E. Kazdin (Eds.), *International handbook of behavior modification and therapy.* NY: Plenum Press.

Lewinsohn, P. M., Hoberman, H. M., Teri, L., & Hautzinger, M. (1985). An integrative theory of depression. In S. Reiss & R. R. Bootzin (Eds.) *Theoretical issues in behavior therapy* (pp. 331–359). New York: Academic Press.

Love, S. R., & Matson, J. L. (1990). Diagnostic instruments for depression in the mentally retarded. In A. Dosen & F. J. Menolascino (Eds.), *Depression in mentally retarded children and adults.* Leiden: Logon.

Lowry, M. A. (1993). A clear link between problem behaviors and mood disorders. *The Habilitative Mental Healthcare Newsletter, 12,* 105–110.

Lowry, M. A. (1994). Functional assessment of problem behaviors associated with mood disorders. *The Habilitative Mental Healthcare Newsletter, 13,* 79–84.

Lowry, M. A., & Sovner, R. (1992). Severe behavior problems associated with rapid cycling bipolar disorder in two adults with profound mental retardation. *Journal of Intellectual Disability Research, 36*, 269–281.

Maier, S. F., & Seligman, M. (1976). Learned helplessness: Theory and evidence. *Journal of Experimental Psychology: General, 105*, 3–46.

Matson, J. L. (1982). The treatment of behavioral characteristics of depression in the mentally retarded. *Behavior Therapy, 13*, 209–218.

Matson, J. L. (1983). Depression in the mentally retarded: Toward a conceptual analysis of diagnosis. *Progress in Behavior Modification, 15*, 39–46.

Matson, J. L., Coe, D. A., Gardner, W. I., & Sovner, R. (1991). A factor analytic study of the Diagnostic Assessment for the Severely Handicapped scale. *Journal of Nervous and Mental Disorders, 179*, 553–557.

Matson, J. L., Dettling, J., & Senatore, V. (1981). Treating depression of a mentally retarded adult. *British Journal of Mental Subnormality, 16*, 86–88.

Matson, J. L., Gardner, W. I., Coe, D. A., & Sovner, R. (1991). A scale for evaluating emotional disorders in severely and profoundly retarded persons. *British Journal of Psychiatry, 159*, 404–409.

Matson, J. L, Kazdin, A., & Senatore, V. (1984). Psychometric properties of the Psychopathology Inventory for Mentally Retarded Adults. *Applied Research in Developmental Disabilities, 5*, 881–889.

Meins, W. (1993). Assessment of depression in mentally retarded adults: Reliability and validity of the Children's Depression Inventory (CDI). *Research in Developmental Disabilities, 14*, 299–312.

Meins, W. (1995). Symptoms of major depression in mentally retarded adults. *Journal of Intellectual Disability Research, 39*, 41–45.

Menolascino, F. J. (Ed.). (1970). *Psychiatric approaches to mental retardation.* New York: Basic Books.

Menolascino, F. J., Levitas, A., & Gilson, S. F. (1986). Issues in the treatment of mentally retarded patients in the community mental health system. *Community Mental Health Journal, 22*, 324–327.

Menolascino, F. J., & McCann, B. M. (Eds.). (1983). *Mental health and mental retardation: Bridging the gap.* Baltimore: University Park Press.

Menolascino, F. J., & Weiler, M. A. (1990). The challenge of depression and suicide in severely mentally retarded adults. In A. Dosen & F. J. Menolascino (Eds.), *Depression in mentally retarded children and adults.* Leiden: Logon.

O'Neill, R. E., Horner, R. H., Albin, R. W., Storey, K., & Sprague, J. R. (1990). *Functional analysis of problem behavior: A practical assessment guide.* Sycamore, IL: Sycamore.

Pawlarcyzk, D., & Beckwith, B. (1987). Depressive symptoms displayed by persons with mental retardation: A review. *Mental Retardation, 1987*, 323–330.

Penrose, L. S. (1963). *The biology of mental defect* (3rd ed.). New York: Grune & Stratton.

Pyles, D. A., Muniz, K., Cade, A., & Silva, R. (1997). A behavioral diagnostic paradigm for integrating behavior-analytic and psycho-pharmacological interventions for people with a dual diagnosis. *Research in Developmental Disabilities, 18*, 185–214.

Reiss, S. (1988). *The Reiss Screen for Maladaptive Behavior test manual.* Worthington, OH: IDS Publishing.

Reiss, S. (1993). Assessment of psychopathology in persons with mental retardation. In J. L Matson & R. P. Barrett (Eds.), *Psychopathology in the mentally retarded* (pp. 17–40). Needham Heights, MA: Allyn & Bacon.

Reiss, S. (1994). *Handbook of challenging behaviors: Mental health aspects of mental retardation.* Worthington, OH: International Diagnostic Systems.

Reiss, S., & Havercamp, S. (1997). The sensitivity theory of aberrant motivation: Why functional analysis is not enough. *American Journal of Mental Retardation, 101,* 553–566.

Reiss, S., & Rojahn, J. H. (1993). Joint occurrence of depression and aggression in children and adults with mental retardation. *Journal of Intellectual Disability Research, 37,* 287–294.

Reiss, S., & Valenti-Hein, D. (1990). *Reiss Scales for Children's Dual Diagnosis: Test manual.* Worthington, OH: IDS Publishing.

Reudrich, S. (1993a). Bipolar mood disorders in persons with mental retardation: Assessment and diagnosis. In R. J. Fletcher & A. Dosen (Eds.), *Mental health aspects of mental retardation: Progress in assessment and treatment* (pp. 111–129). New York: Lexington Books.

Reudrich, S. (1993b). Treatment of bipolar mood disorders in persons with mental retardation. In R. J. Fletcher & A. Dosen (Eds.), *Mental health aspects of mental retardation: Progress in assessment and treatment* (pp. 268–280). New York: Lexington Books.

Reynolds, W., & Baker, J. (1988). Assessment of persons with mental retardation. *American Journal of Mental Retardation, 93,* 93–103.

Rojahn, J. Borthwick-Duffy, S. A., & Jacobson, J. W. (1993). The association between psychiatric diagnoses and severe behavior problems in mental retardation. *Annals of Clinical Psychiatry, 5,* 163–170.

Schloss, P. J. (1982). Verbal interaction patterns of depressed and non-depressed institutionalized mentally retarded adults. *Applied Research in Mental Retardation, 3,* 1–12.

Sovner, R. (1986). Limiting factors in the use of DSM-III criteria with mentally ill/mentally retarded persons. *Psychopharmacology Bulletin, 22,* 1055–1059.

Sovner, R., & Fogelman, S. (1996). Irritability and mental retardation. *Seminars In Clinical Neuropsychiatry, 1,* 105–114.

Sovner, R., Foxx, C. J., Lowry, M. J., & Lowry, M. A. (1993). Fluoxetine treatment of depression and associated self-injury in two adults with mental retardation. *Journal of Intellectual Disability Research, 37,* 301–311.

Sovner, R., & Hurley, A. D. (1982). Diagnosing depression in the mentally retarded. *Psychiatric Aspects of Mental Retardation Reviews, 1,* 1–3.

Sovner, R., & Hurley, A. D. (1983). Do the mentally retarded suffer from affective illness? *Archives of General Psychiatry, 40,* 61–67.

Sovner, R., & Hurley, A. D. (1985). Assessing the quality of psychotropic drug regimens prescribed for mentally retarded persons. *Psychiatric Aspects of Mental Retardation Reviews, 8/9,* 31–38.

Sovner, R., & Lowry, M. A. (1990). A behavioral methodology for diagnosing affective disorders in individuals with mental retardation. *The Habilitative Mental Healthcare Newsletter, 9,* 55–61.

Sovner, R., & Pary, R. J. (1993). Affective disorders in developmentally disabled persons. In J. L. Matson & R. P. Barrett (Eds.), *Psychopathology in the mentally retarded* (2nd ed., pp. 87–147). Needham Heights, MA: Allyn & Bacon.

Stack, L. S., Haldipur, C. V., & Thompson, M. (1987). Stressful life events and psychiatric hospitalization of mentally retarded patients. *American Journal of Psychiatry, 144,* 661–663.

Sturmey, P. (1995). Diagnostic-based pharmacological treatment of behavior disorders
in persons with developmental disabilities:
A review and a decision-making typology.
Research in Developmental Disabilities, 16,
235–252.

Szymanski, L. S., & Biederman, J. (1984).
Depression and anorexia nervosa of
persons with Down syndrome. American
Journal of Mental Deficiency, 89, 246–251.

Wieseler, N. A., Campbell, G. J., & Sonis, W.
(1988). Ongoing use of an affective rating
scale in the treatment of a mentally
retarded individual with a rapid-cycling
bipolar affective disorder. *Research in
Developmental Disabilities, 9,* 47–53.

Young, J. E., Beck, A. T., & Weinberger, A. (1993).
Depression. In D. H. Barlow (Ed.), *Clinical
handbook of psychological disorders* (2nd
ed., pp. 240–277). New York: The Guilford
Press.

Autistic Disorder: Characteristics and Behavioral Treatment

Laura Schreibman
Laura Heyser
University of California
San Diego, CA

Aubyn Stahmer
Children's Hospital and Health Center
University of California
San Diego, CA

In 1943, Dr. Leo Kanner of Johns Hopkins University described 11 children who had surprisingly similar behavioral characteristics but who were qualitatively different from other child clinical populations. Providing detailed descriptions of these children, Kanner published a landmark paper about a disorder he labeled *early infantile autism*.

Behavioral excesses and pervasive behavioral deficits have characterized the psychopathology of children with autism. Over the last five decades, the study of autism has attracted professionals and researchers in virtually every field connected with children and development. This involvement has been due primarily to two factors. The first is that autism is an enigmatic disorder of unknown etiology that affects almost every area of development. The second is the profound impact the disorder has on every aspect of the child and the child's social environment. This chapter describes and discusses the characteristic features of this unique disorder.

Behavioral Characteristics

Deficits in Social Behavior

Perhaps the most characteristic feature of children with autism is a profound and pervasive deficit in social behavior and attachment (Butera & Haywood, 1995; Cox & Mesibov, 1995; Harris, Belchic, Blum, & Celiberti, 1994; Rimland, 1964; Rutter, 1978; Schreibman, 1988). Typically, children with autism do not develop normal social relationships but prefer to be alone. Not only do many autistic children fail to bond with their parents or seek affection from them, they may actively resist (or only passively accept) contact with others. Contact avoided may include eye contact, holding and cuddling, or playing together (e.g., Harris et al., 1994; Sturmey & Sevin, 1994).

During infancy many parents report these children to be "good babies" because they are very quiet, content to be left alone, and do not cry for attention. However, parents also report that their children fail to physically mold and cuddle when held (Schreibman, Koegel, & Koegel, 1989). Most autistic infants either fail to show any anticipation to being held and go limp when picked up or they become stiff and rigid when held and do not conform to the parent's body. One developmental milestone that many infants with autism fail to reach, or are extremely delayed in reaching, is joint attention (Capps & Sigman, 1996; Lord, 1993; Loveland & Landry, 1986; Pierce & Schreibman, 1995). Joint attention involves directing another's eye gaze in order to share experiences with objects and has been shown to be an important behavior for the development of more complex social interactions (Capps & Sigman, 1996).

As children with autism grow older, other social deficits begin to emerge. For instance, children with autism do not derive comfort from their parents, nor do they comfort others (Capps & Sigman, 1996; Dawson & Lewy, 1989). Children with autism generally do not share enjoyable experiences with others (e.g., showing toys, puzzle completion; Capps & Sigman, 1996). Likewise, these children do not exhibit the "separation anxiety" seen in normal children (Le Couteur et al., 1989). They are neither upset if their parents leave nor glad when they return. Although it has been shown that children with autism do engage in some appropriate social behaviors (Capps & Sigman, 1996), much of the apparent social and affectionate behavior has been found to be driven by ulterior motives (e.g., reaching to be picked up so as to gain access to a favored toy or interacting with a parent in a self-stimulatory manner, such as petting hair; Schreibman & Charlop, 1989). As Rimland (1964) and others have pointed out, children with autism may treat people as if they were objects. Instead of developing attachments to people, children with autism often develop attachments to inanimate objects such as lids, toys, or certain books, etc. These attachments can be quite pervasive, and the child usually becomes very upset when a favored object is taken away (Kanner, 1943).

Appropriate peer relations also fail to develop normally. Children with autism show a significant lack of peer contact and interactive play. This may be due partly to their preference for aloneness (Capps & Sigman, 1996), their failure to develop a theory of mind (Baron-Cohen, 1989a; Frith, 1989; Tager-Flusberg, 1994), or their failure to attend to others (Loveland & Landry, 1986; Mundy, Sigman, & Kasari, 1990), which would prevent autistic children from learning through observation or modeling. Children with autism often do not demonstrate imaginative, pretend, or sociodramatic play (Prizant & Wetherby, 1993; Wolfberg & Schuler, 1993). Play that appears to be imaginative is often very scripted and the child will repeat the same script over and over without any alterations. Social behavior in high functioning children with autism is often characterized by a lack of interest in establishing friendships, a failure to consider the interests of others, a lack of responsiveness or complete unawareness of subtle social cues, and a continued interest in being alone (Prizant & Wetherby, 1993; Schreibman & Charlop, 1989; Schreibman et al., 1989; Wolfberg & Schuler, 1993).

Speech and Language

Approximately one half of all children with autism fail to develop functional speech (Charlop & Haymes, 1994; Prizant & Wetherby, 1993; Rutter, 1978), and those children who do acquire speech often develop noncommunicative speech patterns. Such speech patterns are qualitatively different from those of children who develop normally or those who have language disorders (Schreibman, 1988), and as such, language development is often what first alerts parents to the disorder (Gillberg et al., 1990; Le Couteur et al., 1989). It is important to note that no physical basis for these language production deficits has been identified (Rimland, 1964).

One speech anomaly that is frequently associated with autism is *echolalia*. Echolalia is the repetition of words or phrases spoken by others (Fay, 1969) and can either occur immediately after hearing another person speak (immediate echolalia) or be the repetition of something heard in the past (delayed echolalia; [e.g., repeating part of a television commercial days later]). Echolalic speech is often reproduced accurately, and with the same intonation, inflection, and volume as the heard speech. Initial reports contended that the child was likely to have little or no comprehension of what she or he was saying and that echolalic speech was typically noncommunicative in nature (Myklebust, 1995). In fact, echolalia was regarded by Rutter (1968) to be meaningless. Currently, other theories on the use of echolalia are gaining in popularity. Although out-of-context phrases (Charlop & Haymes, 1994) and verbatim repetition of phrases (Ricks & Wing, 1975) have been cited as evidence for the nonfunctional use of echolalia, some aspects of echolalic speech has have been found to be functional (Carr, 1988; McEvoy, Loveland, & Landry, 1988; Prizant & Wetherby, 1993). More specifically, Prizant (e.g., Prizant, 1983) suggests that echolalia may represent a chunking or "gestalt" type of strategy for language acquisition. Echoic speech has also been found to serve functional communication needs in children with limited communicative abilities (Prizant & Wetherby, 1993). For over a decade, Charlop and her colleagues have been investigating functional uses of echolalia. These researchers have tapped echoic speech as another means to facilitate speech training (Charlop & Haymes, 1994). In particular, generalization strategies have been developed using echolalia in actual training and video modeling situations (e.g., Charlop, 1983; Charlop & Milstein, 1989).

Another distinguishing speech characteristic of autistic children is *pronominal reversal* (Bartak & Rutter, 1974; Charlop & Haymes, 1994; Kanner, 1943; Lee, Hobson, & Chiat, 1994; Ricks & Wing, 1975). Autistic children who exhibit pronominal reversal refer to themselves as *you.* The reversal of pronouns may be related to echolalia; that is, in that the child may be echoing the speech of others who have spoken directly to the child (Bartak & Rutter, 1974; Lee et al., 1994). This speech anomaly in autistic children is often pervasive and continues to be problematic during speech training.

Idiosyncratic language and *neologisms* are also frequently observed in the speech of autistic children (Volden & Lord, 1991). Idiosyncratic language is language made up of words that are incorrectly paired with objects, but that still convey meaning (Le Couteur et al., 1989; Lord et al., 1989; Volden & Lord, 1991). For example, a child may refer to a toy by a particular idiosyncratic feature (e.g., call a specific doll a "green shoes"). Children may also replace unknown labels for known labels (e.g., a street lamp overhead could be called the moon). Neologisms, on the other hand, are completely made-up words that autistic children use consistently as if they were real words (Le Couteur et al., 1989; Volden & Lord, 1991). Neologisms are seen in a nonpervasive form in the early development of language in normal children. Words such as "ba-ba" for

bottle or "oogie" for blanket are typically referred to as "baby talk." In normal children, however, they soon develop into the appropriate, correct labels, whereas autistic children may never replace the neologism with the correct word.

An additional speech production abnormality is that the non-content-carrying features of speech are often inappropriate or inaccurate in children with autism (Baltaxe, 1984; Green, Fein, Joy, & Waterhouse, 1995; Paul, 1987). This is called speech *dysprosody* and refers to abnormal intonation, inflection, tone, volume, rhythm, and rate of speech. With all of these impaired features, even extensive language training may not result in the production of normal sounding speech (Koegel, Koegel, & O'Neill, 1989; Schreibman et al., 1989).

Content of speech, in both comprehension and expression, is also altered in children with autism. Speech, especially delayed echolalia, often serves a self-stimulatory function and is heard as repetitive words, phrases, or sounds that are unrelated to the environment or current activity (Lovaas, Newsom, & Hickman, 1987; Lovaas, Varni, Koegel, & Lorsch, 1977; Schreibman et al., 1989). In addition, children with autism are, for the most part, extremely literal and frequently do not understand analogies, metaphors, and sayings with dual or hidden meanings (Charlop & Haymes, 1994; Schreibman & Charlop, 1987, 1989; Wing, 1976). Teasing or humor frequently goes unnoticed or is simply not comprehended. Additionally, even children with well-developed language skills are limited in that they have difficulty discussing events in the past or future even though they may be capable of talking about their immediate situation (Rutter, 1978).

A final area related to speech and language that is affected in children with autism is that of emotion recognition. Children with autism typically have trouble expressing, labeling, and understanding emotions (Bormann-Kischkel, Vilsmeier, & Baude, 1995; Capps, Yirmiya, & Sigman, 1992; Davies, Bishop, Manstead, & Tantam, 1994; Prior, Dahlstrom, & Squires, 1990). Although these findings have been debated, emotion comprehension has been shown to be related to language ability; differences in emotion recognition are small when autistic children are matched for language ability with a control group (see Capps et al., 1992).

Abnormalities in Response to the Sensory Environment

Many parents of children with autism have reported that their children are detached from their immediate surroundings. "He seems almost to draw into his shell and live within himself" is how one parent described his child to Kanner (1943, p. 217). The majority of children with autism appear to have some type of sensory deficit, and many are essentially unresponsive to their environment (James & Barry, 1980; Kinsbourne, 1987; Lincoln, Courchesne, Harms, & Allen, 1995). Typically, this is first evident when children fail to respond to loud noises, bright lights, or their name being called, and many parents initially suspect that their child to is deaf or blind (Schreibman et al., 1989). However, closer observation reveals that many children will respond to quieter sounds like the opening of the refrigerator or to the soft touch, like the touch of a leaf brushing a child's arm as she walks by. This unusual responsivity to the sensory environment is evident in a child's under- and/or overresponsiveness to various sensory stimuli and can also be seen at times with the same stimuli on different occasions (James & Barry, 1980; Ornitz, 1989; Ornitz & Ritvo, 1968; Rincover & Ducharme, 1987). The degree to which a child responds to the sensory environment is therefore highly variable.

Courchesne and his colleagues have investigated auditory sensitivity and have cited evidence of abnormal late auditory event related potentials (ERPs) in subjects with autism (e.g., Courchesne, Lincoln, Yeung-Courchesne, Elmasian, & Grillon, 1989; Lincoln, Courchesne, Harms, & Allen, 1993).

Children with autism have been shown to have difficulty processing and utilizing compound stimulus information. Lovaas, Schreibman, Koegel, and Rehm (1971) demonstrated that these children often attend to only one component of a compound stimulus. Termed *stimulus overselectivity* (Lovaas, Schreibman et al., 1971), this deficit has been tied to behavioral deficits and failures in learning situations (Lovaas, Koegel, & Schreibman, 1979; Rincover & Ducharme, 1987; Schreibman & Lovaas, 1973). It has been suggested that this deficit is the result of a failure to disengage, shift, and reengage attention (Courchesne et al., 1994; Posner, Walker, Friedrich, & Rafal, 1984; Wainwright-Sharp & Bryson, 1993).

Many children have been found to have accentuated responses to spinning objects, and these children may intently watch fans, clothes dryers, tops, or they may spin themselves for hours at a time. Some of these abnormal responses to the sensory environment are cause for great concern for parents. Many children show abnormal reactions to tactile (e.g., soft/painful touch or temperature related) stimuli (Ritvo & Freeman, 1978). For example, a child may be incredibly sensitive to a soft touch but may seem undersensitive to pain. Such a child may not exhibit distress when injured and will not alert her parents to any medical needs. Furthermore, unusual responses to gustatory stimuli may result in unusual or extremely limited food preferences or perhaps the ingestion of nonfood items (e.g., Ritvo & Freeman, 1978). Indeed, such responses or lack of responses to the environment demand increased supervision for the safety of the child.

Not surprisingly, abnormal responsivity interferes with learning. In any environment or learning situation, a large number of cues are presented at one time. These cues can be presented via unimodal or multimodal means and must be processed as a whole in order to understand any given situation. Children with autism may fail to respond to the large number of cues given in a learning situation and tend to respond to only one cue or component of the relevant stimulus (Koegel & Rincover, 1976; Lovaas et al., 1979; Rincover & Ducharme, 1987; Rincover & Koegel, 1975; Schreibman & Lovaas, 1973). In the classroom, for example, a child learning the alphabet must be able to differentiate the letters *O* and *Q*. A child with autism may overselect the circle component of these letters and not respond to the other (discriminating) component of the angular line. Lacking attention to all relevant cues, the child would not recognize the difference between the letters. A more complex example of stimulus overselectivity in the home might be a child who only recognizes his mother by her eyeglasses or certain pairs of shoes. Since learning requires attention to multiple cues simultaneously, overselectivity can greatly impede progress and can interfere with acquisition and generalization of a variety of new skills (e.g., Lovaas et al., 1979; Rincover & Koegel, 1975; Schreibman, Charlop, & Tryon, 1981; Schreibman, Kohlenberg, & Britten, 1986; Schreibman & Lovaas, 1973) Today, there are some procedures that have been shown to increase a child's responsivity to multiple cues and thus help eliminate overselective responding (Koegel & Schreibman, 1977; Rincover, 1978; Schreibman, 1975; Schreibman, Charlop, & Koegel, 1982).

Demand for Sameness in the Environment

In his original diagnostic criteria for autism, Kanner (1943) noted a compulsive demand for the preservation of sameness. Such compulsive behavior is seen in a variety of areas (Baron-Cohen, 1989b). First, many children are highly sensitive to changes in the physical environment (Rutter, 1978; Sturmey & Sevin, 1994). The arrangement of furniture or toys is often very specific. Children often line up toys, blocks, books, and other objects in a repeated and exact fashion (McBride & Panksepp, 1995). Disruption of these arrangements may lead autistic children to become extremely upset (Sturmey & Sevin, 1994). The tantrum that follows such change may continue until the situation is rectified, either by the child or another person, at which point the child usually becomes calm and goes back to the previous activity (which may or may not involve the stimuli that elicited the tantrum). Routes of travel and daily routines can also become limited and rigid. Failures of others to maintain these routines, again, may result in a tantrum.

Toy play with autistic children is limited and may be related to the demand for sameness (Baron-Cohen, 1989b; Rutter, 1978). Typically, these children fail to play with toys appropriately in unstructured settings (Lord, 1993; Stahmer & Schreibman, 1992). Pieces of games or puzzles may be lined up repeatedly, and other toys may be spun intently or sought out for particular features such as texture or color (Van Bourgondien, 1993). Play that is appropriate is often limited in imagination and variation compared to that observed in age-matched children without autism (Rutter, 1978; Sturmey & Sevin, 1994; Ungerer, 1989). One child, for example, while playing with his parents, would reenact movie scenes with toy figures from the movie, but any variation from the movie (by the parents) would not be tolerated.

Many children become obsessively attached to a specific object (Baron-Cohen, 1989b; McBride & Panksepp, 1995; Rutter, 1978; Schreibman & Mills, 1983; Wing, 1976) and search actively for it, demand it all the time, talk obsessively about it, and have tantrums when the object is not accessible or when it is taken away. Objects children obsess over are wide-ranging and may include items of clothing (one child would only wear red clothes), plastic alphabet letters or numbers, rubber bands, a particular television program, belts, and keys. We have encountered a child who was obsessed with vacuum cleaners and who would insist on taking a Dustbuster to bed with him. Another child was reported to eat only McDonald's type french fries and would not eat french fries that were a different shape or size. Because these obsessions and compulsions are so pronounced in the autistic population, research comparing autism with obsessive-compulsive disorder has been on the rise for the last decade (Baron-Cohen, 1989b; Brasic et al., 1994; McBride & Panksepp, 1995; McDougle et al., 1995; Nelson & Pribor, 1993). Although evidence that distinguishes autism from obsessive-compulsive disorders is growing (McDougle et al., 1995), such comparisons have been important in promoting research in the area of drug treatment for the obsessions and compulsions of individuals with autism (e.g., Brasic et al., 1994).

In addition to obsessions with objects, many children with autism develop ritualistic preoccupations with (rote) memorization. Frequent reports are made by parents about their children memorizing calendars, time tables, bus and train schedules or routes, the *TV Guide*, books, songs, and other items (Kanner, 1943; Nelson & Pribor, 1993; Rutter, 1978; Schreibman & Charlop, 1989; Schreibman et al., 1989). We have encountered adult autistic men who ritualistically asked about and memorized personal information (e.g., name, address, phone number, age, date of birth) of any person to whom they were introduced.

Self-Stimulatory (or Stereotypic) Behavior

Self-stimulatory behavior, also referred to as stereotypy, is seen in a wide range of childhood pathologies. It consists of repetitive, persistent behavior that serves no function except to provide sensory feedback (Lovaas, Litrownik, & Mann, 1971; Lovaas et al., 1987; Rincover, 1978). Self-stimulation can be observed in many forms from gross to fine motor movements. The more common examples include body rocking, hand flapping, toe walking, posturing, jumping or darting, spinning, sniffing, and staring at lights out of the corners of the eyes. Self-stimulation may involve objects and include behaviors such as smelling someone else's hair, sifting sand or wood chips, tapping hubcaps, or twirling string. In addition, many children with verbal capabilities engage in verbal stereotypic behavior during which they repeat sounds or words in rapid succession (i.e., delayed echolalia) or insert inappropriate verbalizations into communicative speech (Lovaas et al., 1987). One example is a young man who repeated certain movie quotes to himself throughout the day.

For most children with autism, self-stimulatory behavior is so intrinsically motivating that, if allowed, they may spend most of their day engaged in self-stimulation. Many of these children resist attempts to be redirected to other, more appropriate activities and are often unresponsive to the environment when engaged in stereotypic behavior (Lovaas, Litrownik et al., 1971). As a result, stereotypy can strongly interfere with the acquisition of new skills (Koegel & Covert, 1972; Koegel, Firestone, Kramme, & Dunlap, 1974; Lovaas, Litrownik et al., 1971). However, recent research has shown that the opportunity to engage in self-stimulatory behavior can be used as a motivating reinforcer in learning situations (Runco, Charlop, & Schreibman, 1986). Additionally, other research has suggested that children are not always as oblivious to their environment as they may seem when engaged in such aberrant behavior. Durand and Carr (1987) have suggested that some autistic children may, in fact, use self-stimulatory behavior as a means of escaping or avoiding work or unpleasant demands. That is to say, a functional analysis of stereotyped behaviors has shown factors other than intrinsic motivation to be controlling the behavior (Durand & Carr, 1987; Harris et al., 1994).

Before leaving the subject of self-stimulation, it is important to note that most people engage in self-stimulatory behavior of some kind. Nail biting, finger drumming, hair twirling, thumb twiddling, and foot tapping are all examples of stereotypic behaviors seen in the general population. What makes these behaviors different from those seen in autism is that people in the general population know what behaviors are appropriate to engage in and when. Further, these behaviors are not considered aberrant or self-destructive, nor do they interfere with learning.

Self-Injurious Behavior

Perhaps the most severe and dramatic behavior seen in the autistic population is self-injury. Self-injurious behavior (SIB) is defined as any behavior in which the individual consciously inflicts physical damage to his or her own body (Tate & Baroff, 1966). Like most of the characteristic features already described, the severity of SIB can range widely, from mild to life threatening. The more common behaviors seen in individuals who engage in SIB include hair pulling, slapping, scratching, pinching, eye gouging, self-biting (usually hands or wrists), and head banging (e.g., Rutter & Lockyer, 1967;

Schreibman, 1988; Schreibman & Mills, 1983). By far, self-biting and head banging are the forms of SIB most commonly seen and potentially the most dangerous.

Again, the intensity of SIB varies from one individual to the next, and the damage caused can range from bruises and calluses to broken bones, detached retinas, skull fractures, and removal of large portions of flesh (Carr, 1977). For the more serious cases of SIB, restraints may be necessary, but the prolonged use of such devices can also be detrimental to the physical well-being of the child.

Because of the possible deleterious effects of SIB, it is critical that the behavior be treated quickly and effectively. Functional analyses of self-injury have revealed three possible reasons why self-injurious behavior is maintained (Carr, 1977; Carr & Durand, 1985; Oswald, Ellis, Singh, & Singh, 1994). First, SIB may be a form of self-stimulatory behavior. As with other stereotypes, eliminating SIB when it is self-reinforcing can be a difficult and tedious process. Second, the behavior may be negatively reinforced (Iwata, 1987). Children who engage in self-injury may do so to avoid or escape an unpleasant situation. For example, a child may bite his hand when a learning task gets too challenging. Third, self-injury can be, and often is, positively reinforced (Carr, 1977; Carr & Durand, 1985). Given the dramatic nature of this behavior, many people will run to console and comfort the child just as they would if the child had fallen accidentally. Treatment intervention, particularly that which involves functional communication training, has been successful with SIB that is maintained by both positive and negative reinforcement (Carr & Durand, 1985; Iwata, Dorsey, Slifer, Bauman, & Richman, 1982; Oswald et al., 1994; Schreibman & Charlop, 1989).

Special Skills

Despite the high number of deficits seen in autism and the depressed level of functioning, many autistic individuals are reported as exhibiting isolated areas of skill (Creak, 1961; Mottron & Belleville, 1995). These skills may fall in the range of typical functioning levels but appear special because of the individual's depressed functioning in other areas, or they may in fact be truly exceptional skills. The special skill areas typically seen in autism include musical and artistic, mechanical, and rote memory areas (e.g., Applebaum, Egel, Koegel, & Imhoff, 1979; Rimland & Fein, 1988). In the area of music, some children are able to reproduce a song perfectly after hearing it once and may even be able to play it on multiple instruments. Other children may have exceptional drawing abilities that allow them to reproduce images such as three-dimensional objects, photos, or city skylines (e.g., Mottron & Belleville, 1995). Mechanical skills can be seen in a variety of areas such as VCR programming at an early age or advantaged puzzle completion abilities.

Affect

Frequently, children with autism exhibit affect that is not contextually appropriate (Hobson, 1989; Ricks & Wing, 1975; Rimland, 1964). That is to say, they display emotions that are not consistent with those expected in a given situation. For example, some children may laugh when being punished or cry when praised. Others may experience emotions at extreme levels (Ricks & Wing, 1975). Still other children display a flattened affect, showing relatively little emotion in a variety of situations (Rimland, 1964; Schreibman & Charlop, 1989). Research in the area of affect and emotion recognition has shown that children with autism have difficulty modeling or imitating facial expressions and may be unable to integrate information about emotions and their expression (Capps et al., 1992; Hobson, 1989; see also Capps & Sigman, 1996).

In addition to unusual emotional responses, children with autism often experience irrational fears (Wing, 1976). Like phobias, these fears are intense, irrational, and difficult to overcome. Such fears are usually associated with common objects or situations and have been observed to include items as disparate as "tortillas, pictures of five dogs, ferns, Bill Cosby, and white bread" (Schreibman & Charlop, 1989, p. 109). In contrast, some children with autism seem to have no sense of fear at all.

Intellectual Functioning

Kanner (1943) originally suggested that children with autism were of normal or above-normal intelligence. This view was based on their intelligent facial expressions and good rote memories. However, we now understand that the majority of individuals with autism do have some level of mental retardation. It is estimated that about 75% to 80% of children with autism have some level of mental retardation; that is, only 20% to 25% of autistic individuals have an IQ above 70. Of those who function in the mentally retarded range it has been suggested that approximately 25% have IQs between 50 and 70 and the other 75% have IQs below 50 (*DSM-IV*; American Psychiatric Association, 1994; Ritvo & Freeman, 1978; Sturmey & Sevin, 1994).

It is often difficult to assess the intellectual functioning of a child with autism. First, stereotypy, avoidance, and other competing behaviors interfere with the administration of assessment test batteries (Schreibman & Charlop, 1987, 1989). Second, verbal deficits often prevent the administration of some tests or subtests (Ritvo & Freeman, 1978). Third, theory-of-mind deficits (as opposed to language impairments) may impede performance on some subtests (Happé, 1994). In contrast to these deficits, autistic children generally perform best on visual-spatial or rote memory tasks. Happé (1994) summarized numerous studies which show that children with autism consistently show peak performance on block design subtests of performance assessments. The resulting test profile pattern differentiates the child with autism from children with mental retardation, who generally show a very even pattern of responding across all assessment tests and subtests. A child with autism, on the other hand, typically shows an uneven pattern of responding, performing poorly on some and relatively well on others (Happé, 1994; Ritvo & Freeman, 1978; Schreibman & Charlop, 1989; Schreibman et al., 1989).

Diagnostic Criteria

Evolution

Kanner's original description of autism emphasized extreme autistic aloneness, language abnormalities, and sameness. He also described good cognitive potential and normal physical development, and remarked that the children typically had cold, obsessive, and intelligent parents (a view subsequently dispelled). Although we now know that the parents are not involved in the etiology of autism and that autism is a biologically based disorder, the three primary areas that differentiate autism from other child psychiatric disorders remain the same. Over the years, the criteria for diagnosis have changed from time to time. Although it is interesting to examine the forces behind diagnostic changes, here we are focusing on diagnostic criteria that are used today.

Diagnostic Criteria

According to the *Diagnostic and Statistical Manual of Mental Disorders (DSM-IV;* 1994), autism occurs in approximately 2 to 5 of 10,000 live births, with a male to female ratio of 4:1. Besides its association with mental retardation, autism has been known to co-occur in above-average rates with such disorders as Fragile X syndrome, phenylketonuria, maternal rubella, and seizure disorders. In fact, about one fourth to one third of children with autism develop seizures by adolescence.

For a diagnosis of autism, onset must be evident before the child is 3 years old. This is *not* to say that the child must be diagnosed with autistic disorder before 3 years of age; rather, evidence of the disorder must be present prior to age 3. The diagnostic criteria for autism are divided into three primary areas: social impairments, communication impairments, and stereotyped behavior patterns. Because of the heterogeneity of autism, each child will not exhibit every criterion listed in the *DSM-IV* (1994). Rather, the *DSM-IV* is meant to serve as a guideline, having certain requirements within each category.

Qualitative impairment in social interaction. A large number of children diagnosed with autism exhibit marked impairment in their nonverbal behaviors such as eye-to-eye gaze, facial expression, body postures, and gestures which that regulate social interaction. As mentioned previously, children with autism prefer to be alone and are often content only when left to themselves. Failure to make eye contact or to adopt anticipatory postures before being picked up are extremely common features of autism. These children also typically fail to develop peer relationships appropriate to developmental level and do not spontaneously seek others with whom to share enjoyment, interests, or achievements; nor do they engage in social or emotional reciprocity. These three criteria are all very much related in that without social reciprocity or spontaneous speech, it is very difficult for other children to interact with the autistic child (Harris, 1995). Hence, the child with autism may become further and further removed.

Qualitative impairments in communication. A delay or complete lack of the development of spoken language occurs in approximately 50% of all children with autism. Other children who do develop adequate speech may have impairments in their abilities to commence or prolong a conversation with others. Children with autism may exhibit stereotyped and repetitive use of language, and they may also show an impairment in their ability to institute varied, spontaneous, make-believe play. Various other abnormalities in speech may be present (see discussion under Speech and Language, above), but only these specific impairments are used as criteria for diagnosis.

Restricted repetitive and stereotyped patterns of behavior. Preoccupations with stereotypic patterns of abnormal intensity or focus or of inflexible adherence are characteristic of autism. Such behaviors typically involve motoric mannerisms or preoccupations with parts of objects.

Thus far, this chapter has described the characteristic features of autism in depth and highlighted those features used for diagnosis. Although many of the features described earlier, such as SIB, are not required criteria for diagnostic purposes, these behaviors are important features known to be associated with autism. We now turn to examine how autism differs from other, closely related disorders of childhood.

Differential Diagnosis

According to the *DSM-IV* (1994), autistic disorder is distinguished from other forms of pervasive developmental disorder. Children with the following pervasive developmental disorders share some features with children with autism but may be distinguished based upon the following characteristics. Children with *Rett's disorder* are characterized by a specific pattern of head growth deceleration, loss of previously acquired purposeful hand skills, poorly coordinated gait and trunk movements, and lack of the consistent deficits in social interaction that would likely characterize a child with autism. Further, Rett's disorder has been diagnosed only in females. Autistic disorder differs from *childhood disintegrative disorder* in that the latter is characterized by a distinctive pattern of regression in development that follows a minimum of 2 years of normal development. This is in contrast to autism, where the developmental abnormalities are typically apparent from birth (or at least within the first year). *Asperger's disorder* has in the past been referred to as high-functioning autism, and indeed to this day there is not unanimity in the opinion that it is in fact a distinct disorder. Asperger's cases are best distinguished from autism based on their lack of delay in language development. These individuals do, however, share the deficits in social interaction and the presence of restricted, repetitive, and stereotyped patterns of behavior. In addition, although cognitive impairment is present in most individuals with autistic disorder, it is not a feature in individuals with Asperger's disorder. The diagnosis of *pervasive developmental disorder, not otherwise specified,* is made when the diagnostic criteria for autistic disorder or any of the other subcategories of pervasive developmental disorder are not met but some of the important characteristics, such as severe and pervasive impairment in the development of reciprocal social interaction, deficits in communication, or restricted, repetitive, stereotyped behaviors, are present.

Treatment

Treatment research in the area of autism has been based upon prevailing theories regarding the etiology of the disorder. When he first described the disorder in 1943, Kanner, embracing the prevailing spirit of psychoanalytic theory, hypothesized that early experiences caused autism. This led treatment providers to hypothesize that parental characteristics played a primary role in causing the children's symptoms. Thus, treatment models at that time focused on removing the child from the hostile home environment and placing the child into institutional treatment (e.g., Bettelheim, 1967). Fortunately, the notion of parental causation of autism is known to be erroneous, and now parents typically play an integral role in the providing treatment for their children.

However, while it is now widely recognized that there is a biological basis for autism, the specific etiology for most cases of autistic disorder is unknown. The consensus of most researchers working in this area is that the behavioral syndrome of autism has a variety of causes including genetic causes (Cook et al., 1998), neuroanatomic abnormalities (Courchesne, 1997), viral causes, and environmental causes (such as toxins or pathogens) (Smalley & Collins, 1996). Although researchers are working toward a connection between causation and treatment, there is currently not a good model for linking behavioral manifestations of the disorder to particular biological markers. Therefore the most widely used treatments involve manipulation of environmental events. To date the only form of treatment for autism that has substantial empirical support is treatment based upon a behavioral model (see Schreibman, 1997). This model focuses on the understanding of the behavioral characteristics of individuals with autism and environmental events of which they

are a function. In addition, recent research in the behavioral treatment of autism has emphasized the importance of addressing treatment regimens that may be particularly important for treating the children at an early age.

Recent research with a variety of treatment methods has indicated that early intervention is essential for the treatment of autism. A longitudinal study of children with autism indicated that currently 75% of children with autism are able to remain with their families rather than move into an institution (Hameury et al., 1995). This is in comparison to earlier research indicating that the majority of children with autism (over 60%) were living in hospitals for individuals with mental retardation or in other protective settings (Rutter, 1970). The authors credit early specialized intervention and family support for this amount of success. Clearly, there is a connection between intervention and outcome for children with autism. The difficulty lies in choosing the appropriate treatment for individual children with the disorder. Several behavioral treatment strategies that are considered state-of-the-art in the field today are briefly reviewed below. Additionally, choosing treatments based upon child, family, and behavioral characteristics is a major focus of this section.

Behavioral Treatment

One of the earliest forms of treatment to show successful learning in children with autism was a method based on the principles of applied behavior analysis. This type of treatment represented a change in etiological perspective from a psychodynamic, disease model to viewing the disorder as a syndrome of behaviors that can best be addressed by looking at the behaviors in terms of their functional relationship to the environment. The earliest form of treatment in this area looked at behavioral excesses and deficits in individual children with autism and used basic behavioral principles (e.g., reinforcement, extinction, punishment) to modify these behaviors. Over the years treatment based upon on a behavioral model has developed into a sophisticated and comprehensive set of procedures that address layered units of behavior via treatment packages. These treatment packages emphasize positive behavioral intervention while reducing reliance on the more aversive procedures that have previously been employed in some cases (Schreibman, 1988).

Discrete trial training. Early intensive behavioral treatment for higher functioning children with autism has been reported to be very successful (Lovaas, 1987). Programs following this one-on-one, in-home model typically focus on breaking down complex behaviors into smaller components and teaching them individually through repetition. Children are taught behaviors they do not yet demonstrate. These programs often begin by targeting behaviors such as increasing eye contact and responding to verbal directions such as "sit down" or "look at me." Children learn to match and categorize as well as to vocalize and use verbal language.

New skills are taught by (a) providing an instruction, (b) obtaining a response (either an independent response from the child or one that is prompted by the teacher), and finally (c) administering a consequence (see Maurice, Green, & Luce, 1996, for a complete description of this technique). The instruction must be clear, concise, task-relevant, and consistent across trials. Prompts are often used to evoke a correct response, for example, helping a child sit in a chair after hearing the instruction. Prompts are faded once the child begins to master the task. Positive reinforcement is then administered immediately after a correct response. No rewards are given for incorrect responses. Consequences must be clear, immediate, and effective to ensure behavior change. In a typical discrete trial training (DTT) program, children receive repeated trials of instructions until they have demonstrated mastery of the skill (see Maurice et al., 1996).

Current DTT practice includes providing 20 to 40 hours per week of in-home, one-to-one treatment. There were early reports of excellent progress, with almost 50% of children in the experimental group mainstreaming into a typical first-grade classroom and obtaining IQ scores within the normal range (Lovaas, 1987).

Based upon this research, the use of intensive one-on-one, in-home services has increased dramatically over the past 5 years. In more recent years, however, several researchers have questioned the rigor of this early research (e.g., Mundy, 1993; Schopler, Short, & Mesibov, 1989). Only recently have researchers begun to look at the effect of such a program with children who are functioning at lower IQ levels (Smith, Eikeseth, Klevstrand, & Lovaas, 1997). Additionally, the need for such a high-intensity program has been questioned (Sheinkopf & Siegel, 1998).

Benefits of the DTT program for children with autism include a specific curriculum that is easy to follow and the use of a systematically applied learning methodology that has been shown to be quite useful, especially for teaching complex behaviors. Reported drawbacks of such a program include poor generalization of newly learned skills to areas outside the teaching situation, poor generalization of skills to related behaviors, lack of spontaneity in child responses, and rote memorization rather than naturalistic learning (e.g., Mundy, 1993; Schopler et al., 1989).

Pivotal response training. Pivotal response training (PRT; Koegel, Schreibman et al., 1989) is a behavioral treatment method designed to address some of the problem areas evidenced when using DTT. PRT was designed specifically to increase generalization of new skills and to increase the motivation of children to perform the behaviors being taught to them. Like DTT, this intervention is also based on the principles of learning, but clinicians using PRT methods treat behavioral deficits by addressing more complex and comprehensive behavioral repertoires. Researchers have identified two pivotal behaviors that affect wide ranges of behavior in children with autism: motivation and responsivity to multiple cues. Thus, the focus of this treatment program is on facilitating generalized behavioral changes rather than on teaching each new skill individually (Koegel, O'Dell, & Koegel, 1987).

Due to severe skill deficits in the areas of play and language, and a history of task failure, children with autism typically lack motivation to learn new skills (e.g., Schreibman, 1988). PRT works to increase motivation by including components such as utilizing functional response-reinforcer relationships, reinforcing attempts at appropriate responding, frequently varying task and stimulus materials, usinge of multiple examples, allowing the child to choose the activity, and interspersing maintenance tasks the child has already mastered. PRT has been used to increase language skills (Koegel et al., 1987), play skills (Stahmer, 1995; Thorp, Stahmer, & Schreibman, 1995), and social interaction (Pierce & Schreibman, 1995) in children with autism. This type of program shares features in common with incidental teaching (e.g., McGee, Krantz, & McClannahan, 1985) or the milieu teaching model (Kaiser, Yoder, & Keetz, 1992). All of these approaches involve a more naturalistic set of strategies that utilize the child's typical environment to promote more natural interactions that differ substantially from the highly structured and relatively artificial interactions more characteristic of DTT.

Benefits of this program include increased generalization and maintenance of behavior change, and increases in language and play skills in many children (e.g., Koegel et al., 1987; Stahmer, 1995). Most of the research in this area includes parent training research which indicates that parents are able to learn these techniques and use them to effect change in their children with autism (see Laski, Charlop, & Schreibman, 1988). PRT does not have a curriculum accompanying it because it is a means of teaching whatever curriculum is found most appropriate for the child, and it may not be as successful for behaviors that do not have a natural consequence or that children may not be motivated to perform.

Picture Exchange Communication System.

Other behavioral methods of teaching children with autism often focus on particular areas of skill deficit. For example, the Picture Exchange Communication System (PECS) provides children with an augmentative communication system (Bondy & Frost, 1994). PECS was developed at the Delaware Autistic Program after data indicated that for many students

intensive verbal imitation training, sign language training, and picture-pointing programs were not successful. When using PECS, students hand a picture of a preferred item to a communicative partner in exchange for the item. PECS is similar to PRT in that the child chooses the stimuli, reinforcers are direct, and the technique promotes success, which increases the child's motivation. The PECS system focuses on child-initiated communication by limiting the number of prompts used by the communicative partner, and programming success through the use of two trainers early in treatment. One trainer acts as the communicative partner and controls access to the reinforcer. The other trainer is positioned behind the student and uses physical prompting to encourage success. Once requesting with pictures is firmly established, students are taught to use PECS to comment and form sentences (e.g., "I see the airplane").

Students are taught to use the system spontaneously throughout their environment. This program has been very successful at increasing appropriate communication as well as language skills in children with autism (Bondy & Frost, 1994). The use of PECS appears to facilitate rather than inhibit the use of spoken language in many children with autism who use the system. Drawbacks of the PECS system are that it it is often difficult to teach more complex concepts using the pictures and PECS can be difficult for parents to use at home.

Self-management training. Self-management training is a treatment method that helps children obtain independent control over their own behavior through the use of self-identification of the appropriate and inappropriate behavior, self-recording of progress, and self-reinforcement. Self-management helps to increase generalization of skills to unsupervised settings. Self-management training has been successful in increasing independent work skills (Sainato, Strain, Lefebvre, & Rapp, 1990), decreasing self-stimulatory behavior (Koegel & Koegel, 1990), increasing daily living skills (Pierce & Schreibman, 1994), and increasing social and play skills (Koegel,

Koegel, Hurley, & Frea, 1992; Stahmer & Schreibman, 1992). The specific procedures of self-management vary based upon the ability of the child and the nature of the target behavior. In general, children are taught to identify the target behavior (e.g., appropriate vs. inappropriate greeting skills), monitor their own performance (through frequency count or the use of an interval watch), and to self-reinforce. As the individual becomes better able to manage and record behavior, the intervals of expected appropriate behavior before reinforcement increase. Additionally, the treatment provider is eventually faded from the setting for increasing lengths of time in order to encourage independence.

Self-management is most appropriate for children who have IQ scores greater than 50 and verbal abilities greater than those of nonautistic 2-year-olds. Typically, teaching children to use the system is quite time intensive; however, once the self-management system is in place, children can be taught to modify additional behaviors quite rapidly. Parents who value independence in their children and who have sufficient time to implement the initial stages of the program are most likely to follow- through with these techniques at home. Benefits of the program include decreased stress for parents and increased independence for the individual with autism. However, as noted, this program can be quite time-intensive in the early stages and may be difficult for younger children or children with poor verbal skills (Schreibman & Koegel, 1996).

Functional analysis. Functional analysis is an example of positive behavioral programming developed by behavior analysts to improve the behavior of individuals with behavior problems through more client-centered methods (see O'Neill, Horner, Albin, Storey, & Sprague, 1990). In this approach, treatment providers look for the *function* of a behavior for the individual. For example, behavior problems often occur when individuals have minimal communication skills and use challenging behaviors to communicate needs. Medical and physical variables may affect the behaviors of concern

as well. For example, if a person is ill or injured, behavior may worsen. Aspects of the individual's environment may also elicit problem behaviors. For example, a particularly noisy television show or game may upset some individuals. Functional analysis of behavior problems takes all of these factors into account.

A functional analysis results in an operational description of the problem behaviors, prediction of the times and situations in which these behaviors occur (and do not occur), and definitions of the functions of the behaviors for the individual. Once all of these factors are assessed, behavior can be altered to provide the individual with a functional alternative behavior or the environment can be changed to eliminate the behavior. For example, if the function of a particular behavior is escape from teaching demands, the individual can learn to signal a need for a break. If the function of the behavior is to express frustration (e.g., the individual cannot tie his shoes quickly enough to get to breakfast in time), the expectations may be altered (e.g., provide the individual with shoes that use Velcro instead of laces). Functional analyses can be completed through direct interview with the client or caregiver, direct observation of the behavior, and/or manipulation of the environment (e.g., observing the child in a demand situations vs. a non-demand situation). Often behaviors will serve multiple functions. Typically changes in the environment and changes in antecedent stimuli coupled with increasing skills such as communication can improve behavior dramatically for many individuals. These types of procedures have been used in a variety of different forms to improve quality of life as well as improve community integration (see Koegel, Koegel, & Dunlap, 1996).

Individualized Treatment Approaches

The programs and treatment techniques described here are considered state-of-the-art for children with autism. Each type of programming is used to various degrees, often depending upon the area of the country a child lives in or the focus of a particular treatment provider. However, as mentioned earlier, children with autism are a very heterogeneous group, with very widely differing abilities and needs. Because of these differences among children, researchers and clinicians have begun to adopt a more individualized approach to treatment (Schreibman, 1996), basing their selection of treatment options on the needs of the child and family as well as on the particular target behaviors addressed. For example, a child may have a picture schedule to assist with transitions, receive DTT to learn imitation skills, and receive incidental teaching during free play to increase social and language skills, while her parents conduct PRT to increase language in the home.

Although teachers and clinicians often have chosen to use an eclectic approach when working with children with autism, research in the area of treatment individualization is still in its infancy. Much of the research on particular treatment strategies involves the use of group designs, which typically indicate that one treatment is more effective than the comparison treatment *in most cases*. However, the data typically also indicate that for some children that apparently "best" treatment is not as effective. More recently researchers have begun focusing on which children are responding to particular treatments rather than just the overall efficacy of the treatment itself. It appears that a complex set of variables, including child characteristics (e.g., functioning level, language ability, visual processing), parent/family characteristics (e.g., cultural background, stress level, parenting style), and characteristics of the target behavior (e.g., acquisitions task, behavior excess, task with motivating consequences) all interact to determine treatment effectiveness.

Child Characteristics

The characteristics of the individual being served are the most obvious place to begin when individualizing treatment. Behavioral researchers have a long history of focusing on specific individual needs when designing treatment packages. But the current focus is on

developing a systematic approach to the specification of which treatment(s) may be most beneficial given a particular set of child characteristics. Preliminary research in this area is presented below.

Intellectual ability, especially for very young children with autism, does not appear to differentiate appropriate treatment methods. In general, children who are able to perform well on standardized measures of intelligence or developmental ability have better outcomes using various treatment strategies. However, for most young children with autism (e.g., under age 4), standardized measures of intellectual ability are very unreliable and do not provide specific information regarding best treatment options (Lord & Schopler, 1989).

Clearly, a child's language and communication skills will affect the choice of treatment. Children with better language skills often have a wider variety of complex treatment options available to them, including peer interaction training and self-management training. For example, research indicates that self-management techniques are most effective for children who have verbal comprehension skills greater than 2 years 6 months of age (Schreibman & Koegel, 1996). Language ability before treatment does not appear to be related to a child's success in either PRT or DTT as both are used with children of all language abilities. In contrast, a child with good language production might not be an appropriate candidate for a picture communication system.

Researchers working with PRT have begun to identify particular behaviors associated with success in this type of treatment. Data presented by Sherer and Schreibman (1998) suggest that children with some interest in toys (as indicated by touching toys during a play session), some verbalizations (including babbling, verbal self-stimulation), and low levels of other types of self-stimulatory behaviors (e.g., hand flapping) respond well to PRT programming. Children with high degrees of nonverbal self-stimulation and an absence of interest in toys exhibit a poorer response to this program. Functioning level did not appear to relate to outcome for these children. Similar descriptions of the relationship between program responsiveness and a priori child characteristics are not yet available for the other treatment methods described here. However, this type of research is desperately needed in the field to assist with appropriate treatment planning for children with autism.

Choice of communication medium for children with autism may also be related to child characteristics. For example, children with autism who do not acquire verbal language by the age of 6 years have significantly lower chances of ever using spoken language than younger children. Therefore, an augmentative form of communication (e.g., PECS) would be more appropriate for these older children who lack verbal skills (e.g., Oxman & Konstantareas, 1981). Augmentative communication systems may also be appropriate for some younger children as well. Some young children with autism do not engage in much verbal behavior at all (e.g., babbling, vocal play). The use of vocal language techniques would be very difficult with these children. Additionally, research indicates that augmentative communication systems may facilitate verbal language skills, and at the very least do not inhibit the later acquisition of verbal language (e.g., Carpenter, Charlop-Christy, & LeBlanc, 1998). Deciding whether to target spoken language, picture communication, or sign language currently depends upon the preferences and judgment of the individual treatment provider. More research is currently needed to assess characteristics of children who respond best to various communicative alternatives.

Family Variables

In general, parent training benefits both parent and child. Parent training serves to extend the treatment environment, facilitate the acquisition of new skills, and increase generalization and maintenance of behavior changes (Schreibman, Koegel, Mills, & Burke, 1984). Research indicates that for the majority of parents, naturalistic training strategies (e.g., PRT) lead to reduced stress, increased leisure

time, and more positive parental affect during treatment than more structured techniques such as DTT (e.g., Schreibman, Kaneko, & Koegel, 1991; Schreibman & Koegel, 1996). Additionally, techniques that increase children's independent functioning, such as self-management, typically lead to a greater reduction in parental stress levels (Schreibman & Koegel, 1996). However, as is the case with child characteristics, family variables also mediate the efficacy of a particular treatment.

Research indicates that parental stress levels are negatively correlated with a child's progress in family-oriented programs (Robbins, Dunlap, & Plienis, 1991). Parents with high levels of stress unrelated to their child with autism (e.g., health concerns, isolation, spousal difficulty) had a particularly difficult time learning parent training techniques. For these parents, traditional parent training programs using any treatment technique may not be appropriate. A more effective way to assist these parents might be a new technique called clinician-facilitated parent training currently in development by Drs. Robert Koegel and Laura Schreibman at the University of California. When using clinician-facilitated parent training, clinicians provide the majority of the treatment until other aspects of parental stress can be significantly reduced.

As is true of research looking at individualizing treatment based on child characteristics, few studies have specifically looked at which type of treatments might be a best fit for individual families based on a priori assessment of family variables. An example of some detailed analysis of fit between treatment method and family characteristics can be seen in recent studies of teaching families to implement self-management procedures in the home. Self-management procedures can increase children's independence in many settings, and the techniques can be generalized to additional behaviors with decreased training time (Pierce & Schreibman, 1994). However, relatively intensive training is necessary for a child to initially master the procedure. Therefore a greater amount of parental effort must be exerted early in treatment to obtain the benefits of such training, which suggests that particular parenting styles and concerns may affect parent training in this area. To illustrate: As mentioned earlier, the child characteristic of language predicts success overall in self-management, yet research indicates that some children with poor language actually do well with self-management and others with high language skills do not perform as well as would be expected (Schreibman & Koegel, 1996). Preliminary data indicate that parental factors may play a role in explaining these individual differences. One difference between children who did not meet the profile and those who did seemed to be the motivation of parents. It seems that children with poor language whose parents were highly motivated (as evidenced by amount of time spent working with child, high attendance, and preparation for training sessions) and valued independence in their children (as measured by the *Family Environment Scale;* Moos, 1974) had a better chance of succeeding with the self-management procedures. Parents who were very concerned about their child's dependency (as measured by increased scores on the *Questionnaire on Resources and Stress* [Holroyd, 1974]) were also more likely to have children who succeeded in self-management. These parents were more motivated to promote independence in their children than parents who were not as concerned about overdependence. The improved result probably reflects extra time and efforts spent working on self-management skills in the home. In contrast, children with moderate to high language skills who did not learn the self-management skills as well typically had parents who were not as highly motivated to participate in treatment, or who did not value independence as an important skill for their children. An assessment of parental motivation and values may be an important indicator of the success of self-management training.

Similarly, parental style and value of a particular target behavior may affect a parent's use of other techniques. For example, although most parents prefer naturalistic techniques, some parents anecdotally report they actually prefer more structured programs. It is hypothesized that parents who are less comfortable engaging in unstructured play may be more inclined to choose structured techniques. Additionally, some parents who have not yet accepted their child's diagnosis tend to report they prefer techniques such as floor time, which often feel more similar to an interaction with a typical child. Parents who are very playful and tend to use high affect in their play report more satisfaction with the naturalistic techniques. Currently these hypotheses are based only on anecdotal parental report and await confirmation through controlled research studies.

Target Behavior

Aspects of the target behavior also affect treatment characteristics and outcome. Often children receive more than one type of treatment based upon what is being taught. For example, PRT is especially useful for teaching skills that have natural consequences, such as language and play skills, while DTT may be more appropriate for skills that are not naturally reinforcing, such as shape discrimination or toilet training. An example of differential responding to treatment includes language structures. Researchers have been more successful teaching a first lexicon using variables of PRT (Koegel et al., 1987). In contrast, some structures such as question asking and grammatical features that occur infrequently appear to be enhanced with at least some of the components of a discrete trial model (Koegel, 1994). Behavior problems are often best addressed through the use of functional analysis. Transition difficulties have been successfully reduced using techniques such as picture schedules and video priming (e.g., Whalen & Schreibman, 1998).

Conclusions

There are many different treatment methods available for use with children with autism. This array of options can often be very confusing for parents as well as treatment providers. It is important to rely on treatment procedures that have been empirically validated. Additionally, when it comes to treatment, one size does not fit all. Treatment procedures must be individualized based on a complex set of variables including child, family, and target behavior characteristics. These three areas work in combination to provide practitioners with clues to select the most effective treatment options for each child. Additionally, treatment methods should not be used in isolation. Each procedure has a set of strengths and weaknesses. When the procedures are used in combination, and with consideration of the child variables mentioned above, the most effective treatment for that individual child can be developed.

REFERENCES

American Psychiatric Association. (1994). *Diagnostic and statistical manual of mental disorders* (4th ed.). Washington, DC: Author.

Applebaum, E., Egel, A. L., Koegel, R. L., & Imhoff, B. (1979). Measuring musical abilities of autistic children. *Journal of Autism and Developmental Disorders, 9,* 279–285.

Baltaxe, C. A. (1984). The use of contrastivie stress in normal, aphasic, and autistic children. *Journal of Speech and Hearing Research, 27,* 97–105.

Baron-Cohen, S. (1989a). Are autistic children behaviorists? *Journal of Autism and Developmental Disorders, 19,* 579–600.

Baron-Cohen, S. (1989b). Do autistic children have obsessions and compulsions? *British Journal of Clinical Psychology, 28,* 193–200.

Bartak, L., & Rutter, M. (1974). The use of personal pronouns by autistic children. *Journal of Autism & Childhood Schizophrenia, 4,* 217–222.

Bettelheim, B. (1967). *The empty fortress.* New York: Free Press.

Bondy, A. S., & Frost, L. A. (1994). The picture exchange communication system. *Focus on Autistic Behavior, 9,* 1–19.

Bormann-Kischkel, C., Vilsmeier, M., & Baude, B. (1995). The development of emotional concepts in autism. *Journal of Child Psychology and Psychiatry, 36,* 1243–1259.

Brasic, J. R., Barnett, J. Y., Kaplan, D., Sheitman, B. B., Aisemberg, P., Lafargue, R. T., Kowalik, S., Clark, A., Tsaltas, M. O., & Young, J. G. (1994). Clomipramine ameliorates adventitious movements and compulsions in prepubertal boys with autistic disorder and severe mental retardation. *Neurology, 44,* 1309–1312.

Butera, G., & Haywood, H. C. (1995). Cognitive education of young children with autism: An application of Bright Start. In E. Schopler & G. Mesibov (Eds.), *Learning and cognition in autism* (pp. 269–292). New York: Plenum Press.

Capps, L., & Sigman, M. (1996). Autistic aloneness. In R. D. Kavanaugh, B. Zimmerberg, & S. Fein (Eds.), *Emotion: Interdisciplinary perspectives* (pp. 273–296). Hillsdale, NJ: Erlbaum.

Capps, L., Yirmiya, N., & Sigman, M. (1992). Understanding of simple and complex emotions in non-retarded children with autism. *Journal of Child Psychology and Psychiatry, 33,* 1169–1182.

Carpenter, H. M., Charlop-Christy, M. H., & LeBlanc, L. A. (1998, May). An evaluation of spontaneous speech and verbal imitation in children with autism after learning the Picture Exchange Communication System. Paper presented at the 24th annual meeting of the Association for Behavior Analysis Meeting, Orlando, FL.

Carr, E. G. (1977). The motivation of self-injurious behavior. A review of some hypotheses. *Psychological Bulletin, 81,* 800–816.

Carr, E. G. (1988). Functional equivalence as a mechanism of response generalization. In R. H. Horner, G. Dunlap, & R. L. Koegel (Eds.), *Generalization and maintenance: Life-style changes in applied settings* (pp. 221–241). Baltimore: Brookes.

Carr, E. G., & Durand, V. M. (1985). Reducing behavior problems through functional communication training. *Journal of Applied Behavior Analysis, 18,* 111–126.

Charlop, M. H. (1983). The effects of echolalia on acquisition and generalization of receptive speech in psychotic children. *Journal of Applied Behavior Analysis, 16,* 111–126.

Charlop, M. H., & Haymes, L. K. (1994). Speech and language acquisition and intervention: Behavioral approaches. In J. L. Matson (Ed.), *Autism is in children and adults: Etiology, assessment, and intervention* (pp. 213–240). Pacific Grove, CA: Brooks/Cole.

Charlop, M. H., & Milstein, J. P. (1989). Teaching autistic children conversational speech using video modeling. *Journal of Applied Behavior Analysis, 22,* 275–285.

Cook, E. H., Courchesne, R. Y., Cox, N. J., Lord, C., Gnen, D., Guter, S. J., Lincoln, A., Nix, K., Haas, R., Leventhal, B. L., & Courchesne, E. (1998). Linkage-disequilibruim of Autistic Disorder, with 15q11–13 markers. *American Journal of Human Genetics, 62,* 1077–1083.

Courchesne, E. (1997). Brainstem, cerebellar and limbic neuroanatomical abnormalities in autism. *Current Opinion in Neurobiology, 7,* 269–278.

Courchesne, E., Townsend, J., Akshoomoff, N. A., Saitoh, O., Yeung-Courchesne, R., Lincoln, A. J., James, H. E., Haas, R. H., Schreibman, L., & Lau, L. (1994). Impairment in shifting attention in autistic and cerebellar patients. *Behavioral Neuroscience, 108,* 848–865.

Courchesne, E., Lincoln, A. J., Yeung-Courchesne, R., Elmasian, R., & Grillon, C. (1989). Pathophysiologic findings in nonretarded autism and receptive developmental language disorder. *Journal of Autism and Developmental Disorders, 19,* 1–17.

Cox, R. D., & Mesibov, G. B. (1995). Relationship between autism and learning disabilities. In E. Schopler & G. Mesibov (Eds.), *Learning and cognition in autism* (pp. 57–70). New York: Plenum Press.

Creak, E. M. (1961). Schizophrenic syndrome in children. *Lancet, 2,* 818.

Davies, S., Bishop, D., Manstead, A. S. R., & Tantam, D. (1994). Face perception in children with autism and Asperger's syndrome. *Journal of Child Psychology and Psychiatry, 35,* 1033–1057.

Dawson, G., & Lewy, A. (1989). Arousal, attention, and the socioemotional impairments of individuals with autism. In G. Dawson (Ed.), *Autism: Nature, diagnosis, and treatment* (pp. 49–74). New York: Guilford Press.

Durand, V. M., & Carr, E. G. (1987). Social influences of self-stimulatory behavior. Analysis and treatment application. *Journal of Applied Behavior Analysis, 20,* 119–132.

Fay, W. H. (1969). On the basis of autistic echolalia. *Journal of Communication Disorders, 2,* 38–47.

Frith, U. (1989). *Autism: Explaining the enigma.* Oxford, England: Blackwell.

Gillberg, C., Ehlers, S., Schaumann, H., Jakobsson, G., Dahlgren, S. O., Lindblom, R., Bagenholm, A., Tjuus, T., & Blidner, E. (1990). Autism under age three years. A clinical study of 28 cases referred for autistic symptoms in infancy. *Journal of Child Psychology and Psychiatry, 31,* 921–934.

Green, L., Fein, F., Joy, S., & Waterhouse, L. (1995). Cognitive functioning in autism: An overview. In E. Schopler & G. Mesibov (Eds.), *Learning and cognition in autism* (pp. 57–70). New York: Plenum Press.

Hameury, L., Roux, S., Lenoir, P., Adrien, J. L., Sauvage, D., Barthelemy, C., Lelord, G. (1995). Longitudinal study of autism and other pervasive developmental disorders: Review of 125 cases. *Development and Brain Dysfunction, 8,* 51–65.

Happé, F. G. E. (1994). Wechsler IQ profile and theory of mind in autism: A research note. *Journal of Child Psychology and Psychiatry, 35,* 1461–1471.

Harris, S. L. (1995). Educational strategies in autism. In E. Schopler & G. Mesibov (Eds.), *Learning and cognition in autism* (pp. 293–309). New York: Plenum Press.

Harris, S. L., Belchic, J., Blum, L., & Celiberti, D. (1994). Behavioral assessment of autistic disorder. In J. L. Matson (Ed.), *Autism is in children and adults: Etiology, assessment, and intervention* (pp. 13–31). Pacific Grove, CA: Brooks/Cole.

Hobson, R. P. (1989). Beyond cognition: A theory of autism. In G. Dawson (Ed.), *Autism: Nature, diagnosis, and treatment* (pp. 22–48). New York: Guilford Press.

Holroyd, J. (1974). The Questionnaire on Resources and Stress: An instrument to measure family response to a handicapped family member. *Journal of Community Psychology, 2,* 92–94.

Iwata, B. A. (1987). Negative reinforcement in applied behavior analysis: An emerging technology. *Journal of Applied Behavior Analysis, 20,* 361–387.

Iwata, B. A., Dorsey, M. F., Slifer, K. J., Bauman, K. E., & Richman, G. E. (1982). Toward a functional analysis of self-injury. *Analysis and Intervention in Developmental Disabilities, 2,* 3–20.

James, A. L., & Barry, R. J. (1980). Respiratory and vascular responses to simple visual stimuli in autistics, retardates, and normals. *Psychophysiology, 17,* 541–547.

Kaiser, A. P., Yoder, P. J., & Keetz, A. (1992). Evaluating milieu training. In S. F. Warren & J. Reichle (Eds.), *Causes and effects in communication and language intervention* (pp. 9–47). Baltimore: Brookes.

Kanner, L. (1943). Autistic disturbances of affective contact. *Nervous Child, 2,* 217–250.

Kinsbourne, M. (1987). Cerebral-brainstem relations in infantile autism. In E. Schopler & G. Mesibov (Eds.), *Neurobiological issues in autism* (pp. 107–125). New York: Plenum Press.

Koegel, L. K. (1994). *Teaching children with autism to use a self-initiated strategy to learn expressive vocabulary.* Unpublished doctoral dissertation, University of California, Santa Barbara.

Koegel, L. K., & Koegel, R. L., & Dunlap, G. (1996). Positive behavioral support. Baltimore: Brookes.

Koegel, L. K., & Koegel, R. L., Hurley, C., & Frea, W. D. (1992). Improving social skills and disruptive behavior in children with autism through self-management. *Journal of Applied Behavior Analysis, 25,* 341–353.

Koegel, R. L., & Covert, A. (1972). The relationship of self-stimulation to learning in autistic children. *Journal of Applied Behavior Analysis, 5,* 381–387.

Koegel, R. L., Firestone, P. B., Kramme, K. W., & Dunlap, G. (1974). Increasing spontaneous play by suppressing self-stimulation in autistic children. *Journal of Applied Behavior Analysis, 7,* 521–528.

Koegel, R. L., & Koegel, L. K. (1990). Extended reductions in stereotypical behavior through self-management in multiple community settings. *Journal of Applied Behavior Analysis, 23,* 119–128.

Koegel, R. L., Koegel, L. K., & O'Neill, R. E. (1989). Generalization in the treatment of autism. In L. V. McReynolds & J. E. Spradlin (Eds.), *Generalization strategies in the treatment of communication disorders* (pp. 116–0131). Toronto: B. C. Decker.

Koegel, R. L., O'Dell, M. C., & Koegel, L. K. (1987). A natural language teaching paradigm for nonverbal autistic children. *Journal of Autism and Developmental Disorders, 17,* 187–200.

Koegel, R. L., & Rincover, A. (1976). Some detrimental effects of using extra stimuli to guide responding in normal and autistic children. *Journal of Abnormal Child Psychology, 4,* 59–71.

Koegel, R. L., & Schreibman, L. (1977). Teaching autistic children to respond to simultaneous multiple cues. *Journal of Experimental Child Psychology, 24,* 199–311.

Koegel, R. L., Schreibman, L., Good, A., Cerniglia, L., Murphy, C., & Koegel, L. K. (1989). *How to teach pivotal behavior to children with autism: A training manual.* University of California, Santa Barbara.

Laski, K. E., Charlop, M. J., & Schreibman, L. (1988). Training parents to use the natural language paradigm to increase their autistic children's speech. *Journal of Applied Behavior Analysis, 18,* 15–28.

Le Couteur, A., Rutter, M., Lord, C., Rios, P., Robertson, S., Holdgrafer, M., & McLennan, J. D. (1989). Autism Diagnostic Interview: A standardized investigator-based instrument. *Journal of Autism and Developmental Disorders, 19,* 363–387.

Lee, A., Hobson, R. P., & Chiat, S. (1994). I, you, me, and autism: an experimental study. *Journal of Autism and Developmental Disorders, 24,* 155–176.

Lincoln, A. J., Courchesne, E., Harms, L., & Allen, M. (1993). Contextual probability evaluation in autistic, receptive developmental language disorder and control children: ERP evidence. *Journal of Autism and Developmental Disorders, 23,* 37–58.

Lincoln, A. J., Courchesne, E., Harms, L., & Allen, M. (1995). Sensory modulation of auditory stimuli in children with autism and receptive developmental language disorder: Event-related brain potential evidence. *Journal of Autism and Developmental Disorders, 25,* 521–539.

Lord, C. (1993). Early social development in autism. In E. Schopler, M. E. Van Bourgondien, & M. M. Bristol (Eds.), *Preschool issues in autism* (pp. 61–94). New York: Plenum Press.

Lord, C., Rutter, M., Goode, S., Heemsbergen, J., Jordan, H., & Mawhood, L. (1989). Autism diagnostic observation schedule: A standardized observation of communicative and social behavior. *Journal of Autism and Developmental Disorders, 19,* 185–212.

Lord, C., & Schopler, E. (1989). The role of age at assessment, developmental level, and test in the stability of intelligence scores in young autistic children. *Journal of Autism & Developmental Disorders, 19,* 463–499.

Lovaas, O. I. (1987). Behavioral treatment and normal educational and intellectual functioning in young autistic children. *Journal of Consulting and Clinical Psychology, 55,* 3–9.

Lovaas, O. I., Koegel, R. L., & Schreibman, L. (1979). Stimulus overselectivity in autism. A Review of research. *Psychological Bulletin, 86,* 1236–1254.

Lovaas, O. I., Litrownik, A., & Mann, R. (1971). Response latencies to auditory stimuli in autistic children engaged in self-stimulatory behavior. *Behaviour Research and Therapy, 9,* 39–49.

Lovaas, O. I., Newsom, C., & Hickman, C. (1987). Self-stimulatory behavior and perceptual reinforcement. *Journal of Applied Behavior Analysis, 20,* 45–68.

Lovaas, O. I., Schreibman, L., Koegel, R. L., & Rehm, R. (1971). Selective responding by autistic children to multiple sensory input. *Journal of Abnormal Psychology, 77,* 211–222.

Lovaas, O. I., Varni, J., Koegel, R. L., & Lorsch, N. C. (1977). Some observations on the non-extinguishability of children's speech. *Child Development, 48,* 1121–1127.

Loveland, K. A., & Landry, S. H. (1986). Joint attention and language in autism and developmental language delay. *Journal of Autism and Developmental Disabilities, 16,* 335–349.

Maurice, C., Green, G., & Luce, S. C. (1996). *Behavioral intervention for young children with autism.* Austin, TX: Pro-Ed.

McBride, J. A., & Panksepp, J. (1995). An examination of the phenomenology and the reliability of ratings of compulsive behavior in autism. *Journal of Autism and Developmental Disorders, 25,* 381–396.

McDougle, C. J., Kresch, L. E., Goodman, W. K., Naylor, S. T., Volkmar, F. R., Cohen, D. J., & Price, L. H. (1995). A case-controlled study of repetitive thoughts and behavior in adults with autistic disorder and obsessive-compulsive disorder. *American Journal of Psychiatry, 152,* 772–777.

McEvoy, R. E., Loveland, K. A., & Landry, S. H. (1988). The functions of immediate echolalia in autistic children: A developmental perspective. *Journal of Autism and Developmental Disorders, 18,* 657–668.

McGee, G. G., Krantz, P. J., & McClannahan, L. E. (1985). The facilitative effects of incidental teaching on preposition use by autistic children. *Journal of Applied Behavior Analysis, 18,* 17–31.

Moos, R. H. (1974). *Family Environment Scale: Preliminary Manual.* Palo Alto, CA: Consulting Psychologists Press.

Mottron, L., & Belleville, S. (1995). Perspective production in a savant autistic draughtsman. *Psychological Medicine, 25,* 639–648.

Mundy, P. (1993). Normal functioning versus high-functioning status in children with autism. *American Journal on Mental Retardation, 97,* 381–384.

Mundy, P., Sigman, M., & Kasari, C. (1990). A longitudinal study of joint attention and language development in autistic children. *Journal of Autism and Developmental Disorders, 20,* 115–128.

Myklebust, H. R. (1995). Verbal and nonverbal cognitive processes: A comparison of learning disability and autistic children. In E. Schopler & G. Mesibov (Eds.), *Learning and cognition in autism* (pp. 33–55). New York: Plenum Press.

Nelson, E. C., & Pribor, E. F. (1993). A calendar savant with autism and Tourette syndrome: Response to treatment and thoughts on the interrelationships of these conditions. *Annals of Clinical Psychiatry, 5,* 135–140.

O'Neill, R. E., Horner, R. H., Albin, R. W., Storey, K., & Sprague, J. R. *Functional analysis of behavior: A practical assessment guide.* Pacific Grove, CA: Brooks/Cole.

Ornitz, E. M. (1989). Autism at the interface between sensory and information processing. In G. Dawson (Ed.), *Autism: Nature, diagnosis, and treatment* (pp. 174–207). New York: Guilford Press.

Ornitz, E. M., & Ritvo, E. R. (1968). Perceptual inconstancy in early infantile autism. *Archives of General Psychiatry, 18,* 76–98.

Oswald, D. P., Ellis, C. R., Singh, N. N., & Singh, Y. N. (1994). Self-injury. In J. L. Matson (Ed.), *Autism is in children and adults: Etiology, assessment, and intervention* (pp. 147–164). Pacific Grove, CA: Brooks/Cole.

Oxman, J., & Konstantareas, M. M. (1981). On the nature and variability of linguistic impairment in autism. *Clinical Psychology Review, 1,* 337–352.

Paul, R. (1987). Communication. In D. J. Cohen, & A. M. Donnellan (Eds.), *Handbook of autism and pervasive developmental disorders* (pp. 61–84). New York: Wiley.

Pierce, K., & Schreibman, L. (1994). Teaching daily living skills to children with autism in unsupervised settings through pictorial self-management. *Journal of Applied Behavior Analysis, 27,* 471–481.

Pierce, K., & Schreibman, L. (1995). Increasing complex social behaviors in children with autism: Effects of peer-implemented pivotal response training. *Journal of Applied Behavior Analysis, 28,* 285–295.

Posner, M. I., Walker, J. A., Friedrich, F. J., & Rafal, R. D. (1984). Effects of parietal injury on covert orienting of attention. *Journal of Neuroscience, 4,* 1863–1874.

Prior, M., Dahlstrom, B., & Squires, T. (1990). Autistic children's knowledge of thinking and feeling states in other people. *Journal of Child Psychology and Psychiatry, 31,* 587–601.

Prizant, B. M. (1983). Language acquisition and communicative behavior: Toward an understanding of the "whole" of it. *Journal of Speech and Hearing Disorders, 48,* 296–307.

Prizant, B. M., & Wetherby, A. M. (1993). Communication in preschool autistic children. In E. Schopler, M. E., Van Bourgondien, & M. M. Bristol (Eds.), *Preschool issues in autism* (pp. 94–128). New York: Plenum Press.

Ricks, D. M., & Wing, L. (1975). Language communication, and the use of symbols in normal and autistic children. *Journal of Autism and Childhood Schizophrenia, 5,* 191–221.

Rimland, B. (1964). *Infantile autism.* New York: Appleton-Century-Crofts.

Rimland, B., & Fein, D. (1988). Special talents of autistic savants. In L. K. Obler & D. Fein (Eds.), *The exceptional brain: Neuropsychology of talented and special abilities.* New York: Guilford Press.

Rincover, A. (1978). Variables affecting stimulus-fading and discriminative responding in psychotic children. *Journals of Abnormal Psychology, 87,* 541–553.

Rincover , A., & Ducharme, J. M. (1987). Variables influencing stimulus overselectivity and "tunnel vision" in developmentally delayed children. *American Journal of Mental Deficiency, 91,* 422–430.

Rincover, A., & Koegel, R. L. (1975). Setting generality and stimulus control in autistic children. *Journal of Applied Behavior Analysis, 8,* 235–246.

Ritvo, E. R., & Freeman, B. J. (1978). National Society for Autistic Children definition of the syndrome of autism. *Journal of Autism and Childhood Schizophrenia, 8,* 162–167.

Robbins, F. R., Dunlap, G., & Plienis, A. J. (1991). Family characteristics, family training and the progress of young children with autism. *Journal of Early Intervention, 15,* 173–184.

Runco, M. A., Charlop, M. H., & Schreibman, L. (1986). The occurrence of autistic children's self-stimulation as a function of familiar versus unfamiliar stimulus conditions. *Journal of Autism and Developmental Disorders, 16,* 31–44.

Rutter, M. (1968). Concepts of autism. *Journal of Child Psychiatry and Psychology, 46,* 241–249.

Rutter, M. (1970). Autistic children: Infancy to adulthood. *Seminars in Psychiatry, 2,* 435–450.

Rutter, M. (1978). Diagnosis and definition of childhood autism. *Journal of Autism and Childhood Schizophrenia, 8,* 139–161.

Rutter, M., & Lockyer, L. (1967). A five to fifteen year follow-up study of infantile psychosis. I. Description of sample. *British Journal of Psychiatry, 113,* 1169–1182.

Sainato, D. M., Strain, P. S., Lefebvre, D., & Rapp, N. (1990). Effects of self-evaluation on the independent work skills of preschool children with disabilities. *Exceptional Children, 56,* 540–549.

Schopler, E., Short, A., & Mesibov, G. (1989). Relation of behavioral treatment to normal functioning: Comment on Lovaas. *Journal of Consulting and Clinical Psychology, 57,* 162–164.

Schreibman, L. (1975). Effects of within-stimulus and extra-stimulus prompting on discrimination learning in autistic children. *Journal of Applied Behavior Analysis, 8,* 91–112.

Schreibman, L. (1988). *Autism.* Newbury Park, CA: Sage.

Schreibman, L. (1996). Brief report: The case for social and behavior intervention research. *Journal of Autism and Developmental Disorders, 26,* 247–250.

Schreibman, L. (1997). Theoretical perspectives on behavioral intervention for individuals with autism. In D. J. Cohen & F. R. Volkmar (Eds.), *Handbook of autism and pervasive developmental disorders,* (2nd ed., pp. 920–933). New York: Wiley.

Schreibman, L., & Charlop, M. H. (1987). Autism. In V. B. Van Hasselt & M. Hersen (Eds.), *Psychological evaluation of the developmentally and physically disabled* (pp. 155–177). New York: Grune & Stratton.

Schreibman, L., & Charlop, M. H. (1989). Infantile autism. In T. H. Ollendick & M. Hersen (Eds.), *Handbook of child psychopathology* (pp. 105–129). New York: Plenum Press.

Schreibman, L., Charlop, M. H., & Koegel, R. L. (1982). Teaching autistic children to use extra-stimulus prompts. *Journal of Experimental Child Psychology, 33,* 475–496.

Schreibman, L., Charlop, M. H., & Tryon, A. S. (1981, August). *The acquisition and generalization of appropriate spontaneous speech in autistic children.* Paper presented at the annual meeting of the American Psychological Association, Los Angeles, CA.

Schreibman, L., Kaneko, W. M., & Koegel, R. L. (1991). Positive affect of parents of autistic children: A comparison across two teaching techniques. *Behavior Therapy, 22,* 479–490.

Schreibman, L., & Koegel, R. L. (1996). Fostering self-management: Parent-delivered pivotal response training for children with autistic disorder. In E. D. Hibbs & P. S. Jensen (Eds.), *Psychosocial treatment for child and adolescent disorders: Empirically based strategies for clinical practice* (pp. 525–552). Washington, DC: American Psychological Association.

Schreibman, L., Koegel, L. K., & Koegel, R. L. (1989). Autism. In M. Hersen (Ed.), *Innovations in child behavior therapy* (pp. 395–428). New York: Springer.

Schreibman, L., Koegel, R. L., Mills, J. I., & Burke, J. C. (1984). Training parent-child interactions. In E. Schopler & G. B. Mesibov (Eds.), *The effects of autism on the family* (pp. 123–149). New York: Plenum Press.

Schreibman, L., Kohlenberg, B. S., & Britten, K. R. (1986). Differential responding to content and intonation components of a complex auditory stimulus by nonverbal and echolalic autistic children. Special Issue: Stimulus control research and developmental disabilities. *Analysis & Intervention in Developmental Disabilities, 6,* 109–125.

Schreibman, L., & Lovaas, O. I. (1973). Overselective response to social stimuli by autistic children. *Journal of Abnormal Child Psychology, 1,* 152–168.

Schreibman, L., & Mills, J. I. (1983). Infantile autism. In T. J. Ollendick & M. Hersen (Eds.), *Handbook of child psychopathology* (pp. 123–149). New York: Plenum Press.

Sheinkopf, S. J., & Siegel, B. (1998). Home based behavioral treatment of young children with autism. *Journal of Autism & Developmental Disorders, 28,* 15–23.

Sherer, M., & Schreibman, L. (1998, May). *Deciphering variables related to positive treatment outcome: Reports of intensive Pivotal Response Training therapy for young children with autism.* Paper presented at the 24th annual meeting of the Association for Behavior Analysis Meeting, Orlando, FL.

Smalley, S. L., & Collins, F. (1996). Brief report: Genetic, prenatal and immunologic factors. *Journal of Autism and Developmental Disorders, 26,* 195–198.

Smith, T., Eikeseth, S., Klevstrand, M., & Lovaas, O. I. (1997). Intensive behavioral treatment for preschoolers with severe mental retardation and pervasive developmental disorder. *American Journal on Mental Retardation 102,* 238–249.

Stahmer, A. C. (1995). Teaching symbolic play to children with autism using pivotal response training. *Journal of Autism and Developmental Disorders, 25,* 123–141.

Stahmer, A. C., & Schreibman, L. (1992). Teaching children with autism appropriate play in unsupervised environments using a self-management treatment package. *Journal of Applied Behavior Analysis, 25,* 447–459.

Sturmey, P., & Sevin, J. A. (1994). Defining and assessing autism. In J. L. Matson (Ed.), *Autism is in children and adults: Etiology, assessment, and intervention* (pp. 13–36). Pacific Grove, CA: Brooks/Cole.

Tager-Flusberg, H. (1994). The relationship between language and social cognition: Lessons from autism. In Y. Levy (Ed.), *Other children, other languages: Issues in the theory of language acquisition* (pp. 359–381). Hillsdale, NJ: Erlbaum.

Tate, B. G., & Baroff, G. S. (1966). Aversive control of self-injurious behavior in a psychotic boy. *Behaviour Research and Therapy, 4,* 281–287.

Thorp, D. M., Stahmer, A. C., & Schreibman, L. (1995). Teaching sociodramatic play to children with autism using pivotal response training. *Journal of Applied Behavior Analysis, 25,* 265–282.

Ungerer, J. A. (1989). The early development of autistic children: Implications for defining primary deficits. In G. Dawson (Ed.), *Autism: Nature, diagnosis, and treatment* (pp. 75–91). New York: Guilford Press.

Van Bourgondien, M. E. (1993). Behavior management in the preschool years. In E. Schopler, M. E., Van Bourgondien, & M. M. Bristol (Eds.), *Preschool issues in autism* (pp. 129–145). New York: Plenum Press.

Volden, J., & Lord, C. (1991). Neologisms and idiosyncratic language in autistic speakers. *Journal of Autism and Developmental Disorders, 21,* 109–130.

Wainwright-Sharp, J. A., & Bryson, S. E. (1993). Visual orienting deficits in high-functioning people with autism. *Journal of Autism and Developmental Disorders, 23,* 1–13.

Whalen, C., & Schreibman, L. (1998, May). *Easing transitional difficulties of children with autism using video priming techniques.* Paper presented at the 24th annual meeting of the Association for Behavior Analysis Meeting, Orlando, FL.

Wing, L. (1976). Diagnosis, clinical description, and prognosis. In L. Wing (Ed.), *Early childhood autism* (pp. 15–48). London: Pergamon Press.

Wolfberg, P. J., & Schuler, A. L. (1993). Integrated play groups: A model for promoting the social and cognitive dimensions of play in children with autism. *Journal of Autism and Developmental Disorders, 23,* 467–489.

Author Note

Preparation of this chapter was facilitated by U.S. Public Service Research Grant MH39434 from the National Institute of Mental Health.

The Causes of Self-Injurious Behavior and Their Clinical Implications

Stephen R. Schroeder
R. Matthew Reese
Jessica Hellings
Pippa Loupe
R. E. Tessel
University of Kansas
Lawrence, KS

In this chapter we review hypotheses and factors related to the probable causes of self-injurious behavior (SIB) among people with mental retardation and developmental disabilities. We do not review treatments for SIB. Over the past 25 years, thousands of studies, hundreds of reviews, and more recently several treatment manuals for treating SIB have been published. Since 1990, publications on SIB have been tracked by an abstract service, *Self-Injury Abstracts and Reviews.*[1] Perhaps the overriding question still remains, however: Why do people do it? Why do they choose these particularly counterintuitive forms of behavior, as opposed to temper tantrums or aggression? That is the question we explore in this chapter.

SIB Defined

By SIB we mean acts directed toward oneself that result in tissue damage (Tate & Baroff, 1966). SIB is a heterogeneous response class, multiply caused and multiply affected (Schroeder, Mulick, & Rojahn, 1980). Rojahn (1994) reviewed several large-scale prevalence studies that reported 38 different topographies, the most frequent being head banging, biting self, scratching self, and hitting self with objects. There does not seem to be much overlap with self-mutilation, such as enucleation of an eye or limb removal, which is often observed in psychiatric populations (Favazza, 1987). Mortality among persons with SIB does not differ significantly from that of a population matched for age, gender, mental age, but without SIB (Borthwick-Duffy 1994; Wieseler, Hanson, & Nord, 1995). SIB often is life-threatening, however.

Probable Causes Defined

It is still not unusual to read in the literature statements such as, "The literature overwhelmingly supports the view that SIB is acquired," or, "Behavioral assessment procedures do not take into account the underlying causes of SIB." Both of these views are anachronisms. One might as well ask, "Which contributes more to the area of a rectangle—its length or its width?" Causality in clinical practice is based on finding the stimulus antecedents to behavior (or symptoms and signs, in medical terms). This fact does not preclude the search for genetic or neurobiological causes. Indeed, when all antecedents are consistent across domains of knowledge, the plausibility of probable causes is greatly enhanced; when they disagree, plausibility is decreased. In considering the relative contribution of biological and environmental causes, it is helpful to visualize a two-by-two contingency table in which one compares the effect of each alone and in

---

[1]   *Self-Injury Abstracts and Reviews* (1992–present). Oxford Publishing Group, P. O. Box 974, Oxford, MS 38655.

combination compared to unknown causes (see Figure 4.1). As a matter of fact, there is substantial literature to fill each of these four contingency panels, and this should not surprise us. Each may be correct under some circumstances.

Moreover, causes are often inferred from successful treatment with environmental or biomedical interventions. However, in statistical terms, or from the viewpoint of external validity, confirmation of a hypothesis in this manner may have only specificity while lacking sensitivity. One cannot predict who will or who will not respond among the people yet to be treated. Experimental manipulation is severely restricted for ethical reasons because of the danger to the client. Withholding a highly probable effective treatment is also often ethically problematic.

Under restricted conditions such as those described above, hypothesis-testing of probable causes for SIB is usually an observational multivariate procedure in which a host of independent variables, interacting variables, and confounding variables are weighed to assess their relative influence in causing the target behavior. Environmental causes may be eliciting stimuli (e.g., a fear or avoidance stimulus), response-produced or chained stimuli (e.g., previously reinforced SIB), and setting events or social ecologies (e.g., a mealtime or a pathogenic environment). Biological causes may be genetic or neurodevelopmental disorders that increase

susceptibility to SIB, physical impairments that affect communication, or treatable medical conditions. Environmental causes are usually explored by a number of operant procedures collectively labeled "functional analysis." Biological causes are usually explored in a step-down algorithm in which all previously known biomedical antecedents are reviewed and ruled out until likely causal candidates are found, tested, and treated (Gualtieri, 1989). We will call these probable causes risk factors and explore them in the next section.

Genetic Risk Factors

The term *behavioral phenotype* was introduced by Nyhan (1972, p. 1) to describe an observable behavior pattern so characteristic of a person with a genetic disorder that its presence suggests an underlying genetic condition and structural deficits in the central nervous system. Over the past 25 years the study of such specific behavioral patterns characteristic of single-gene and polygenic developmental disorders has become increasingly important (Dykens, 1995). Here we review briefly disorders with a higher incidence of SIB relative to similar comparison groups.

Lesch-Nyhan Syndrome

Lesch-Nyhan syndrome (Lesch & Nyhan, 1964) is the most distinctive genetic disorder with a behavioral phenotype in which almost 100% of the cases show a predisposition to compulsive self-biting. It is a sex-linked recessive disorder of purine metabolism caused by absence of the enzyme hypoxanthine-guanine phosphoribosyltransferase (HPRT) in the purine salvage pathway. Other features are hyperuricemia, cerebral palsy, choreoathetosis, spasticity, dystonia, dysarthric speech, and mental retardation (Lesch & Nyhan, 1964). Because people with Lesch-Nyhan syndrome are difficult to test, it may be that their intelligence is underestimated (Anderson, Ernst, & Davis, 1992). Because the disorder is so rare, perhaps 1 in 100,000 (Crawhall, Henderson, & Kelly, 1981), there are only a few study groups of more than 50 cases in the United States. So there are wide variations in prevalence estimates.

Figure 4.1. Causes of self-injurious behavior (SIB).

BIOLOGICAL CAUSES

Known   Unknown

ENVIRONMENTAL CAUSES

Known: SIB   SIB

Unknown: SIB   SIB

The characteristic forms of SIB are biting of the lips, tongue, fingers, arms, and shoulders as well as head banging, back arching and head snapping, eye poking, getting fingers and toes caught in one's wheelchair (Nyhan, 1967). The biting is often fierce and disfiguring, apparently very difficult to inhibit. The person often begs for restraints when at risk. Sometimes, such begging is followed by aggressive hitting and insulting the caregiver, then apologizing for being out of control.

No psychotropic medications or replacement therapies (e.g., enzyme therapy, gene therapy) have been very successful for Lesch-Nyhan syndrome, although many have been tried (Nyhan, 1994). Lasting behavioral interventions have been successful under restricted conditions among milder cases, but not among severe cases. Perhaps this is because SIB in Lesch-Nyhan disease is the result of an interaction of an X-linked genetic predisposition, maturational variables, and environmental variables. For an environmental intervention alone to have much effect, it might have to be very comprehensive, intensive, and extensive over infancy and childhood, and targeted toward the specific neurobiological dysfunctions related to SIB.

A considerable amount is known about the neurobiology of SIB in Lesch-Nyhan syndrome (see Harris, 1995, for a review). The metabolic abnormality is a genetic deficiency of the enzyme HPRT, resulting in excessive uric acid and gout unless it is treated with allopurinol. This treatment does not affect SIB, however. It is believed that disruption of the neurotransmitter dopamine in the basal ganglia is the cause of the SIB. Postmortem studies of Lesch-Nyhan cases by Lloyd et al. (1981) showed a significant loss of dopamine neurons in nigrostriatal and mesolimbic dopamine terminal areas. Similar results were found by Wong et al. (1996) using in vivo PET scanning. Furthermore, the depletion was larger for the D_1 dopamine receptor subtype than for other dopamine receptors. This is partial confirmation of results found in a rodent model for Lesch-Nyhan self-biting in rats by Breese and his colleagues (see Breese et al., 1995, for a review).

The Breese rat model of SIB has been a very heuristic model for examining the causes of self-biting in Lesch-Nyhan syndrome and perhaps other forms of SIB. First, it suggests that some SIB may be primarily mediated by D_1 dopamine receptor dysfunction. Therefore, D_1 dopamine modulating drugs (e.g., primarily atypical neuroleptics such as clozapine) may be more efficacious in decreasing SIB. Secondly, it suggests that, in cases where early (neonatal or perinatal) depletion of dopamine is related to onset of SIB, early intervention with SIB is very important to later modulation of SIB. SIB may be more readily preventable if intervention is begun earlier rather than if it is begun later in childhood.

There is also a mouse model for HPRT deficiency in Lesch-Nyhan syndrome; however, these animals show no motor deficiencies or SIB (Breese et al., 1995). However, these animals will be valuable in studying the neurodegenerative process in Lesch-Nyhan syndrome.

Cornelia de Lange Syndrome

Cornelia de Lange syndrome (also called Brachmann-de Lange syndrome) is an autosomal dominant disorder with no distinctive biochemical or chromosomal markers. Discovered in 1933 (de Lange, 1933), the initial clinical features noted were dwarfism, distinctive facies, hirsutism, microcephaly, short forearms, abnormal hands and feet, severe feeding disorders, hearing loss, vision problems, sleep problems, seizures, severe growth, and mental retardation (IQ range 30–85).

The behavioral phenotype of Cornelia de Lange syndrome includes limited speech, avoidance of being held, stereotyped movements (e.g., whirling) that have autistic-like features, and retarded social development (Harris, 1992). Surveys of parent associations in Denmark (Beck, 1987), Germany (Sarimski, 1997), and the United States (Gualtieri, 1991; Hawley, Jackson, & Kurnit, 1985) suggest a prevalence between 1 in 50,000 and 1 in 100,000 live births.

Although the majority of Cornelia de Lange cases are placid and good-natured, a significant number show irritability, aggression, destructiveness, and SIB. In the above-cited surveys SIB was noted in 17% (Beck, 1987), 40% (Sarimski, 1997) and 64% (Gualtieri, 1991) of the cases. The Beck study surveyed 36 families and Sarimski, 27 families. Gualtieri studied 700 families of the Cornelia de Lange Foundation that reside mostly in the United States and other English-speaking countries. Differences in prevalence estimates may be related to sampling procedures.

According to Gualtieri (1991), who has conducted the most in-depth survey to date, antecedents for SIB in Cornelia de Lange syndrome appear to reflect immature patterns of social development (i.e., the SIB occurred when the person was angry, frustrated, sick, or in pain) or for attention or in response to unreasonable demands. The most common topographies were self-biting, hitting, slapping, hair pulling, head banging, picking, scratching, and gouging, sometimes resulting in mild injuries. But the uncontrollable, fierce self-biting seen in Lesch-Nyhan syndrome did not occur. Parents reported SIB beginning at ages 2, 3, 4 and worsening into later childhood and early adulthood and decreasing thereafter. This time-course parallels that of most SIB cases without a known genetic syndrome. Gualtieri's (1991) view is that their SIB mainly grows out of immature behavior patterns, a temperamental nature, and sensitivity to aversive stimuli. No particular psychotropic medication has proven very successful in treating their SIB, but few controlled case studies have addressed this issue.

Rett's Syndrome

Rett (1966) initially described this disorder in 22 girls. It consists of severe mental retardation, stereotyped hand-wringing movement, dementia, autistic behavior, lack of facial expression, ataxic gait, cortical atrophy, seizures, and hyperammonemia. It only received international recognition after similar cases were noted in Sweden by Hagberg, Aicardi, Dias, and Ramos (1983) and two international conferences, one in Vienna and one in the United States, followed in 1984 and 1985.

Prevalence is estimated at 1 in 10,000 to 1 in 15,000 (Naidu, 1992). Rett syndrome occurs predominantly in females, but there are

as yet no known genetic markers. Possibly it is an autosomal dominant mutation that is lethal in males. At least two cases of monozygotic twins and two cases of sisters have been reported (Naidu, 1992). It is often misdiagnosed as autism. It is probably better classified as a degenerative neurological disorder than as a genetic syndrome whose main effect is mental retardation (Gillberg, 1987; Tsai, 1992).

From a developmental perspective, infants with Rett's syndrome appear normal at birth. Between 6 and 18 months there appears to be stagnation in growth followed by regression and deterioration until 36 months; a plateau occurs in the school years, and deterioration with spasticity and scoliosis resumes in adulthood (Kerr, 1992). Brain neurochemistry studies and postmortem neuropathology studies have noted reduced levels of choline acetyltransferase (CHAT) and biogenic amines and metabolites (Wenk, Naidu, & Moser, 1989), low brain weight, and small, densely packed cells with limited dendritic branching in a variety of brain regions, suggesting arrested maturation (Bauman, 1991).

SIB in Rett's syndrome, according to a parent survey, appears to arise out of anxiety, panic, agitation, and crying for no apparent reason. Mild self-injury by hand mouthing and biting occurred in 38% of cases (Sansom, Krishnan, Corbett, & Kerr, 1993). However, head banging and more serious SIB also occur at much lower frequencies. The biting is not fierce and driven as in Lesch-Nyhan syndrome.

Behavioral treatments aimed at SIB in Rett's syndrome have met with mixed success (Iwata, Pace, Willis, Gamache, & Hyman, 1986; Oliver, Murphy, Crayton, & Corbett, 1993; Smith, Klevstrand, & Lovaas, 1995). Treatments aimed at avoidance of anxiety attacks and agitation seem to work best at present. Psychotropic medications have not been selectively successful for SIB in Rett's syndrome (Harris, 1995).

Riley-Day Syndrome (Congenital Insensitivity to Pain)

Disorders involving congenital insensitivity to pain such as Riley-Day syndrome (Riley, Day, Greeley, & Langford, 1949) may be associated with a subset of people who self-injure because pain perception is absent at birth over the entire body, while other sensory modalities are intact (Harris, 1992). SIB may be accidental or due to lack of caution. It does not follow the developmental syndromal pattern as the previously discussed genetic disorders related to SIB seem to do.

Riley-Day syndrome is an autosomal recessive disorder estimated to occur in 1 in 10,000 to 1 in 20,000 live births. Mental retardation occurs in about one third of them. There appears to be a reduction in dopamine—hydroxylase, the enzyme that converts dopamine to epinephrine. The opioid system also seems to be involved (Dehen, Willer, Boureau, & Cambier, 1977). Dehen et al. (1977) found that naloxone reduced the pain threshold and nociception reflex in these patients with congenital insensitivity to pain, but these results have not been replicated. This syndrome seems to be a natural one for studying the opioid system and SIB, which is currently a topic of considerable interest (Sandman & Hetrick, 1995; Thompson, Symons, Delaney, & England, 1995).

Prader-Willi Syndrome

As described by Prader, Labhart, and Willi (1956), Prader-Willi syndrome is a congenital syndrome involving chromosomal translocations in the region of chromosome 15 in 80% of cases. A small percentage appear to have neither deletions nor disomy (Holm, 1996). There are nearly 30 diagnostic symptoms of which the major ones are neonatal and infantile hypotonia, feeding problems in infancy, excessive weight gain between 12 and 72 months of age, distinctive facial features, hypogonadism, developmental delay, hyperphagia, foraging, obsession with food, high pain threshold, and behavior problems. It occurs in 1 in 10,000 to 1 in 20,000 live births (Harris, 1992).

Behavior problems involve emotional lability, stubbornness, and tantrums that are often related to food seeking and gorging. Anxiety, aggression, and compulsive behavior are common (Stein, Keating, & Zar, 1993). In this survey of 369 cases Stein et al. (1993) also found that skin picking is the most common form of SIB, occurring in 19.6% of cases. Other lower frequency SIB topographies were nose picking, nail biting, lip biting, and hair pulling. Treatment approaches involve behavior management, family interventions, and pharmacological interventions to control hoarding, overeating, weight gain, and psychiatric disorders. Stein et al. (1993) found that 17.5% were receiving serotonin reuptake inhibitors; 20.8% neuroleptics; and 25% stimulants. Recently, a few studies have successfully treated severe skin picking in Prader-Willi syndrome with fluoxetine (Tu, Hartridge, & Izawa, 1992; Warnock & Kestenbaum, 1992). A comprehensive intervention program is needed to address all of the needs of these children.

Tourette's Syndrome

Although Tourette's syndrome may have been known in the 1600s, it got its name from a report of nine cases by Georges Gilles de la Tourette in 1885 (Lees, Robertson, Trimble, & Murphy, 1984). The main features were multiple frequent motor and verbal tics, involuntary movements, echolalia, and coprolalia (spontaneously spoken obscenities). Onset usually ranges between 2 and 15 years. Likely implications of genetic involvement come from twin studies. It is probably an autosomal single dominant gene with incomplete penetrance, and its prevalence is estimated at 1 in 2,000 (Van de Wetering & Heutink, 1993).

Features of Tourette's syndrome include obsessive-compulsive behavior, hyperactivity attention deficit disorder (27%), and learning disorders (24%). Sometimes it is accompanied by antisocial behavior, exhibitionism, inappropriate sexual behavior, and SIB (13–53%). Severity of SIB is related to severity of Tourette's symptoms. The wide range of prevalence estimates probably is due to referral bias to specialty clinics (see Robertson, 1992, for a review). Robertson, Trimble, and Lees (1989) did an in-depth study of an outpatient clinic cohort of 90 Tourette's cases, 33% of which did 23 topographies of SIB similar to those observed among people with more severe mental retardation (i.e., head banging, head-to-object hitting, self-biting, self-scratching, hair pulling, poking objects into bodily orifices, and a variety of less frequent topographies). These prevalences of SIB in Tourette's (> 30%) are much higher than in other community psychiatric populations or among people with mental retardation living in the community (< 7%) (Robertson et al., 1989).

No consistent abnormalities in neuro-anatomy, neuropharmacology, or neurochemistry have been found, although hypotheses abound. Abnormalities of the dopamine system have received the most support (Singer, 1992). The treatment choice appears to be pharmaco-therapy with dopamine antagonists, chief among which is haloperidol (Seignot, 1961); this treatment has been known for over 35 years. The behavioral intervention literature for Tourette's syndrome is very limited.

Fragile X Syndrome

Fragile X syndrome is a familial X-linked disorder first reported by Martin and Bell (1943). Recently the gene FMR-1 was cloned in DNA by Verkerk et al. (1991). Over the past 50 years, Fragile X syndrome has come to be recognized as the second most common form of heritable mental retardation behind Down syndrome. Its prevalence is estimated at 1 in 1,250 in males and 1 in 2,500 in females. Its primary clinical manifestations in males are mental retardation, abnormal facial features (long jaw and big ears), prominent forehead, macrorchidism, mitral valve prolapse, gaze aversion, and language delay. No specific neurochemical abnormalities have been found (Hagerman & Silverman, 1991).

Behavioral problems in Fragile X syndrome involve impulsivity, hyperactivity, autism (in 7% of cases), stereotyped behavior, aggression, and SIB (Hagerman, 1990). Hagerman, Jackson, Levitas, Rimland, and Braden (1986) found 66% hand flapping, 74% hand biting, and 84% unusual hand mannerisms in 50 males with Fragile X; but these figures have not been compared to a comparable group without the syndrome. Behavioral and pharmacological interventions have not proven selectively more efficacious in the Fragile X population compared to the general population of people with mental retardation.

Other Syndromes

Other conditions that have involved SIB are Down syndrome, autism, cri-du-chat syndrome, congenital rubella, prematurity, fetal alcohol syndrome, postnatal brain injury, and 47XYY and 49XXXXY chromosomal anomalies (Hyman, 1996). Whether the incidence of SIB is higher in these syndromes than in comparable groups without them is not known. Perhaps they are related to mediating variables such as seizures and severity of mental retardation, which are highly related to prevalence and severity of SIB.

Neurobiological Risk Factors

Seizures and Degenerative Neurological Conditions

Many of the previous genetic disorders involve a history of seizures and a degenerative neurological condition that may be related to a distinctive behavior phenotype for SIB. SIB prevalence has also been found to be higher in the rest of the mentally retarded population without a known genetic syndrome (Borthwick-Duffy, 1994; Bruininks, Olson, Larson, & Lakin, 1994; Jacobson, 1990; Rojahn, 1994; Schroeder, Schroeder, Smith, & Dalldorf, 1978). The association is related more to the severity than the type of the seizure or degenerative condition. In one study, Gedye (1989) argued that SIB was caused by frontal lobe seizures; however, Coulter (1990) has disputed this view. Further study and replication are needed. The problem is that SIB cases with frontal lobe seizures are relatively rare, so that it is difficult to find a sufficient number to compare SIB among people with different types of neurological disorders. Nevertheless one would expect from the literature on animal models for SIB that focal lesions in the nigrostriatal and mesolimbic dopamine systems might be related to SIB (see Breese et al., 1995, for a review).

Psychiatric Risk Factors

A number of prevalence studies show a higher incidence of psychiatric disorders among people with SIB (Borthwick-Duffy, 1994;

Rojahn, 1994). Which is cause and which is effect is often difficult to determine because there is little overlap of *Diagnostic and Statistical Manual of Mental Disorders* (*DSM-IV*; American Psychiatry Association, 1994) diagnoses and aberrant behaviors such as SIB among people with mental retardation (Schroeder, Tessel, Loupe, & Stodgell, 1997). It is difficult to study their interaction in a controlled way with a large enough population to allow subtyping of psychiatric disorders. Psychiatric disorders are treated in another chapter of this volume and are not discussed in detail here.

Environmental and Behavioral Risk Factors

Several chapters in this volume are devoted to functional assessment of environmental and behavioral antecedents that set the occasion for SIB or act as a discriminative stimulus for SIB. We will not repeat this material here. Suffice it to say that functional assessment technology grew out of the study of SIB because SIB was recognized as a heterogeneous response class, which is multiply caused and multiply affected. The standardization of a procedure by Iwata, Dorsey, Slifer, Bauman, and Richman (1982) allowed subtyping of a number of environmental stimuli and circumstances that could reliably evoke SIB, to which an appropriate treatment could then be matched. Today many tools and functional analysis schemes exist for assessing the functions of SIB. The one we like best is that of Mace and Mauk (1995), which describes five behavioral models for SIB: (a) positive reinforcement of SIB by restriction of attention, (b) positive reinforcement of SIB by restriction of tangible items, (c) negative reinforcement of SIB by escape or avoidance of demands, (d) reinforcement of SIB by sensory consequences, (e) SIB reinforced by multiple functions. Mace and Mauk (1995) have been able to use these subtypes in combination with several biomedical models of SIB to form biobehavioral intervention strategies for a wide range of SIB cases.

General Medical Risk Factors

There are now several lists of medical conditions that precipitate SIB among someone so inclined and that result in decreasing SIB when removed (Bailey & Pyles, 1989; Carr & Smith, 1995; Gardner & Sovner, 1994; Gualtieri, 1991; Reese, Hellings, & Schroeder, in press). Most sources are case reports involving conditions causing pain, discomfort, aversive emotional states, disease states, or metabolic disturbances (e.g., changes in blood sugar levels or electrolyte concentrations altering central nervous system [CNS] function). SIB may be a nonspecific response to irritability, mood change, arousal, rage attacks, disturbances in attention, or supersensitivity related to psychotropic medication (e.g., withdrawal, anxiety, depression, akathisia, dyskinesia). Adverse drug reactions may exacerbate existing SIB tendencies (Gardner & Sovner, 1994). Most of this work is anecdotal, and only a few experimental studies have been done.

Menses

Taylor, Rush, Hetrick, and Sandman (1993) examined the role of the endogenous opiate system in the association between the menstrual cycles and SIB of nine women with mental retardation residing at Fairview Hospital. They found that the highest frequency of SIB occurred in the early and late follicular phases rather than in the early or late luteal phases and was related to changing peripheral and central endorphin and pain threshold during the menstrual cycle.

Otitis Media

Several investigators have suggested a link between otitis media and ear banging, but there is only one documented case study relating middle-ear infection and head banging known to us (Gunsett, Mulick, Fernald, & Martin, 1989).

Developmental Risk Factors

Chronological Age

SIB (head banging, crib banging) begins in normal children at around 6 months and is mostly gone by 60 months (de Lissavoy, 1961;

Kravitz, Rosenthal, Teplitz, Murphy, & Thesser, 1960). Except for Lesch-Nyhan syndrome and a few other genetic disorders, SIB in people with mental retardation is generally brought to the attention of clinicians around the age of 2 years or later increasing into adulthood, then declining in the 50s and 60s (Borthwick-Duffy, 1994; Oliver, Murphy, & Corbett, 1987; Rojahn, 1994). As Rojahn (1994) noted, it may be underreported during infancy and early childhood. Early onset and chronicity tend to be correlated with severity of SIB (Schroeder et al., 1978).

Level of Mental Retardation

There is good agreement that frequency and severity of SIB are generally positively related to severity of mental retardation (Borthwick-Duffy, 1994; Jacobson, 1990; Maisto, Baumeister, & Maisto, 1978; Oliver et al., 1987; Rojahn, 1994; Schroeder et al., 1978). This rule, however, does not necessarily hold for the different genetic disorders associated with SIB that were examined in the previous section. The relation between level of mental retardation and SIB frequency and severity tends to differ somewhat for each syndrome. This fact suggests that level of mental retardation may be a surrogate variable that is multicollinear with several other disabling conditions like seizures, brain damage, and communication deficits.

Sensory and Communication Deficits

Visual, auditory, and language impairments were all found to be risk factors for SIB by Schroeder et al. (1978). This result was replicated for lack of expressive communication associated with SIB (Borthwick-Duffy, 1994; Griffin, Williams, Stark, Altmeyer, & Mason, 1986; Gunter, 1984). Whether communication deficits in SIB are collinear with level of mental retardation is uncertain. Studying SIB in syndromes where receptive or expressive language and mental retardation level are less well correlated (e.g. autism, Williams syndrome, Prader-Willi syndrome, etc.) would be of interest. A number of studies have shown that differential reinforcement of communica-

tion can decrease SIB in some cases (see Carr et al., 1994, for a review); but there has been no longitudinal developmental study showing that SIB decreases as the capacity to communicate increases. This is an interesting question to study.

Biobehavioral Models for Sib[2]

There are numerous behavioral models for how SIB is learned and how it develops: (a) arrested sensory-motor maturation related to self-stimulation and self-regulation, (b) avoidance of aversive situations, (c) attention getting, (d) dysfunctional arousal or homeostasis related to physiological state conditions, (e) frustration, (f) stress, (g) elicited self-aggression, (h) failure to communicate (Schroeder, 1991). Many of these hypotheses are now testable by using functional analysis methodology and by confirming them on a case-by-case basis (*JABA*, 1994). There still remains a number of severe chronic cases, perhaps 25% to 40%, who remain refractory to behavioral treatment alone and for whom biobehavioral interventions need to be considered. These treatments usually involve rational pharmacotherapy alone or in combination with behavioral interventions based upon biological hypotheses related to biological causes for SIB. We review these biobehavioral models for SIB in the next section.

Physiological States and SIB

Physiological state conditions (e.g., arousal) have often been invoked as preventable conditions that may set the occasion for SIB (see Schroeder, Bickel, & Richmond, 1986, for a review). However, it was only recently that a developmental model for SIB based upon physiological states was proposed by Guess and Carr (1991).

Guess and Carr (1991) proposed a three-level biobehavioral model to explain the development of rhythmic stereotypy and self-injury. Level I consists of rhythmic behaviors, such as sleep, waking, and crying patterns, that are internally regulated states common in

---

[2]   The section on Biobehavioral Models borrows heavily from a recent chapter by Schroeder, Tessel, Loupe, & Stodgell (1997) with permission from the authors.

normally developing infants but abnormal or delayed in onset among children with handicapping conditions. Level II involves the development of self-regulation of arousal and homeostasis wherein stereotypy and self-injury are viewed as adaptations to under- or over-stimulating environments. Level III represents stereotypy and self-injury as learned behavioral tendencies that come to control the behavior of others. Behavior develops in a sequence from Level I to III. There are fluid transitions between levels. Delayed, abnormal, or arrested development represents a risk factor for pathology. Interventions that facilitate the transitions to age-appropriate levels are likely to prevent behavior problems. For instance, it may be that infants or children who are at Level I may not respond well to behavioral interventions. Premature inhibitory interventions of Level I behavior states may be counterproductive, until the child has the ability to respond appropriately.

The Guess and Carr (1991) model is a biobehavioral descriptive model that attempts to integrate a variety of diverse findings about state conditions related to stereotypy and SIB. Although it has its critics (Lovaas & Smith, 1991; Mulick & Meinhold, 1991), it is the first attempt to show how self-injury *may develop* from rhythmic behavior states. Chaos theory (Guess & Sailor, 1993) is used to analyze phase changes and differentiation of behavior response classes. This is a very innovative but unproven idea. Thus far, Guess and colleagues (Guess et al., 1993; Guess & Siegel-Causey, 1995) have concentrated on differentiating Level I state conditions among people with severe and profound mental retardation. They have not as yet demonstrated the emergence of SIB as implied by their theory, nor have they shown how the levels of state conditions interact to improve their prediction of selected forms of SIB. This would be an important test of their theory and methodology.

Compulsive Behavior Hypothesis for SIB

The compulsive behavior hypothesis holds that for some individuals self-injury is a compulsive behavior that occurs in the context of cerebral damage (Gedye, 1992; King, 1993). According

to King (1993), it is based on four observations: (a) cerebral damage sometimes causes compulsive behavior; (b) severity of mental retardation may reflect the degree of underlying cerebral impairment; (c) persons with self-injurious or compulsive behavior susceptibility both react similarly to stress, anxiety, and task demands; (d) some serotonergic drugs (e.g., clomipramine, fluoxetine, buspirone) appear to ameliorate obsessive-compulsive disorders (OCD) and self-injury (Bodfish & Madison, 1993; Lewis, Bodfish, Powell, & Golden, 1995; Lewis, Bodfish, Powell, Parker, & Golden, 1996).

The compulsive behavior hypothesis is almost entirely speculative and without conclusive empirical support. While it is interesting, like all other existing hypotheses of SIB, it has had no disjunctive or exclusive test to prove its specificity. Nevertheless it may be correct for a given subpopulation of SIB cases. Several of the neurobiological and behavioral histories of OCD and SIB may overlap in some cases. How and to what degree they overlap are the big questions. Recently, Bodfish and his colleagues have set out to establish the existence of compulsive behaviors as an independent response class among people with mental retardation (Bodfish & Madison, 1993; Bodfish, Crawford et al., 1995). In a sample of 210 medically stable, ambulatory persons with severe or profound mental retardation, they found considerable overlap in the prevalence of stereotypy (60.9%), self-injury (46.6%), and compulsive behaviors (40%). The instrument they used to assess compulsive behaviors was Gedye's (1992) Compulsive Behavior Checklist, an unvalidated staff rating instrument. Examples of items are arranges objects, closes doors, hand-washing, taps floor, and licks objects. The stereotypy checklist they used contained items from the Timed Stereotypies Rating Scale (Campbell, 1985). An adaptation of the SIB Questionnaire by Maurice and Trudel (1982) was used. None of these instruments has had any formal validity study, yet the data are promising that compulsive behavior can be reliably identified in this population and may be associated with some SIB cases.

King (1993) cites as evidence the high incidence of self-injury and compulsive tics in

Tourette's syndrome. (We have discussed SIB in Tourette's syndrome in a previous section.) Research is needed to show how much overlap there is between people with SIB and Tourette's syndrome and people with SIB and no Tourette's syndrome and how similarly they respond to the same psychopharmacological and behavioral interventions. For instance, haloperidol, pimozide, and fluphenazine, the most effective drugs for treating motor and verbal tics in Tourette's disorder (Robertson, 1992), have had a much more inconsistent effect on SIB in the mentally retarded population (Aman, 1993). SIB in Tourette's syndrome may represent a distinct subtype of SIB.

Neonatal Dopamine Depletion Hypothesis of SIB

Breese et al. (1995) published a review of their SIB model. Breese and Traylor (1970) found that injecting an adult rat with the neurotoxin 6-hydroxydopamine (6-OHDA) in the corpus striatum created a selective lesion of dopamine neurons resulting in supersensitivity. If the rats were then challenged with a dopamine agonist such as L-DOPA or apomorphine, they became aggressive and hyperactive. If, however, these lesions were performed at age 5 to 15 days and then the rats were challenged as adults with a dopamine agonist, such as L-DOPA or apomorphine, they began biting themselves severely. Breese and Baumeister recognized this as a potential model for self-biting in Lesch-Nyhan syndrome (Breese, Baumeister, McGowan, Emerick, Frye, & Mueller, 1984a,b). Examination of postmortem brain tissues of Lesch-Nyhan cases by Lloyd et al. (1981) showed indeed a large depletion of dopamine in the corpus striatum and elevated serotonin levels in the substantia nigra, as would be predicted by the Breese-Baumeister model. Similar results have been found in PET scanning studies with live Lesch-Nyhan patients (Wong et al., 1996).

The question then arose as to why dopamine blockers such as haloperidol and chlorpromazine do not decrease SIB among humans very well (Aman, 1993). Breese et al. (1984b) posited that these drugs blocked primarily D_2 dopamine receptor subtypes, while SIB is primarily a D_1 dopamine receptor

phenomenon. Using the experimental drug SCH 23390, a specific D_1 receptor antagonist, he was able to block SIB in neonatal dopamine depleted rats who had been challenged with apomorphine.

Unfortunately, there is no pure D_1 receptor antagonist available for clinical use as yet in the United States to test the neonatal dopamine depletion model in human SIB cases. The dopamine system has been implicated in repetitive behavior disorders, such as SIB (Bodfish, Powell, Golden, & Lewis, 1995; Lewis, Bodfish, Powell, Wiest et al., 1996). Clinical trials with D_1 and D_2 receptor blockers fluphenazine (Gualtieri & Schroeder, 1989) and clozapine (see Schroeder, Hammock, Mulick, Rojahn, Walson et al., 1995, for a review) have both been successful, but all of these drugs have serious side effects. Clozapine also has an affinity for other dopamine (D_4) and serotonin receptors in addition to D_1 and D_2 dopamine receptors. These drugs are, therefore, not an unambiguous test of the neonatal dopamine depletion hypothesis, even though Criswell, Mueller, and Breese (1989) showed that clozapine at low doses was a relatively selective D_1 blocker in the Breese model. Nevertheless, this work points to atypical neuroleptic drugs such as clozapine, risperidone, and olanzapine as potentially efficacious for treating SIB.

Serotonin Hypothesis for SIB

Serotonin is another major central nervous system (CNS) neurotransmitter that often acts in a reciprocal relationship with dopamine. Mizuno and Yugari (1974) found that giving 5-hydroxytryptophan (5-HTP), a serotonin agonist, to four Lesch-Nyhan boys had a dramatic effect for a few weeks. Other investigators failed to replicate this finding until Nyhan, Johnson, Kaufman, and Jones (1980) gave 5-HTP along with carbidopa and imipramine to prevent rapid excretion in the urine. They also found a dramatic effect, which disappeared after 3 months and could not be recovered.

More recently, in uncontrolled clinical trials, a number of serotonin reuptake inhibitors have been found to suppress SIB and aggression in persons with mental retardation. Examples of these drugs are fluoxetine, trazodone, buspirone, sertraline, and related drugs (see Baumeister, Todd, & Sevin, 1993, for review). Because these studies were not methodologically sound, they do not offer unequivocal support for the specificity of the serotonin hypothesis. But they do merit a closer examination in future research (Schroeder & Tessel, 1994). Lewis and colleagues recently found in a double-blind comparison with placebo that clomipramine reduced stereotypy, hyperactivity, and irritability among people with severe and profound mental retardation (Lewis et al., 1995; Lewis, Bodfish, Powell, Parker, & Golden, 1996). Serotonin dysregulation also occurs in many psychiatric disorders in persons without mental retardation.

Recent studies of risperidone for aggression and SIB among people with mental retardation (Simon, Blubaugh, & Pippidis, 1996; Van den Borre et al., 1993) suggest that drugs affecting serotonin and dopamine and their interactions might be very efficacious. Double-blind studies are now under way with risperidone by our group.

Opioid Peptide Hypotheses of SIB

Two hypotheses by Sandman et al. (1983) are based on the clinical observation that some SIB cases appear to be insensitive to pain or even to seek painful stimuli. Perhaps their pain regulatory system is not working normally. Perhaps stimulation of their pain receptors results in production of excessive amounts of opioid peptides, the neurotransmitters involved in pain regulation.

The first hypothesis, *the pain hypothesis,* proposes that SIB is a symptom of general sensory depression, including hypoalgesia, caused by chronic elevation of endogenous opiates. If a person has elevated pain threshold, the SIB might be a form of self-stimulation to reach it. Opiate blockers, such as naloxone and naltrexone, on the other hand, reduce the pain threshold and thereby lower self-stimulatory SIB rate.

The second hypothesis, *the addiction hypothesis,* suggests that SIB subjects are addicted to their opiate system and that they engage in SIB to secure pain-induced release of opiates, producing a reinforcing opiate "high."

Opiate blockers might attenuate SIB by increasing pain and reducing the subsequent high.

Sandman (1990/91) reviewed 16 studies of naloxone and naltrexone involving 45 subjects, most of whom had autism and 28 of whom had SIB. Of the SIB cases, 24 had varied positive responses, averaging about 50%. These studies varied widely in methodological quality.

Two more recent large-scale, well-conducted studies merit close examination.

Sandman et al. (1993) performed a 10-week double-blind cross-over study of naltrexone among 24 adults with SIB and mental retardation at Fairview Developmental Center. In the institutional population of 1,200 there were 129 SIB cases; from these, the 24 with the highest SIB rates were chosen. Other psychoactive medications (used in 43% of the residents) were kept constant during the trial. Different orders of weekly treatments of placebo, 0.5, 1.0, and 2.0 mg/kg of naltrexone were assigned randomly to subjects. Video-taped observations, neurological examinations, ratings of adaptive and maladaptive behavior, as well as a discrimination learning task were conducted. Only the videotaped observations and the discrimination task yielded significant results. There was a dose-response effect of naltrexone on change scores of SIB ranging from 10% to 90% reduction in 18 of 21 cases. The median was 50% at optimal dose. There was also improvement on the discrimination task secondary to reduction of SIB while on naltrexone. Use of change scores did not allow one to see the absolute baseline SIB levels. The potential pharmacological interactions between multiple psychoactive medications which subjects were using were also not studied. Nevertheless this is an impressive study.

An excellent double-blind cross-over study of the effects of naltrexone on SIB in eight adults with severe or profound mental retardation was performed by Thompson, Hackenberg, Cerutti, Baker, and Axtell (1994). Five-minute behavioral samples were taken one-per-hour for 7 hours each day over four 2-week phases (baseline, placebo, 50 mg, and 100 mg) in randomly assigned order. Half of the subjects also received 0.3 mg per day of clonidine along with naltrexone in order to control for possible confounding due to opiate-like withdrawal symptoms that may accompany naltrexone administration. The results showed no psychotropic effects of clonidine, but significantly reduced high intensity head banging and self-biting from 23% to 100% in 6 of 8 subjects. There was no improvement in eye, nose, or throat poking or face slapping. The largest effects were on hand-to-head hitting and head-to-object hitting. Few physiological side effects of naltrexone were observed except that sleep increased from 5.34 hours to 6.72 hours per night.

Taken together, the studies of naltrexone on SIB show a highly consistent dose effect averaging about a 50% reduction in SIB in 60% to 80% of cases that is related to intensity and topography. This is the best documented selective neuropharmacological hypothesis to date for some types of SIB.

Self-Injurious Behavior as Endogenous Neurochemical Self-Administration

Thompson et al. (1995) published a new and compelling account of SIB based upon the mechanisms of addiction and the commonalties in behavior patterns among persons who perform SIB and among people addicted to cocaine and morphine. Citing the operant technology to study drug addiction in animals, they draw many parallels between people performing SIB and opiate and cocaine self-administration in animals in terms of (a) response requirements to maintain a constant blood level under a given schedule of reinforcement, (b) relationships between route of administration and unit dose, (c) availability of alternative reinforcers, (d) the primary reinforcing properties of dopamine and opioid ligand binding, (e) the role of stressful and painful events, (f) the interplay between social and neurochemical events. They draw models to show how interoceptively conditioned and exteroceptively conditioned stimuli sometimes work together, sometimes against each other, to reinforce and maintain SIB.

There are common denominators between SIB and opiate and cocaine self-administration: (a) They are both mediated by dopamine binding in the nucleus accumbens and ventral tegmental area (VTA); (b) the reinforcing properties of exogenous and endogenous opioids have been demonstrated. SIB may come under the control of these neurochemical consequences; (c) SIB may be maintained in order to avoid withdrawal distress due to decrease in dopamine and opioid release.

The endogenous neurochemical self-administration hypothesis of SIB is a very heuristic and plausible account that bears further study to test its validity and limits. As yet there is little research in the SIB literature that is based directly on it except for the studies of the effects of naltrexone on SIB.

Isolate-Rearing Model of SIB

Kraemer (1992) has posited a comprehensive psychobiological attachment theory (PAT) in which disruptions between the infant and its caretaker set the stage in the CNS for social dysfunction in later life. He summarized 25 years of research at the Harlow laboratories on isolate rearing of infant rhesus monkeys. This research shows that if an infant monkey is separated from its mother for the first 22 months of life, it develops a variety of dysfunctional behaviors (e.g., abnormal motor patterns, hyperphagia, hyper-responsivity to change, stereotyped rocking, self-injurious biting and head banging, and aggressive attacks when later confronted with normal monkeys [Kraemer & Clarke, 1990]). These behaviors have been related to the decoupling in the brain of the "tuning" process effected by the norephinephrine (NE) system, of the "switching" processes by the dopamine (DA) system and by the "gatekeeping" or "enabling" functions effected by the serotonin (5HT) system (Kraemer, Ebert, Schmidt, & McKinney, 1989, p. 187). Social isolation is thought to produce cytoarchitectural changes in these brain biogenic amine systems that result in their dysregulation, such that the animal is not prepared to respond appropriately to normal social stimuli, but performs inappropriate behaviors instead.

PAT is a very heuristic model that attempts to integrate a wide variety of disparate findings from the animal literature and from human infant attachment theories such as Bowlby (1969) and Ainsworth, Blehar, Waters, and Wall

(1978). It also has many critics, as was evident from the open peer commentary following Kraemer's article (Kraemer et al., 1989). Probably the most controversial idea is that attachment systems alter neurobiological structures in the brain. This idea is supported only modestly by direct evidence. Most of it is indirect evidence inferred from assays of neurotransmitters, their precursors, and their metabolites in cerebrospinal fluid of live monkeys (Mason, 1992). Nevertheless, Kraemer's approach begins to reflect the complexity of the effects of environmental and biological interactions on the development of stereotypy, self-injury, and aggression, and points to future directions for research in terms of the neuroplasticity of SIB and the possibility of modifying it through behavioral and pharmacological interventions.

Neural Oscillator Model of Stereotyped Behavior, SIB, and Aggression

Lewis and Baumeister (1982), in their review of animal and human models of stereotypy, put forth a cohesive view first posited for infants by Wolff (1967): that stereotyped movements are the behavioral expression of a central motor program controlled by neural pattern generators or oscillators. This hypothesis is an outgrowth of extensive biological research showing that the CNS does not need sensory feedback to generate sequenced rhythmic movements. Such a theory fits well with some other regulatory theories of stereotypy. For an excellent book on these theories, see Sprague and Newell (1996).

Support for the oscillator model comes from (a) the regularity of number of bouts, bout length, and periodicity of much stereotyped body rocking, head weaving, etc.; (b) presence of ultradian rhythms in people who perform stereotypies; (c) the apparent lack of discrete environmental stimulus control over stereotypy; and (d) the fact that, once triggered, stereotyped action patterns appear to run to completion independent of environmental stimulus control. This holds not only for moment-to-moment fluctuations (Lewis et al., 1984), but also for longer periods of time (Lewis, MacLean, Johnson, & Baumeister, 1981). In fact, Lewis, Silva, and Silva (1995)

have now extended this analysis to stereotyped SIB and aggression occurring over 3- and 5-month cycles in large institutional populations. Lewis interprets these rhythmic cycles as representing a shift from environmental stimulus control to internal self-regulation primarily under CNS control.

The presence of cyclicity in the occurrence of aberrant behaviors is certainly noteworthy and important to caregivers. The theoretical explanations for cyclicity and stereotyped behavior are still a matter of much speculation (Sprague & Newell, 1996). There have been no direct observations of neural pattern generators in the CNS; they must be inferred indirectly from behavioral or neurophysiological methods. This will be a growing area for research in the future.

Genetic and Perinatal Risk Factors and Rodent Models of Stress-Induced Destructive Behavior

Tessel and colleagues (Loupe, Schroeder, & Tessel, 1995; Stodgell, Schroeder, Hyland, & Tessel, 1995; Stodgell, Schroeder, & Tessel, 1996; Tessel, Schroeder, Loupe, & Stodgell, 1995; Tessel, Schroeder, Stodgell, & Loupe, 1995) have combined the effects of isolate rearing with three rodent models for stress-induced destructive behavior: (a) a genetic model of aggression using the spontaneously hypertensive rat (SHR), (b) a model of stereotyped behavior using methylazoxymethanol (MAM) injected prenatally to induce microcephaly in rat offspring, (c) a model of SIB using the Breese-Baumeister neonatal dopamine depletion model in rats.

Tessel and colleagues (Stodgell et al., 1995) have found that, under conditions when rats were administered periodic unavoidable shock, members of the SHR group initially demonstrated aggressive responses by biting the bars of the chamber; soon after, within the same session, SHR rats displayed marked increases in freezing behavior. MAM rats under the same conditions became hyperactive and engaged in stereotypic rearing behavior. No self-injurious behavior was observed in any group during shock sessions. However, when 6-OHDA rats who had experienced shock were exposed to apomorphine, self-injurious biting did occur.

Periodic food delivery to food-deprived rats induced nonrearing stereotypies among SHR rats and rearing and hyperactivity among both SHR and MAM rats. Together these data suggest that *specific aberrant behavior patterns are associated with the different models.* Now the question occurs: Will drug or other treatments serve to reduce the aberrant behavior associated with the various models?

Another set of fascinating data derives from observations related to fixed ratio (FR) discrimination training. Initially subjects were taught to discriminate between FR-1 and FR-16 schedules (Tessel et al., 1995). This procedure involved having subjects respond to a center lever and then, when that lever was retracted and one of two side levers was presented, respond to the left lever if the center lever had one ratio requirement and to the right lever if the center lever had another ratio requirement. When the discrimination started with the easy FR-1 versus FR-16 discrimination and then gradually progressed to FR-8 versus FR-16, all groups learned the discriminations and their learning curves were essentially identical. However, when the discrimination was reversed, MAM rats reversed more slowly than the subjects of the other three groups. Moreover, when the fixed ratio discrimination started with the FR-8 versus FR-16 discrimination, MAM and SHR rats learned the discrimination at a significantly slower rate than controls.

Analysis of brain structures and chemicals, however, yielded the most exciting findings (Tessel et al., 1995). The 6-OHDA rats who had been given fixed ratio training showed *a reversal of cerebral and striatal catecholamine depletion.* Similarly, MAM animals that had been given FR discrimination training showed *a partial reversal of hippocampal hypoplasia (reversal of MAM-induced hippocampal weight and protein concentration reduction). These observations are the first to suggest the possibility that susceptibility to chronic aberrant behavior and the presence of cognitive deficits may not only be amenable to prevention, they may be amenable to reversal.* While changes in behavior must be associated with changes in the brain, no one has previously shown such

specific and massive changes related to training. Moreover, the fact that changes were in the direction of normality for animals with specific lesions was totally unexpected.

These changes raise a number of important questions. First, are the changes related to a specific kind of training involving progressive increase in problem difficulty or would training on simple repetitive tasks result in the brain changes? Second, are such changes restricted to rats or do they occur in other animals including humans? Are these changes in brain structure and chemistry accompanied by more generalized changes in behavior? For example, do MAM animals that have been through fixed ratio discrimination training engage in less stereotyped rearing or do 6-OHDA animals no longer engage in self-biting when administered apomorphine and electric shock? Is it possible that such training will have a more generalized effect?

The combined approach of isolate rearing in different risk models may help Tessel and colleagues to increase the specificity of their hypotheses related to animal models of the development of aberrant behavior. This promises to be a fruitful line of research for the future.

Implications and Conclusions

The research discussed in this chapter offers considerable hope that approaches to diagnosis and treatment of SIB are reaching a level of complexity and sophistication that will make possible a range of clinically significant treatments resulting in lasting changes in this behavior.

Better Assessment and Diagnosis

It is apparent that much SIB serves a social function and is readily changed by altering social occasions for SIB and the reinforcement contingencies that maintain it without necessarily addressing the biological conditions that set the occasion for it. There are also cases of SIB, however, that may originally have been occasioned by social stimuli or contingencies but which, through extensive practice, have now altered interoceptive stimuli (e.g., dopamine or opioid release) the functions of which must also be altered in order to allow social contingencies to be effective in treating

SIB. In still other cases (e.g., Lesch-Nyhan syndrome) there may be a strong genetic or neuro- biologically based predisposition toward SIB. In these cases, using social contingencies without considering neurochemical deficiencies and maturational variables is very unlikely to produce lasting effects.

The study of behavioral phenotypes in genetic syndromes associated with SIB gives us hope that there are subtypes of SIB that, if considered sufficiently, will allow us to tune our algorithms in the treatment and prognosis for SIB.

The biobehavioral models for SIB also give plausible accounts for the variety of forms and functions of SIB. In some cases the independent variable is behavioral (e.g., isolate rearing); in other cases, it is biological (e.g., dopamine dysregulation) in still other cases, the model is mixed (e.g., Guess and Carr's [1991] biobehavioral state model). A given SIB case might fit one or several of these models depending on his or her genetic, neurobiological, and behavioral history.

The tools we have for exploring the above risk factors continue to improve. We now have better rating scales (Aman, 1991). The various methods of functional analysis (*JABA,* 1994) have been a major advance in our armentarium. The study of genetic behavioral phenotypes with new genetic techniques such as linkage analysis (Brzustowicz, 1996) is another tool. The use of neurochemical assays of neurotransmitter functions (e.g. Lewis, Bodfish, Powell, Wiest et al. [1996]) may also aid in predicting who will respond best to which drug treatment. Together these tools will also help us with efforts to prevent SIB.

The Role of Animal Models

Animal models play a key role in discovering the biological causes and treatments for different types of SIB. They are critical for our understanding the mechanisms by which adverse events cause SIB and mental retardation (Crnic & Nitkin, 1996). They permit us to experiment with therapies that would never be permitted on humans without such prior testing. Finally, we can check our behavioral findings with genetic and neurobiological techniques too invasive to be used on humans. To be sure, care must be used in comparing a particular animal phenotype with an appropriate homology in humans. But once homology is established, one can then experiment with the methods of producing, preventing, and curing the disorder. For instance, gene therapy for Lesch-Nyhan syndrome is a real possibility for the future, but currently it requires study of the HPRT mouse model to understand the purine salvage pathway in Lesch-Nyhan syndrome and how the genetic defect can be cured or prevented.

Better Treatments and Prognoses

It is easy to forget that only 40 years ago, the SIB cases of the type discussed in this paper were written off as hopeless, confined to physical and chemical restraints in highly restrictive environments. Today there are humane and effective interventions for *the majority* of SIB cases in mostly unrestricted settings. That is a paradigm shift in treatment and prognosis that was brought about by the behavioral analytic revolution. We now think differently about and have different expectations for people with mental retardation and SIB.

It is only 20 years since our knowledge of the neurobiological causes of SIB began to grow, and the rate of growth has been exponential ever since. We now have a few drugs based on a clear neurobiological rationale that selectively improve SIB without serious side effects (e.g., naltrexone, the atypical neuroleptics, and the serotonin reuptake inhibitors). We now have behavior phenotypes whose SIB is differentially affected by selected drugs. There are now drugs coming on the market that are likely to work even better. There is even the prospect of gene therapy for certain SIB-related genetic syndromes. Lastly, there is a prospect of noninvasive, training-induced recovery from lesion-induced susceptibilities to SIB. Truly we have come a long way with research on SIB, but we still have a long way to go in order to address all of the aspects of this multiply caused and multiply affected devastating disorder.

REFERENCES

Ainsworth, M. D. S., Blehar, M. C., Waters, E., & Walls, S. (1978). *Patterns of attachment: A psychological study of the strange situation.* Hillsdale, NJ: Erlbaum.

Aman, M. G. (1991). *Assessing psychopathology and behavior problems in persons with mental retardation: A review of available instruments.* Rockville, MD: U.S. Department of Health and Human Services.

Aman, M. G. (1993). Efficacy of psychotropic drugs for reducing self-injurious behavior in developmental disabilities. *Annals of Clinical Psychiatry, 5,* 177–188.

Anderson, L. T., Ernst, M., & Davis, S. V. (1992). Cognitive abilities of patients with Lesch Nyhan disease. *Journal of Autism and Developmental Disorders, 22,* 189–203.

Bailey, J. S., & Pyles, D. A. M. (1989). Behavioral diagnostics. In E. Cipani (Ed.), The treatment of severe behavior disorders. *Monographs of the American Association on Mental Retardation, 12* (pp. 85–107). Washington, DC: American Association on Mental Retardation.

Bauman, M. (1991, June). *Neuropathology of Rett's syndrome.* Rett's syndrome symposium. Kennedy Institute, Baltimore.

Baumeister, A. A., Todd, M. E., & Sevin, J. A. (1993). Efficacy and specificity of pharmacological therapies for behavioral disorders of persons with mental retardation. *Clinical Neuropharmacology, 16,* 271–294.

Beck, B. (1987). Psycho-social assessment of 36 de Lange patients. *Journal of Mental Deficiency Research, 31,* 251–257.

Bodfish, J. W., Crawford, T. W., Powell, S. B., Parker, D. E., Golden, R. N., & Lewis, M. H. (1995). Compulsions in adults with mental retardation: Prevalence, phenomenology, and comorbidity with stereotypy and self-injury. *American Journal on Mental Retardation, 100,* 183–192.

Bodfish, J. W., & Madison, J. T. (1993). Diagnosis and treatment of compulsive behavior disorder of adults with mental retardation. *American Journal on Mental Retardation, 98,* 360–367.

Bodfish, J. W., Powell, S. B., Golden, R. N., & Lewis, M. H. (1995). Blink rate as an index of dopamine function in adults with mental retardation and repetitive behavior disorders. *American Journal on Mental Retardation, 99,* 334–335.

Borthwick-Duffy, S. A. (1994). Epidemiology and ontogeny of destructive behavior. In T. Thompson & D. Gray (Eds.), *Destructive behavior in developmental disabilities* (pp. 13–23). Thousand Oaks, CA: Sage.

Bowlby, J. (1969). *Attachment and loss: Separation, anxiety, and anger.* New York: Basic Books.

Breese, G. R., Baumeister, A. A., McCowan, T. J., Emerick, S., Frye, G. D., Crotty, K., & Mueller, R. A. (1984a). Behavioral differences between neonatal- and adult-6-hydroxydopamine-treated rats to dopamine agonists: Relevance to neurological symptoms in clinical syndromes with reduced brain dopamine. *Journal of Pharmacology and Experimental Therapeutics, 231,* 343–354.

Breese, G. R., Baumeister, A. A., McCowan, T. J., Emerick, S., Frye, G. D., & Mueller, R. A. (1984b). Neonatal-6-hydroxydopamine treatment: Model of susceptibility for self-mutilation in the Lesch-Nyhan syndrome. *Pharmacology Biochemistry and Behavior, 21,* 459–461.

Breese, G. R., Criswell, H. E., Duncan, G. E., Moy, S. S., Johnson, K. B., Wong, D. F., & Meuller, R. E. (1995). Model for reduced dopamine in Lesch-Nyhan syndrome and the mentally retarded: Neurobiology of neonatal-6-hydroxydopamine-lesioned rats. *Mental Retardation and Developmental Disabilities Research Reviews, 1,* 111–119.

Breese, G. R., & Traylor, T. D. (1970). Effects of 6-hydroxydopamine on brain norepineph-rine and dopamine: Evidence of selective degeneration of catecholamine neurons. *Journal of Pharmacology and Experimental Therapeutics, 174,* 413–420.

Bruininks, R. H., Olson, K. M., Larson, S. A., & Lakin, C. (1994). Challenging behaviors among persons with mental retardation in residential settings: Implications for policy, research, and practice. In T. Thompson & D. Gray (Eds.), *Destructive behavior in developmental disabilities* (pp. 24–48). Thousand Oaks, CA: Sage.

Brzustowicz, L. (1996). Looking for language genes: Lessons from complex language studies. In M. L. Rice (Ed.), *Toward a genetics of language* (pp. 3–26). Mahwah, NJ: Erlbaum.

Campbell, M. (1985). Timed stereotypies rating scale. *Psychopharmacology Bulletin, 21,* 1082–1085.

Carr, E. G., Levin, L., McConnachie, G., Carlson, J. I., Kemp, D. C., & Smith, C. E. (1994). *Communication-based intervention for problem behavior: A user's guide for producing positive change.* Baltimore: Brookes.

Carr, E. G., & Smith, C. E. (1995). Biological setting events for self-injury. *Mental Retardation and Developmental Disabilities Research Reviews, 1,* 94–98.

Coulter, D. A. (1990). Frontal lobe seizures: No evidence of self-injury. *American Journal on Mental Retardation, 96,* 81–84.

Crawhall, J. C., Henderson, J. F., & Kelley, W. N. (1981). Diagnosis and treatment of Lesch-Nyhan syndrome. *Pediatric Research, 6,* 504–524.

Criswell, H. E., Mueller, R. A., & Breese, G. R. (1989). Clozapine antagonism of D-1 and D-2 dopamine receptor-mediated behaviors. *European Journal of Pharmacology, 159,* 141–147.

Crnic, L. S. & Nitkin, R. M. (1996). Animal models of mental retardation: An overview. *Mental Retardation and Developmental Disabilities Research Reviews, 2,* 185–187.

Dehen, H., Willer, J. C., Boureau, F., & Cambier, J. (1977). Congenital insensitivity to pain, and endogenous morphine-like substances. *Lancet, 11,* 293–294.

de Lange, C. (1933). Sur un type nouveau degeneration (typus Amstelodamensis). *Archives de Medicine des Infants, 36,* 713–719.

de Lissavoy, V. (1961). Head-banging in early childhood. *Journal of Pediatrics, 58,* 803–805.

Dykens, E. M. (1995). Measuring behavioral phenotypes: Provocations from the "New Genetics." *American Journal on Mental Retardation, 99,* 522–532.

Favazza, A. (1987). *Bodies under siege.* Baltimore: Johns Hopkins University Press.

Gardner, W. I., & Sovner, R. (1994). *Self-injurious behaviors.* Willow Street, PA: VIDA.

Gedye, A. (1989). Extreme self-injury attributed to frontal lobe seizures. *American Journal on Mental Retardation, 94,* 20–26.

Gedye, A. (1992). Recognizing obsessive-compulsive disorder in clients with developmental disabilities. *The Habilitative Mental Health Care Newsletter, 11,* 73–77.

Gillberg, C. (1987). Autistic symptoms in Rett syndrome: The first two years according to mothers' reports. *Brain Development, 9,* 499–501.

Griffin, J. C., Williams, D. E., Stark, M. T., Altmeyer, B. K., & Mason, M. (1986). Self-injurious behavior: A state-wide prevalence survey of the extent and circumstances. *Applied Research in Mental Retardation, 7,* 105–116.

Gualtieri, C. T. (1989). The differential diagnosis of self-injurious behavior in mentally retarded people. *Psychopharmacology Bulletin, 25,* 358–363.

Gualtieri, C. T. (1991). *Neuropsychiatry and behavioral pharmacology.* New York: Springer-Verlag.

Gualtieri, C. T., & Schroeder, S. R. (1989). Pharmacotherapy of self-injurious behavior: Preliminary tests of the D-1 hypothesis. *Psychopharmacology Bulletin, 25,* 364–371.

Guess, D., & Carr, E. (1991). Emergence and maintenance of stereotypy and self-injury. *American Journal on Mental Retardation, 96,* 299–320.

Guess, D., Roberts, S., Siegel-Causey, E., Ault, M., Guy, B., & Thompson, B. (1993). Analysis of behavior state conditions and associated environmental variables among students with profound handicaps. *American Journal on Mental Retardation, 97,* 634–653.

Guess, D., & Sailor, W. (1993). Chaos theory and the study of human behavior: Implications for special education and developmental disabilities. *Journal of Special Education, 27,* 16–34.

Guess, D., & Siegel-Causey, D. (1995). Attractor dimensions of behavior state changes among individuals with profound disabilities. *American Journal on Mental Retardation, 99,* 642–663.

Gunsett, R. P., Mulick, J. A., Fernald, W. B., & Martin, J. L. (1989). Brief report: Indications for medical screening prior to behavioral programming for severely and profoundly mentally retarded clients. *Journal of Autism and Developmental Disorders, 19,* 167–172.

Gunter, P. L. (1984). Self-injurious behaviour: Characteristics, etiology, and treatment. *The Exceptional Child, 31,* 91–98.

Hagberg, B., Aicardi, J., Dias, K., & Ramos, D. (1983). A progressive syndrome of autism, dementia, ataxia, and loss of purposeful hand use in girls: Rett's syndrome: Report of 35 uses. *Annals of Neurology, 14,* 471–479.

Hagerman, R., Jackson, A. W., Levitas, A., Rimland, B., & Braden, M. (1986). An analysis of autism in 50 males with fragile X syndrome. *American Journal of Medical Genetics, 23,* 359–374.

Hagerman, R. J. (1990). The association between autism and fragile X syndrome. *Brain Dysfunction, 3,* 218–227.

Hagerman, R. J., & Silverman, A. C. (Eds.). (1991). *Fragile X syndrome: Diagnosis, treatment, and research.* Baltimore: Johns Hopkins University Press.

Harris, J. C. (1992). Neurobiological factors in self-injurious behavior. In J. Luiselli, J. L. Matson, & N. Singh (Eds.), *Self injurious behavior: Analysis, assessment, and treatment* (pp. 59–92). New York: Spring-Verlag.

Harris, J. C. (1995). *Developmental neuropsychiatry* (Vol. 2). New York: Oxford University Press.

Hawley, P., Jackson, L., & Kurnit, D. (1985). Sixty-four patients with Brachmann-de Lange syndrome: A survey. *American Journal of Medical Genetics, 20,* 453–459.

Holm, V. A. (1996). Prader-Willi syndrome. In A. J. Capute & P. J. Accardo (Eds.), *Developmental disabilities in infancy and childhood* (2nd ed., Vol. 2, pp. 245–254). Baltimore: Brookes.

Hyman, S. I. (1996). A transdisciplinary approach to self-injurious behavior. In A. J. Capute & P. J. Accardo (Eds.), *Developmental disabilities in infancy and childhood* (2nd ed., Vol. 2, pp. 317–333). Baltimore: Brookes.

Iwata, B. A., Dorsey, M. F., Slifer, K. J., Bauman, K. E., & Richman, G. S. (1982). Toward a functional analysis of self-injury. *Analysis and Intervention in Development Disabilities, 2,* 3–20.

Iwata, B. A., Pace, G. M., Willis, K. D., Gamache, T. B., & Hyman, S. L. (1986). Operant studies of self-injurious hand biting in Rett syndrome. *American Journal of Medical Genetics, 24* (suppl.), S157–166.

JABA. (1994). Special Issue on functional analysis approaches to behavioral assessment and treatment. *Journal of Applied Behavior Analysis, 27,* 196–418.

Jacobson, J. W. (1990). Assessing the prevalence of psychiatric disorders in a developmentally disabled population. In E. Dibble & D. B. Gray (Eds.), *Assessment of behavior problems with persons with mental retardation living in the community* (pp. 19–70). Rockville, MD: Department of Health and Human Services, National Institutes of Health, Public Health Service, Alcohol, Drug Abuse, and Mental Health Administration.

Kerr, A. M. (1992). *The significance of the Rett syndrome phenotype.* In "From Genes to Behavior," Society for the Study of Behavioral Phenotypes, 2nd International Symposium, Welshpool, UK, November 19–21, Paper No. 1.

King, B. H. (1993). Self-injury by people with mental retardation: A compulsive behavior hypothesis. *American Journal on Mental Retardation, 98,* 93–112.

Kraemer, G. W. (1992). A psychobiological theory of attachment. *Behavioral and Brain Sciences, 15,* 493–541.

Kraemer, G. W., & Clarke, H. S. (1990). The behavioral neurobiology of self-injurious behavior in rhesus monkeys. *Progress in Neuropsychopharmacology and Biological Psychiatry, 14,* 141–168.

Kraemer, G. W., Ebert, M. H., Schmidt, D. E., & McKinney, W. T. (1989). A longitudinal study of the effect of different social rearing conditions on cerebrospinal fluid norepinephrine and biogenic amine metabolites in rhesus monkeys. *Neuropsychopharmacology, 2,* 175–189.

Kravitz, H., Rosenthal, Y., Teplitz, Z., Murphy, I., & Thesser, R. (1960). A study of headbanging in infants and children. *Diseases of the Nervous System, 21,* 203–208.

Lees, A. J., Robertson, M., Trimble, M. R., & Murray, N. M. (1984). A clinical study of gilles de la Tourette syndrome in the United Kingdom. *Journal of Neurology, Neurosurgery and Psychiatry, 47,* 1–8.

Lesch, M., & Nyhan, W. L. (1964). A familial disorder of uric acid metabolism and central nervous system 22 function. *American Journal of Medicine, 36,* 561–570.

Lewis, M. H., & Baumeister, A. A. (1982). Stereotyped mannerisms in mentally retarded persons: Animal models and theoretical analyses. In N. R. Ellis (Ed.), *International review of research in mental retardation* (Vol. 12, pp. 123–161). New York: Academic.

Lewis, M. H., Bodfish, J. W., Powell, S. B., & Golden, R. N. (1995). Clomipramine treatment for stereotypy and related repetitive movement disorders associated with mental retardation. *American Journal on Mental Retardation, 100,* 299–312.

Lewis, M. H., Bodfish, J. W., Powell, S. B., Parker, D. E., & Golden, R. N. (1996). Clomipramine treatment for self-injurious behavior of individuals with mental retardation: A double-blind comparison with placebo. *American Journal on Mental Retardation, 100,* 654–665.

Lewis, M. H., Bodfish, J. W., Powell, S. B., Wiest, K., Darling, M., & Golden, R. N. (1996). Plasma HVA in adults with mental retardation and stereotyped behavior: Biochemical evidence for a dopamine deficiency model. *American Journal on Mental Retardation, 100,* 413–417.

Lewis, M. H., MacLean, W. E., Jr., Bryson-Brockmann, W., Arendt, R., Beck, B., Fidler, P. S., & Baumeister, A. A. (1984). Time-series analysis of stereotyped movements: Relationship of body rocking to cardiac activity. *American Journal on Mental Retardation, 89,* 287–294.

Lewis, M. H., MacLean, W. E., Jr., Johnson, W. L., & Baumeister, A. A. (1981). Ultradian rhythms in stereotyped and self-injurious behavior. *American Journal of Mental Deficiency, 85,* 601–610.

Lewis, M. H., Silva, J. R., & Silva, S. G. (1995). Cyclicity of aggression and self-injurious behavior in individuals with mental retardation. *American Journal on Mental Retardation, 99,* 436–444.

Lloyd, K. C., Hornykiewicz, O., Davidson, L., Shannak, K., Farley, I., Goldstein, M., Shibuya, M., Kelley, W., & Fox, I. H. (1981). Biochemical evidence of dysfunction of brain neurotransmitters in the Lesch-Nyhan syndrome. *New England Journal of Medicine, 305,* 1106–1111.

Loupe, P., Schroeder, S. R., & Tessel, R. E. (1995). FR discrimination training effects in SHR and microcephalic rats. *Pharmacology, Biochemistry, and Behavior, 51,* 869–876.

Lovaas, O. I., & Smith, T. (1991). There is more to operant theory and practice: Comment on Guess and Carr. *American Journal on Mental Retardation, 96,* 324–326.

Mace, F. C., & Mauk, J. E. (1995). Bio-behavioral diagnosis and treatment of self-injury. *Mental Retardation and Developmental Disabilities Research Reviews, 1,* 104–110.

Maisto, C. R., Baumeister, A. A., & Maisto, A. A. (1978). An analysis of variables related to self-injurious behavior among institutionalized retarded persons. *Journal of Mental Deficiency Research, 22,* 27–36.

Martin, J. P., & Bell, J. (1943). A pedigree of mental defect showing sex-linkage. *Journal of Neurology and Psychiatry, 6,* 151–154.

Mason, W. A. (1992). Does function imply structure? *Behavioral and Brain Sciences, 15,* 519–520.

Maurice, P., & Trudel, G. (1982). Self-injurious behavior: Prevalence and relationship to environmental events. In J. H. Hollis & C. E. Meyers (Eds.), *Life-threatening behavior: Analysis and intervention* (pp. 81–103). Washington, DC: American Association on Mental Retardation.

Mizuno, T. L., & Yugari, Y. (1974). Self-mutilation in the Lesch-Nyhan syndrome. *Lancet, 1,* 761.

Mulick, J. A., & Meinhold, P. M. (1991). Evaluating models for the emergence and maintenance of stereotypy and self-injury. *American Journal on Mental Retardation, 96,* 327–384.

Naidu, S. (1992). Rett syndrome: An update. In Y. Fukuyama, Y. Suzuki, S. Kamashita, & P. Casaer (Eds.), *Fetal and perinatal neurology* (pp. 79–92). Basel, Switzerland: Karger.

Nyhan, W. (1967). The Lesch-Nyhan Syndrome: Self-destructive biting, mental retardation, neurological disorder, and hyperuricemia. *Developmental Medicine and Child Neurology, 9,* 563–572.

Nyhan, W. (1972). Behavioral phenotypes in organic genetic disease. Presidential address to Society of Pediatric Research, May 1, 1971. *Pediatric Research, 6,* 1–9.

Nyhan, W. L., (1994). The Lesch-Nyhan disease. In T. Thompson & D. Gray (Eds.), *Destructive behavior in developmental disabilities* (pp. 181–197). Thousand Oaks, CA: Sage.

Nyhan, W. L., Johnson, H. G., Kaufman, I. A., & Jones, K. L. (1980). Serotonergic approaches to the modification of behavior in the Lesch-Nyhan syndrome. *Applied Research in Mental Retardation, 1,* 25–40.

Oliver, C., Murphy, G. H., & Corbett, J. A. (1987). Self-injurious behavior in people with mental handicap: A total population study. *Journal of Mental Deficiency Research, 31,* 147–162.

Oliver, C., Murphy, G., Crayton, L., & Corbett, J. (1993). Self-injurious behavior in Rett syndrome: Interactions between features of Rett syndrome and operant conditioning. *Journal of Autism and Developmental Disorders, 23,* 91–109.

Prader, A., Labhart, A., & Willi, H. (1956). Ein syndrom von adipositas, kleinwachs, kryptorchismus und oligophrenie nach myatonicartigem zustand in neugeborenalter. *Schineizerische Medizinische Wochenschrift, 86,* 1260–1261.

Reese, R. M., Hellings, J., & Schroeder, S. R. (in press). Treatment methods for destructive and aggressive behavior in people with severe mental retardation/developmental disabilities. In N. Bouras (Ed.), *Psychiatric and behavioural disorders in developmental disabilities and mental retardation.* London: Cambridge University Press.

Rett, A. (1966). Uber ein eigenartiges hirnatrophisches syndrom bei hyperammoniamie in kindesalter. *Weiner Medizinische Wochenschrift, 116,* 723–738.

Riley, C. M., Day, R. L., Greeley, D. M., & Langford, W. S. (1949). Central autonomic dysfunction with defective lacrimation. *Pediatrics, 3,* 468–478.

Robertson, M. M. (1992). Self-injurious behavior and Tourette syndrome. In T. N. Case, A. J. Friedhoff, & D. J. Cohen (Eds.), *Advances in neurology* (Vol. 58, pp. 105–114). New York: Raven.

Robertson, M. M., Trimble, M. R., & Lees, A. J. (1989). Self-injurious behavior and the Gilles de la Tourette syndrome: A clinical study and review of the literature. *Psychological Medicine, 19,* 611–625.

Rojahn, J. (1994). Epidemiology and topographic taxonomy of self-injurious behavior. In T. Thompson & D. Gray (Eds.), *Destructive behavior and developmental disabilities* (pp. 49–67). Thousand Oaks, CA: Sage.

Sandman, C. A. (1990/1991). The opiate hypothesis in autism and self-injury. *Journal of Child and Adolescent Psychopharmacology, 1,* 237–248.

Sandman, C. A., Datta, P., Barron, J. L., Hoehler, F., Williams, C., & Swanson, J. (1983). Naloxone attenuates self-abusive behavior in developmentally disabled subjects. *Applied Research in Mental Retardation, 4,* 5–11.

Sandman, C. A., & Hetrick, W. P. (1995). Opiate mechanisms in self-injury. *Mental Retardation and Developmental Disabilities Research Reviews, 1,* 130–136.

Sandman, C. A., Hetrick, W. P., Taylor, D. V., Barron, J. L., Touchette, P., Lott, I., Crinella, F., & Martinazzi, V. (1993). Naltrexone reduces self-injury and improves learning. *Experimental and Clinical Psychopharmacology, 1,* 242–258.

Sansom, D., Krishnan, V. H. R., Corbett, J., & Kerr, A. (1993). Emotional and behavioral aspects of Rett syndrome. *Developmental Medicine and Child Neurology, 35,* 340–345.

Sarimski, K. (1997). Communication, social-emotional development and parenting stress in Cornelia-de-Lange syndrome. *Journal of Intellectual Disability Research, 41,* 70–75.

Schroeder, S. R. (1991). Self-injury and stereotypy. In J. L. Matson & J. A. Mulick (Eds.), *Comprehensive handbook of mental retardation* (2nd ed., pp. 240–259). New York: Pergamon.

Schroeder, S. R., Bickel, W. K., & Richmond, G. (1986). Primary and secondary prevention of self-injurious behavior. In K. Gadow & I. Bialer (Eds.), *Advances in learning and behavioral disabilities* (Vol. 5, pp. 65–87). Greenwich, CT: JAI.

Schroeder, S. R., Hammock, R. G., Mulick, J.A., Rojahn, J., Walson, P., Fernald, W., Meinhold, P., & Sarphare, G. (1995). Clinical trials of D_1 and D_2 dopamine modulating drugs and self-injury in mental retardation and developmental disability. *Mental Retardation and Developmental Disablities Research Review, 1,* 120–129.

Schroeder, S. R., Mulick, J. A., & Rojahn, J. (1980). The definition, taxonomy, epidemiology, and ecology of self-injurious behavior. *Journal of Autism and Developmental Disorders, 10,* 417–432.

Schroeder, S. R., Mulick, J. A., Rojahn, J., Walson, P., & Hammock, R. (1995). Clinical trials of D_1 and D_2 dopamine modulating drugs and self-injury. *Mental Retardation and Developmental Disabilities Research Reviews, 1,* 120–129.

Schroeder, S. R., Schroeder, C., Smith, B., & Dalldorf, J. (1978). Prevalence of self-injurious behavior in a large state facility for the retarded. *Journal of Autism and Childhood Schizophrenia, 8,* 261–269.

Schroeder, S. R., & Tessel, R. (1994). Dopaminergic and serotonergic mechanisms in self injury and aggression. In T. Thompson & D. Gray (Eds.), *Treatment of destructive behavior in developmental disabilities* (pp. 198–212). Newbury Park, CA: Sage.

Schroeder, S. R., Tessel, R. E., Loupe, P., & Stodgell, C. (1997). Severe behavioral problems in developmental disabilities. In W. E MacLean (Ed.), *Handbook of mental deficiency* (3rd ed., pp. 439–465). Hillsdale, NJ: Erlbaum.

Seignot, M. J. N. (1961). Un cas de maladie de tics de Gilles de la Tourette gueri par le R. - 1625. *Annales Medico-Psychologicues* (Paris), *119,* 578–579.

Simon, E. W., Blubaugh, K. M., & Pippidis, M. (1996). Substituting traditional antipsychotics with risperidone for individuals with mental retardation. *Mental Retardation, 34,* 359–366.

Singer, H. S. (1992). Neurochemical analysis of post-mortem cortical and striatal brain tissue in patients with Tourette syndrome. *Advances in Neurology, 58,* 135–144.

Smith, T., Klevstrand, M., & Lovaas, O. I. (1995). Behavioral treatment of Rett's disorder: Ineffectiveness in three cases. *American Journal on Mental Retardation, 100,* 317–322.

Sprague, R. L., & Newell, K. M. (1996). *Stereotyped movements: Brain and behavior relationships.* Washington, DC: American Psychological Association.

Stein, D. J., Keating, J., & Zar, H. (1993, May). Compulsive and impulsive symptoms in Prader-Willi syndrome. *Abstracts in New Research* (NR 33). Annual Meeting of the American Psychiatric Association, San Francisco, CA.

Stodgell, C. J., Schroeder, S. R., Hyland, J. M., & Tessel, R. E. (1995). Effect of repeated footshock stress, apomorphine and their combination on the incidence of apomorphine (APO)-elicited self-injurious behavior (SIB) in juvenile neonatal 6-hydroxydopamine (6HD)-treated rats. *Neuroscience Abstracts, 20,* 507.

Stodgell, C. J., Schroeder, S. R., & Tessel, R. E. (1996). FR discrimination training reverses 6HD-induced striatal dopamine depletion of a rat with Lesch-Nyhan syndrome. *Brain Research, 713,* 246–252.

Tate, B. G., & Baroff, G. S. (1966). Aversive control of self-injurious behavior in a psychotic boy. *Behavior Research and Therapy, 4,* 281–287.

Taylor, D. V., Rush, D., Hetrick, W. P., & Sandman, C. A. (1993). Self-injurious behavior within the menstrual cycle of women with developmental delays. *American Journal on Mental Retardation, 97,* 659–664.

Tessel, R. E., Schroeder, S. R., Loupe, P. S., & Stodgell, C. J. (1995). Reversal of 6HD-induced neonatal brain catecholamine depletion after operant training. *Pharmacology, Biochemistry, and Behavior, 51,* 861–868.

Tessel, R. E., Schroeder, S. R., Stodgell, C. J., & Loupe, P. S. (1995). Rodent models of mental retardation: Self-injury, aberrant behavior and stress. *Mental Retardation and Developmental Disabilities Reviews, 1,* 99–103.

Thompson, T., Hackenberg, T., Cerutti, D., Baker, D., & Axtell, S. (1994). Opioid antagonist effects on self-injury in adults with mental retardation: Response form and location as determinants of medication effects. *American Journal on Mental Retardation, 99,* 85–102.

Thompson, T., Symons, F., Delaney, D., & England, C. (1995). Self-injurious behavior as endogenous neurochemical self-administration. *Mental Retardation and Developmental Disabilities Research Reviews, 1,* 137–148.

Tsai, L. (1992). Is Rett syndrome a subtype of pervasive developmental disorders? *Journal of Autism and Developmental Disorders, 22*, 551–561.

Tu, J. B., Hartridge, C., & Izawa, J. (1992). Psychopharmacogenetic aspects of Prader-Willi syndrome. *Journal of the American Academy of Child and Adolescent Psychiatry, 31*, 1137–1140.

Van den Borre, R., Vermote, R., Buttins, M., Thiry, P., Dierick, G., Gentjens, J., Sieben, G., & Heylen, S. (1993). Risperidone as add-on therapy in behavioural disturbance in mental retardation: A double-blind placebo-controlled cross-over study. *Acta Psychiatrica Scandinavica, 87*, 167–171.

Van de Wetering, B. J. M., & Heutink, P. (1993). The genetics of Gilles de la Tourette syndrome: A review. *Journal of Laboratory and Clinical Medicine, 121*, 638–645.

Verkerk, A. J. M. H., Pieretti, M., Sutcliffe, J. S., Fu, Y. H., Kuhl, D. P., Pizzuti, A., Reiner, O., Richards, S., Victoria, M. F., Zhangi, F. P., Eussen, B., van Ommen, G., Blonden, L., Riggins, G., Chastain, J., Kunst, C., Galjaard, H., & Warren, S. (1991). Identification of a gene (FMR-1) containing a CGG repeat coincident with a break-point cluster region exhibiting length variation in fragile X syndrome. *Cell, 65*, 905–914.

Warnock, J. K., & Kestenbaum, M. D. (1992). Pharmacologic treatment of severe skin-picking behaviors in Prader-Willi syndrome. *Archives of Dermatology, 128*, 1623–1625.

Wenk, G. L., Naidu, S., & Moser, H. (1989). Altered neurochemical markers in Rett syndrome. *Annals of Neurology, 26*, A466–468.

Wieseler, N. H., Hanson, R. H., & Nord, G. (1995). An investigation of mortality and morbidity associated with self-injurious behavior. *American Journal on Mental Retardation, 100*, 1–4.

Wolff, P. (1967). The role of biological rhythms in early psychological development. *Bulletin of the Menninger Clinic, 31*, 197–218.

Wong, D. F., Harris, J. C., Naidu, S., Yokoi, F., Marenco, S., Dannals, R. F., Ravert, H. T., Yaster, M., Evans, A., Rousset, O., Bryan, R. N., Gjedde, A., Kuhar, M. J., & Breese, G. R. (1996). Dopamine transporters are markedly reduced in Lesch-Nyhan disease *in vivo. Proceedings of the National Academy of Science, 93*, 5539–5543.

Author Note

We wish to acknowledge Grants HD 02528 and HD 26927 from the National Institute of Child Health and Human Development as well as Maternal and Child Health Grant MCJ 944 and Administration on Developmental Disabilities Grant 07DD0365 for financial assistance during the writing of this paper.

Facts and Fictions Concerning Mental Illness in People With Mental Retardation and Developmental Disabilities

Robert Sovner[1]
Anne DesNoyers Hurley
Tufts University School of Medicine,
Boston, Massachusetts

A number of prevalent myths about behavior and mental illness greatly influence professional practice in the field of mental retardation and developmental disabilities (MR/DD). Many of these myths are reflected in some regulations, like those by the Health Care Financing Administration (HCFA, 1988). Much of the current treatment of psychiatric disorders in people with MR/DD is based on a misconception from the 1960s and 70s that people with MR/DD were protected from mental illness (King, State, Shah, Davanzo, & Dykens, 1997a; Moss, Emerson, Bouras, & Holland, 1997; Sovner & Hurley, 1983).

Fiction: All Behavior Is Functionally Defined

The traditional view posited that people with MR/DD displayed maladaptive behavior because they lived in deprived environments (Moss et al., 1997). It was believed to remedy this situation, it was necessary only to provide an enriched lifestyle, value each person as an individual, and enhance self-esteem. If problems persisted, a behavioral program would help retrain the person to a more adaptive behavior pattern. The belief was that these interventions would eliminate all the challenging behaviors (see Table 5.1); clinically, however, this is not always the case.

This antiquated view is built into HCFA regulations and especially impacts pharmacotherapy. The provision of psychosocial treatment implies that some functional purpose of the behavior accounts for its etiology. For example, the assumption is that if the person is provided with more alternatives to communicate his or her needs, to respond in different ways, and to have more meaningful daily life experiences, he or she will not engage in challenging behaviors. This is true for some people with MR/DD; but for many, it is *not* true. Manic overactivity, for example, is not a functional response to the environment but is totally driven by biological neurochemical structures and pathways (Akiskal, 1995; Berrettini & Pekkarinen, 1996). When in a

---

[1] Robert Sovner passed away March 4, 1997, at the age of 52. He made an extraordinary contribution to the field of mental retardation through his efforts to write and lecture about the mental health needs of people with mental retardation and other developmental disabilities. Dr. Sovner believed that people with disabilities suffered from the same mental illnesses that impact all people, and that people with disabilities deserve the same attention from psychiatry, as well as the right to benefit from appropriate pharmacological treatments.

manic state, individuals need little sleep. Once awakened and feeling uncomfortable, the person in a manic state may begin to roam around the house, which may attract the attention of housemates or staff. In this situation, misguided caregivers have assumed that such behavior is attention-getting and that it will respond to a behavior program.

The reality is that some behavior is involuntary. It is not under the control of the individual and may not respond to social consequences. Behavioral symptoms may be managed, but this is not the same as treating the underlying biological condition. The irony is that psychosocial and behavioral interventions may not be active treatment and may serve as containment that keeps the person safe, but only during the time the programmatic restrictions are enforced. In many instances, pharmacological intervention may be the treatment of choice and may be the active and necessary component for healthful change.

Consideration should be given to determining if the target behavior is driven by internal or external stimuli and whether it represents an adaptive response for the person. A good model for making this distinction is Tourette's disorder, a neuropsychiatric condition characterized by vocal and motor tics. Motor and vocal tics may occur many times, daily, in bouts. Severity and frequency may wax and wan, often with stress, but the tics remain a lifelong condition. Tourette's disorder is a useful model because it combines both neurological and psychiatric features. First, stress makes it worse. Like many extrapyramidal disorders including drug-induced Parkinsonia and tardive dyskinesia, the movements worsen with increased arousal. An individual with Tourette's disorder in a stressful situation displays more tics. Thus, someone may have a neurobiologically determined behavioral disorder that also has an environmentally sensitive component.

From this we can understand that someone with MR/DD may have a mental illness that responds in some ways to environmental influences, but that response to environmental influences does not mean that the condition is not biologically driven.

Many behaviors that are biologically driven may also be somewhat responsive to voluntary control. Again, in Tourette's disorder we have an example of this in premonitory urges, which are sensory phenomena prior to the onset of a tic. A tic can be voluntarily suppressed by certain movements, and if the person's arm is going to tic, moving the arm or performing some other action may suppress that particular tic (Leckman, Walker, & Cohen, 1993). Thus, voluntary strategies may be successful, but this success does not negate in any way the biological etiology of the problem.

Unfortunately, many federal and state regulations and guidelines are based on the assumption that challenging behavior is functional and requires an environmental

TABLE 5.1

Myth 1 About Behavior and Mental Illness in People With MR/DD

Myth: Behavior always has funcitonal significance and is under the control of the affected individual.

Premise	Behavior is an adaptive response to an external or internal stimulus.
Reality	Some behavior is involuntary and nonadaptive, (e.g., tics and vocalizations of Tourette's disorder).
Treatment implications	Involuntary behavior may not respond to psychosocial interventions.

Myth 2 About Behavior and Mental Illness in People With MR/DD

Myth: If a behavior has functional significance it is unlikely to be related to a psychiatric disorder.

Premise	Determining the "meaning of the behavior" means that it can be explained in behavioral terms.
Reality	Behavior may represent an adaptive response to stress associated with psychiatric disorder. (The onset of the illness may produce state-dependent behavior or result in an increase in state-exacerbated behavior).
Treatment implications	State-dependent and state-exacerbated behavior should be managed with treatment directed toward the underlying psychiatric disorder.

intervention. HCFA regulations require a behavior program to manage the target behavior in order to eventually discontinue medication. To argue the alternative assumption (that is, that the challenging behaviors may be driven by abnormalities in the neurobiological substrate), and that a behavior plan is not necessary, may result in a regulatory citation.

Fiction: The Behavioral/Biological Dichotomy

The second myth dichotomizes psychiatric disorders and environmentally influenced behavior. Thus, if a behavior has functional significance (i.e., the behavior is voluntary), care providers assume that it is not a symptom of psychiatric illness (see Table 5.2). Generally, care providers do not ask these questions: Why does the person need the attention now? Why hasn't this always been the case? Why 6 months ago did his attention-getting behavior increase in frequency and severity? It is not an either/or situation. The answer to the question, "Is it behavior or is it mental illness?" should be, "Why can it not be both?"

A dysfunctional behavior may have functional significance and it may be an adaptive response at some level. The person with MR/DD may be able to moderate either internal or external stress in the case of a psychiatric disorder by performing a dysfunctional behavior. For example, a person suffering from a major depressive episode may avoid social contact because of the discomfort and negative self-thoughts generated by socialization. The social avoidance behavior serves to reduce the discomfort. This adaptive-maladaptive response has a strong functional relationship to the environment, but it is associated with major depression. Recommended treatment usually consists of cognitive-behavioral psychotherapy in concert with antidepressant medication (Beck, Rush, Shaw, & Emery, 1979; Harrington, Whittaker, & Shoebridge, 1998; Katon et al., 1997; Rush et al., 1998).

If a target behavior is a manifestation of a psychiatric illness, then the active treatment should be directed to the underlying psychiatric illness, not just the behavioral manifestations. The treatment of first choice for a drug-responsive psychiatric disorder is pharmacotherapy. Sometimes a disservice is performed by insisting that behavior therapy is the active treatment and that pharmacotherapy is just a containment measure necessary until the active treatment takes effect. In the case of severe depression, the person will generally be unable to initiate any self-correcting behavioral or other therapeutic measures. Once pharmacotherapy has lessened the physical symptoms associated with depression, the person will be more able to address difficulties in life and change any cognitive or behavioral habits that contribute to the depression.

If service providers are not fully trained in mental health, consultations may be misguided. For example, if a person with MR/DD has become irritable, disruptive, and aggressive, a behavioral consultation may be sought. During the assessment, it may become apparent that the individual reacts negatively with aggression in response to task demands. At this point, many consultants would conclude that the functional significance observed calls for a purely behavioral explanation and implementation of a reward program to curb the behavior. This is often a myopic conclusion. Care providers often overlook conducting a comprehensive assessment that addresses other determinants or conditions. For example, it is important to ask about sleep patterns because the person could be depressed or manic. Other physical symptoms could be present suggesting a medical condition. The presence of a psychiatric disorder or another medical condition needs to be fully explored.

A useful conceptual framework for diagnostic purposes fully encompasses understanding of *state-dependent* and *state-exacerbated* behavior. State-dependent symptoms are behavior that is transitory and only occurs during illness episodes (e.g., someone becomes irritable and loud only during a major depressive episode). State-exacerbated symptoms are behavior that is always present, but that worsens with the onset of a psychiatric illness (e.g., a person with autism engages in a low frequency of self-injury that escalates during a major depressive episode).

A parallel between behavior and personality can be made. Personality is the product of learned expectations, biological endowment, and temperament that is genetically determined and modified through the person's environmental history. For example, the life experiences a person has been exposed to—such as how the person was nurtured or how he or she experienced school—interact with the person's genetic complement to determine whether that person is a good athlete, develop-

mentally disabled, autistic, or short-tempered. The personality is constantly interacting with an individual's physiological brain function. Genes do not stop affecting behavior after childhood. Experiences and stressors also affect brain function. When an individual is exposed to stress, that individual's perception of the stressor interacts with brain function, modified by genetic constitution, and often produces challenging behaviors as well as psychiatric illness. Thus, challenging behaviors may serve an environmental function; however, this does not mean the behavior is purely environmentally determined.

Fiction: Cognitive Limitations Preclude Psychiatric Diagnoses

The third myth is a form of severity of disability discrimination. Prior to the last decade, it was widely believed that people with MR/DD could not develop psychiatric disorders; that due to their cognitive limitations they were protected from the stresses everyone experiences (King et al., 1997a; Moss et al., 1997; Sovner & Hurley, 1983). This is not true, but unfortunately the criteria for diagnosing mental illness are based on self-reported information by people of normal intelligence. This does not imply the disorder is a function of intelligence (see Table 5.3). The nonverbal person with severe or profound mental retardation cannot say that he or she feels distressed. Typically, a depressed person with MR/DD cannot derive pleasure, feels "down," does not look forward to any future or any event that would justify getting out of bed in the morning. If one is quite depressed and perceiving oneself as a failure, a variety of self-abusive behaviors may result. Feelings of rage, hopelessness, and helplessness can be manifested in people with severe disabilities, but often without the verbalizations that accompany such behavior in people of normal intelligence. The nonverbal person with MR/DD cannot describe negative feelings or will not express them in the typical manner (Charlot, 1998; Hurley, 1996a; Lowry, 1997, 1998; Sovner & Hurley, 1982; Sovner & Pary, 1993).

Research has shown that self-injury is associated with depressive disorders in people with MR/DD. Meins (1995) identified 32 people with MR/DD who met the criteria for a major depressive episode, and found one third of the sample was self-injurious, another third was assaultive, and a little less than a third was engaging in property destruction. A quarter of the sample had tantrums, and a quarter had stereotypic behavior. In his sample of subjects diagnosed with a depressive disorder, Meins observed relatively high rates of maladaptive behaviors as one of the presenting symptoms. In addition, Meins found a difference due to the severity of the disability. Three of the behavioral categories (self-injury, assaultive behaviors, and tantrums) were more prominent in people with severe developmental disabilities. This prominence suggests that the greater the intellectual disability, the more undifferentiated are responses to life, perhaps because of a limited repertoire of responding. Thus, people with severe MR/DD cannot do what many people do when they feel depressed because of limited coping skills and restrictions in ability to express discomfort. The person who is severely cognitively impaired, whether constipated, suffering from a migraine headache, or feeling depressed, frequently displays discomfort by exhibiting three or four different challenging behaviors.

Psychiatric disorders can be diagnosed in people with severe or profound disabilities, but they may not display the full syndrome (that is, meet all of the criteria necessary) because many of the criteria require the ability to verbalize and self-report symptoms. Partial criteria may be met, and a diagnosis given. A person with MR/DD should not receive psychoactive medications without a *DSM-IV* (1994) formulation, even if the individual has severe or profound disabilities. This includes specifying if there is a major psychiatric disorder or other conditions that may be the focus of attention (Axis I), personality disorders and learning disabilities (Axis II), medical conditions (Axis III), psychosocial and environmental problems (Axis IV), and a global assessment of functioning (Axis V).

T A B L E 5 . 3

Myth 3 About Behavior and Mental Illness in People With MR/DD

Myth: A person with severe or profound disabilities is too impaired to develop classic psychiatric disorders.

Premise	Because impairments in communication and functional skills preclude obtaining information about many psychiatric symptoms (e.g., suicidal ideation), people with severe impairments cannot manifest psychiatric disorders such as major depression.
Reality	*DSM-IV* diagnostic criteria represent only approximations of syndromes, many of which have biochemical underpinnings. Criteria are based on the assumption that the diagnostically relevant behaviors and emotional experiences are highly associated.
Treatment implications	All patients, irrespective of the severity of their disabilities, who are being treated with psychotropic drug therapy should have a *DSM-IV* diagnostic formulation.

Fiction: Bizarre Behavior Indicates Psychosis

Developmental delay, limited cognitive organization, stress, and prior traumatic experiences can all result in behaviors that are regularly misdiagnosed as psychotic. Behavior must be considered in a neurodevelopmental perspective prior to being diagnosed as psychotic, and other possible precipitating factors must be examined. A number of pseudopsychotic features of mental illness, presented in Table 5.4, cannot be considered signs of psychosis per se. During the diagnostic evaluation, the mental health clinician considers how organized the person's behavior appears; however, the norms for making that determination were developed from people of normal intelligence. Thus, what may be very normal organization for a person with moderate to profound MR/DD can be confused with the disorganized psychotic behavior of (e.g., a person with schizophrenia) particularly when the examining clinician is unfamiliar with developmental disabilities.

In stressful situations, people with MR/DD often become overwhelmed and suffer cognitive deterioration. A similar situation, called pseudodementia, is well-known in geriatric psychiatry (Cavenar, Maltbie, & Austin, 1979; Haggerty et al., 1998; Raskind, 1998). Memory problems may be seen, as well as apathy and loss of hygiene or adaptive daily living skills. In these cases, an elderly person suffering from a major depressive episode shows dramatic deterioration and may frequently be misdiagnosed with dementia, thought to occur because of neurobiological changes in the aging brain. People with MR/DD suffer the same *cognitive disintegration* under stress or when suffering from a mental illness, but mental health clinicians are not at all as aware of this situation, frequently misdiagnosing psychotic conditions (Sovner, 1986).

Developmental delay impacts behavior among people with MR/DD (see Table 5.5), and several phenomenon are regularly misdiagnosed as psychotic behavior (Hurley, 1996b). Talking out loud to oneself is quite disconcerting to caregivers. From a developmental perspective, however, this is quite normal, as all small children talk to themselves out loud. As they mature, these verbalizations are subsumed and referred to as private speech (Vygotsky, 1988). Children with attention-deficit/hyperactivity disorder (ADHD) also do this beyond the typical ages (Berk & Potts, 1991), and all of us do this at times. (Have you ever muttered to yourself out loud when upset about something and was this pointed out to you by someone?) The frequency of this behavior among people with MR/DD is quite high and is to be expected. During times of anger or distress, such talk will increase in emotional tone, which should be seen as normal coping from a developmental perspective, rather than as abnormal.

The imaginary friend is also a normally observed phenomenon in children, seen in possibly as much as 60% of 3- and 4-year-olds (Manosevitz, Preston, & Wilson, 1973). People with MR/DD may also talk to a person as if that person were there, a situation quite troubling to caregivers, employers, and families. This habit can be a long-developed coping skill, or it may be directly related to an unfulfilled need for close companionship.

Fantasy play among children is normal and encouraged. Fantasy in adults with MR/DD takes the form of wish-fulfillment. For example, the person with MR/DD may lie or exaggerate about friends or romantic liaisons that do not exist. Frequently, overengagement with TV

T A B L E   5 . 4

Pseudopsychotic Features of Mental Illness in MR/DD

1. Disorganized thinking
2. Disorganized and/or bizarre behavior
3. Monologue
4. Imaginary friends
5. Fantasy
6. Stress-induced hallucinations
7. Flashbacks

Myth 4 About Behavior and Mental Illness in People With MR/DD

Myth: Bizarre behaviors, such as talking to yourself out loud, fantasy play, or talking to an imaginary friend, represent manifestations of psychosis.

Premise	Bizarre behaviors indicate the presence of delusions or hallucinations.
Reality	Talking to yourself out loud, fantasy play and imaginary friends are best considered to be normal developmental behaviors that have persisted.
Treatment implications	These behaviors do not respond to antipsychotic drug therapy.

characters (e.g., stars of soap operas or fantasy shows) is observed and of great concern only because the developmental perspective has not been considered.

It is also important to understand the breadth of hallucinations as phenomena. From a developmental perspective, young children may experience hallucinations (Schreier & Libor, 1986). Under unusual and traumatic stress, many normal adults experience stress and decompensation. Soldiers at the battlefront often decompensate and have hallucinations and delusions, which are usually successfully treated by several days in the unit hospital with support and nurturing. Further, Tien (1991) reported that in the National Institute of Mental Health catchment area study 10 to 30 individuals per 1,000 reported having hallucinations. Romme and his colleagues in Great Britain reported on a self-help network, Resonance, in which members, who suffer hallucinations, have learned to deal cognitively with their mental perceptions (Romme, Honig, Noorthoorn, & Escher, 1992). Thus, the frequent overreaction of caregivers to people with MR/DD who may talk to themselves or report hearing voices or having friendships that do not exist may be unwarranted. Such observed behavior does not equate with a diagnosis of a psychotic disorder but should be considered within the context of the person's developmental level and present quality of life. The existence of delusions must also be examined within a context. Some would posit

that monodelusional disorders (e.g., possible abduction by a UFO) are common and not consistent with a psychotic disorder or mental illness (Munro, 1991).

People with MR/DD may experience visual hallucinations, for example, "When I go to bed at night, I see the head of my stepfather raping me," or, "I think there are people outside my room who are going to come in." It is important to ascertain whether the individual has been exposed to abuse. There may be a documented history of physical or sexual abuse. What is usually ascribed to this phenomenon is that the person has been exposed to documented experiences of sexual or physical abuse. These situations may be flashbacks, more accurately diagnosed as post traumatic stress disorder than as psychosis.

Lastly, hallucinations and delusions occur with a variety of mental illnesses and medical conditions. People suffering depression may hear voices making self-deprecating statements, and those with mania have delusions of grandeur. Substance abuse may regularly result in hallucinations. Thus, for people with MR/DD, clinicians must not make the mistake of diagnosing a psychotic disorder because of extraneous presentation that is "different" due to the person's disability. A diagnostic treatment approach called the *false negative strategy* has been recommended by Hurley (1996a). It is a diagnostic strategy that considers it better to miss a diagnosis of psychosis than to overdiagnose it because of the great risks of treating with antipsychotic medication and missing the common illnesses of depression and anxiety disorders.

Fiction: Behavioral Therapy Is Always Superior to Pharmacotherapy

This final myth considers pharmacotherapy to be a restrictive form of treatment and asserts that there must be a behavioral plan and a timetable for discontinuing the medication (see Table 5.6). Pharmacotherapy is therapeutic and may be the first-choice treatment for some mental illnesses. For major depression, manic states, and schizophrenia, pharmacotherapy must be offered and encouraged as the first treatment. Thus, for people with MR/DD and severe disabilities, problematic behavior noted may be secondary to the psychiatric disorder. If this is the case, the treatment of the psychiatric disorder is the primary consideration while the behavior program focuses primarily on containment.

For people of normal intelligence, no timetable to end medication is mandated. People suffering from mental illness work out their treatment with the physician using a team approach. If side effects are difficult, the regimen may be adjusted and the patient may want to work toward discontinuing medication. Often, the physician suggests tapering or discontinuing medication, but the person of normal intelligence resists, having suffered and felt relief with treatment. People of normal intelligence can easily voice the benefits and costs of treatment. If after treatment for depression and discontinuation of medication, the person begins to feel depressed again, he or she can easily contact the physician and reinstate medication. Most people with MR/DD cannot do this and must therefore wait until their symptoms are so difficult that they have seriously decompensated. In the meantime, they may have to endure treatment aimed at making their behavior more adaptive. Such an approach is a form of disability discrimination.

Because of advances in biological psychiatry and neurobiology, it is now understood that mental illness is strongly influenced by brain neurochemistry. Many, and perhaps the vast majority of, people with MR/DD may have neurobiological brain abnormalities as the cause of their disability, either due to prenatal and perinatal difficulties, the effects of toxins, illness, accidents, or genetic factors (Baumeister & Woodley-Zanthos, 1996; King et al., 1997b; Macmillan, 1998). Therefore, it is more likely that these abnormalities would contribute to an increased incidence of mental illness. The field of MR/DD should not, therefore, be prejudiced against the existence of mental illness and the need for pharmacotherapy for these individuals.

TABLE 5.6

Myth About Behavior and Mental Illness in People With MR/DD

Myth: Drug therapy is a restrictive form of behavior control. All regimens must, therefore, include a behavior plan and a timetable for discontinuing treatment.

Premise	Drug therapy directly affects behavior.
Reality	Behavior such as self-injury and aggression are too nonspecific to be considered as direct targets for drug therapy.
Treatment implications	The appropriate targets for drug therapy are the changes in neurophysiological function that mediate behavior associated with psychiatric disorders and central nervous system dysfunction.

Final Comments

People with severe mental retardation and developmental disabilities should not be denied access to state-of-the-art psychiatric care due to prejudice that they are different from others. Their dependence on others for care should not relegate them to behavior plans as the primary focus of treatment. Because people with severe MR/DD cannot articulate their inner feelings and needs, caregivers should not assume that clients cannot suffer from the effects of mental illness. Serious changes in behavior may indeed herald the development of an underlying, and treatable, psychiatric disorder.

Today, due to advances in pharmacotherapy, the general population has access to a wide array of medications that can treat mental illness. The understanding of mental illness has radically changed in the last 20 years: from a simplistic dichotomy between neuroses and psychoses to a complex and specific nomenclature of conditions. Much research has advanced the understanding of the development of mental illness, with treatments to address many disorders specifically. For many conditions, drug therapy is the primary treatment of choice, and for some conditions (such as manic states), drug therapy is the only active treatment. Because people with MR/DD have received inadequate general habilitative care in this country until recent years, advocates have erroneously focused on pharmacotherapy as a treatment to be avoided. Today, pharmacotherapy is among the most effective treatments available for mental illness, and it should be available for all individuals with intellectual disabilities.

REFERENCES

Akiskal, H. S. (1995) Mood disorders: Clinical features. In H. I. Kaplan, & B. J. Sadock, *Comprehensive textbook of psychiatry (Vol. 2, 6th ed., pp. 1123–1152).* Philadelphia: Williams & Wilkins.

American Psychiatric Association. (1994*). Diagnostic and statistical manual of mental disorders* (4th ed.). Washington, DC: Author.

Baumeister, A. A., & Woodley-Zanthos, P. (1996). Prevention: Biological factors. In J. W. Jacobson & J. A. Mulick (Eds.), *Manual of diagnosis and professional practice in mental retardation* (pp. 229–242). Washington DC: American Psychological Association.

Beck, A. T., & Rush, A. J. (1995). Cognitive therapy. In H. I. Kaplan & B. J. Sadock (Eds.), *Comprehensive textbook of psychiatry (Vol. 2, 6th ed.,* pp. 1847–1857). Philadelphia: Williams & Wilkins.

Beck, A. T., Rush, A. J., Shaw, B. F., & Emery, G. (1979). *Cognitive therapy of depression.* New York: Guilford Press.

Bentall, R., & Shade, P. D. (1985). Reality testing and auditory hallucinations. *British Journal of Clinical Psychology, 24,* 159–169.

Berk, L. E., & Potts, M. K. (1991). Developmental and functional significance of private speech among attention-deficit hyperactivity disordered and normal boys. *Journal of Abnormal Child Psychology, 19,* 357–377.

Berrettini, W. H., & Pekkarinen, P. H. (1996). Molecular genetics of bipolar disorder. *Annals of Medicine, 28,* 191–194.

Cavenar, J. O., Maltbie, A. A., & Austin, L. (1979). Depression simulating organic brain disease. *American Journal of Psychiatry 136,* 521–524.

Charlot, L. R. (1998). Developmental effects on mental health disorders in persons with developmental disabilities. *Mental Health Aspects of Developmental Disability, 1,* 29–39.

Haggerty, J. J., Golden, R. N., Evans, D. L., & Janowsky, D. S. (1998). Differential diagnosis of pseudodementia in the elderly. *Geriatrics, 43,* 61–69.

Harrington, R., Whittaker, J., & Shoebridge, P. (1998). Psychological treatment of depression in children and adolescents. A review of treatment research. *British Journal of Psychiatry, 173,* 291–298.

Health Care Financing Administration. (1988). In *Federal register* (pp. 20495–20505). Washington DC: U.S. Department of Health and Human Services.

Hurley, A. D. (1996a). Identifying psychiatric disorders in persons with mental retardation: A model illustrated by depression in Down syndrome. *Journal of Rehabilitation, 15,* 6–31.

Hurley, A. D. (1996b). The misdiagnosis of hallucinations and delusions in persons with mental retardation: A neurodevelopmental perspective. *Seminars in Clinical Neuropsychiatry, 2,* 1–13.

Kalachnik, J. E., Leventhal, B. L., James, D. H., Sovner, R., Kastner, T. A., Walsh, K., Weisblatt, S. A., & Klitzke, M. G. (1998). Guidelines for the use of psychotropic medication. In S. Reiss & M. G. Aman (Eds.), *Psychotropic medication and developmental disabilities. The international consensus handbook* (pp. 45–72). Columbus: Ohio State University Nisonger Center.

Katon, W., VonKorff, M., Lin, E., Simon, G., Walker, E., Bush, T., & Ludman, E. (1997). Collaborative management to achieve depression treatment guidelines. *Journal of Clinical Psychiatry, 58 (*Suppl. 1), 20–23.

King, B. H., State, M. W., Shah, B., Davanzo, P., & Dykens, E. (1997a). Mental retardation: A review of the past 10 years. Part I. *Journal of the American Academy of Child and Adolescent Psychiatry, 36,* 1656–1663.

King, B. H., State, M. W., Shah, B., Davanzo, P., & Dykens, E. (1997b). Mental retardation: A review of the past 10 years. Part II. *Journal of the American Academy of Child and Adolescent Psychiatry, 36,* 1664–1671.

Leckman, J. F., Walker, D. E., & Cohen, D. J. (1993). Premonitory urges in Tourette's syndrome. *American Journal of Psychiatry, 150,* 98–102.

Lowry, M. A. (1997). Unmasking mood disorders: Recognizing and measuring symptomatic behaviors. *Habilitative Mental Healthcare Newsletter, 16,* 1–6.

Lowry, M. A. (1998). Assessment and treatment of mood disorders in persons with developmental disabilities. *Journal of Developmental and Physical Disabilities, 10,* 387–406.

Macmillan, C. (1998). Genetics and developmental delay. *Seminars in Pediatric Neurology, 5,* 39–44.

Manosevitz, M., Prentice, N. M., & Wilson, F. (1973). Individual and family correlates of imaginary companions in preschool children. *Developmental Psychology, 8,* 72–79.

Meins, W. (1995). Symptoms of major depression in mentally retarded adults. *Journal of Intellectual Disability Research, 39,* 41–45.

Moss, S., Emerson, E., Bouras, N., & Holland, A. (1997). Review: Mental disorders and problematic behaviours in people with intellectual disability: Future directions for research. *Journal of Intellectual Disability Research, 41,* 440–447.

Munro, A. (1991). Phenomenological aspects of monodelusional disorders. *British Journal of Psychiatry, 159,* 62–64.

Raskind, M. A. (1998). The clinical interface of depression and dementia. *Journal of Clinical Psychiatry 59* (Suppl. 10), 8–12.

Romme, M. A. J., Honig, A., Noorthoorn, E. O., & Escher, A. D. M. A. C. (1992). Coping with hearing voices: An emancipatory approach. *British Journal of Psychiatry, 161,* 99–103.

Rush, A. J., Crismon, M. L., Toprac, M. G., Trivedi, M. H., Rago, W. B., Shon, S., & Altshuler, K. Z. (1998). Consensus guidelines in the treatment of major depressive disorder. *Journal of Clinical Psychiatry, 59* (Suppl. 20), 73–84.

Schreier, H. A., & Libor, J. A. (1986). Acute phobic hallucinations in very young children. *Journal of the American Academy of Child Psychiatry, 25,* 574–578.

Sovner, R. (1986). Limiting factors in the use of DSM-III criteria with mentally ill-mentally retarded persons. *Psychopharmacology Bulletin, 22,* 1055–1059.

Sovner, R., & Hurley, A. D. (1982). Diagnosing depression in the mentally retarded. *Psychiatric Aspects Mental Retardation, 1,* 1–4.

Sovner, R., & Hurley, A. D. (1983). Do the mentally retarded suffer from affective illness? *Archives of General Psychiatry, 40,* 61–67.

Sovner, R., & Pary, R. J. (1993). Affective disorders in developmentally disabled persons. In J. L. Matson & R. P. Barret (Eds.), *Psychopathology in the mentally retarded* (2nd ed.). Needham Heights, MA: Allyn & Bacon.

Tien, A. Y. (1991). Distributions of hallucinations in the population. *Social Psychiatry & Psychiatric Epidemiology, 26,* 287–292.

Vygotsky, L. S. (1988). *The collected works of L. S. Vygotsky: Vol 1. Problems of general psychology, including volume thinking and speech.* (R. W. Rieber, A. S. Caton, N. Minick, Trans). New York: Plenum Press.

PART TWO

Pharmacotherapy

Psychopharmacotherapy for People With Profound and Severe Mental Retardation and Mental Disorders

Cynthia A. Kern
Southern Cities Community Health Clinic
Faribault, Minnesota

Significant behavioral symptoms in individuals with profound and severe mental retardation may be best treated with pharmacotherapy conjunctive to social environmental interventions. Many psychiatric disorders are highly drug-responsive, and drug treatment should not be withheld in lieu of nondrug approaches. Treatment, nevertheless, is frequently complex due to multiple psychiatric diagnoses combined at times with multiple medical diagnoses. Also, drug response tends to be more unpredictable in this population than in the general population (Arnold, 1993).

Psychotropic Drugs

All classes of psychotropic medications have been shown to be useful in treating psychiatric disorders in clients with profound and severe mental retardation (Gabriel, 1994). Psychotropic medication classes include antidepressants, mood stabilizers, antipsychotics, anxiolytics, stimulants, and others (e.g., opiate antagonists and antihypertensives). Antiepileptic medications may also have pronounced behavioral effects (see Chapter 7, this volume). The more available drugs there are, the more options and opportunities exist for successful treatment of mental health disorders. In addition, the more recently released medications may allow for either more effective treatment or an improved side effect profile or both.

Clinical Drug Treatment

Psychiatric diagnosis has become the primary indication for psychotropic drug treatment. Unfortunately, because diagnosis is difficult, selection of psychotropic drug treatment in clients with profound and severe mental retardation is complicated. The complex nature of this process necessitates the use of psychotropic drug trials. Specific medications are chosen based on information described in the following paragraphs.

Generally, diagnosis is based on target behaviors and symptoms, which are interrelated. These target behaviors and symptoms guide treatment toward reasonable drug choices. Defining the meaning of the target behaviors is challenging. For example, if the client is agitated, is this a symptom of a mood disorder or does the agitation stem from depression or an agitated mania? The agitation could be associated with a psychotic disorder, or perhaps an anxiety disorder. Drug trials are utilized because of this unclear origin of symptoms. If a drug trial is effective, it often assists in clarifying the diagnosis (Mikkelsen, 1997).

Drug history information is extremely important in developing medication trials, because it can provide information that increases the possibility of success (Tomb, 1995). Every effort should be made to acquire information relating to previous effective and ineffective treatments, along with any adverse effects that have occurred. Repeating ineffective drug trails needs to be avoided. In some cases, adverse effects can be minimized by using newer drugs with fewer side effects.

Due to some amount of genetic linkage, family history of mental disorders may provide beneficial information (Tomb, 1995). For example, the diagnostic history of family members treated effectively for mood disorders or schizophrenia can provide insight into drug trial development for the client.

Target behaviors are identified and prioritized, baseline behavioral data are collected, and the client is treated symptomatically. Behaviorally defined target behaviors and quantified severity levels are extremely useful for assessing treatments. Drugs that can treat an array of symptoms are likely to be primary choices. The goals of pharmacological treatment are to (a) keep drug treatment as simple as possible, (b) provide the client with the greatest chance for success early in therapy, and (c) use the safest drug available to avoid side effects (Mikkelsen, 1997).

Initiating Drug Treatment

Psychotropic drugs should be initiated at low doses and slowly titrated to avoid side effects. Clients with profound and severe mental retardation are frequently found to be especially sensitive to the effects of medications. Toxicity may occur in the typical dosage range used for psychiatric clients without cognitive disabilities. Additionally, drug response can be observed at lower than usual doses. If the drug is well-tolerated, the drug trial may last 1 to 6 months or longer, depending on the specific drug. This period allows time for an evaluation of the drug response based on empirical data on index behaviors.

Side Effects Versus Disorder

Once a drug is initiated, it is often difficult or even impossible to determine whether a client is having side effects from the medication. Clients with profound or severe mental retardation are not able to communicate information directly about side effect discomfort. Staff need to be familiar with the common side effects of the psychotropic medication and consider how these might affect behaviors. With the clinician's advisement, more frequent and regular monitoring of drug specific effects is very important for this population. Baseline laboratory values and vital signs before and after the initiation of some medications are also helpful.

Side effects may manifest as increases in target behaviors. This may occur with antipsychotic drugs that cause akathisia (i.e., a subjective feeling of restlessness). In a client who otherwise has anxious symptoms or becomes easily agitated, akathisia would likely cause increased rates of target behaviors. The selective serotonin reuptake inhibitors (SSRIs), like fluoxetine (Prozac), can cause some nervousness or agitation, but this is more often observed at higher doses. Buspirone (Buspar), an anxiolytic, may cause some agitation with dose increases or at high doses. Also, a client with mood symptoms and target behaviors of screaming and crying may display more screaming and crying if experiencing a headache as a medication side effect.

Side effects may produce emergent novel behaviors. For instance, a client with self-injurious biting may suddenly start banging his head because the medication is causing headaches.

Side effects of medications can also result in decreased behaviors. Sedation and fatigue are adverse effects of many psychotropic drugs, including the antipsychotics, antidepressants, mood stabilizers, anxiolytics, and antihypertensives (e.g., beta-blockers). The resultant chemical restraint from sedation is not an acceptable outcome of drug treatment.

When mild side effects occur, tolerance of them can develop over time. Common side effects, like nausea, sedation, agitation, and blood pressure changes, often subside over time. In some cases, the dose can be decreased to lessen the adverse effect or the medication may need to be discontinued. If a drug is effective but its side effects are a concern, another drug in the same class may be substituted.

Psychotropic Drug Classes and Specific Drugs

As previously mentioned, psychotropic drugs consist of antidepressants, mood stabilizers, antipsychotics, anxiolytics, stimulants, and others. These drugs may be used in combination in cases of comorbidity or as augmentation treatment. It is important to remember that psychotropic medications have the potential to interact with one another and also to interact with a multitude of other nonpsychotropic drugs, both prescription and nonprescription medications. When a drug interaction is significant, it may result in treatment failure or toxic effects. A comprehensive review of potential drug interaction is beyond the scope of this paper. However, it is important to recognize that drug interactions may result in serious untoward effects, either behavioral or medical or both, and consultation with a knowledgeable health professional is essential.

Antidepressants

Antidepressant medications include selective serotonin reuptake inhibitors (SSRIs), tricyclic antidepressants (TCAs), monoamine oxidase inhibitors (MAOIs), and other miscellaneous agents. Antidepressants can be useful in treating depression, anxiety, panic, obsessive-compulsive disorders, eating disorders, and sleep disturbances (Mikkelsen, Albert, Emens, & Rubin, 1997). Currently, TCAs and MAOIs are not considered first-line treatments. TCAs can be difficult to tolerate due to side effects and can have increased risk of toxic effects. MAOIs also may not be tolerated well due to numerous side effects, and in addition they can interact with certain foods to produce serious, life-threatening reactions. Both TCAs and MAOIs require more monitoring than the newer antidepressants. Because the newer antidepressant agents will be more frequently prescribed, only the newer antidepressants are discussed here.

Selective serotonin reuptake inhibitors (SSRIs). Selective serotonin reuptake inhibitor antidepressants include fluoxetine (Prozac), sertraline (Zoloft), paroxetine (Paxil), fluvoxamine (Luvox), and citalopram (Celexa). In clients with profound and severe mental retardation, these medications are generally considered first-line treatment for depressive symptoms. Agitation, compulsiveness, impulsiveness, anxiousness, aggression, self-injury, panic symptoms, changes in appetite, and sleep problems may all suggest the need for an SSRI trial (Hellings, Kelley, Gabrielli, Kilgore, & Shah, 1996; Meins, 1995; Mikkelsen et al., 1997). Fluvoxamine has been shown to be effective in reducing symptoms of autism (McDougle, Naylor, Cohen, & Volkmar,1996; Sovner, Fox, Lowry, & Lowry, 1993). Some of the more common side effects of SSRIs are headache, nausea, nervousness or sedation, diarrhea or constipation, and sexual dysfunction (Bernstein, 1995; Gelman, Rumack, & Sayre, 1997; Olin et al., 1995-1997; Stahl, 1997). If one SSRI trial fails or the side effects are intolerable, a different SSRI may succeed.

Miscellaneous antidepressants. Trazodone (Desyrel) and nefazodone (Serzone) are antidepressants that can have concomitant antianxiety effects. For this reason, these drugs may be beneficial in clients with agitated behaviors. Both of these medications can also be useful for treating sleep problems. In fact, trazodone sometimes cannot be tolerated at the doses needed to treat depression due to its sedative effect. Nefazodone may be less sedating than trazodone and can actually improve sleep cycles and, thus, the quality of sleep. Notable side effects are daytime sedation, dizziness, orthostatic hypotension, and alterations in heart rate (Bernstein, 1995; Gelman et al., 1997; Olin et al., 1995-1997).

Mirtazapine (Remeron) is a relatively new antidepressant that may have antianxiety effects. It is useful for treating clients with depressive disorder who exhibit agitation, diminished appetite with weight loss, or have sleep disturbances. Sedation, dizziness, increased appetite, and weight gain are the more common side effects of mirtazapine. It has minimal anticholinergic effects (i.e., dry mouth, blurred vision, urinary retention, and constipation) (Gelman et al., 1997; Olin et al., 1995-1997).

Venlafaxine (Effexor) may be reserved for more difficult to treat depressed clients or those with concomitant anxiety (Silverstone & Ravindran, 1999). The dosing schedule is two to three times daily for the immediate-release (IR) form, or once daily for the extended-release (XR) form. Effexor XR is preferred over the IR form because it is easier to dose, better tolerated, and may be more effective (Cunningham, 1997). Blood pressure should be monitored regularly for possible sustained increases especially at high doses or if the client has a history of hypertension. Common side effects are nausea, nervousness, somnolence, insomnia, dizziness, anorexia, and sexual dysfunction (Bernstein, 1995; Gelman et al., 1997; Guze et al., 1995; Olin et al., 1995-1997; Stahl, 1997).

Bupropion (Wellbutrin) is available in an extended-release (XR) form that can be given once or twice daily, compared to two to three times daily for the immediate-release (IR) form. Use of the XR form results in more even drug levels with fewer side effects than with the IR form. Bupropion may increase the risk for seizures; therefore, it may be contraindicated for use in clients who are known to have low seizure thresholds. Clients with profound and severe mental retardation have a higher incidence of seizures (see Chapter 7, this volume), so bupropion has not been a first-line option in their treatment. Also, agitation and restlessness, which often are presenting symptoms in this client population, may be side effects. Other common side effects are headache, insomnia, and nausea (Kaplan & Sadock, 1996). Bupropion may pose less risk of a switch to mania in clients with bipolar disorder (Guze, Ferng, Szuba, & Richeimer, 1995; Haykal & Akiskal, 1990; Wright, Galloway, & Kim, 1985).

Antidepressant treatment, if tolerated by the client, should continue for 6 to 8 weeks after a therapeutic dose is reached. This provides sufficient time to collect data on target behaviors and determine if the medication is beneficial. Minimum effective doses do not apply to antidepressants, in that the maintenance dose is the initial effective dose. If others perceive that the effect of an antidepressant has ameliorated over time, options include increasing the dose, switching to a different antidepressant agent, or augmenting with buspirone.

Mood Stabilizers

Current established mood stabilizers include lithium, valproate (e.g., valproic acid [Depakene] and divalproex sodium [Depakote]), and carbamazepine (Tegretol). Adjunctive drug treatment might include an antipsychotic, a benzodiazepine, or an antidepressant, depending on symptoms. If traditional mood stabilizers are not well tolerated by the client, second-line mood stabilizing agents include gabapentin (Neurontin), calcium channel blockers (e.g. verapamil), or trazodone (Gelman et al., 1997; Kaplan & Sadock, 1996; McElroy et al., 1997; Olin et al., 1995-1997). Mood stabilizers can be very useful for treating bipolar disorder in individuals with profound and severe mental retardation (Kastner, Friedman, & Plummer, et al., 1990; Sovner, 1989). Treatable target behaviors may include agitation, irritability, aggression, decreased sleep, decreased appetite, self-injury, increased vocalizations, increased sexual displays, and decreased attention span (Langee, 1989; Sovner et al., 1991). Mood swings are most easily recognized by graphing prevalent target behaviors on a chart over time. In appropriately aged females, if mood symptoms cycle monthly and are associated with menses, the pharmacotherapy may be quite different for treating this premenstrual dysphoric disorder (Bazire & Benefield, 1997).

Even though lithium has been the classic mood stabilizing agent since the 1960s, valproate is also now considered a first-line therapy (Bazire & Benefield, 1997). Valproate has been shown to be as efficacious as lithium and it often produces fewer side effects than either lithium or carbamazepine. It has a wider therapeutic range, less risk of toxicity, and requires less laboratory monitoring. It can also be used simultaneously to treat seizure disorders (as can carbamazepine), whereas lithium can lower the seizure threshold. Additionally, carbamazepine can be very difficult to use because of the multitude of drug interactions involved when individuals are on concomitant drug therapies. Clients with rapid cycling or mixed state mood disorders may be more likely to benefit from valproate (Goldberg, Harrow, & Grossman, 1995).

Acute manic episodes also can be effectively treated with valproate by cautiously using a loading dose strategy that is given in divided doses. Manic episodes with psychotic features can be treated with antipsychotics. Benzodiazepines are used to treat insomnia and to decrease anxious symptoms. Depressive episodes can be treated with an antidepressant (such as an SSRI or mirtazapine) in combination with a mood stabilizer if needed. Depressive episodes with psychotic features may also require the addition of an antipsychotic.

Higher drug doses are generally required to treat acute episodes. Treatment of bipolar disorder requires maintenance doses of mood stabilizers and sometimes requires mood stabilizers used in combination to prevent recurring acute episodes.

It is noteworthy that the minimum effective dosage principle does not apply to mood stabilizing agents. Dosages are prescribed according to blood levels maintained within a specific therapeutic range (Bernstein, 1995).

Antianxiety Agents

Antianxiety drugs include buspirone (Buspar), some of the antidepressants, and, most notably, the benzodiazepines (e.g., lorazepam [Ativan], clonazepam [Klonopin]). Treatable conditions in individuals with profound or severe mental retardation may be behaviorally defined nervous or anxious behaviors, panic-type behaviors, aggression, or self-injurious behaviors.

Benzodiazepines should be used only in the short term as they can have a paradoxical disinhibitory effect on behavior, resulting in increased agitation and aggression. They can also cause considerable sedation and impair cognitive abilities. If benzodiazepines are used regularly, tolerance can occur where increasingly higher doses may be needed. Benzodiazepines can also be very difficult medications to discontinue, especially if used daily for more than a week or two. Even a very gradual taper can result in increased behavior rates with each small decrease. Generally, it is advisable to avoid long-term daily use of benzodiazepines. However, they can be effective in managing episodic agitation or sleep problems on an intermittent basis (Guze et al., 1995).

Buspirone is a good first-line treatment for anxiety symptoms, especially for generalized anxiety disorder. As previously mentioned, it can be used augmentatively with SSRIs for treating depression or obsessive-compulsive disorder. When combined with pindolol (Visken), a beta-adrenergic blocker, buspirone may be an effective antidepressant (Kaplan & Sadock, 1996). Agitation, aggression, self-injury, anxiousness or nervousness, hyperactivity, and impulsiveness or compulsiveness are symptoms that might respond to buspirone treatment (Gelman et al., 1997).

Unlike the benzodiazepines, buspirone is associated much less with sedation and adverse cognitive side effects. It has no apparent abuse potential, nor does it build tolerance. Overall, buspirone has a desirable safety profile with some of the more common side effects reported to be headache, nausea, dizziness, and lightheadedness (Bernstein, 1995; Gelman et al., 1997; Kaplan & Sadock, 1996; Olin et al., 1995-1997). Because buspirone has some dopaminergic action, there have been reports of movement disorders, but these are rare (Gelman et al., 1997). Infrequently, increased agitation may occur with dose increases, but the agitation tends to be only temporary. When buspirone is initiated, the dose is gradually increased over time, with full clinical benefits taking up to 4 weeks to become apparent. A buspirone trial may require 2 months or longer (Kaplan & Sadock, 1996).

SSRIs can be effective for treating various anxiety disorders (Stavrakaki & Mintsioulis, 1997). Paroxetine and fluvoxamine are more sedating and less stimulating than fluoxetine, sertraline, and citalopram. Citalopram is the most selective SSRI and may be associated with fewer side effects and drug interactions. SSRIs have proven efficacy in anxiety associated with depression, panic disorder, and obsessive compulsive disorder. Encouraging findings have been reported in social phobia, post-traumatic stress disorder, and premenstrual dysphoric disorder (Stahl, 1997).

Antipsychotics

These include the older typical antipsychotics (e.g., chlorpromazine [Thorazine], thioridazine [Mellaril], haloperidol [Haldol]) and the newer atypical antipsychotic agents. Atypical antipsychotics are clozapine (Clozaril), risperidone (Risperdal), olanzapine (Zyprexa), and quetiapine (Seroquel). Others are awaiting U.S. Food and Drug Administration (FDA) approval or are in clinical trials. The atypical agents are considered the best antipsychotic treatments currently available. Clozapine is not considered a first-line antipsychotic because it requires weekly to biweekly laboratory monitoring of the white blood cell count due to a 1-2% risk of agranulocytosis, which can be fatal. Risperidone, olanzapine, and quetiapine are first-line antipsychotic treatments and superior to typical antipsychotics, because they can often be more effective, particularly in terms of treating the negative symptoms of schizophrenia (blunted affect, apathy, social and emotional withdrawal, and anhedonia). The side effect profiles of risperidone, olanzapine, and quetiapine are also improved compared to typical antipsychotics, with less risk of extrapyramidal (i.e., akathisia, dystonias, tremors, and cogwheel rigidity) and probably less risk for tardive dyskinesia. The incidence of extrapyramidal effects may increase with higher risperidone doses; however, these side effects do not seem to occur as frequently with higher doses of olanzapine and quetiapine.

It can be very difficult, and at times impossible, to assess whether psychotic symptoms exist in a person with profound or severe mental retardation. If psychosis is suspected, treatment with an antipsychotic may be helpful. Risperidone, olanzapine, or quetiapine may be initiated at a low dose and gradually increased over a period of days or weeks to an effective dose. Orthostatic hypotension and sedation can be early side effects, but these generally subside over time. No regularly scheduled laboratory monitoring is required for these drugs unless there are specific problems. Risperidone is more likely than olanzapine or quetiapine to cause increases in prolactin levels and amenorrhea in females. Other reasons for an abnormal prolactin level should be eliminated, as there may be other medical causes. If it is determined to be a drug side effect, the risperidone dose can be minimized as much as possible or olanzapine or quetiapine can be substituted. Prolactin levels should be monitored as determined by the clinician.

Some individuals, particularly elderly clients tend to be very sensitive to medications in terms of therapeutic response and sensitivity to side effects. These individuals may require very low doses of an antipsychotic, whereas others may require high doses. Persons taking carbamazepine in combination with an antipsychotic may require higher antipsychotic doses because carbamazepine induces metabolic enzymes that increase the metabolism of many other drugs. Consequently, antipsychotics may be less effective at customary doses when taken with carbamazepine (Kaplan & Sadock, 1996).

Many clients with profound and severe mental retardation referred for psychiatric services are already receiving an antipsychotic medication and often have an extensive medication history. If their current medication regimen consists of an older, typical antipsychotic (e.g., thioridazine or haloperidol), it can be switched to risperidone, olanzapine, or quetiapine by doing a cross-taper that may take several weeks. In individuals with severe behavior problems, major medication changes may involve risk of increased self-injury or aggression to others. The treatment team must weigh the possible risks against the possible benefits of using a safer and possibly more effective drug.

Antipsychotics can be effective for diminishing psychotic symptoms related to schizophrenia, dementia, psychotic depression, and mania. Risperidone has been useful for treating behavioral disturbances, such as aggression, agitation, hyperactivity, and self-injury in individuals with profound or severe mental retardation (Vanden Borre et al., 1993). Olanzapine and quetiapine are comparatively newer and, although demonstrated to be effective in a population without mental retardation, empirical validation in this population of persons with mental retardation is needed. Other medications used in combination with antipsychotics to treat side effects may be anticholinergics (e.g., benztropine [Cogentin], diphenhydramine [Benadryl], trihexyphenidyl [Artane]) for extrapyramidal effects, or a beta-adrenergic blocker (e.g., propranolol [Inderal]) for akathisia or restlessness. Benzodiazepines (e.g., lorazepam [Ativan]) can be used in combination with antipsychotics for treating comorbid sleep or anxiety disorders, or an antidepressant or mood stabilizer can also be used for affective disorders (Kaplan & Sadock, 1996).

In conclusion, newer atypical antipsychotics (i.e., risperidone, olanzapine, or quetiapine) are preferred over traditional antipsychotics for treating psychotic symptoms and significant behavioral disturbances because they produce fewer side effects and may be more effective (Tollefson et al., 1997). For individuals with profound or severe mental retardation, they can be associated with cognitive improvements and increased functioning.

Other Agents

Beta-blockers (e.g., propranolol [Inderal]) can be used to treat akathisia, a side effect of antipsychotic drugs. They can be effective at relatively low doses for treating tremors induced by lithium or valproate (Kaplan & Sadock, 1996). Propranolol, pindolol (Visken), and other beta-blockers have been used to successfully treat aggressive and impulsive behaviors in individuals with mental retardation (Ratey & Lindem, 1991).

Naltrexone (ReVia), an opiate antagonist, has been effective in diminishing self-injurious behavior in this population (Barrett et al., 1989; Bernstein, Hughes, & Mitchell, 1987; Deutsch, 1986; Herman, 1990, 1991; Herman, Hammock, Arthur-Smith et al., 1987, Herman, Hammock, & Egan et al., 1989; Kars, Broekema, & Glaudemans-Van Geleren, 1990; Leboyer, Bouvard, & Dugas, 1988; Sandman, 1988). A mechanism for this may involve blocking the release of endogenous or naturally occurring opiates that are normally released in the body in response to painful stimuli (Herman, 1991).

Clonidine (Catapres), an antihypertensive drug, has had some use in autistic and other developmentally disabled children with hyperactivity and behavioral disturbances (Ahmed & Takeshita, 1996).

Summary

The medications used to treat this dually diagnosed population are many and varied in terms of their uses, side effect profiles, and resultant individual responses. Diagnosis is extremely difficult for many of these clients, and frequently drug trials are required. Many times, it is necessary to have several drug trials before arriving at a medication regimen that produces the desired effects and allows the client the best quality of life.

REFERENCES

Ahmed, I. & Takeshita, J. (1996). Clonidine: A critical review of its role in the treatment of psychiatric disorders. *CNS Drugs, 6,* 53-70.

Arnold, L. E. (1993). Clinical pharmacological issues in treating psychiatric disorders of patients with mental retardation. *Annals of Clinical Psychiatry, 5*(3), 189-197.

Barrett, P. R., Feinstein, D., & Hole, W. T. (1989). Effects of naloxone and naltrexone on self-injury: A double blind, placebo controlled analysis. *American Journal on Mental Retardation, 93,* 644-651.

Bazire, S., & Benefield, W. H., Jr. (1997). *Psychotropic drug directory: The mental health professional's handbook.* Tewkesbury, UK: Beshara Press Ltd.

Bernstein, J. G. (1995). *Drug therapy in psychiatry.* St. Louis: Mosby-Year Book.

Bernstein, G. A., Hughes, J. R., Mitchell, J. E. (1987). Effects of narcotic antagonists on self-injurious behavior: A single case study. *Journal of the American Academy of Child and Adolescent Psychiatry, 26,* 886-889.

Cunningham, L. A. (1997). Once-daily venlafaxine extended release (xr) and venlafaxine immediate release (ir) in outpatients with major depression. *Annals of Clinical Psychiatry, 9*(3), 157-164.

Deutsch, S. I. (1986). Rationale for administration of opiate antagonists in treating infantile autism. *American Journal of Mental Deficiency, 90,* 631-635.

Gabriel, S. R. (1994). The developmentally disabled, psychiatrically impaired client. Proper treatment of dual diagnosis. *Journal of Psychosocial Nursing and Mental Health Services, 32*(9), 35-39.

Gelman, D. R., Rumack, B. H., Sayre, N. K. (Eds.). (1997, September-November) DRUGDEX® System. Englewood, CO: Micromedex.

Goldberg, J. F., Harrow, M., & Grossman, L. S. (1995). Course and outcome in bipolar affective disorder. *American Journal of Psychiatry, 152,* 379-384.

Guze, B. H., Ferng, H., Szuba, M. P., & Richeimer, S. (1995). *The psychiatric drug handbook.* St. Louis: Mosby-Year Book.

Haykal, R. F., & Akiskal, H. S. (1990). Bupropion as a promising approach to rapid cycling bipolar II patients. *Journal of Clinical Psychiatry, 51,* 450-455.

Hellings, J. A., Kelley, L. A., Gabrielli, W. F., Kogore, E., & Shah, P. (1996). Sertraline response in adults with mental retardation and autistic disorder. *Journal of Clinical Psychiatry, 57,* 333-336.

Herman, B. H. (1990). A possible role of proopiomelanocortin peptides in self injurious behavior. *Progress in Neuro-Psychopharmacology and Biological Psychiatry, 14,* 109-139.

Herman, B. H. (1991). Effects of opioid receptor antagonists in the treatment of autism and self-injurious behavior. In J. J. Ratey (Ed.), *Mental retardation: Developing pharmaco-therapies* (pp. 107-162). Washington, DC: American Psychiatric Press.

Herman, B. H., Hammock, M. K., Arthur-Smith, A. et al. (1987). Naltrexone decreases self-injurious behavior in children. *Annals of Neurology, 22,* 550-552.

Herman, B. H., Hammock, M. K., Egan, J. et al. (1989). A role of opioid peptides in self-injurious behavior: dissociation from autonomic nervous system functioning. *Developmental Pharmacology and Therapeutics, 12,* 118-127.

Kaplan, H. I., & Sadock, B. J. (1996). *Pocket handbook of psychiatric drug treatment.* Baltimore: Williams & Wilkins.

Kars, H., Broekema, W., Glaudemans-Van Geleren, I. et al (1990). Naltrexone attenuates self-injurious behavior in mentally retarded subjects. *Biological Psychiatry, 27,* 741-746.

Kastner, T., Friedman, D. L., Plummer, A. T. et al. (1990). Valproic acid for the treatment of children with mental retardation and mood symptomatology. *Pediatrics, 86,* 467-472.

Langee, H. R. (1990). A retrospective study of mentally retarded patients with behavioral disorders who were treated with carbamagozine. *American Journal on Mental Retardation, 93*(6), 640-643.

Leboyer, M., Bouvard, M. P., & Dugas, M. (1988). Effects of naltrexone on infantile autism. *Lancet, 1,* 715.

McDougle, C. J., Naylor, S. T., Cohen, D. J., & Volkmar, F. R. (1996). A double-blind, placebo-controlled study of fluvoxamine in adults with autistic disorder. *Archives of General Psychiatry, 53,* 980-983.

McElroy, S. L., Soutullo, C. A., Keck, P. E., Jr., & Kmetz, G. F. (1997). A pilot trial of adjunctive gabapentin in the treatment of bipolar disorder. *Annals of Clinical Psychiatry, 9*(2), 99-103.

Meins, W. (1995). Symptoms of major depression in mentally retarded adults. *Journal of Intellectual Disability Research, 39,* 41-45.

Mikkelsen, E. J. (1997). Risk-benefit analysis in the use of psychopharmacologic interventions for difficult-to-diagnose behavioral disorders in individuals with mental retardation. *Psychiatric Annals, 27,* 207-212.

Mikkelsen, E. J., Albert, L. G., Emens, M., & Rubin, E. (1997). The efficacy of antidepressant medication for individuals with mental retardation. *Psychiatric Annals, 27,* 198-206.

Olin, B. R. et al. (Eds.). (1995-1997). *Facts and comparisons drug information.* St. Louis: Wolters Kluwer.

Ratey, J. J., & Lindem, K. J. (1991). Beta-blockers as primary treatment for aggression and self-injury in the developmentally disabled. In J. J. Ratey (Ed.), *Mental retardation: developing pharmacotherapies* (pp. 51-81). Washington, DC: American Psychiatric Press.

Sandman, C. A. (1988). Beta-endorphin dysregulation in autistic and self-injurious behavior: a neurodevelopmental hypothesis. *Synapse, 2,* 193-199.

Silverstone, P. H., & Ravindran, A. (1999). Once-daily venlafaxine extended release (xr) compared with fluoxetine in outpatients with depression and anxiety. *Journal of Clinical Psychiatry, 60,* 22-28.

Sovner, R. (1989). The use of valproate in the treatment of mentally retarded persons with typical and atypical bipolar disorders. *Journal of Clinical Psychiatry, 50,* 40-43.

Sovner, R. (1991). Use of anticonvulsant agents for treatment of neuropsychiatric disorders in the developmentally disabled. In J. J. Ratey (Ed.), *Mental retardation: developing pharmacotherapies* (pp. 83-106). Washington, DC: American Psychiatric Press.

Sovner, R., Fox, C., Lowry, M. J., & Lowry, M. A. (1993). Fluoxetine treatment of depression and associated self-injury in two adults with mental retardation. *Journal of Intellectual Disability Research, 37,* 301-311.

Stahl, S. M. (1997). *Psychopharmacology of antidepressants* (pp. 39-60). London: Martin Dunitz.

Stavrakaki, C., & Mintsioulis, G. (1997). Implications of a clinical study of anxiety disorders in persons with mental retardation. *Psychiatric Annals, 27,* 182-189.

Tollefson, G. D., Beasley, C. M., Tran, P. V., Street, J. S., Krueger, J. A., Tamura, R. N., Graffeo, K. A., & Thieme, M. E. (1997). Olanzapine versus haloperidol in the treatment of schizophrenia and schizoaffective and schizophreniform disorders: Results of an international collaborative trial. *American Journal of Psychiatry, 154,* 457-465.

Tomb, D. A. (1995). *Psychiatry.* Baltimore: Williams & Wilkins.

Vanden, Borre, R., Vermote, R., Buttiens, M. et al. (1993). Resperidone as add-on therapy in behavioural disturbances in mental retardation: A double-blind placebo-controlled cross-over study. *Acta Psyciatrica Scandinavica, 87,* 167-171.

Wright, G., Galloway, L., Kim, J. et al. (1985). Bupropion in the long-term treatment of cyclic mood disorders: mood stabilizing effects. *Journal of Clinical Psychiatry, 46,* 22-25.

Adverse Behavioral Effects of Antiepileptic Medications in People With Developmental Disabilities

John R. Gates
Minnesota Epilepsy Group, PA
and University of Minnesota
Minneapolis, MN

The association of epilepsy with cognitive impairment is significant. As reviewed by Hauser and Hesdorffer (1990), studies of people with mental retardation reveal a 6% to 19% prevalence of epilepsy in cases of mild to moderate mental retardation and 24.5% to 33% in severe mental retardation. This far exceeds the prevalence of epilepsy reported in the typical noncognitively impaired population (range 2.7–6 per 1,000).

Similarly, approximately 33.9% of children with cerebral palsy were found to have epilepsy and, conversely, cerebral palsy was present in 19% of children with epilepsy. These proportions, as cited by Hauser and Hesdorffer (1990), are more than 35 times greater than the cumulative incidences of epilepsy reported in Oakland, California, in a nondisabled group of similar age.

When cerebral palsy and mental retardation coexist, seizure risk is higher. The incidence of afebrile seizures among children with both mental retardation and cerebral palsy found in the Oakland study was 50%, which is a relative risk factor of 53. The corresponding frequency of seizures in a similar dually diagnosed Bronx, New York, population was 50.7%, a relative risk factor of 92. Thus, children with both mental retardation and cerebral palsy have a 53 to 92 times increased risk of developing seizures (Hauser & Hesdorffer, 1990).

This association is evident as both mental retardation and cerebral palsy are indicators of neurologic abnormality. Therein lies the critical challenge of assessing the effects of antiepileptic medication in this population. Clinicians are dealing with an injured cerebrum that is evidenced by the mental retardation or cerebral palsy (or both), and it is known that behavioral consequences can arise from this substrate alone. When antiepileptic drugs are added to the equation, it becomes even more complicated.

Dodrill (1991) has carefully reviewed the issue of effects of antiepileptic drugs on behavior and reached this conclusion:

> The area of behavioral effects of antiepileptic drugs is poorly defined, lacks recognized and validated methods of assessment, and has suffered from a number of methodological limitations, especially including the use of experimental designs which have led to the contamination of drug effects and subject effects. (p. 44)

Given these limitations, Dodrill (1991) was able to draw the following conclusions:

1. The best controlled study showed that the behavioral effects of antiepileptic drugs are quite limited.

2. The benzodiazepines have the most consistently favorable effect, but they are of limited utility in epilepsy as

they are not typically administered on a long-term basis.

3. Carbamazepine is associated with a favorable behavior change, but this change is seen most consistently in groups who do not have epilepsy.

4. Relatively few studies have been conducted using valproic acid. Those studies reported are associated with limited positive behavioral change.

5. Phenytoin is not associated with either a consistently positive or consistently negative change.

6. The barbiturates are clearly associated with the most negative behavioral change. (p. 44) Dodrill (1991) further suggested that a substantial commitment of resources be directed to overcome the major methodological limitations to provide an important scientific clarification of the effects of these medications.

Overview of Adverse Effects

When discussing any pharmacological agent, adverse effects can be categorized into three basic groupings: (a) dose-concentration related, (b) inherent side effects, and (c) idiosyncratic reactions. A fourth category is often pertinent to the antiepileptic drugs and that is the additive effects of combination therapy, which can result in toxicity for almost half of patients receiving three concurrent antiepileptic medications (Brodie & Dichter, 1996; Levy, Mattson, Meldrum, Penry, & Dreifuss, 1995).

As will be discussed briefly for each medicine, the idiosyncratic reactions are of greatest concern because these can be potentially life-threatening. These include an allergic dermatitis, which can progress in some cases to a Stevens Johnson syndrome, with systemic symptoms including pain, exfoliation, and mucous membrane involvement; lupus erythematosus; diffuse bone marrow suppression; hepatotoxicity; renal failure; pancreatitis; or encephalopathy (Brodie & Dichter, 1996; Levy et al., 1995).

The inherent side effects of these medications often include phenomena such as lethargy, decreased attention span, sleep pattern changes, impotency, and leukopenia. These side effects can produce their own behavioral consequences. Similarly, the dose-related adverse effects of sedation, mental dullness, ataxia, diplopia, and headache can produce behavioral effects. The ability of the cognitively impaired, mentally ill patient to articulate these concerns may be severely limited. A change in behavior may be the only way the patients express their concerns. Each medication must be evaluated on its own merits, considering its profile of dose-related, non-dose-related, and idiosyncratic reactions. Here we review the profiles of phenytoin, carbamazapine, valproic acid, phenobarbitol, gabapentin, felbamate, lamotrigine, topirimate, and tigabine.

Phenytoin

As discussed by Dodrill (1991), phenytoin (Dilantin) appears essentially devoid of any significant general behavioral impact. Some studies have shown positive effects and some have shown negative effects.

However, in the case of people with mental retardation, phenytoin can cause significant dose-related cognitive impairment, as well as ataxia, poor coordination, and dyskinesia that can consist principally of choreiform disturbances. Non-dose-related effects can include significant cosmetic effects (e.g., darkening or increasing of body hair, coarsening of facial features, worsening of acne or gingival hyperplasia), which may have significant behavioral consequences. With chronic use, a significant concern can be osteopenia (thinning of bones), as well as folic acid deficiency (Fröscher et al., 1995), which also may result in behavioral consequences (Bruni, 1995).

The idiosyncratic reactions are principally allergic dermatitis, hepatic failure, aplastic anemia (which is extremely rare), a lupus reaction, and a pseudolymphoma state, which is very uncommon (Bruni, 1995).

The other particular challenge unique to phenytoin is its nonlinear kinetics. Figure 7.1

(Browne & LeDuc, 1995) demonstrates that, unlike the so-called ideal antiepileptic drug, which has linear kinetics (i.e., a change in dose at any point along the dosing curve resulting in the same change of blood level), phenytoin, for most patients, changes from first-order kinetics to saturation kinetics in the lower end of the therapeutic range. Consequently, a small increase in dose at the lower end of the therapeutic range can result in a dramatic increase in blood level.

Significant drug interactions can also occur because of phenytoin's significant protein binding (Browne & LeDuc, 1995). For patients with cognitive impairments, significant drug interactions with psychotropic medications, antibiotics, or other antiepileptic drugs can result in a significant change in the level due to this saturation kinetic interaction, resulting in toxicity that may manifest only as behavior change.

Carbamazepine

Carbamazepine (Tegretol) has resulted in many reports of favorable behavioral change (Dodrill, 1991). The most commonly reported changes are decreased anxiety, depression, and aggression with increased cooperation and generally improved behavior.

The principal dose-related effects of carbamazepine include double vision usually at about 2.5 hours after dose, which is the time of the peak absorption of the drug (T-max). Other side effects are cognitive viscosity, lethargy, and movement disorders, which can occur as dose-related phenomena. Non-dose-related side effects include hyponatremia, which when pronounced can cause an exacerbation of seizures or behavioral consequence of its own. Often observed is a mild suppression of white blood cell count, which is rarely clinically significant unless the total white count is less

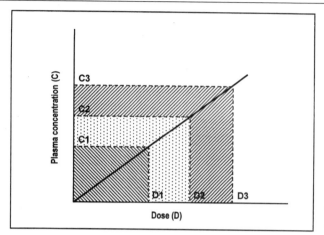

1A. First-order kinetics—the ideal antiepileptic drug

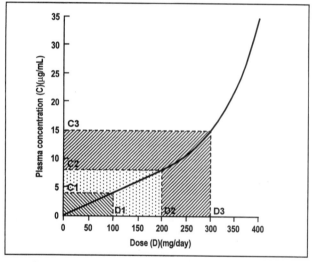

1B. Phenytoin—saturation kinetics
(D1 − D2 = D3 − D2 for 1A.,
but C3 − C2 > C2 − C1 for phenytoin)

Figure 7.1. Comparison of linear kinetics of the ideal antiepileptic drug with nonlinear kinetics of phenytoin. A small increase in dose at the lower end of the therapeutic range can result in a dramatic increase in blood level.

than 3,000 and the absolute neutrophil count is below 1,000 (Brodie & Dichter, 1996; Tohen, Castillo, Baldessarini, Zarate, & Kando, 1995).

Idiosyncratic reactions include aplastic anemia (approximately 1 in 50,000 patients), allergic dermatitis (1 in 20 patients), Stevens Johnson syndrome, as well as hepatic and renal failure (rare incidence). Generally, carbamazepine has demonstrated a reasonable profile. The effectiveness has been demonstrated in treating bipolar affective disorders. A few isolated case reports (Holmes, 1995; Scull & Trimble, 1995) have identified carbamazepine as possibly precipitating mania with its discontinuation, as well as an isolated case report of oculogyric crisis induced by carbamazepine, resolved with appropriate reduction (Gormann & Barkley, 1995).

Valproic Acid

Although fewer studies have been done with valproic acid (Depakene) than with carbamazepine, valproic acid has demonstrated a positive behavioral effect (Dodrill, 1991). Its side-effect profile in the dose-related category can include gastrointestinal upset, tremor, elevation of ammonia, some somnolence, cognitive viscosity, and thrombocytopenia (Dreifuss, 1995). The hyperammonemia and secondary liver effects can result in a confusional-irritable state, especially in cognitively impaired patients who cannot verbally label their symptoms. However, Murphy and Marquard (1982) have observed hyperammonemia without apparent consequence in many patients. Supplementing carnitine can ameliorate this effect in many patients. Cognitive impairment is mostly associated with very high blood levels (Dreifuss, 1995). The thrombocytopenia is a concern as the thrombocyte can be as low as 30,000 as a dose-related phenomena. This usually becomes critical only in the situation of an anticipated elective surgical procedure, where reducing the dose of valproic will elevate the platelet count within a week or two, or in patients with atonic, tonic, or tonic-clonic seizures with precipitous falls (Dreifuss, 1995).

The non-dose-related effects include weight gain, nausea, and a change in hair texture with hair loss. This cosmetic effect can have secondary effects on behavior in that the individual can become concerned about physical appearance and behave accordingly (Dreifuss, 1995).

Idiosyncratic reactions include a confusional syndrome that can progress to coma or stupor, as well as pancreatitis (Buzan, Firestone, Thomas, & Dubovsky, 1995; Evans, Miranda, Jordan, & Krolikowski, 1995) and hepatic failure (Dreifuss, 1995). Of particular concern is that valproic acid can cause hepatic failure in a polypharmacy regimen in 1 of 500 patients under the age of 2 years (Dreifuss, 1995). For patients older than 2 years, even in a polypharmacy regimen, the risk of hepatic failure appears to be dramatically less (1 in 12,000) (Dreifuss, 1995).

From a behavioral aspect, the most pertinent concern is the confusional state that can progress to coma or stupor (Sackellares, Lee, & Dreifuss, 1979). This progression is most dramatic and obviously would require prompt medical intervention with discontinuation of the medication. This can occur in the absence of elevation of ammonia or liver functions. It is diagnosed by the presence of high-voltage frontal delta activity on an electroencephalogram. A variant of this is seen fairly frequently at the Minnesota Epilepsy Group, with a case presenting about once every month of an individual with a confusional state or behavior that is not quite right, often masquerading as possible pseudomentia. On closer inspection, the patient is found to be suffering from valproic encephalopathy. Sometimes this condition is associated with hyperammonemia. In all cases, the patients have improved considerably intellectually with the discontinuation of valproic acid. A variant of this syndrome has been described by Papazian and his colleagues (1995). There was even evidence of brain atrophy in the two cases they reported, with reversal as seen from brain imaging 1 year after discontinuation of the medication.

Phenobarbital

The barbiturates are the drugs most clearly associated with negative behavioral changes (Dodrill, 1991). Several studies have demonstrated increased depression, irritability, unhappiness, inattentiveness, argumentativeness, stubbornness, or aggression. The barbiturates have also been associated with the most negative cognitive effects among the antiepileptic drugs.

The most convincing studies have been conducted with children. Domizo, Verrotti, Ramenghi, Sabatino, & Morgese (1993) studied 300 children ages 3.1 to 15.9 years in Italy. While 197 children were treated with phenobarbital, 103 were treated with other antiepileptic medications. From questionnaires completed by parents it was determined that 76% of the group of patients treated with phenobarbital showed one or more behavior disturbances, such as hyperactivity, irritability, disturbances of sleep, and drowsiness, versus 31% of the patients receiving other antiepileptic drugs. The most frequent behavioral disturbance mentioned was hyperactivity.

The report from the Committee on Drugs (1995) published in *Pediatrics* examined the issue of behavior and cognitive effects of anticonvulsant therapy. One study of 39 children with epilepsy, evaluated by psychiatric interview, suggested a high rate of major depressive disorder following the initiation of phenobarbital therapy in children with a family history of affective disorder. In another study, phenobarbital was discontinued in 14% of the sample due to the display of severe behavior problems (Committee on Drugs, 1995).

The observation of clinicians at the Minnesota Epilepsy Group in St. Paul of patients receiving barbiturates, especially those with cognitive impairment, prompted the collaborative writing of the Report on the Behavioral Side Effects of Barbiturate Antiepileptic Drugs for the State of Minnesota (Kalachnik & Hanzel, 1995; Kalachnik, Hanzel, Harder, Bauernfeind, & Engstrom, 1995). This monograph identified profiles of behavior which may result from antiepileptic medication use in cognitively impaired patients, who displayed challenging behaviors of irritability, aggression, self-injury, depression, disruptive vocalizations, sleep disturbance, and temper tantrums. All of these behaviors can occur in cognitively impaired patients as possible side

effects of antiepileptic medications or for social-environmental reasons. However, with the use of phenobarbital, the possibility that these behaviors are drug induced is very high.

Generally, the dose-related adverse effects of phenobarbital include sedation, and in children, cognitive impairment, hyperactivity, and aggressive behavior. In addition, hyperactivity can be a non-dose-related phenomena, as can depression and decreased attention span and lethargy (Cramer & Mattson, 1995).

As with all the other antiepileptic medications, the possibility exists of allergic dermatitis, Stevens Johnson syndrome, hepatic failure, and dupytrens contractures (Cramer & Mattson, 1995).

Gabapentin

Gabapentin (Neurontin) is a new antiepileptic medication that was designed as a gamma-aminobutyric acid (GABA) mimetic; however, the mechanism of action is not through that pathway and remains unknown. As a relatively new medication, its behavioral side effects are only beginning to be understood. Its usual dose-related and non-dose-related side effects include somnolence, dizziness, ataxia, fatigue, and nystagmus, with incidences ranging from 8% to 20% (Ramsay, 1995). In a study conducted at the Minnesota Epilepsy Group of 119 patients with refractory epilepsy who were receiving gabapentin, on a mean dosage of 3,136 mg/day for a mean of 8.25 months, the side effect of irritable aggressive behavior was observed in 15 patients (13%). Nine patients had a full-scale IQ under 70, 6 patients above 70, and 7 patients had a prior history of irritability or behavioral problems on other antiepileptic medication. When gabapentin was discontinued in 11 patients, the irritability or behavioral problem resolved (Doherty, Gates, Penovich, & Moriarty, 1995).

The negative behavioral effects of gabapentin have been observed by other investigators. Tallian, Nahata, Lo, and Tsao (1996) described two children who developed intolerable aggressive behavior requiring dose reduction or drug discontinuation. In one case, hypomania was induced by gabapentin (Short & Cooke, 1995). Consequently, although this medication has a very important role, it needs to be used cautiously in patients with cognitive impairment and very cautiously in patients with a history of previous irritable or aggressive behavior.

Felbamate

Felbamate (Felbatol) was distributed in 1993 following 15 years without the release of a new antiepileptic drug. It was enthusiastically endorsed by the epilepsy community and began to gain market share rapidly in the marketplace. After approximately 100,000 patients were on felbamate, it was discovered this medicine has an irreversible idiosyncratic side effect, aplastic anemia, with an incidence of approximately 1 in 5,000 (Theodore, Jensen, & Kwan, 1995). This has significantly limited the use of this medication. However, many patients who had been on the medicine for more than a year apparently have continued on the drug. Approximately 12,000 patients in the country are still receiving felbamate, without evidence of developing aplastic anemia.

Nonetheless, the Minnesota Epilepsy Group did report, as have others, behavioral side effects of this drug. There was an incidence of approximately 8% (Mason, Alexander, Palas, Penovich, & Gates, 1994) of an exacerbation of behavior, especially in cognitively impaired patients. Consequently, because of the risk of aplastic anemia, it is prudent not to utilize this medication for new patients except in desperate circumstances. When using this drug, practitioners need to be cognizant of a possible behavior exacerbation in patients with cognitive impairment and a history of previous medication-induced behavioral exacerbations.

Lamotrigine

Another new antiepileptic agent recently approved by the U.S. Food and Drug Administration (FDA) is lamotrigine (Lamictal). This medication provides two completely different profiles depending upon whether the patient is on inducing agents (e.g., phenytoin or carbamazepine) or valproic acid, an inhibiting agent. With the inducing agents, the half-life is 14 hours; but on the valproic acid, it increases

to 58 to 69 hours (Yuen, 1995). As a consequence, the dose required to maintain a therapeutic level most likely ranges between 2 and 20 mcg/ml. In a recent study presented at the American Epilepsy Society Meeting by the Minnesota Epilepsy Group, the mean dose of lamotrigine for 12 patients on valproic acid was 325 mg for 24 hours with a range of 100 mg to 600 mg. This was necessary to achieve a mean level of 12.37 mcg/ml. The mean dose of lamotrigine for 37 patients on inducing agents was 855 mg for 24 hours ranging from 100 mg to 2100 mg to achieve a mean level of 8.2 mcg/ml. Remarkable efficacy results were observed with 58% of the patients who had this medicine added to a mean 1.25 concomitant antiepileptic medication regimes. They achieved a 50% or greater reduction of their seizure frequency (28% becoming seizure free). The principal side effects observed were a rash in 8% (4 patients), intolerable movement disorder in 4% (2 patients), ataxia in one (2%) and decreased appetite in another (2%). Adverse behavioral consequences were not observed. Dose-related somnolence is significant, but usually can be ameliorated by slowly increasing the dosing (Gates, Penovich, Moriarty, & Doherty, 1996).

The idiosyncratic reactions of the allergic dermatitis rash can be significant; to date, in 1 in 1,000 adult patients it can progress to Stevens Johnson syndrome, and in children, 1 in 200 may develop the complication (Personal communication, Glaxco Pharmaceutical). This appears to be an antigen-loading phenomenon that is unique to this drug (i.e., the more rapidly the drug is loaded, the more likely the complication of the rash with the possibility of progression to Stevens Johnson syndrome) (Richens, 1995). Consequently, meticulous adherence to the dosing regimen described in the package insert is very important when prescribing this medication. An isolated case report of Lamictal encephalopathy was reported by Hennessey and Wiles (1996), though none was observed in the Minnesota study (Gates et al., 1996). The usual side effects consisted of ataxia, headache, diplopia, and a vision abnormality. Another study presented at the Minnesota Epilepsy Society Meeting also documented an increase in movement disorders in children receiving lamotrigine. This was a dose-related phenomena (Frost, Ritter, Hoskin, Mims, & Espe-Lillo, 1996).

Topiramate

Another new antieplileptic agent recently approved by the FDA is topiramate (Topamax). This medication has demonstrated a remarkable efficacy profile in the published reports to date. One recent study by Privitera (1995) demonstrated that in a 24-month follow-up, 58% of patients had a greater than 50% reduction. Mean scores on tests of cognitive function in the same study declined slightly over time, but appeared to be minimal.

Other studies such as Baldev et al. (1998), from Medical College of New York, also showed remarkable efficacy in that 12 of 20 patients had a greater than 50% reduction in seizure frequency with two patients becoming seizure-free with topiramate as an add-on therapy in patients with mental retardation and developmental disabilities. In another study by Svendsen (1998), 45 of the 91 patients who had a preexisting diagnosis of medically refractory had a greater than 50% seizure reduction, with four patients becoming seizure-free. Thirty of the patients had to stop the medication because of lack of efficacy or side effects with 14 of the 91 having significant slowed thinking, 13 drowsiness, and 13 with significant behavioral disturbance.

In the clinical experience at the Minnesota Epilepsy Group, topiramate does appear to be well tolerated in the cognitively impaired population. However, in our observations, a number of patients exhibited significant slowed thinking phenomena, which can limit the medication significantly. A maximal dose of 200 mg used for the typical 70-kilogram patient, appears to be well advised unless the patient is highly induced by concomitant medications such as carbamazepine or phenytoin. Then the dose must be increased carefully lest cognitive viscosity be affected by the increased dose of topiramate, further

limiting the drug. At doses of 200 mg/day or below, however, most patients appear to tolerate this drug quite well.

Tiagabine

Tiagabine (Gabitril) doses up to 64 mg/day, have demonstrated an efficacy profile comparable to established antiepileptic drugs with patients in add-on studies demonstrating greater than 50% seizure reductions in the 27% to 50% range, with patients on higher doses demonstrating a greater efficacy (Ben-Menachem, 1995). In a postmarketing study, Jacqueline French (1998) demonstrated that in 99 patients, 69 with partial epilepsy, seizures were rated as much improved in 34%, stayed the same in 41%, and worsened in 17%. The most common adverse effects were fatigue in 19%, nausea and GI upset in 9%, dizziness in 7%, and insomnia in 7%. Dodrill et al. (1998) performed neuropsychological tests on individuals taking tiagabine, phenytoin, or carbamazepine. In a series of 82 patients tested on tiagabine, he concluded that the test battery showed few differences between adjunctive tiagabine and phenytoin or carbamazepine, except the motor speed was slightly faster with tiagabine than with phenytoin or carbamazepine. Also, verbal fluency was slightly better with tiagabine. Finally, a study from Litzinger (1997) reviewed the effect of lamotrigine, tiagabine, and topiramate in an institutionalized population with epilepsy. For 131 patients on lamotrigine, 60% were still on the drug and doing well. For the 65 on tiagabine, 70% were still on it and doing well. Only 7 patients were on topiramate at the time of the study. The author concluded that lamotrigine and tiagabine seemed to do well in the institutionalized population group.

The experience to date with tiagabine has been brief due to its very recent approval by the FDA. As a consequence, the effects on the cognitively impaired population have been too briefly observed at the Minnesota Epilepsy Group to comment at this time.

Currently Unapproved Drugs

A number of medications are on the near horizon, including vigabatrin, oxcarbazepine, losigamone, pregabalix, and rufinamiol. Additional experience with these investigational medications is necessary to make informed observations. The exception is vigabatrin, which has been used in Europe (Monaco, 1996; Sander, Trevistol-Bittencourt, Hart, & Shorvon, 1990). Recent studies have suggested a psychotic break and depression risk associated with vigabatrin, though more recent studies suggest this may not be as common as previously thought, following a slower titration regimen (Fisher & Kerrigan, 1995). A lack of sufficient experience prevents any commentary on oxcarbazepine, losigamone, pregabalix, and rufinamiol.

Conclusion

Every anticonvulsant medicine has behavioral consequences. The clinician needs to balance seizure control with minimizing the side-effect profile of the medicine chosen for the specific seizure type. The most important strategy for therapeutics is to choose the appropriate medicine for the seizure type and epilepsy syndrome. Additionally, it is important to maximize a single drug before considering the addition or substitution of alternative medication. It is prudent to avoid the barbiturates in the cognitively impaired, behaviorally challenged patient. Other medicines should each be considered as appropriate given their possible behavioral side effects.

REFERENCES

Baldev, K. S. et al. (1998). Role of topiramate (Topamax) in adults with intractive epilepsy, mental retardation, and developmental disabilities. *Epilepsia, 39* (Suppl. 6), 55.

Ben Menachem, E. (1995). International experience with tiagabine add-on therapy. *Epilepsia, 36,* (Suppl. 6), 14-21.

Brodie, M. D., & Dichter, M. A. (1996). Antiepileptic drugs. *New England Journal of Medicine, 334,* 168–175.

Browne, T. R., & LeDuc, B. (1995). Chemistry and biotransformation. In R. H. Levy, R. H. Mattson, B. S. Meldrum, J. K. Penry, & F. E. Dreifuss (Eds.), *Antiepileptic drugs* (4th ed., pp. 283–300). New York: Raven Press.

Bruni, J. (1995). Toxicity. In R. H. Levy, R. H. Mattson, B. S. Meldrum, J. K. Penry, & F. E. Dreifuss (Eds.), *Antiepileptic drugs* (4th ed., pp. 345–350). New York: Raven Press.

Buzan, R. D., Firestone, D., Thomas, M., & Dubovsky, S. L. (1995). Valproate-associated pancreatitis and cholecystitis in six mentally retarded adults. *Journal of Clinical Psychiatry, 56,* 529–532.

Committee on Drugs. (1995). Behavioral and cognitive effects of anticonvulsant therapy. *Pediatrics, 96,* 538–540.

Cramer, J. A., & Mattson, R. H. (1995). Toxicity. In R. H. Levy, R. H. Mattson, B. S. Meldrum, J. K. Penry, & F. E. Dreifuss (Eds.), *Antiepileptic drugs* (4th ed., pp. 409–420). New York: Raven Press.

Dodrill, C. B. (1991). Effects of antiepileptic drugs on behavior. In O. Devinsky & W. H. Theodore (Eds.), *Epilepsy and behavior: Vol. 12. Frontiers of clinical neuroscience* (pp. 37–46). New York: Wiley-Liss.

Dodrill, C. B. (1998). Adjunctive tiagabine, phenytoin, and carbamazepine, and neuropsychological tests in a multi-center trial for partial seizures. *Epilepsia, 39* (Suppl. 6), 147.

Doherty, K. P., Gates, J. R., Penovich, P. E., & Moriarty, G. L. (1995). Gabapentin in a medically refractory epilepsy population: Seizure response and unusual side effects. *Epilepsia, 36,* (Suppl. 4), 71.

Domizo, S., Verrotti, A., Ramenghi, L. A., Sabatino, G., & Morgese, G. (1993). Antiepileptic therapy and behaviour disturbances in children. *Child's Nervous System, 9,* 272–274.

Dreifuss, F. E. (1995). Toxicity. In R. H. Levy, R. H. Mattson, B. S. Meldrum, J. K. Penry, & F. E. Dreifuss (Eds.), *Antiepileptic drugs* (4th ed., pp. 641–648). New York: Raven Press.

Evans, R. J., Miranda, R. N., Jordan, J., & Krolikowski, F. J. (1995). Fatal acute pancreatitis caused by valproic acid. *American Journal of Forensic Medicine and Pathology, 16,* 62–65.

Fisher, R. S., & Kerrigan, J. F. (1995). Toxicity. In R. H. Levy, R. H. Mattson, B. S. Meldrum, J. K. Penry, & F. E. Dreifuss (Eds.), *Antiepileptic drugs* (4th ed., pp. 931–939). New York: Raven Press.

French, J. et al. (1998). Postmarketing experience with tiagabine. *Epilepsia, 39,* (Suppl. 6), 56.

Fröscher, W., Maier, V., Laage, M., Wolfersdorf, M., Straub, R., Rothmeier, J., Steinert, A., Fiaux, U., Frank, U., & Grupp, D. (1995). Folate deficiency, anticonvulsant drugs, and psychiatric morbidity. *Clinical Neuropharmacology, 18,* 165–182.

Frost, M. D., Ritter, F. J., Hoskin, C., Mims, J., & Espe-Lillo, J. (1996). Movement disorder associated with lamotrigine treatment in children and adolescents. *Epilepsia, 37,* (Suppl. 5), 112.

Gates, J. R., Penovich, P. E., Moriarty, G. L., & Doherty, K. (1996). Efficacy and dosing of lamotrigine in a medically refractory epilepsy population. *Epilepsia, 37,* (Suppl. 5), 166.

Gormann, M., & Barkley, G.L. (1995). Oculogyric crisis induced by carbamazepine. *Epilepsia, 36,* 1158–1160.

Hauser, W. A., & Hesdorffer, D. C. (1990). *Epilepsy: Frequency, causes, and consequences.* New York: Demos.

Hennessy, M. J., & Wiles, C. M. (1996). Lamotrigine encephalopathy. *Lancet, 347,* 974–975.

Holmes, G. L. (1995). Toxicity. In R. H. Levy, R. H. Mattson, B. S. Meldrum, J. K. Penry, & F. E. Dreifuss (Eds.), *Antiepileptic drugs* (4th ed., pp. 567–579). New York: Raven Press.

Kalachnik, J. E., & Hanzel, T. E. (1995). *Educational bulletin: Report on the behavioral side effects of barbiturate antiepileptic drugs.* A Report by the Office of the Ombudsman for Mental Health and Mental Retardation, State of Minnesota.

Kalachnik, J. E., Hanzel, T. E., Harder, S. R., Bauernfeind, J. D., & Engstrom, E. A. (1995). Antiepileptic drug behavioral side effects in individuals with mental retardation and the use of behavioral measurement techniques. *Mental Retardation, 33,* 374–382.

Levy, R., Mattson, R., Meldrum, B., Penry, J. K., & Dreifuss, F. E. (Eds). (1995). *Antiepileptic drugs* (4th ed.). New York: Raven Press.

Litzinger, M. J. (1997). Aggressive behaviors controlled by sublingual lorazepam in persons with developmental delay or mental retardation and epilepsy. *Epilepsia, 38* (Suppl. 8).

Mason, S., Alexander, B., Palas, J., Penovich, P., & Gates, J. (1994). Psychological disturbance as a contributing factor for felbamate discontinuation. *Epilepsia, 35,* (Suppl. 8), 32.

Monaco, F. (1996). Cognitive effects of vigabatrin. *Neurology, 47,* S6–S11.

Murphy, J. V., & Marquard, K. (1982). Asymptomatic hyperammonemia in patients receiving valproic acid. *Archives of Neurology, 39,* 591–592.

Papazian, O. P., Cañizales, E., Alfonso, I., Archila, R., Duchowny, M., & Aicardi, J. (1995). Reversible dementia and apparent brain atrophy during valproate therapy. *Annals of Neurology, 38,* 687–691.

Penovich, P. E. et al. (1997). Clinical experience with topiramate: Correlation of serum levels with efficacy and adverse events. *Epilepsia, 38* (Suppl. 8), 181.

Privatera, M. (1995). Long-term cognitive effects of topiramate. *Epilepsia, 36* (Suppl. 3), S152.

Ramsay, R. E. (1995). Toxicity. In R. H. Levy, R. H. Mattson, B. S. Meldrum, J. K. Penry, & F. E. Dreifuss (Eds.), *Antiepileptic drugs* (4th ed., pp. 857–860). New York: Raven Press.

Richens, A. (1995). Toxicity. In R. H. Levy, R. H. Mattson, B. S. Meldrum, J. K. Penry, & F. E. Dreifuss (Eds.), *Antiepileptic drugs* (4th ed., pp. 897–902). New York: Raven Press.

Sackellares, J. C., Lee, S. I., & Dreifuss, F. E. (1979). Stupor following administration of valproic acid to patients receiving other antiepileptic drugs. *Epilepsia, 20,* 697–703.

Sander, J. W., Trevistol-Bittencourt, P. C., Hart, Y. M., & Shorvon, S. D. (1990). Evaluation of vigabatrin as an add-on drug in the management of severe epilepsy. *Journal of Neurology, Neurosurgery, and Psychiatry 53,* 1008–1010.

Scull, D. A., & Trimble, M. R. (1995). Mania precipitated by carbamazepine withdrawal. *British Journal of Psychiatry, 167,* 698.

Short, C., & Cooke, L. (1995). Hypomania induced by gabapentin. *British Journal of Psychiatry, 166,* 679–680.

Svendsen, T. (1998). Topiramate in refractory epilepsy. *Epilepsia,* (Suppl. 6).

Tallian, K. B., Nahata, M. C., Lo, W., & Tsao, C. Y. (1996). Gabapentin associated with aggressive behavior in pediatric patients with seizures. *Epilepsia, 37,* 501–502.

Theodore, W. H., Jensen P. K., & Kwan, R. M. F. (1995). Clinical use. In R. H. Levy, R. H. Mattson, B. S. Meldrum, J. K. Penry, & F. E. Dreifuss (Eds.), *Antiepileptic drugs* (4th ed., pp. 818–822). New York: Raven Press.

Tohen, M., Castillo, J., Baldessarini, R. J., Zarate, C., & Kando, J. C. (1995). Blood dyscrasias with carbamazepine and valproate: A pharmacoepidemiological study of 2,228 patients at risk. *American Journal of Psychiatry, 152,* 413–418.

Yuen, A. W. C. (1995). Interactions with other drugs. In R. H. Levy, R. H. Mattson, B. S. Meldrum, J. K. Penry, & F. E. Dreifuss (Eds.), *Antiepileptic drugs* (4th ed., pp. 883–888). New York: Raven Press.

Neurobehavioral Mechanisms of Drug Action

Travis Thompson
John F. Kennedy Center
Peabody College, Vanderbilt University
Nashville, Tennessee

Frank J. Symons
Frank Porter Graham Child Development Center
University of North Carolina
Chapel Hill, NC

Destructive Behavior in Developmental Disabilities

Although many people with mental retardation, autism, and related disabilities learn the necessary life skills to participate in integrated educational, vocational, residential, and recreational settings, a significant minority do not, and lead restrictive lives because they injure themselves or others, or destroy property. Such destructive behavior limits the integration of people with developmental disabilities into community settings and often leads to reinstitutionalization (Davidson, et al., 1996; Intagliata & Willer, 1981; Vitello, Atthowe, & Cadwell, 1983). For these people, community integration means very little because often they live in isolated settings or in highly specialized treatment centers and are subjected to sedating medications or mechanical restraints as forms of behavior control. Practitioners are confronted often with people displaying complex behavior problems resulting from several interacting causes. The challenges for treatment are especially difficult because our understanding of behavior disorders and specific mental health or psychiatric disorders among people with mental retardation are imprecise, which can result in our applying the same treatments to people with behavior problems that appear similar but, in fact, are not related.

The most common forms of destructive behavior include aggressive assault, self-injury, and property destruction. Some destructive behavior is of special concern because of its pervasiveness, high frequency, and possibility of tissue damage (e.g., repetitive skin-picking), whereas other problem behavior is significant because of the immediate harm caused by even a few instances (e.g., physical assault, self-biting) (Schroeder, Tessel, Loupe, & Stodgell, 1997). Consequences of such behavior problems can include disfigurement and almost permanent application of mechanical restraints (e.g., self-mutilation in Lesch-Nyhan syndrome). Schroeder, Rojahn, and Oldenquist (1991) reported the prevalence of aggressive behavior in people with mental retardation and developmental disabilities as ranging from approximately 9% to 23%, and reported property destruction in 4% to 14% of this population. More recent surveys reveal similar if not higher prevalence rates of destructive behavior including self-injury (Bruininks, Olson, Larson, & Lakin, 1994). It is an understatement to say we face a grave problem when from one quarter to one third of people with mental retardation and related disabilities display significant destructive behavior.

Treatments for severe destructive behaviors have included intrusive punishment procedures such as applying faradic skin shock, facial screening, squirts in the face with water mist, manual overcorrection, and other physically aversive interventions. Although these procedures can produce rapid reductions in severe destructive behavior (Cataldo, 1991), they are not socially acceptable and their use has been the object of considerable debate (Repp & Singh, 1990). Positive behavioral intervention procedures using more socially acceptable methods have been designed to reduce behavior problems of people with developmental disabilities by teaching the individual functional skills to control events in their surroundings (Horner et al., 1990). Positive behavioral interventions often involve reducing difficult task demands (e.g., Weeks & Gaylord-Ross, 1981), increasing functional alternative communication skills (e.g., Carr & Durand, 1985a; Reichle & Wacker, 1993), and increasing reinforcement contingent on appropriate adaptive skills and social behavior (e.g., Tarpley & Schroeder, 1979).

The most widely researched interventions were reviewed critically as part of a National Institutes of Health (NIH) Consensus Development Conference on Destructive Behavior in Developmental Disabilities (NIH, 1991). The report concluded that many behavior problems may involve both biological and environmental components. And, although several types of treatments produce temporary reductions in problem behavior, in many cases the destructive behavior begins again after treatment is stopped. Treatments typically have been designed based on the assumption of a single type of cause for the behavior problem (most often *either* biological or environmental, but rarely with both combined). Many of the most difficult to treat destructive behaviors, however, are likely regulated by factors in the person's social environment as well as by biological or biochemical factors. Because of the likelihood of this dual control, our assessment and treatment efforts should consider the possibility of both behavioral and biomedical treatments (see Figure 8.1). In this chapter, our purpose is to discuss the behavioral effects that

psychotropic medication may have when treating the destructive behavior of people with developmental disabilities by considering both the motivational properties of the behavior problem and the ways in which pharmacologic treatment can affect these different properties.

Psychotropic Medications and Destructive Behavior

Numerous investigators have documented the effects of psychotropic drugs on behavior problems in mental retardation (Aman & Singh, 1988; Lipman, 1970; Sprague & Werry, 1971). Schaal and Hackenberg (1994) suggest that despite the widespread prescription of psychotropic medication to treat the destructive behavior of people with developmental disabilities, the most confident statement we can make about the therapeutic effects of psychotropic medication is that sometimes they help and sometimes they do not. The purpose of administering psychotropic treatments is to improve a person's functioning by modifying the way in which he or she typically responds to naturally occurring events in the environment. By doing so, challenging behavior is made unnecessary and improbable. Effective use of psychotropic medications enables the person to respond to daily environmental events in a more normalized manner. If pharmacological interventions are successful, it may make it possible for the person to adjust successfully to a wider range of typical settings that do not or are not able to provide environmental supports or modifications. For example, if a client suffers from anxiety related to novel situations, an effective pharmacological treatment might include an antianxiety or anxiolytic drug that allows that client to tolerate novel environments and behave in ways that are motivated less by avoiding situations perceived to be frightening. In the past, little attention has been paid to deciding what factors may help identify people with mental retardation and related developmental disabilities who respond favorably to one type of medication treatment from those who would not benefit from the same or similar treatment. This kind of behavioral pharmacology research has been advocated for

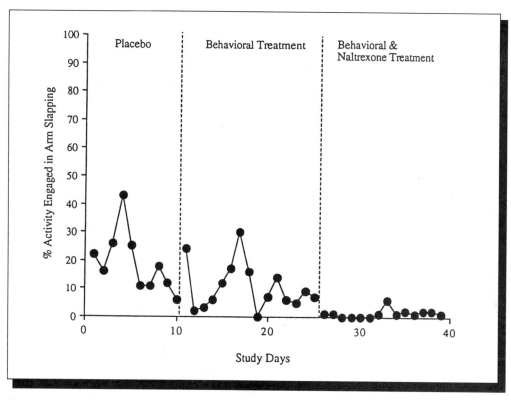

Figure 8.1. Percentage of time Matthew, a 12-year-old boy with severe mental retardation living in a large residential facility, engaged in severe arm slapping. Observational data were collected in real time for four 10-minute intervals each study day using hand-held optical bar-code readers. Data presented here were collected during a structured activity designed to teach Matthew how to set a dining room table in his cottage's dining area. Modest reductions in arm slapping occurred during behavioral treatment when Matthew was taught how to functionally communicate and request a break. With the addition of naltrexone hydrochloride (1.4 mg/kg/day), Matthew's time spent arm slapping during the activity was reduced to almost zero.

and is beginning to emerge (Schaal & Hackenberg, 1994; Thompson, 1986; Thompson, Hackenberg, & Schaal, 1991).

Functional Interpretations of Destructive Behavior

A functional approach to behavioral assessment and treatment identifies factors associated with and controlling the person's destructive behavior (Carr, 1977; Donnellan, Mirenda, Mesaros, & Fassbender, 1984; Iwata, Dorsey, Bauman, & Richman, 1982; O'Neill, Horner, Albin, Storey, & Sprague, 1989; Repp & Karsh, 1990). These factors typically include environmental events immediately preceding or following the behavior problem as well as features of specific settings in which the behavior problem occurs. If hitting a staff

member reliably results in attention from other staff, then staff attention may eventually reinforce hitting and make future instances of hitting more likely. Staff attention contingent on the client's hitting reinforces hitting. Behavior motivated by access to staff attention is said to be attention-motivated. Events prior to the occurrence of behavior problems (i.e., antecedents) can also gain control over destructive behavior (e.g., task demands). A client with no spoken language may bite his hand when staff ask him to brush his teeth. It is likely the staff person will stop asking the client to brush his teeth when biting occurs and, furthermore, may brush his teeth for him. If toothbrushing is difficult for the client or is an activity he dislikes, in the future he is more likely to bite himself when he is asked to brush his teeth. Biting is an efficient way to escape or avoid having to brush one's teeth. In this case, biting is escape motivated. In both previous examples, the challenging behavior was neither random nor indicative of a psychiatric disorder, but instead was predictably related to the functions the behavior served in managing the person's social environment. In these examples, appearance of the behavior (i.e., hitting) was less important than the function of the behavior (i.e., the effect the behavior had on the social environment).

Much of the destructive behavior of people with developmental disabilities comes under control of both antecedent and consequent events (Iwata et al., 1994). Many of our most effective environmentally-based treatments therefore are designed to change the way we interact with individuals with behavior problems (Carr et al., 1994). Knowing the function of a problem behavior is important in designing habilitative or educational programs to promote alternative adaptive behaviors while reducing the problem behaviors (Carr, Newsom, & Binkoff, 1976; Gaylord-Ross, Weeks, & Lipner, 1980; Iwata et al., 1982; Repp, Felce, & Barton, 1988; Weeks & Gaylord-Ross, 1981). Several comprehensive accounts exist describing in detail the functional assessment and treatment of problem behavior (e.g., see Chapter 11 and Chapter 12, this volume).

Biochemical Interpretations of Destructive Behavior

There are other cases, however, in which destructive behavior is neither attention nor escape motivated. Other factors are at work. Barbara, a 32-year-old woman with moderate mental retardation who enjoys her daily household chore of washing the dishes, occasionally explodes into fits of uncontrollable self-injurious behavior. In such cases, Barbara's outbursts seem unpredictable. Several theories suggest that biological or biochemical factors may be involved in such severe destructive behavior.

Three main neurochemical theories of destructive behavior by people like Barbara have been proposed implicating three different brain chemical systems that involve the neurochemical transmitters dopamine, serotonin, and the neuropeptide opioids. The dopamine theory was proposed following the observation that patients with Lesch-Nyhan syndrome who exhibit very severe self-mutilation have markedly lower levels of the neurotransmitter dopamine in the central nervous system than people without the syndrome (Lloyd et al., 1981). It has been suggested that the self-injury exhibited by these individuals may result from the dopamine receptors being very sensitive to even small amounts of dopamine (referred to as dopamine supersensitivity), particularly involving the D_1 dopamine receptor (e.g., Goldstein et al., 1986). Receptors are specialized proteins located in the cell membrane of nerve cells. Neurotransmitter molecules fit into the receptors like keys into locks. When neurotransmitters attach to the receptors on the cells surface (i.e., when there are enough keys in enough locks), the nerve cells are activated.

The opioid receptor theory was proposed following the observation that painful stimulation causes release of naturally occurring (endogenous) substances referred to as opioids, which bind or connect with opioid receptors in the brain (Willer, Dehen, & Cambier, 1981). Either by modulating normal pain sensation or because of the rewarding effects of the opioid molecules binding to opiate receptors (e.g., Cataldo & Harris, 1982; Stein & Belluzi, 1989), the self-injurious behavior producing self-inflicted pain becomes repetitive.

The serotonin theory is based on several observations. First, about one third of children with autism display elevated blood serotonin levels (Anderson & Hoshino, 1997; Ritvo et al., 1970). Moreover, there is a relation between serotonin blood levels and the amount of disturbed behavior exhibited by people with autism (Campbell et al., 1975; Coleman & Gillberg, 1985; Schain & Freedman, 1961). Another line of evidence indicates some antidepressant drugs bind to the receptors that transport serotonin from the spaces between nerve cells back up into the presynaptic cells so the serotonin can be reused. The selective serotonin reuptake inhibitors (SSRIs) are often effective in reducing symptoms of obsessive-compulsive behavior in autism (McDougle, 1997) and Prader-Willi syndrome (Stein, Keating, Zar, & Hollander, 1994). Finally, serotonin agonists reduce aggression in animals (Miczek, Mos, & Olivier, 1989; White, Kucharik, & Moyer, 1991) as well as in humans. Impulsive aggression related to personality disorder was reduced by the serotonin agonist buspirone (Coccaro, Gabriel, & Siever, 1990).

Psychopathology, Dual Diagnosis, and Functional Analysis of Behavior Problems

Major mental illnesses occur among people with mental retardation with a higher incidence than among non-developmentally disabled comparison groups (Matson & Barrett, 1993; Rojahn & Tasse, 1996). Although differences in prevalence rates of major psychiatric disorders in people with developmental disabilities arise because of methodological differences across studies in subject selection and defintional issues, a consensus is emerging that far more attention needs to be directed toward psychiatric disorders in evaluating and treating individuals with mental retardation and related developmental disabilities (Romanczyk, Lockshin, & Harrison, 1993).

Although existing nosological schemes such as the *Diagnostic and Statistical Manual of Mental Disorders* (4th ed.) *(DSM-IV;* American Psychiatric Association, 1994) and the diagnoses they lead to may be appropriate for people with mild and sometimes moderate mental retardation, they are often inadequate for describing and understanding the disturbances of people with severe mental retardation (MacLean, 1993). The psychiatric diagnostic process is further complicated by the cognitive and language limitations inherent in mental retardation and related developmental disabilities, and the associated problems in obtaining reliable self-reports.

Biological brain disorders (e.g., seizure disorders), some of which are genetically determined, often require specific medications for treatment and management. Similarly, major psychiatric illnesses, such as schizophrenia, bipolar disorder, and major depressive disorder, all appear to involve biological factors

that are effectively managed using specific psychotropic medications (Meltzer, 1987). When these disorders co-occur among people with mental retardation, pharmacotherapy is equally appropriate as with other people.

Psychiatric disorders, such as major depressive disorder, profoundly alter the ability to interact effectively with the environment. Typical social reinforcers are not as effective for seriously depressed individuals and the anhedonia seen in later stages of simple schizophrenia makes most secondary reinforcers ineffective (Ayllon & Azrin, 1965; Thompson & Hollon, 1999). A behavioral analysis of environmental variables can extend our understanding of the way in which biological brain disorders alter people's ability to manage their daily transactions with the world around them (Salzinger, 1990, 1992). However, a thorough discussion of behavioral mechanisms of psychotropic drug action in treating people with major mental illnesses is beyond the scope of this chapter. Instead, this chapter is concerned with primary presenting behavioral problems and learned adjustments to environmental circumstances. We also explore mood disorders as they arise within that context.

Neurobehavioral Pharmacology of Destructive Behavior

Behavioral Mechanisms of Drug Action

Choosing an effective behavioral treatment depends on the results of a functional assessment of the antecedent conditions preceding and consequent events typically following destructive behavior. This procedure is seldom used in clinical applications or even research projects designed to evaluate the effectiveness of pharmacological treatments (Cerutti & Thompson, 1990; Schaal & Hackenberg, 1994). A functional analysis strategy has been described elsewhere as an element in the analysis of *behavioral mechanisms of drug action* (Thompson & Schuster, 1968; Thompson, 1984). In their review of the use of psychotropic medications for people with developmental disabilities, Schaal and Hackenberg (1994) showed that virtually no attention has been given to combining functional assessment approaches with drug treatment. Although the reasons for this neglect are unclear, it may be related to unreasonable expectations for immediate behavior change and limited resources for conducting empirically based functional assessments. This neglect probably has been compounded by psychotropic medications being prescribed almost solely on the basis of the destructive behavior's appearance rather than its current cause.

A functional diagnostic approach attempts to evaluate the most probable behavioral and biological variables that may be contributing to the behavior of concern. A behavioral function may involve a consistent pattern of staff attention to head banging which maintains the problem behavior whereas a biological function may be related to the release of endogenous opioids when the client strikes her head. The same form of destructive behavior may be influenced and controlled by different mechanisms. Self-injury that is pain-elicited or dopaminergically-driven may appear the same (e.g., hand biting), but the neurochemical mechanisms regulating each type can be very different. Problem behavior that is positively reinforced (e.g., attention from staff) or negatively reinforced (e.g., removal of an aversive task demand) may respond differently to pharmacological treatments.

Therapeutic drugs influence a person's health by modulating normal or abnormal physiological or biochemical processes. Drugs moderate the body's natural physiological responses yielding quantitatively different outcomes. If a person prone to hypertension walks too rapidly up several flights of stairs, it may result in his blood pressure increasing to dangerous levels. A specific medication for blood pressure, such as clonidine, increases the diameter of peripheral blood vessels and therefore reduces the degree to which blood pressure increases when the person again takes the stairs two steps at a time. In comparison, the manner in which psychotropic drugs often are prescribed to alter the destructive behavior of people with developmental disabilities seldom reflects foregoing reasoning. Instead,

practitioners and family members often act as though a medication can produce a qualitatively different patient outcome independent of the cause. Inappropriate prescriptions often arise from a prevalent theoretical misconception, namely *that drugs alter brain chemicals or physiological processes and cause behavior to change independent of the environmental circumstances within which the person functions.* It is true that the brain's neurochemistry and the body's physiology set the limits at which external environmental processes and events exert their effects, but this does not happen in a vacuum. In some circumstances a drug may have one kind of behavioral effect, whereas under different circumstances the same drug may have a different behavioral effect. This differential behavioral effect is because part of what determines a drug's effect is the person's current and previous environmental circumstances (e.g., their reinforcement history). To better understand the neurobehavioral mechanisms of action of psychotropic drugs in people with developmental disabilities, we must better understand their behavioral and medical histories as well as the current circumstances influencing their behavior (e.g., whether the problem behavior is maintained by positive or negative reinforcement). These variables create the foundations upon which drugs are able to produce their behavioral effects.

If we choose behavioral treatments based on a functional assessment of the environmental conditions controlling behavior problems, a similar approach should also be adopted to select appropriate pharmacotherapies. Few physicians would consider pharmacologically treating a patient with an inflamed throat without first obtaining an accurate measure of body temperature, palpating the neck for signs of enlarged and tender lymph glands, otoscopically examining the eardrum, and taking an appropriate personal history. Yet physicians routinely prescribe psychotropic medication to treat the behavior problems of people with developmental disabilities without the comparable information required for an adequate functional diagnosis. Not only is this problem often misunderstood, the implications for assessment and treatment are often compromised because of limited resources. The clinical alternative has resulted in treating in the dark, or what has euphemistically been referred to as "treating empirically."

By adopting a functional diagnostic approach, influential behavioral and environmental factors are identified that may interact with a behaviorally active medication to improve the person's ability to function independently and adaptively in addition to reducing the person's destructive responses to aversive environmental stimuli and stressors. The goal is to treat the underlying behavioral and biological mechanisms, not just the appearance of the behavior problem.

Types of Consequences Maintaining Destructive Behaviors

Positive and negative reinforcers. The same psychotropic medication can differentially affect behavior maintained by different types of consequences. Positive reinforcers are defined by their effects on maintaining behavior and typically include contingent attention from staff or peers and access to tangible items, such as food and drink, or preferred activities, such as playing with toys or using playground equipment (Carr & Durand, 1985b; Durand & Crimmins, 1988; Edelson, Taubman, & Lovaas, 1983; Lovaas, Freitag, Gold, & Kassorla, 1965). Behavioral treatment of destructive behavior maintained by positive reinforcers involves teaching the person the skills to gain attention or request desired items in socially accepted ways. Treatment by removal of negative reinforcers maintaining some forms of destructive behavior includes avoidance of difficult instructional demands made on the person (e.g., Carr, Newsom, & Binkoff, 1976, 1980) and terminating or attenuating the level of discomfort associated with an illness or infections, as in the case of an ear infection (e.g., DeLissovoy, 1963; O'Reilly, 1997). A behavioral approach to treatment might decrease the aversiveness of instructional demands in the first example, and a biomedical strategy may involve reducing the discomfort associated with the ear infection by administering an antibiotic in the second instance. Sensory changes arising from self-injurious or stereotypic behavior (such as visual, tactile, or vestibular feedback) may also increase the probability of particular forms of destructive behaviors (e.g., Carr, 1977; Favell, McGimsey, & Schell, 1982; Iwata et al., 1982; Rincover & Devaney, 1982). A functionally based treatment approach for problem behaviors controlled by the mechanism of sensory stimulation often requires teaching alternative, functionally equivalent ways of producing similar sensory experiences (e.g., playing hand-held video games, twirling on a merry-go-round, etc.).

Neuroleptic effects on destructive behavior maintained by positive and negative reinforcers. Neuroleptic medications (e.g., thioridazine, haloperidol) are most commonly used for treating schizophrenia, but they are also used for treating the destructive behavior of people with mental retardation. Although there has been increasing interest in dual diagnosis among people with developmental disabilities, neuroleptics are most commonly administered to them to suppress destructive behavior without compelling evidence of the presence of schizophrenic symptoms. Even though neuroleptics may decrease problem behavior under some circumstances, this effect is more likely due to general sedation rather than to improving a specific biochemical disturbance (e.g., Aman & Singh, 1988; McConahey, Thompson, & Zimmerman, 1977; Thompson et al., 1991).

Behavioral pharmacology research with animals has shown that neuroleptics reduce a wide range of learned behavior that is maintained by positive reinforcement (Heyman & Monaghan, 1987; Zarevics & Setler, 1979). Neuroleptics weaken reinforcer effectiveness (Wise, 1982). Parents and other caregivers often inadvertently positively reinforce self-injurious or aggressive behavior with attention provided contingently following bouts of destructive behavior. If a previous functional assessment showed some forms of destructive behavior were maintained by such positive reinforcement, then it is possible neuroleptics could weaken those destructive actions by reducing the effectiveness of positive reinforcement as well as nonspecifically decreasing other motor behavior.

Neuroleptic medications also interfere with learned avoidance behavior at doses having minimal effects on escape behavior. Laboratory animals are less likely to avoid an aversive signal such as a warning signal preceding a shock if they are administered chlorpromazine (Cook & Weidley, 1957; Posluns, 1962). Neuroleptics weaken or interfere with avoidance behavior by disrupting the tendency to avoid unpleasant situations. Neuroleptic-induced reductions in avoidance do not appear to be the result of a general sedation or impaired motor ability, because once the avoidance begins, it proceeds as it would normally (Cook & Catania, 1964; Cook & Sepinwall, 1975; Davidson & Weidley, 1976). Similar findings have also been found in human laboratory tests (Fischman & Schuster, 1979).

It is difficult to attribute reductions in self-injury and aggression following neuroleptic drug treatment to any single mechanism. Destructive behavior that is positively rein-forced (e.g., attention from staff or access to preferred commodities) or negatively rein-forced (e.g., removal or delay of aversive task demands) could reasonably be expected to decrease for some individuals following neuroleptic treatment. Other adaptive behav-iors maintained by the same consequences would very likely be impaired as well, including household chores and communica-tion with family, peers, and staff.

Self-injury maintained by endogenous reinforcers. Self-injury has been reduced following treatment with the opiate antagonists naloxone and naltrexone hydrochloride (Bernstein, Hughes, Mitchell, & Thompson, 1987; Sandman et al., 1983). Although self-injury may develop early in life for a variety of reasons, over time a child with disabilities may repeatedly injure him- or herself with sufficient severity to cause the release of the body's natural painkillers. These painkillers, or endogenous opioids (endorphins, enkepha-lins), are produced naturally by the body in response to painful stimulation and bind to the same brain receptors as drugs like heroin or morphine. Endogenous opioids not only reduce pain (Loh, Tseng, Wie, & Li, 1976; Tseng, Loh, &

Li, 1976), but are also effective reinforcers, so much so that laboratory animals that have previous experience taking opiate drugs will work to self-administer endogenous opioids (Woods, Herling, & Young, 1981). As with repeated heroin or morphine use, physical dependence can result following repeated administration of endogenous opioids (Wei & Loh, 1976).

Thus, some self-injury may be considered "addictive" behavior, maintained in part by the contingent relation between the self-injurious response (e.g., hand biting), the subsequent endogenous opioid release, and the same brain nerve cell receptors being activated. Some research has shown that some people with autism have atypical levels of endogenous opioids or endorphins (Gillberg, Terenius, & Lonnerhold, 1985; Herman et al., 1989; Weizman et al., 1984). It may be for some individuals with severe and repetitive self-injury that with the passage of time, their self-injury is progressively influenced and con-trolled by the reinforcing properties of endor-phins. If that happens, then the self-injurious individual may become dependent upon the release and binding of the opioids to the brain's opiate receptors following each bout of self-injury, much as a heroin addict becomes dependent upon the binding of opioids following injections of the drug. Repetitive, stereotyped movements of animals (including self-injurious behavior) can be reduced by the administration of antagonist medication that blocks the effects of the opioids (Cronin, Wiepkema, & van Ree, 1985). Opiate blockers (antagonists) such as naltrexone reduce some forms of self-injury (see, e.g., Barrett, Feinstein, & Hole, 1989; Bernstein et al., 1987; Davidson, Kleene, Carroll, & Rockowitz, 1983; Richardson & Zeleski, 1983; Sandman & Hetrick, 1995; Sandman et al., 1983; Sandyk, 1985; Thomp-son, Hackenberg, Cerutti, Baker, & Axtell, 1994). Although the weight of evidence suggests that for some individuals, opiate antagonists reduce self-injury, it is equally clear that they are not effective for all forms of self-injury, and currently it is difficult to predict who will respond favorably to these medications (Beckwith, Couk, & Schumacher, 1986;

Willemsen-Swinkels, Buitelaar, Weijnen, Thijssen, & Van Engeland, 1996).

Negative reinforcement, punishment, and possible antisuppressive effects of benzodiazepines.

Self-injurious behavior can be reinforced by terminating or preventing the occurrence of aversive demand situations. If a client is asked to carry out a difficult or unfamiliar task, his or her noncompliance with similar demands in the past may have resulted in reprimands or the loss of promised privileges by caregivers. This behavioral history can establish the verbal demand or request as a conditioned negative reinforcer, and termination or removal of the request can maintain the behavior leading to its termination. A staff member who is teaching language skills to a child with profound mental retardation may cease language training whenever the child appears anxious, frustrated, and bites himself. If the training task is sufficiently aversive to the child, the self-biting may be negatively reinforced by avoiding the beginning of the task or escaping from it altogether (Carr et al., 1976). Eventually, the child may learn to bite himself even before the training sessions actually begin (such as at the sight of the language training material), thereby successfully avoiding the task entirely.

Drugs that are used to treat anxiety (e.g., benzodiazepines) may decrease destructive behavior maintained by negative reinforcement such as that described above. But if the aversive stimuli (e.g., teacher demands) also function as behavior suppressing punishers in the same context, then it would not be surprising if benzodiazepine administration actually increased learned self-injury in some cases because benzodiazepine reduces the suppressive properties of aversive stimuli. With administration of benzodiazepines, such as chlordiazepoxide, punishers are not as punishing and, therefore, behavior that was previously suppressed by punishment increases. There is abundant evidence from laboratory animal research showing this to be the case (Cook & Catania, 1964; Heise & Boff, 1962; Randall et al., 1960).

Some individuals who self-injure display violent bouts of self-injury following administration of benzodiazepines and other sedative hypnotics (Barron & Sandman, 1983, 1985). These drugs counteract suppressive effects of aversive consequences in studies with laboratory animals and people (Carlton, Siegel, Murphree, & Cook, 1981; DiMascio, Shader, & Harmatz, 1967; Jeffery & Barrett, 1979; Salzman, DiMascio, Shader, & Harmatz, 1969; Sepinwall & Cook, 1978). In other words, strength of behavior increases if those actions were previously reduced by contingent aversive consequences (i.e., punishment). Gardos (1980) described a woman whose depression symptoms were not responsive to treatment with tricyclic antidepressants. Diazepam (a benzodiazepine antianxiety medication) was prescribed for her anxiety symptoms. Over several weeks, she experienced sexual and aggressive impulses. In response, she increased her consumption of diazepam, resulting in acting out aggressively. Aggressive behaviors included verbal and physical assault of family and therapist, property destruction, and head banging. These behaviors were reduced following cessation of benzodiazepine treatment.

If the normal consequence for a person with mental retardation who self-injures is the painful feedback consequent upon that action, one might assume the painful stimulation functions, at least in part, as a punisher (i.e., it suppresses the behavior that if follows). During or immediately following a bout of self-injury, teachers and parents often verbally reprimand and restrain the person, which may also suppress the behavior. The fact that benzodiazepines and other sedative hypnotics may reduce or make less punishing the suppressive effects of these typical consequences for self-injury is not really paradoxical as it is consistent with laboratory research findings showing that these drugs reduce the suppressive effects of punishment (Olivier, Mos, & Miczek, 1991).

Destructive behavior, punishment, anxiety, and serotonin agonists.

Research with laboratory animals has suggested that reduced levels of the brain chemical (neurotransmitter) serotonin (5-hydroxytryptamine [5-HT]) may be related to self-injurious behavior (Kraemer & Clarke, 1990) and aggression (Soubrie, 1986). Drugs that increase serotonin have reduced some forms of aggression in laboratory animals (White et al., 1991). Similar drugs have reduced aggressive and self-injurious behavior of people with developmental disabilities. Several investigators have reported reductions in destructive behavior including aggression, self-injury, as well as anxiety, obsessive-compulsive behaviors, and impulsive behaviors (Cook, Roulett, Jaselskis, & Beventhal, 1992; Gedye, 1991; Markowitz, 1992; Ratey, Sovner, Parks, & Rogentine, 1991; Ratey et al., 1992). If aggressive and self-injurious behaviors are associated with reductions in the activity of serotonin, it may result in the reduced efficacy of naturally occurring punishers that would normally decrease such behavior. In other words, events that normally function to punish or decrease behavior may be less effective if there are reduced levels of serotonin. Experimental research with laboratory animals have found results consistent with this idea (Kantak, Hegstrand, & Eichelman, 1981; Katz, 1980; Sewell, Gallus, Gault, & Cleary, 1982; Waldbillig, 1979). Thus, the behavioral effects of events functioning as aversive antecedent stimuli or punishers may be modulated, in part, by the neurotransmitter serotonin and by psychotropic medication that affect this neurochemical system.

Reinforcement Schedules Maintaining Destructive Behavior

Intermittent schedules. The probability of a given behavior occurring is related directly to the pattern of consequences maintaining the behavior under investigation. It has been well established in behavioral pharmacology laboratory research that drug effects on performance depend critically on the specific arrangement of consequences (positive reinforcers, negative reinforcers, or punishers) (Dews, 1955; Thompson & Schuster, 1968). A specific dose of a given drug (e.g., pentobarbital or methamphetamine) will increase or decrease the performance rate depending on the schedule of consequences maintaining the behavior. Few investigations have been done in clinical, residential, or educational settings to evaluate this well-established laboratory phenomena. This is surprising, because it is

likely adaptive or maladaptive behavior in schools (Martens, Lockner, & Kelly, 1992; Picker, Poling, & Parker, 1979; Pierce & Epling, 1995) and other settings (McDowell, 1982) is related, in part, to the relative distribution of reinforcement (often in the form of attention). Parents, teachers, and other caregivers often attend intermittently to aggressive, self-injurious, or other forms of destructive behavior (sometimes necessarily). Frequently reinforced behavior is more resistant to the effects of many of the drugs (e.g., neuroleptics) typically used for treating behavior problems in mental retardation (Heyman, 1983). The identical dose of the identical drug may have very different effects on the destructive behavior of a person with a developmental disability, depending on how frequently the behavior problem receives attention from significant others. On days when staff are not overworked, they are more likely to quickly respond to a client's aggressive outburst, but the behavior persists at a high frequency despite the 8 mg of haloperidol the person is receiving. When staff are overworked, due to understaffing, the same individual may receive very little attention, and even though he has repeated outbursts, the overall frequency of outbursts may decline. Such apparently unpredictable variability in response to psychotropic medications may be accounted for, in part, by the type and pattern of reinforcement maintaining the problem behavior. In such situations, staff typically contend that they had not changed anything in the way they treated the client, when in fact, the observed effect was because of an interaction between the medication dosage and the intermittent social reinforcement schedule contingent on episodes of aggressive outbursts.

Concurrent schedules. Destructive behavior such as aggression often occurs sporadically and seemingly unpredictably. Consider a student who intermittently hits other students around her in an inclusive classroom in which she receives special education services. Observational assessment indicates she receives approximately four times as much attention in the same amount of time when she hits other students when she is doing academically relevant activities. The teachers and behavior specialists recommend to her parents that she should be evaluated by a physician. Following a visit to the doctor and subsequent treatment with thioridazine for her outbursts, the teaching staff soon discover that while her outbursts decrease by 25%, her academically relevant activities almost completely cease. Such results might have been predicted by considering the research literature on *concurrent reinforcement schedules*.

A concurrent reinforcement schedule arranges for reinforcers to be available concurrently for two or more different responses. Each response is maintained by an independent schedule of reinforcement (Catania, 1963; Ferster & Skinner, 1957; Thompson & Grabowski, 1972). Analyses of concurrent reinforcement schedules provide practical ways of understanding how behavior is distributed among several available activities and their associated reinforcement alternatives. The relation between relative rates of behavior and relative reinforcement rates contingent on the behavior is described by a mathematical model called the Matching Law which holds that the relative amount of behavior is proportional to relative reinforcement rates for two concurrent activities (Herrnstein, 1961). The amount of time engaged in a particular behavior and activities depends on the rate at which those different adaptive and maladaptive behaviors are reinforced. Because the reinforcement rate for hitting was four times higher than for academically appropriate behavior, it is not surprising that the problem behavior was more resistant to the neuroleptic drug effects than the adaptive performance, which was seldom reinforced.

There have been several demonstrations in laboratory, residential, and classroom settings showing that animals and people perform differently under concurrent reinforcement schedules (Pierce & Epling, 1995). Psychotropic drugs interact with concurrent reinforcement schedules to differentially affect behavior (Galizio & Allen, 1991; Higgins & Stitzer, 1988), which could have important implications for individuals with destructive behaviors in everyday living and learning environments.

Classrooms and employment settings provide a wide variety of alternative and concurrently available activities, each with its own reinforcement conditions. An individual may be relatively free to engage in a variety of different behaviors, some of which are considered socially appropriate and others considered inappropriate (Mace & Shea, 1990). In many cases, the individual is most likely to engage in the option resulting in the highest reinforcement rate (Martens, Lockner, & Kelly, 1992). When high reinforcement rates favor destructive behavior, there are higher rates of problem behavior and less time spent in socially appropriate behavior. This effect is important because if behavioral interventions interrupt only the reinforcement contingencies for problem behavior, they may not be effective over time if the relative reinforcement rate for appropriate behavior is ignored (e.g., Stanford & Nettlebeck, 1982).

Destructive behavior maintained by a concurrent reinforcement schedule may be influenced by a variety of factors including reinforcers differing in value, interactions between positive and negative reinforcement contingencies, and uncontrolled or unknown reinforcement histories (Pierce & Epling, 1983; Sprague & Horner, 1992). In evaluating the effects of psychotropic medications, careful attention must be given to the maintaining reinforcement contingencies. Behavioral factors that affect or influence the way in which problem behaviors occur relative to occurrences of appropriate behaviors may include, but are not limited to, the physical effort required by the competing responses, the value of competing reinforcers, the dimensions of competing reinforcement schedules, and the comparative time delay between discriminative stimuli and the reinforcer. It is possible that the effects of psychotropic treatments for individuals with destructive behavior and developmental disabilities would be moderated by these and other factors.

Multiple schedules. All psychotropic medication will eliminate destructive behavior at some dose. The problem, of course, is that those doses are frequently associated with sedative effects that interfere with learning and lead to problematic changes in other nonde-structive behavior (Ortiz & Gershon, 1986). Demonstrating the specificity of a drug effect for given certain type of behavior, but not another, can be accomplished using a *multiple reinforcement schedule* (Ferster & Skinner, 1957). Multiple reinforcement schedules consist of two or more independent reinforce-ment schedules presented successively (one after another), each in the presence of a distinctive stimulus or environmental cue (Ferster & Skinner, 1957; Thompson & Grabowski, 1972). McConahey et al. (1977) examined the effects of chlorpromazine on appropriate and inappropriate behavior of women with mental retardation during a multiple schedule in which appropriate behavior was reinforced in one component of the schedule (i.e., a morning training period), but was not systematically reinforced during a second component (i.e., an afternoon unstruc-tured period) and found that drug effects depended in part on the presence or absence of the positive reinforcement schedule (see the section on contextual control, below).

Recurring evocative stimuli and schedule-induced behavior. Problem behavior also can be exacerbated by periodic schedules of intermittent positive reinforcement, even though they are not related directly to the reinforcement contingency. Such behavior is said to be *adjunctive* or *schedule-induced* (Falk, 1971; Thompson & Lubinski, 1986). If water is freely available, rats will consume up to 10 times their normal daily water intake when lever-pressing for food pellets under interval reinforcement schedules (Falk, 1961). The excessive behavior that is displayed, such as water drinking, during a concurrent intermit-tent reinforcement schedule depends on the properties of the reinforcer itself and the temporal (i.e., time-based) properties of the reinforcer's presentation. Infrequent destruc-tive or other repetitive behavior may escalate when people are placed in situations where powerful positive reinforcers are available only periodically. Wieseler, Hanson, Chamberlain, and Thompson (1988) showed that the frequency of repetitive self-stimulatory behavior increased as the time between

successive consumable reinforcement deliveries increased for completing a table-top task. Emerson and Howard (1992) also described schedule-induced stereotypies among people with mental retardation. Stereotyped behaviors increased when reinforcement for performing simple experimental tasks was available for fixed intervals of time (FI) or differential reinforcement of low response rate (DRL) schedules. If the same overall number of reinforcers were given in a single lump sum, however, no changes in stereotypy were observed. Paradoxically, it may be that reinforc-ing adaptive behaviors under some conditions with a particularly valued reinforcer leads to increased frequency and intensity of certain forms of maladaptive behavior. Thus, in addition to identifying antecedents and consequences of destructive behavior, an analysis of contextual reinforcement conditions may also be required.

Falk (1986) hypothesized that schedule-induced behavior might involve conflicting response tendencies, namely the tendency to remain in close proximity to a source of a valued reinforcer and the tendency to leave as the likelihood of being reinforced appears progressively less. The value of adjunctive behaviors may be to prevent one from leaving an environment prematurely when persistence may pay off. On the other hand, if reinforcers occur too infrequently, adjunctive behavior is not evoked, likely because remaining in such situations would likely be unsuccessful.

For many people with severe developmen-tal disabilities, it is likely that the variety and frequency of positive reinforcers is restricted. Behavioral programs based on positive reinforcement often occur in the context of an otherwise impoverished reinforcement environment. Because of this, the programmed reinforcement conditions will probably increase adaptive appropriate behaviors, but may also evoke nonadaptive behaviors by enhancing the reinforcing efficacy of the opportunity to engage in self-stimulation or self-injury. Drugs that appear to alter reinforcer effectiveness, such as neuroleptics, might reduce the ability of the fixed-time schedule to evoke adjunctive behavior. Drugs that affect the timing patterns of responses, such as stimulants, may affect the temporal relation between reinforcer presentation and responding, and produce changes in schedule-induced responding (Pellon & Blackman, 1992). Drugs that block endogenous opiates, possibly affecting the acquisition of adjunctive behavior, may not only reduce behaviors maintained by endogenous opiate release and binding (e.g., self-injurious behavior), but may also interfere with the reinforcing properties of the events maintaining adjunctive behavior.

Psychotropic Medications and Contextual Control of Destructive Behavior

Although different forms of destructive behavior can be influenced by discrete environmental events and stimuli, such as staff demands placed on the individual (e.g., Carr et al., 1980), crowding (e.g., Boe, 1977; McAfee, 1987), staff change (Touchette, MacDonald, & Langer, 1985), task repetition (e.g., Winterling, Dunlap, & O'Neill, 1987), and even stimulation arising from certain items of clothing (e.g., Rojahn, Mulick, McCoy, & Schroeder, 1978), it is important to evaluate a broader range of environmental setting factors including the typical physical and social context setting the occasion for problem behavior, as well as events occurring within the individuals involved (Schroeder et al., 1991). Such an assessment would consider numerous factors including the health and physical discomfort of the individual (e.g., menstrual cramps or pain from a middle ear infection), time since last meal, or the presence of a particular staff member. By conducting a contextual assessment of health and setting factors, more useful information is gathered to assist in evaluating the appropriateness of specific psychotropic medications.

Contextual variables can determine drug effects in other more general ways as well. Chlorpromazine (i.e., Thorazine) is one of the most widely prescribed drugs to treat people with mental retardation who display destructive behavior. But does chlorpromazine reliably reduce aggressive behavior of people with moderate to severe retardation? One might

assume that the answer to this question must be obvious, but it isn't. McConahey et al. (1977) administered chlorpromazine and placebo treatments sequentially for alternating 4-week blocks (ABAB) to individuals with behavior problems in a large public residential setting, and did so within the context of a multiple reinforcement schedule and blind evaluation conditions. During one component of the daily schedule (each morning) 22 women with moderate to severe mental retardation participated in several functional activities for which they received tokens under high-density reinforcement schedules. The tokens were exchanged at the conclusion of each morning's session for toiletries, magazines, and other personal items. During afternoons, there were no programmed reinforcement conditions in place; although similar daily activities were available, residents participated in them without staff initiation or feedback. During afternoons, the unit on which they lived functioned in a fashion nearly identical to the way it had prior to the onset of the study. Similar staff ratios prevailed during both periods.

There was little aggressive behavior during the morning component when positive reinforcement was contingent on participation in functional activities, such as grooming, art, household skills, and preacademic skills. Chlorpromazine had no significant effect on the modest amount of aggression that occurred during the mornings. During afternoons when no programmed contingencies were in place, five times as much aggression occurred, and chlorpromazine markedly reduced the aggression that did occur compared with placebo. Whether chlorpromazine reduces aggression depends on the environmental circumstances in which the behavior is being examined and in which the drug is administered. Presumably the brain's dopamine receptors do not change five-fold from morning to afternoon, so differences in chlorpromazine effects must reflect differences in environmental conditions.

Usually we focus on specific social cues and reinforcement contingencies when evaluating environmental factors that interact with medications to determine behavioral outcomes. However, antecedent and ongoing environmental cues more broadly play a role in the degree of adaptive or maladaptive behavior displayed. Hendrickson, Akkerman, Speggen, and Thompson (1985) studied a group of women with moderate mental retardation in a large, county-operated residential facility that was divided into individual buildings accommodating 16 to 24 residents. Typically the women ate lunch in a large congregate dining room. They displayed frequent inappropriate mealtime behavior (e.g., food grabbing, food throwing, aggression against others, shouting) and limited appropriate mealtime skills (e.g., eating properly with utensils, wiping mouth with napkin). Hendrickson et. al. used an ABAB design to serve lunches on trays in the congregate dining hall for a block of several weeks, then they served lunch family style, four women per table in their own home building. Immediately on switching to family-style dining in their own building, at the very first meal, appropriate mealtime skills emerged and maladaptive mealtime behavior plummeted to an extremely low level. There was no learning of new skills involved in the behavior change. The display of appropriate mealtime skills was clearly under control of familiar cues of a typical family meal setting, which most of the women must have learned at home as children.

Had a drug evaluation been conducted to determine whether a psychotropic medication would reduce maladaptive behavior at mealtimes, the answer would have been that it would clearly depend on the environmental setting. More recently, Thompson, Robinson, Dietrich, Farris, and Sinclair (1996) found that behavior problems of adults with mental retardation were less frequent and more competent behavior was displayed in more homelike community residences ("homelike" as judged by architectural features), and conversely, stereotypies, aggression, and lethargy were more common in the more institutional community residences. In these studies, the investigators statistically controlled for differences in the types of residents and program staff characteristics in the more homelike and institutional residences. Any attempt to evaluate the effects of psychotropic medications independent of the setting in which the medications were administered would have yielded uninterpretable results.

Exteroceptive Stimuli and Attention

We have suggested that neurochemical systems interact with behavioral and environmental factors to alter the way in which environmental stimuli affect behavior, destructive or otherwise. A student who doesn't seem to pay attention is considered to have an attentional problem because his behavior is controlled poorly by certain environmental stimuli that typically result in most children behaving in a conventional manner (e.g., following a teacher's instructions). Children with attention-deficit/hyperactivity disorder (ADHD) often appear to ignore adults (teachers or parents) when they make requests or provide instructions such as "Carlos, put your shoes away." This represents a weakening of stimulus control, which can be enhanced by the use of stimulant medications, such as methylphenidate or amphetamine. From a clinical vantage point, if Carlos begins to follow more instructions and requests, the child's parents and teachers conclude that he is more compliant, but we can also say the threshold for stimulus control has been lowered by the medication. Laboratory studies show that children with ADHD also manifest narrower stimulus control on tasks requiring vigilance and attention to detail, so the effects are not limited to social cues and compliance situations.

The more well-established the stimulus control, the more resilient a learned performance is to the effects of psychotropic medications. An individual in a supported employment setting who is just learning a new job will be more disrupted at work by the atypical neuroleptic resperidone than he is in carrying out his household chores at home, which he has done the same way for several years. Even a small dose of medication may disrupt discriminative skills that are in the transitional stages of being learned, while the same dose of the same medication may have little or no effect on overlearned skills (Laties & Weiss, 1966).

Internal Cues: Rage, Anxiety, and Panic Attacks

Environmental conditions that are provocative, demanding, or otherwise stressful can often elicit internal stimulus changes. Some of these feelings, such as anger, rage, or hostility, may be terminated following an outburst of aggressive behavior (e.g., Berry & Pennebaker, 1993; Sinha, Lovallo, & Parsons, 1992) and may serve as a negative reinforcement function. In other words, the person may feel less angry following an aggressive outburst; removal of the angry feelings constitutes negative reinforcement, thereby increasing the likelihood of aggression under similar circumstances in the future. People with mental retardation often have difficulty learning socially acceptable ways to behave in response to internal emotional cues, for example, by expressing their feelings verbally ("I'm angry!") or asking someone to stop bothering them. In situations where it would be difficult to change many of the external cues that may be disturbing, such as at an integrated job site, pharmacological treatments may reduce the frequency and/or intensity of explosive outbursts by decreasing the magnitude of the initial internal responses and associated unpleasant cues. Propranolol, a nonselective beta-adrenergic receptor blocker, has been used to treat the destructive behaviors of patients with psychiatric disorders (Lader, 1988) and people with mental retardation (Ruedrich, Grush, & Wilson, 1990). Many early reports of propranolol's efficacy in reducing explosive rage outbursts have been methodologically weak and should be interpreted cautiously (e.g., case studies lacking placebo controls and blind drug administration). However, using a double-blind crossover design with placebo controls, Greendyke, Kanter, Schuster, Verstreate, and Wooton (1986) demonstrated that daily propranolol administration resulted in reduced assaultive behavior in people with organic brain damage.

Behavioral Mechanisms of Drug Action: A Hypothetical Case Study

Let us explore a hypothetical case to illustrate the way a functional analysis of variables regulating behavior can be informative in predicting the effects of behaviorally active medications. Our purpose is not to recommend treatments, but to illustrate the decision-making process that underlies a treatment based on an understanding of the behavioral mechanisms of drug action.

David is a 16-year-old young man with a history of destructive behavior including self-injury dating from around 3 years of age and increasingly aggressive behavioral outbursts. He functions in the severe range of mental retardation with no spoken language and limited daily living skills. David has relatively competent fine motor skills for his level of retardation (e.g., he can open a can of his favorite soft drink) and, at times, it seems as if he understands far more that is spoken by his teachers, parents, and friends than might be expected. At various times he has been diagnosed as having autism, organic personality disorder, and conduct disorder. David lives at home with his mother, father, and cousin and attends his neighborhood school, where he is part of a self-contained special-education classroom. His teachers say he frequently rocks his upper torso when sitting, bangs his head against table tops, bites his hands and wrists, and strikes the bridge of his nose with his fist until it bleeds. When he is excited or seems to be apprehensive, he becomes very agitated, waving and flapping his arms and hands and making screeching sounds.

David's family doctor is most concerned about his self-injury and increasing aggression. The physician is considering a variety of psychoactive medications to treat David's behavior problems. A functional assessment is conducted in an attempt to make predictions about the most promising medications for treating David's problem behavior. Behavioral observations are made at school between 8:30 A.M. and 3:30 P.M. for 10 days. During each hour, one 15-minute period is observed randomly during which instances of adaptive behavior, self-injury, aggression, and other behavior (i.e., rocking, staring, flicking his fingers in front of his face) are recorded. It turns out that most of David's self-injury occurs when he is alone or when no social interactions occur either before or after self-injury, although some instances reliably follow teacher requests. Moreover, very little of his self-injury is followed by teaching staff attention, suggesting that it is not maintained by attention, a generalized positive reinforcer. On the other hand, 64% of David's aggression is directed toward teaching staff, and primarily when he is asked to do something he apparently does not want to do, or when material objects are taken away from him or if he is interrupted while busy with a preferred activity. David's aggressive behavior seems to be an effective escape or avoidance response because when he is aggressive his teachers stop making demands of him or allow him to continue a preferred activity. Similarly, aggressive behavior toward other students, though less frequent, tends to occur when other students crowd him (e.g., getting on or off the school bus, in a line-up, at an assembly). Once again, aggressive behavior seems to serve a social avoidance function.

Although David's adaptive behavior (e.g., classroom activities, self-care) occurred relatively frequently (in roughly one quarter of the observed intervals), on 65% of those instances, his adaptive behavior resulted in no positive social consequences, and it was occasionally punished (11%), such as when David attempted to help with preparing a meal but was admonished by staff and who told him not to touch the spoons. If we examine the relation between David's adaptive and maladaptive behavior as performance maintained under a concurrent reinforcement schedule, his appropriate adaptive behavior is only occasionally reinforced when compared with his aggressive behavior, which is reinforced to a relatively greater extent and on many more occasions. Finally, David spends a large of amount of his time (39%) in "other" behavior, including a variety of stereotyped movements. These apparently nonfunctional activities commonly are displayed by people with autism when they are not provided with anything else to do. Although some of these repetitive movements may be driven by neurochemical mechanisms (e.g., dopamine supersensitivity), they also may be learned adaptations in the absence of anything meaningful or constructive to do.

If David is given a *neuroleptic* medication, his self-injury may be reduced, but because only a proportion of this behavior appears to be maintained by negative reinforcement, the most effective dosage may interfere with adaptive behavior. Self-injury also is more probable when David is unoccupied, which suggests that his self-injury is regulated by other mechanisms. David's aggression appears to be largely avoidance motivated, and may also respond to treatment with a dopamine antagonist (i.e., a neuroleptic). But, because so much of David's everyday living skills are infrequently positively reinforced, those performances will be disproportionately weakened by a dopamine antagonist, and his adaptive skills would be expected also to diminish. Finally, David's stereotyped behaviors would most likely be reduced by administering a neuroleptic. But because he is unoccupied for large periods of his day, the medication's sedative side effect will likely result in David becoming drowsy and possibly falling asleep during part of the school day.

Compared with a neuroleptic, a *beta blocker* such as propanolol or *alpha adrenergic agonist* such as clonidine will be less likely to have any direct effects on David's destructive behavior. There is no reason to believe such a medication would affect David's self-injury if his behavior is being regulated by neurochemicals such as dopamine or opioids. A beta blocker, however, may increase David's tolerance threshold for reacting violently when his personal space is violated or losing his temper when asked to do something he doesn't want to do. This would be particularly true if the activity was something he finds anxiety-provoking (e.g., going somewhere new, meeting new people). Such medications should have little effect on the importance of positive reinforcers and therefore should not be detrimental for adaptive behavior. Finally, propanolol may reduce some of David's agitation resulting in reduced self-stimulatory behavior when he is excited or apprehensive about an upcoming activity or event (e.g., a school visit by a parent), but would be very unlikely to have favorable effects on such behavior otherwise (e.g., when he is simply bored with little to do).

The *opiate antagonist* naltrexone is likely to have a specific effect on self-injury if endogenous opioids are involved, with no direct effects on maladaptive or adaptive behavior. Naltrexone would probably reduce intense or frequent self-biting and head hitting, but not other superficial forms of self-injury (Thompson et al., 1994). More detailed analysis would be required to determine whether the superficial forms of self-injury seem to serve an avoidance function (approximately 29% of his self-injury).

Finally, a *serotonin reuptake blocker,* such as fluvoxamine, may have beneficial effects on aggression and possibly reduce stereotyped behavior, but would be less likely to reduce self-injury. Serotonin reuptake inhibitor medications appear to specifically affect repetitive avoidance behaviors (e.g., obsessive-compulsive rituals) and modulate thresholds for engaging in explosive aggressive behavior. It is possible fluvoxamine would elevate the threshold for David to tolerate other clients crowding him so that he no longer had aggressive outbursts during such times. If David's "other" behavior included skin picking, hair pulling, and other common compulsive rituals, they could possibly be reduced.

It is important to keep in mind that the four psychotropic treatment strategies outlined above to treat David's behavior problems may involve overlapping categories of problem behavior that appear different but serve the same function under similar circumstances. Moreover, the effects on one behavior may influence the outcome seen with others (i.e., some self-injury and aggression may actually belong in the same functional category of behavior because sometimes they affect the social environment in similar ways). A treat-ment that reduces avoidance-motivated self-injury may also reduce avoidance-motivated aggression, or a treatment that reduces only aggression may lead to an increase in self-injury. If a behavioral treatment is implemented and directed toward only one type of behavior problem (e.g., aggression), other members of that same class that go untreated may worsen (Schroeder & MacLean, 1987). If a time-out procedure were used to treat attention-maintained aggression, self-injury that was maintained by the same consequence (i.e., attention) may increase. If a medication were simultaneously administered (e.g., naltrexone) and no effects were reported, one might erroneously conclude the medication had no effect. In reality, however, the lack of a decrease in self-injury might reflect a behavioral contrast effect in response to the suppression of attention-maintained aggression.

Conclusion

Clinical behavioral pharmacologists are trying to understand the range of individual differences and the conditions under which psychotropic medications change destructive and adaptive behavior of people with developmental disabilities (Thompson, 1986). We must increase the precision with which we identify the people who stand to gain the most from specific treatments and consider carefully the unintended side effects. These goals can be achieved by combining principles from behavioral pharmacology with new advances in neurochemistry and neuropharmacology, along with the existing robust behavioral principles permitting the analysis of environmental variables influencing the destructive and adaptive behavior of people with developmental disabilities. The result will be a taxonomy of destructive behavior and corresponding treatment strategies based on an analysis of neurobehavioral mechanisms of drug action.

REFERENCES

Aman, M. G., & Singh, N. N. (Eds.). (1988). *Psychopharmacology of the developmental disabilities.* New York: Springer-Verlag.

American Psychiatric Association. (1994). *Diagnostic and statistical manual of mental disorders* (4th ed.). Washington, DC: Author.

Anderson, G. M., & Hoshino, Y. (1997). Neuro-chemical studies of autism. In D. J. Cohen & F. R. Volkmar (Eds.), *Handbook of autism and pervasive developmental disorders* (pp. 325–343). New York: Wiley.

Ayllon, T., & Azrin, N. H. (1965). The measurement and reinforcement of behavior of psychotics. *Journal of the Experimental Analysis of Behavior, 8,* 357–383.

Barrett, R. P., Feinstein, C., & Hole, W. T. (1989). Effects of naloxone and naltrexone on self-injury: A double-blind placebo controlled analysis. *American Journal on Mental Retardation, 93,* 644–651.

Barron, J., & Sandman, C. (1983). Relationship of sedative-hypnotic response to self-injurious behavior and stereotypy for mentally retarded clients. *American Journal of Mental Deficiency, 88,* 177–186.

Barron, J., & Sandman, C. A. (1985). Paradoxical excitement to sedative-hypnotics in mentally retarded clients. *American Journal of Mental Deficiency, 90,* 124–129.

Beckwith, B. E., Couk, D. I., & Schumacher, K. (1986). Failure of naloxone to reduce self-injurious behavior in two developmentally disabled females. *Applied Research in Mental Retardation, 7,* 183–188.

Bernstein, G. A., Hughes, J. R., Mitchell, J. E., & Thompson, T. (1987). Effects of narcotic antagonists on self-injurious behavior: A single case study. *Journal of the American Academy of Child and Adolescent Psychiatry, 26,* 886–889.

Berry, D. S., & Pennebaker, J. W. (1993). Nonverbal and verbal emotional expression and health. *Psychotherapy and Psychosomatics, 59,* 11–19.

Boe, R. B. (1977). Economical procedures for the reduction of aggression in a residential setting. *Mental Retardation, 15,* 25–28.

Bruininks, R. H., Olson, K. M., Larson, S. A., & Lakin, K. C. (1994). Challenging behaviors among persons with mental retardation in residential settings: Implications for policy, research, and practice. In T. Thompson & D. B. Gray (Eds.), *Destructive behavior in developmental disabilities: Diagnosis and treatment* (pp. 24–48). Thousand Oaks, CA: Sage.

Campbell, M., Friedman, E., Green, W. H., Collins, P. J., Small, A. M., & Breuer, H. (1975). Blood serotonin in schizophrenic children: A preliminary study. *International Pharmacopsychiatry, 10,* 213–221.

Carlton, P. L., Siegel, J. L., Murphree, H. B., & Cook, L. (1981). Effects of diazepam on operant behavior in man. *Psychopharmacology, 73,* 314–317.

Carr, E. G. (1977). The motivation of self-injurious behavior: A review of some hypotheses. *Psychological Bulletin, 84,* 800–816.

Carr, E. G., & Durand, V. M. (1985a). Reducing behavior problems through functional communication training. *Journal of Applied Behavior Analysis, 18,* 111–126.

Carr, E. G., & Durand, V. M. (1985b). The social-communicative basis of severe behavior problems in children. In S. Reiss & R. Bootzin (Eds.), *Theoretical issues in behavior therapy* (pp. 219–254). New York: Academic Press.

Carr, E. G., Levin, L., McConnachie, G., Carlson, J. I., Kemp, D. C., & Smith, C. E. (1994). *Communication-based intervention for problem behavior: A user's guide for producing positive change.* Baltimore: Brookes.

Carr, E. G., Newsom, C. D., & Binkoff, J. A. (1976). Stimulus control of self-destructive behavior in a psychotic child. *Journal of Abnormal Child Psychology, 4,* 139–153.

Carr, E. G., Newsom, C. D., & Binkoff, J. A. (1980). Escape as a factor in the aggressive behavior of two retarded children. *Journal of Applied Behavior Analysis, 13,* 101–117.

Cataldo, M. (1991). The effects of punishment and other behavior reducing procedures on the destructive behaviors of persons with developmental disabilities. *Treatment of destructive behaviors in persons with developmental disabilities* (pp. 231–341) (NIH Publication No. 91-2410). Bethesda, MD: National Institutes of Health.

Cataldo, M., & Harris, J. (1982). The biological basis for self-injury in the mentally retarded. *Analysis and Intervention in Developmental Disabilities, 2,* 21–39.

Catania, A. C. (1963). Concurrent performances: Reinforcement interaction and response independence. *Journal of the Experimental Analysis of Behavior, 6,* 253–263.

Cerutti, D., & Thompson, T. (1990). Drug therapy in mental retardation: "Artificial hibernation" evolved. [Review of M. Aman's and N. H. Singh's *Psychopharmacology of the developmental disabilities*] *Contemporary Psychology, 35,* 1148–1150.

Coccaro, E. F., Gabriel, S., & Siever, L. J. (1990). Buspirone challenge: Preliminary evidence for a role for central 5-HT 1a receptor function in impulsive aggressive behavior in humans. *Psychopharmacology Bulletin, 26,* 393–405.

Coleman, M., & Gillberg, C. (1985). *The biology of the autistic syndromes.* New York: Praeger.

Cook, E. H., Rowlett, R., Jaselskis, D. O., & Beventhal, B. L. (1992). Fluoxetine treatment of children and adults with autistic disorder and mental retardation. *Journal of the American Academy of Child and Adolescent Psychiatry, 31,* 739–745.

Cook, L., & Catania, A. C. (1964). Effects of drugs on avoidance and escape behavior. *Federation Proceedings, 23,* 818–835.

Cook, L., & Sepinwall, J. (1975). Psychopharmacological parameters of emotion. In L. Levi (Ed.), *Emotions—their parameters and measurement* (pp. 379–404). New York: Raven Press.

Cook, L., & Weidley, E. (1957). Behavioral effects of some psychopharmacological agents. *Annals of the New York Academy of Sciences, 66,* 740–752.

Cronin, G. M., Wiepkema, P. R., & van Ree, J. M. (1985). Endogenous opioids are involved in abnormal stereotyped behavior of tethered sows. *Neuropeptides, 6,* 527–530.

Davidson, P. W., Kleene, B. M., Carroll, M., & Rockowitz, R. J. (1983). Effects of naloxone on self-injurious behavior: A case study. *Applied Research in Mental Retardation, 4,* 1–4.

Davidson, A. B., & Weidley, E. (1976). Differential effects of neuroleptics and other psychotropic agents on acquisition of avoidance in rats. *Life Science, 18,* 1279–1284.

Davidson, P. W., Cain, N. N., Sloane-Reeves, J. E., Giesow, V. E., Quijano, L. E., & Houser, K. D. (1996). Factors predicting re-referral following crisis intervention for community-based persons with developmental disabilities and behavioral and psychiatric disorder. *American Journal on Mental Retardation, 101,* 109–117.

DeLissovoy, V. (1963). Head banging in early childhood: A suggested cause. *Journal of Genetic Psychology, 102,* 109–114.

Dews, P. B. (1955). Studies on behavior: I. Differential sensitivity to pentobarbital of pecking performance in pigeons depending on the schedule of reward. *Journal of Pharmacology and Experimental Therapeutics, 113,* 393–401.

DiMascio, A., Shader, R. I., & Harmatz, J. (1967). Psychotropic drugs and induced hostility. *Psychosomatics, 10,* 46–47.

Donnellan, A. M., Mirenda, P. L., Mesaros, R. A., & Fassbender, L. L. (1984). Analyzing the communicative functions of aberrant behavior. *Journal of the Association of Persons With Severe Handicaps, 9,* 201–212.

Durand, V. M., & Crimmins, D. B. (1988). Identifying the variables maintaining self-injurious behavior. *Journal of Autism and Developmental Disorders, 18,* 99–117.

Edelson, S. M., Taubman, M. T., & Lovaas, I. O. (1983). Some social contexts of self-destructive behavior. *Journal of Abnormal Child Psychology, 11,* 299–312.

Emerson, E., & Howard D. (1992). Schedule-induced stereotypy. *Research in Developmental Disabilities, 13,* 335–361.

Falk, J. L. (1961). Production of polydipsia in normal rats by an intermittent food schedule. *Science, 133,* 195–196.

Falk, J. L. (1971). The nature and determinants of adjunctive behavior. *Physiology and Behavior, 6,* 577–588.

Falk, J. L. (1986). The formation and function of ritual behavior. In T. Thompson & M. Zeiler (Eds.), *Analysis and integration of behavioral units* (pp. 335–355). Hillsdale, NJ: Erlbaum.

Favell, J. E., McGimsey, J. F., & Schell, R. M. (1982). Treatment of self-injury by providing alternate sensory activities. *Analysis and Intervention in Developmental Disabilities, 2,* 83–104.

Ferster, C. B., & Skinner, B. F. (1957). *Schedules of reinforcement.* New York: Appleton-Century-Crofts.

Fischman, M. W., & Schuster, C. R. (1979). The effects of chlorpromazine and pentobarbital on behavior maintained by electric shock or point loss avoidance in humans. *Psychopharmacology, 66,* 3–11.

Galizio, M., & Allen, A. R. (1991). Variable-ratio schedules of timeout from avoidance: Effects of *d*-amphetamine and morphine. *Journal of the Experimental Analysis of Behavior, 56,* 193–203.

Gardos, G. (1980). Disinhibition of behavior by antianxiety drugs. *Psychosomatics, 21,* 1025–1026.

Gaylord-Ross, R. J., Weeks, M., & Lipner, C. (1980). An analysis of antecedent, response, and consequence events in the treatment of self-injurious behavior. *Education and Training of the Mentally Retarded, 15,* 35–42.

Gedye, A. (1991). Buspirone alone or with serotonergic diet reduced aggression in a developmentally disabled adult. *Biological Psychiatry, 30,* 88–91.

Gillberg, C., Terenius, L., & Lonnerhold, G. (1985). Endorphin activity in childhood psychosis: Spinal fluid levels in 24 cases. *Archives of General Psychiatry, 42,* 780–783.

Goldstein, M., Kuga, S., & Kusano, N., Meller, E., Dancis, J., & Schwarcz, R. (1986). Dopamine agonist induced self-mutilative biting behavior in monkeys with unilateral ventromedial tegmental lesions of the brainstem: Possible pharmacological model for Lesch-Nyhan syndrome. *Brain Research, 367,* 114–119.

Greendyke, R. M., Kanter, D. R., Schuster, D. B., Verstreate, S., & Wooton, J. (1986). Propranolol treatment of assaultive patients with organic brain disease. *Journal of Nervous and Mental Disease, 174,* 290–294.

Heise, G. A., & Boff, E. (1962). Continuous avoidance as a base-line for measuring behavioral effects of drugs. *Psychopharmacologia, 3,* 264–282.

Hendrickson, K. C., Akkerman, P.S., Speggen, L., & Thompson, T. (1985). Dining arrangements and behavior of severely mentally retarded adults. *Applied Research in Mental Retardation, 6,* 379–388.

Herman, B. H., Hammock, M. K., Egan, J., Arthur-Smith, A., Chatoor, I., & Werner, A. (1989). Role for opioid peptides in self-injurious behavior: Dissociation from autonomic nervous system functioning. *Developmental Pharmacology and Therapeutics, 12,* 81–89.

Herrnstein, R. J. (1961). Relative and absolute strength of response as a function of frequency of reinforcement. *Journal of the Experimental Analysis of Behavior, 13,* 267–272.

Heyman, G. M. (1983). A parametric evaluation of the hedonic and motor effects of drugs: Pimozide and amphetamine. *Journal of the Experimental Analysis of Behavior, 40,* 154–161.

Heyman, G. M., & Monaghan, M. M. (1987). Effects of changes in response requirement and deprivation on the parameters of the matching law equation: New data and review. *Journal of Experimental Psychology: Animal Behavior Processes, 13,* 384–394.

Higgins, S. T., & Stitzer, M. L. (1988). Time allocation in a concurrent schedule of social interaction and monetary reinforcement: Effects of *d*-amphetamine. *Pharmacology, Biochemistry, and Behavior, 31,* 227–231.

Horner, R. H., Dunlap, G., Koegel, R. L., Carr, E. G., Sailor, W., Anderson, J., Albin, R. W., & O'Neill, R. E. (1990). Toward a technology of "nonaversive" behavioral support. *Journal of the Association for Persons with Severe Handicaps, 15,* 125–132.

Intagliata, J., & Willer, B. (1981). Reinstitutionalization of mentally retarded persons successfully placed into family-care and group homes. *American Journal of Mental Deficiency, 87,* 34–39.

Iwata, B. A., Dorsey, M. F., Bauman, K. E., & Richman, G. S. (1982). Towards a functional analysis of self-injury. *Analysis and Intervention in Developmental Disabilities, 2,* 3–20.

Iwata, B. A., Pace, G. M., Dorsey, M. F., Zarcone, J. R., Vollmer, T. R., Smith, R. G., Rodgers, T. A., Lerman, D. C., Shore, B. A., Mazaleski, J. L., Goh, H. L., Cowdery, G. E., Kalsher, M. J., McCosh, K. C., & Willis, K. D. (1994). The functions of self-injurious behavior: An experimental-epidemiological analysis. *Journal of Applied Behavior Analysis, 27,* 215–240.

Jeffery, D. R., & Barrett, J. E. (1979). Effects of chlordiazepoxide on comparable rates of punished and unpunished responding. *Psychopharmacology, 64,* 9–11.

Kantak, K. M., Hegstrand, L. R., & Eichelman, B. (1981). Facilitation of shock-induced fighting following intraventricular 5,7-dihydroxytryptamine and 6-hydroxy DOPA. *Psychopharmacology, 74,* 157–160.

Katz, R. J. (1980). Role of serotonergic mechanisms in animal models of predation. *Progress in Neuro-Psychopharmacology, 4,* 219–231.

Kraemer, G. W., & Clarke, A. S. (1990). The behavioral neurobiology of self-injurious behavior in rhesus monkeys. *Progress in Neuro-Psychopharmacology and Biological Psychiatry, 14,* S141–S168.

Lader, M. (1988). b-adrenergic antagonists in neuropsychology: An update. *Journal of Clinical Psychiatry, 49,* 213–223.

Laties, V. G., & Weiss, B. (1966). Influence of drugs on behavior controlled by internal and external stimuli. *Journal of Pharmacology and Experimental Therapeutics, 152,* 388–396.

Lipman, R. S. (1970). The use of psychopharmacological agents in residential facilities for the retarded. In F. J. Menolascino (Ed.), *Psychiatric approaches to mental retardation* (pp. 387–398). New York: Basic Books.

Lloyd, K. G., Hornykiewicz, O., Davidson, L, Shannak, K., Farley, I., Goldstein, M., Shibuya, M., Kelley, W. N., & Fox, I. H. (1981). Biomedical evidence of dysfunction of brain neurotransmitters in the Lesch-Nyhan Syndrome. *New England Journal of Medicine, 305,* 1106–1111.

Loh, H. H., Tseng, L. F., Wie, E., & Li, C. H. (1976). b-endorphin is a potent analgesic agent. *Proceedings of the National Academy of Science, 73,* 3308–3310.

Lovaas, O. I., Freitag, G., Gold, V. J., & Kassorla, I. C. (1965). Experimental studies in childhood schizophrenia: Analysis of self-destructive behavior. *Journal of Experimental Child Psychology, 2,* 67–84.

Mace, F. C., & Shea, M. C. (1990). New directions in behavior analysis for the treatment of severe behavior disorders. In S. L. Harris & J. S. Handleman (Eds.), *Aversive and non-aversive interventions: Controlling life threatening behavior by the developmentally disabled* (pp. 57–79). New York: Springer.

MacLean, W. E. (1993). Overview. In J. L. Matson & R. P. Barrett (Eds.), *Psychopathology in the mentally retarded* (pp. 1–16). Needham Heights, MA: Allyn & Bacon.

Markowitz, P. I. (1992). Effect of fluoxetine on self-injurious behavior in the developmentally disabled: A preliminary study. *Journal of Clinical Psychopharmacology, 12,* 27–31.

Martens, B. K., Lockner, D. G., & Kelly, S. Q. (1992). The effects of variable interval reinforcement on academic engagement: A demonstration of matching theory. *Journal of Applied Behavior Analysis, 25,* 143–151.

Matson, J. L., & Barrett, R. P. (Eds.). (1993). *Psychopathology in the mentally retarded.* Needham Heights, MA: Allyn & Bacon.

McAffe, J. K. (1987). Classroom density and the aggressive behavior of handicapped children. *Education and Treatment of Children, 10,* 134–145.

McConahey, O. L., Thompson, T., & Zimmerman, R. (1977). A token system for retarded women: Behavior therapy, drug administration, and their combination. In T. Thompson & J. Grabowski (Eds.), *Behavior modification of the mentally retarded* (2nd ed., pp. 167–234). New York: Oxford University Press.

McDougle, C. J. (1997). Psychopharmacology. In D. J. Cohen & F. R. Volkmar (Eds.), *Handbook of autism and pervasive developmental disorders* (2nd ed., pp. 707–729). New York: Wiley.

McDowell, J. J. (1982). The importance of Herrnstein's mathematical statement of the law of effect for behavior therapy. *American Psychologist, 37,* 771–779.

Meltzer, H. Y. (Ed). (1987). *Psychopharmacology: The third generation of progress.* New York: Raven Press.

Miczek, K. A., Mos, J., & Olivier, B. (1989). Serotonin, aggression, and self-destructive behavior. *Psychopharmacology Bulletin, 25,* 399–403.

National Institutes of Health. (1991). *Treatment of destructive behaviors in persons with developmental disabilities* (NIH Publication No. 91-2410). Bethesda, MD: Author.

Olivier, B., Mos, J., & Miczek, K. A. (1991). Ethopharmacological studies of anxiolytics and aggression. *European Neuropsychopharmacology, 1,* 97–100.

O'Neill, R. E., Horner, R. H., Albin, R. W., Storey, R., & Sprague, J. R. (1989). *Functional analysis: A practical assessment guide.* University of Oregon.

O'Reilly, M. F. (1997). Functional analysis of episodic self-injury correlated with recurrent otitis media. *Journal of Applied Behavior Analysis, 30,* 165–168.

Ortiz, A., & Gershon, S. (1986). The future of neuroleptic psychopharmacology. *Journal of Clinical Psychiatry, 47,* 3–11.

Pellon, R., & Blackman, D. E. (1992). Effects of drugs on the temporal distribution of schedule-induced polydipsia in rats. *Pharmacology Biochemistry & Behavior, 43,* 689–695.

Picker, M., Poling, A., & Parker, A. (1979). A review of children's self-injurious behavior. *Psychological Record, 29,* 435–452.

Pierce, W. D., & Epling, W. F. (1983). Choice, matching, and human behavior: A review of the literature. *Behavior Analyst, 6,* 57–76.

Pierce, W. D., & Epling, W. F. (1995). The applied importance of research on the matching law. *Journal of Applied Behavior Analysis, 28,* 237–241.

Posluns, D. (1962). An analysis of chlorpromazine-induced suppression of the avoidance response. *Psychopharmacologia, 3,* 361–373.

Randall, L. O., Schallek, W., Heise, G. A., Keith, E. F., & Bagdon, R. E. (1960). The psychosedative properties of methaminodiazepoxide. *Journal of Pharmacology and Experimental Therapeutics, 129,* 163–171.

Ratey, J. J., Sorgi, P., O'Driscoll, G. A., Sands, S., Daehler, M. L., Fletcher, J. R., Kadish, K. J., Spuiell, G., Polakoff, S., Lindem, K. J., Bemporad, J. R., Richardson, L., & Rosenfeld, B. (1992). Nadolol to treat aggression and psychiatric symptomatology in chronic psychiatric inpatients: A double-blind placebo-controlled study. *Journal of Clinical Psychiatry, 53,* 41–46.

Ratey, J. J., Sovner, R., Parks, A., & Rogentine, K. (1991). Buspirone treatment of aggression and anxiety in mentally retarded: A multiple-baseline, placebo lead-in study. *Journal of Clinical Psychiatry, 52,* 159–162.

Reichle, J., & Wacker, D. P. (1993). *Communicative alternatives to challenging behavior: Integrating functional assessment and intervention strategies.* Baltimore: Brookes.

Repp, A. C., Felce, D., & Barton, L. E. (1988). Basing the treatment of stereotypic and self-injurious behavior on hypotheses of their causes. *Journal of Applied Behavior Analysis, 21,* 281–289.

Repp, A. C., & Karsh, K. G. (1990). A taxonomic approach to the nonaversive treatment of maladaptive behavior of persons with developmental disabilities. In A. C. Repp & N. N. Singh (Eds.), *Perspective in the use of nonaversive and aversive interventions with developmental disabilities.* Sycamore, IL: Sycamore.

Repp, A. C., & Singh, N. N. (1990). *Perspectives on the use of nonaversive and aversive interventions for persons with developmental disabilities.* Sycamore, IL: Sycamore.

Richardson, J. S., & Zeleski, W. A. (1983). Naloxone and self-mutilation. *Biological Psychiatry, 18,* 99–101.

Rincover, A., & Devaney, J. (1982). The application of sensory extinction procedures to self-injury. *Analysis and Intervention in Developmental Disabilities, 2,* 67–81.

Ritvo, E. R., Yuwiler, A., Geller, E., Ornitz, E. M., Saeger, K., & Plotkin, S. (1970). Increased blood serotonin and platelets in infantile autism. *Archives of General Psychiatry, 23,* 566–572.

Rojahn, J., Mulick, J. A., McCoy, D., & Schroeder, S. R. (1978). Setting effects, adaptive clothing, and the modification of head banging and self-restraint in two profoundly retarded adults. *Behavioral Analysis and Modification, 2,* 185–196.

Rojahn, J., & Tasse, M. J. (1996). Psychopathology in mental retardation. In J. W. Jacobson & J. A. Mulick (Eds.), *Manual of diagnosis and professional practice in mental retardation* (pp. 147–156). Washington, DC: American Psychological Association.

Romanczyk, R. G., Lockshin, S. B., & Harrison, K. (1993). Schizophrenia and autism. In J. L. Matson & R. P. Barrett (Eds.), *Psychopathology in the mentally retarded* (pp. 151–178). Needham Heights, MA: Allyn & Bacon.

Ruedrich, S. L., Grush, L., & Wilson, J. (1990). Beta adrenergic blocking medications for aggressive or self-injurious mentally retarded persons. *American Journal on Mental Retardation, 95,* 110–119.

Salzinger, K. (1990). The behavioral mechanism to explain abnormal behavior. *Annals of the New York Academy of Sciences, 340,* 66–87.

Salzinger, K. (1992). Connections: A search for bridges between behavior and the nervous system. *Annals of the New York Academy of Sciences, 658,* 276–286.

Salzman, C., DiMascio, A., Shader, R. I., & Harmatz, J. S. (1969). Chlordiazepoxide, expectation and hostility. *Psychopharmacologia, 14,* 38–45.

Sandman, C. A., Datta, P. C., Barron, J. Hoehler, F. K., Williams, C., & Swanson, J. M. (1983). Naloxone attenuates self-abusive behavior in developmentally disabled clients. *Applied Research in Mental Retardation, 4,* 5–11.

Sandman, C. A., & Hetrick, W. P. (1995). Opiate mechanisms in self-injury. *Mental Retardation and Developmental Disabilities Research Reviews, 1,* 130–136.

Sandyk, R. (1985). Naloxone abolishes self-injuring in a mentally retarded child (letter). *American Journal of Psychiatry, 17,* 520.

Schaal, D. W., & Hackenberg, T. (1994). Toward a functional analysis of drug treatment for behavior problems of people with developmental disabilities. *American Journal on Mental Retardation, 99,* 123–134.

Schain, R., & Freedman, D. (1961). Studies of 5-hydroxindol metabolism in autistic and other mentally retarded children. *Journal of Pediatrics, 58,* 315–320.

Schroeder, S. R., & MacLean, W. (1987). If it isn't one thing, its another: Experimental analysis of covariation in behavior management data of severe behavior disturbances. In S. Landesman & P. M. Vietze (Eds.), *Living Environments and Mental Retardation* (pp. 315–338). Washington, DC: American Association on Mental Retardation.

Schroeder, S. R., Rojahn, J., & Oldenquist, A. (1991). Treatment of destructive behaviors among people with mental retardation and developmental disabilities: An overview of the problem. In *Treatment of destructive behaviors in persons with developmental disabilities* (pp. 125–172) (NIH Publication No. 91-2410). Bethesda, MD: National Institutes of Health.

Schroeder, S. R., Tessel, R. E., Loupe, P. S., & Stodgell, C. J. (1997). Severe behavior problems among people with developmental disabilities. In W. E. MacLean (Ed.), *Ellis' handbook of mental deficiency, psychological theory and research* (3rd ed., pp. 439–464). Mahwah, NJ: Erlbaum.

Sepinwall, J., & Cook, L. (1978). Behavioral pharmacology of antianxiety drugs. In L. L. Iversen, S. D. Iversen, & S. H. Snyder (Eds.), *Handbook of psychopharmacology* (Vol. 13, pp. 345–393). New York: Plenum Press.

Sewell, R. G., Gallus, J. A., Gault, F. P., & Cleary, J. P. (1982). p-chlorophenylalanine effects on shock-induced attack and pressing responses in rats. *Pharmacology Biochemistry & Behavior, 17,* 945–950.

Sinha, R., Lovallo, W. R., & Parsons, O. A. (1992). Cardiovascular differentiation of emotions. *Psychosomatic Medicine, 54,* 422–435.

Soubrie, P. (1986). Reconciling the role of central serotonin neurons in human and animal behavior. *Behavioral and Brain Sciences, 9,* 319–364.

Sprague, J. R., & Horner, R. H. (1992). Covariation within functional response classes: Implications for treatment of severe problem behavior. *Journal of Applied Behavior Analysis, 25,* 735–746.

Sprague, R. L., & Werry, J. S. (1971). Methodology of psychopharmacological studies with the retarded. In N. R. Ellis (Ed.), *International review of research in mental retardation* (Vol. 5, pp. 147–210). New York: Academic Press.

Stanford, D., & Nettlebeck, T. (1982). Medication and reinforcement within a token programme for disturbed mentally retarded residents. *Applied Research in Mental Retardation, 3,* 21–36.

Stein, D. J., Keating, J., Zar, H. J., & Hollander, E. (1994). A survey of the phenomenology and pharmacology of compulsive and impulsive-aggressive symptoms in Prader-Willi syndrome. *Journal of Neuropsychiatry, 6,* 23–29.

Stein, L., & Belluzi, J. D. (1989). Cellular investigations of behavioral reinforcement. *Neuroscience and Biobehavioral Reviews, 13,* 69–80.

Tarpley, H. D., & Schroeder, S. R. (1979). Comparison of DRO and DRI on rate of suppression of self-injurious behavior. *American Journal of Mental Deficiency, 84,* 188–194.

Thompson, T. (1984). Behavioral mechanisms of drug dependence. In T. Thompson, P. B. Dews, & J. E. Barrett (Eds.), *Advances in behavioral pharmacology* (pp. 2–45). Orlando, FL: Academic Press.

Thompson, T. (1986). Issues in developmental behavioral pharmacology. In N. A. Krasnegor, D. B. Gray, & T. Thompson (Eds.), *Developmental behavioral pharmacology: Vol. 8. Advances in Behavioral Pharmacology* (pp. 3–20). Hillsdale, NJ: Erlbaum.

Thompson, T., & Grabowski, J. G. (1972). *Reinforcement schedules and multioperant analysis.* New York: Appleton-Century-Crofts.

Thompson, T., Hackenberg, T., Cerutti, D., Baker, D., & Axtell, S. (1994). Opioid antagonist effects on self-injury in adults with mental retardation: Response form and location as determinants of medication effects. *American Journal of Mental Retardation, 99,* 85–102.

Thompson, T., Hackenberg, T. D., & Schaal, D. W. (1991). Pharmacological treatments for behavior problems in developmental disabilities. *Treatment of destructive behaviors in persons with developmental disabilities* (pp. 343-440) (NIH Publication No. 91-2410). Bethesda, MD: National Institutes of Health.

Thompson, T., & Hollon, S. D. (1999). Behavioral and cognitive-behavioral interventions. In M. H. Ebert, P. T. Loosen, & B. Nurcombe (Eds.), *Current diagnosis and treatment in psychiatry.* New York: Appleton & Lange.

Thompson, T., & Lubinski, D. (1986). Units of analysis and kinetic structure of behavioral repertoires. *Journal of the Experimental Analysis of Behavior, 46,* 219–242.

Thompson, T., Robinson, J., Dietrich, M., Farris, M., & Sinclair, V. (1996). Architectural features and perceptions of community residences for people with mental retardation. *American Journal on Mental Retardation, 101,* 292–313.

Thompson, T., & Schuster, C. R. (1968). *Behavioral pharmacology.* Englewood Cliffs, NJ: Prentice Hall.

Touchette, P. E., MacDonald, R. F., & Langer, S. N. (1985). A scatter plot for identifying stimulus control of problem behavior. *Journal of Applied Behavior Analysis, 18,* 343–351.

Tseng, L., Loh, H. H., & Li, C. H. (1976). b-endorphin as a potent analgesic by intravenous injection. *Nature, 263,* 239–240.

Vitello, S. J., Atthowe, J. M., & Cadwell, J. (1983). Determinants of community placement of institutionalized mentally retarded persons. *American Journal of Mental Deficiency, 87,* 539–545.

Waldbillig, R. J. (1979). The role of the dorsal and medial raphe in the inhibition of muricide. *Brain Research, 160,* 341–346.

Weeks, M., & Gaylord-Ross, R. (1981). Task difficulty and aberrant behavior in severely handicapped students. *Journal of Applied Behavior Analysis, 14,* 449–463.

Wei, E., & Loh, H. (1976). Physical dependence on opiate-like peptides. *Science, 193,* 1262–1263.

Weizman, R., Weizman, A., Tyano, S., Szekely, G., Weissman, B. A., & Sarne, Y. (1984). Humoral-endorphin blood levels in autistic, schizophrenic, and healthy subjects. *Psychopharmacology, 82,* 368–370.

White, S. M., Kucharik, R. F., & Moyer, J. A. (1991). Effects of serotonergic agents on isolation-induced aggression. *Pharmacology Biochemistry & Behavior, 39,* 729–736.

Wieseler, N. A., Hanson, R. H., Chamberlain, T. P., & Thompson, T. (1988). Stereotypic behavior of mentally retarded adults adjunctive to a positive reinforcement schedule. *Research in Developmental Disabilities, 9,* 393–403.

Willemsen-Swinkels, S. H., Buitelaar, J. K., Weijnen, F. G., Thijssen, J. H., & Van Engeland, H. (1996). Plasma beta-endorphin concentrations in people with learning disability and self-injurious behavior and/or autistic behavior. *British Journal of Psychiatry, 168,* 105–109.

Willer, J. C., Dehen, H., & Cambier, J. (1981). Stress induced analgesia in humans. *Science, 212,* 680–691.

Winterling, V., Dunlap, G., & O'Neill, R. E. (1987). The influence of task variation on the aberrant behaviors of autistic students. *Education and Treatment of Children, 10,* 105–119.

Wise, R. A. (1982). Neuroleptics and operant behavior: The anhedonia hypothesis. *Behavioral and Brain Sciences, 5,* 39–53.

Woods, J. H., Herling, S., & Young, A. M. (1981). Comparison of discriminative and reinforcing stimulus characteristics of morphine-like opioids and two met-enkephalin analogues. *Neuropeptides, 1,* 409–419.

Zarevics, P., & Setler, P. E. (1979). Simultaneous rate-independent assessment of intracranial self-stimulation: Evidence for direct involvement of dopamine in brain reinforcement mechanisms. *Brain Research, 169,* 499–512.

Author Note

The authors gratefully acknowledge the support provided in part by Public Health Service Core Grant P30 HD15052 and Research Grant R01 HD22415 from the National Institute of Child Health and Human Development of Health to Vanderbilt University. Portions of this chapter are based on "Neurobehavioral Mechanisms of Drug Action in Developmental Disabilities" by T. Thompson, M. Egli, F. J. Symons, & D. Delaney, 1994, in T. Thompson & D. B. Gray (Eds.), *Destructive Behavior in Developmental Disabilities: Diagnosis and Treatment* (pp. 133–180), ©1994 by Sage. Reprinted by permission of Sage Publications, Inc.

Monitoring Psychotropic Medication
"You Tell Me It's the Institution, Well, You Know, You Better Free Your Mind Instead"

John E. Kalachnik
University of South Carolina
Columbia, SC

The purpose of this chapter is not to disparage the community model or advocate a return to an institutional model. Rather, it is to review proper psychotropic medication monitoring concepts no matter what the location to ensure that individuals with developmental disabilities are professionally served in this area. The chapter is organized into four sections: reasons for concern, brief historical perspective, basic concepts, and applied methods. The goal is to provide *workable, believable, and effective* information allowing the reader to objectively review psychotropic medication monitoring views and practices. Within the chapter, the terms *psychopharmacologic* and *psychotropic* are used interchangably. [1]

Reasons for Concern

The unusual title of this chapter originates from the song "Revolution" (Beatles, 1968). The point of the recording, at least to the author, was that efforts to effect mass change become excessively enthusiastic, exclusively assign causes of problems to existing institutions, and expediently assume that change in and of itself solves a problem. Underlying questions and rudimentary procedures necessary to correct or minimize a problem are overlooked, and, as a result, the problem insidiously manifests itself over time in the new system.

Over the past 25 years, a literal revolution has occurred in the field of mental retardation and developmental disabilities in that a community-based model has replaced a state-operated institutional model. Over 40 state institutions have closed, and closures continue. The number of individuals residing in state-operated facilities will be fewer than 55,000 by the year 2000 compared to 149,169 in 1977 (Braddock, Fujiura, Hemp, Mitchell, & Bachelder, 1991). While the benefits of this change are obvious, the community-based model is not immune from "Revolution's" message. For example, the source of problems and the assignment of blame is vividly captured by the title of MacNamara's (1994) article, "The Mansfield Training School Is Closed: The Swamp Has Been Finally Drained." The difficulty of objectively examining underlying questions and the possibility that fundamental procedures may have been overlooked are exemplified by the considerable controversy generated by the suggestion that mortality rates may be higher in the community-based model (Gettings, 1996; Strauss & Kastner, 1996). In short, "it can't possibly be" (*you tell me it's the institution*) when an underlying issue may have been overlooked (*you better free your mind instead*).

---

[1] The term *psychoactive drug* is often used interchangeably with *psychotropic drug* or *psychopharmacologic drug*. Technically, however, a psychoactive drug is defined as any substance that produces behavioral, emotional, or cognitive change, whereas a psychotropic drug is restricted to psychoactive drugs specifically prescribed to produce such change (Aman, 1984). In this schema, the caffeine in a cup of coffee is a psychoactive drug because it may produce behavioral, emotional, or cognitive change, but it is not a psychotropic drug because it is not specifically prescribed to produce such change. Fluoxetine (Prozac), on the other hand, is a psychotropic drug (as well as a psychoactive drug) since it is specifically prescribed to produce behavioral, emotional, or cognitive change in relation to depression.

Over this same 25 years (1972–1997), the use of psychotropic medication with individuals with developmental disabilities has been the focus of considerable controversy and legal activity (Beyer, 1988; Singh, Guernsey, & Ellis, 1992; Sprague, 1982). Three facts characterized the use of psychotropic medication with individuals with developmental disabilities in the late 1960s and 1970s. First, little scientific evidence existed for the efficacy of psychotropic medication in treating behavior problems of individuals with mental retardation (Sprague & Werry, 1971). Second, over 50% of residents in state-operated facilities were prescribed psychotropic medication with antipsychotic medication comprising the overwhelming majority of use (Lipman, 1970; Lipman, DiMascio, Reatig, & Kirson, 1978). And third, little or no data existed as to the extent of psychotropic medication use in community-based facilities (Lipman, 1982). Most of the controversy and activity, therefore, revolved around antipsychotic medication use in state-operated institutions (Plotkin & Gill, 1979). This was logical because this was where most people with mental retardation who received nonfamily-based residential support lived. A massive amount of litigation and regulation subsequently occurred to correct the misuse of psychotropic medication in state institutions (Singh et al., 1992; Sprague, 1982; Sprague & Galliher, 1988).

In view of this activity and the deinstitutionalization movement, it is seductive to conclude that psychotropic medication misuse was an institutional problem (*you tell me it's the institution*), especially in light of national survey data that show lower psychotropic medication use in community-based compared to state-operated facilities and lower psychotropic medication use in smaller compared to larger congregate care settings (Harper & Wadsworth, 1993; Hill, Balow, & Bruinicks, 1985). However, four items, each relatively insipid until taken as a whole and placed within the current social and economic trends, suggest that unless basic monitoring questions are asked, psychotropic medication misuse may insidiously become just as much a major concern over the next 25 years in the community-based model as it was over the past 25 years in the state-operated model (*you better free your mind instead*). These items relate to the extent of psychotropic medication, use-setting size differences, regulatory oversight, and physician concerns.

Psychotropic Medication Use

The first item involves close examination of national data on psychotropic medication use data in community-based and state-operated facilities. While overall psychotropic medication use has decreased since the early 1970s, the difference between community-based and state-operated facilities is only about 10%, at 29% and 39% respectively (Hill et al., 1985). At least some of this difference is due to higher antipsychotic medication use for state-operated facility admissions and readmissions compared to discharges (Harder, Kalachnik, Jensen, & Feltz, 1987; Wigal et al., 1994).

Approximately 80% of those prescribed a psychotropic medication, whether in community-based or state-operated facilities, are still prescribed an antipsychotic medication (Hill, Balow, & Bruinicks, 1985). A recent nonnational study of 1,101 clients in 120 community group homes indicated these figures have not dramatically changed, in that 27% of clients were prescribed a psychotropic medication, and, of these, 78% were prescribed an antipsychotic medication (Aman, Sarphare, & Burrow, 1995). Therefore, whether in community-based or state-operated facilities, antipsychotic medications continue to comprise the overwhelming majority of psychotropic medication use despite advances in the functional analysis of problem behavior, especially aggression and self-injurious behavior, in terms of representing either a specific behavioral-pharmacological hypothesis or an underlying psychiatric condition such as depression, bipolar disorder, or obsessive-compulsive disorder where other medications would be more appropriate (Gedye, 1992; Lewis, Bodfish, Powell, & Golden, 1995; Lowry, 1994; Schaal & Hackenberg, 1994; Sovner & Lowry, 1990; Thompson, Egli, Symons, & Delaney, 1994).

Smaller and Larger Settings

The second item involves close examination of lower psychotropic medication use in smaller group settings compared to larger congregate care settings. *Congregate* is usually defined as 15 beds or more, and *smaller group* is usually defined as fewer than 15 beds. Approximately 42% of community group homes are 15 beds or more (Cunningham & Mueller, 1991). Historically, congregate settings have provided for more severe disabilities under more restrictive conditions (Aman, Field, & Bridgman, 1985). Even when comparisons are controlled for behavior severity, individuals living in congregate settings are older and reside there longer (Harper & Wadsworth, 1993). These characteristics coincide with recent data suggesting high psychotropic drug use with elderly adults with mental retardation (Pary, 1993). Researchers such as Harper and Wadsworth (1993) and Aman and Singh (1991) stress that the use of psychotropic medication in any setting is a complex phenomenon involving caregivers' perceptions and attitudes, staff educational level, agency treatment philosophy, prescriber expertise and prescribing habits, and living environment quality. A recent community-based antipsychotic medication reduction study found the only significant variable associated with the successful reduction of antipsychotic medication (defined as 50% or more of the study entry dose) was a greater level of staff training on how to deal with problem behaviors and how to prevent them in the first place (Ahmed, 1997). Overall, a smaller community-based facility in comparison to a state-operated facility does not in and of itself guarantee lower and proper psychotropic medication use.

Regulatory Oversight

The third item involves close examination of regulatory oversight of community-based and state-operated facilities. Rinck, Guidry, and Calkins (1989) found in a review of all 50 states plus the District of Columbia that fewer states had psychotropic medication statutes or regulations (64% vs. 84%) and department operation manuals (37% vs. 69%) for individuals residing in community-based facilities

compared to state-operated facilities. Further, these investigators noted that fewer states required community-based facilities to adhere to basic psychotropic medication monitoring principles. For example, only 58% of states required community-based facilities to provide psychotropic medication target behaviors (vs. 90% for institutions), only 62% required community-based facilities to use specific methods to evaluate psychotropic medication efficacy in a plan (vs. 96% for institutions), only 56% required community-based facilities to provide periodic behavioral data (vs. 90% for institutions), only 58% required community-based facilities to inform a client's guardian about potential benefits and risks when a psychotropic medication was first prescribed (vs. 88% for institutions), and only 18% required community-based facilities to conduct formal side-effect assessments such as for tardive dyskinesia when antipsychotic medication was prescribed (vs. 61% for institutions). Within this context, in a number of states community-based, Medicaid-waivered sites are being exempted from and not surveyed under federal regulations for intermediate care facilities for the mentally retarded (ICF-MR). Regulation to the point of creative interference, excessive paper compliance, micromanagement, and an antimedication attitude must be guarded against (Holburn, 1992; Jacobson & Otis, 1992). Overall, however, history teaches that regulation usually occurs because of system failure and the inability of professionals to put their own houses in order (Sparr & Smith, 1990) and that without some form of regulatory oversight, it is only a matter of time before problems emerge, reemerge, or intensify (e.g., the savings and loan crisis, meat inspection, etc.).

Physician Concerns

The fourth item involves close examination of physician observations related to the community-based model. In a survey of 342 Maine physicians serving individuals with mental retardation in the community, Minihan, Dean, and Lyons (1993) found that psychotropic medication was the second most frequent treatment strategy. Ninety percent of physicians indicated the greatest obstacle to proper clinical management was the poor quality of medical records and information. Other problems were cognitive and verbal limitations of clients that hindered diagnosis and treatment (77%), difficulty communicating with multiple caregivers (57%), and not knowing who was authorized to give informed consent (53%). Further, 91% described Medicaid reimbursement as inadequate to cover the costs of managing the care of patients with mental retardation, 70% identified as a priority training to help caregivers and parents to become better medical informants, and 75% identified as a priority the need for a pamphlet describing a state's informed consent policies. Next to clinical options for behavior problem treatment (51%) and seizure disorder management (49%), physicians rated the prescribing and monitoring of psychotropic medication (46%) as the highest priority for their own continuing education. Overall, physicians recognized existing problems and necessary actions surrounding proper psychotropic medication use and monitoring with developmentally disabled individuals in community-based facilities.

Social and Economic Trends

Placing these issues within formal and informal social and economic trends increases the potential for psychotropic medication misuse in the community-based model. As state-operated facilities close, more severely behaviorally challenged individuals are being transferred to community-based facilities. Fewer professional staff such as nurses, behavior analysts, psychologists, and other types of therapists are on-site. Funding and reimbursement are being decreased. The multidisciplinary team model is being strained due to physical separation of members and the time and communication problems resulting from such separation. Antiregulatory views predominate, and state regulatory oversight and educational efforts are being replaced by

managed health care contracts. The *magic bullet*[2] has reemerged because of economic pressures, newer psychotropic medications, and the view that these newer and safer medications make concern about overuse and misuse a concern of the past. Staff educational requirements are being reduced, as could be predicted by a higher community-based facility turnover rate and wages averaging 31% less than state-operated facilities which is only 3% above the poverty line for a family of three (Mitchell & Braddock, 1993, 1994).

Historical Perspective

This section presents a brief history of psychotropic medication, the development of concern in relation to individuals with developmental disabilities, and the major events defining the proper use and monitoring of psychotropic medication. In relation to monitoring, we present the recent International Consensus Conference on Psychopharmacology guidelines (Kalachnik et al., 1998) and Health Care Financing Administration (HCFA, 1996) general safety precautions. This section may prove useful for readers who are not familiar with the history surrounding the development of contemporary psychotropic medication use and monitoring concepts.

Development of Psychotropic Medication

The development of chlorpromazine (Thorazine) in 1952 is heralded as the beginning of the modern psychopharmacology era. However, a number of discoveries occurred prior to this, including the use of chloral hydrate (1869), paraldehyde (1882), barbiturates (1903), rauwolfia serpentina—the natural basis for reserpine used to treat psychosis (1931), amphetamine (1937), phenytoin (1940), and lithium (1949). Indeed, human beings' attempts to alter behavior go back to antiquity with history and folklore recounting the use of laudanum (preparations

---

[2] The phrase *magic bullet* originated from a 1906 address by Paul Ehrlich in which he used the term to describe a specific chemical agent seeking out a specific target in an organism without any other effects or side effects. It originally was presented in terms of infection and bacterium. The term gained popularity as treatments for syphilis dramatically lowered the death rate (Lennard, Epstein, Bernstein, & Ransom, 1973; Silverman & Lee, 1974). Used in the vernacular, it generally refers to a perfect intervention which easily and conveniently solves a problem, does not create other problems, and makes other interventions or concerns unnecessary.

containing opium or a solution of opium in alcohol), alcohol, and herb use for purposes of stupor, sedation, or hypnosis (Ayd, 1991; Baldessarini, 1980; Gadow & Poling, 1988; Harvey, 1980; Kaplan & Sadock, 1988).

Few published studies of individuals with developmental disabilities occurred before the modern era other than Cutler's report on stimulants and Albert's report on glutamic acid in the 1940s (Gadow & Poling, 1988; Scheerenberger, 1983). Paraldehyde and hypnotic drugs such as chloral hydrate were generally prescribed to manage behavior before the modern era and were likely used with individuals with mental retardation as well (Thompson, Hackenberg, & Schaal, 1989).

The discovery of chlorpromazine in 1952 was rapidly followed by meprobamate (Miltown) in 1954 which represented the beginning of modern sedatives with antianxiety properties; iproniazid (no longer available) as an antidepressant in 1957 which represented the beginning of monoamine oxidase inhibitors; chlordiazepoxide (Librium) development in 1957 which represented the beginning of benzodiazepine antianxiety agents; imipramine (Tofranil) in 1958 which represented the beginning of tricyclic antidepressant agents; and haloperidol (Haldol) in 1958, which represented the development of antipsychotic agents other than phenothiazines. As time has continued, newer medications with fewer side effects (e.g., the selective serotonin reuptake inhibitors such as the antidepressant sertraline [Zoloft]) or able to help a treatment-resistant subgroup (e.g., the antipsychotic clozapine [Clozaril]) have been developed in these classes.

Development of Psychotropic Medication Concerns

Given these events, concerns about the misuse of psychotropic medication with individuals with mental retardation appeared as early as 1958 when Theodore Greiner observed:

...in the years to come, the retarded may claim an all-time record, of having the greatest variety and the largest tonnage of chemical agents shoveled into them....If your aim is

helping the retarded, I urge you to avoid the casual clinical trial of drugs. Make them good trials, or don't make them at all. (Greiner as cited in Gadow & Poling, 1988, p. 13)

Two seminal studies established a scientific basis for the concerns surrounding the use of psychotropic medication. In 1967 Lipman conducted the first scientific survey of psychotropic medication use with individuals with mental retardation. He concluded:

Unless the writer's radar equipment has seriously failed, it would seem that, to an overwhelming degree, psychotropic drugs instead of paraldehyde and camisoles [straight-jackets] are being used for controlling the behavior of the aggressive, assaultive, difficult-to-manage hyperactive patient. (Lipman, 1967; 1970, p. 393)

In 1971 Sprague and Werry reviewed more than 180 published psychotropic drug studies with individuals with developmental disabilities in terms of scientific methodology and concluded:

Very few empirically verified generalizations can be made about psychotropic drugs with the mentally retarded, yet it is just as clear that this series of methodologically weak, experimentally poor, and statistically inept studies have not provided a fair, sensitive measure of the behavioral effects of the drugs, effects which are routinely assumed to be present considering the widespread use of these drugs. (p. 168)

These concerns went largely unheeded and set the stage for literally dozens of individual and class-action lawsuits (Sprague, 1975, 1982; Sprague & Galliher, 1988).

Events Defining Proper Psychotropic Medication Use and Monitoring

The foundation for proper psychotropic medication use and monitoring with individuals with developmental disabilities derives

TABLE 9.1

Major Events Defining Proper Use and Monitoring of Psychotropic Medication With Individuals With Developmental Disabilities

Year	Source [1]	Type	Comment
1970	Freeman	Professional	One of the earliest set of professional recommendations. Emphasized: (1) environmental analysis and differentiation between situations requiring psychotropic medication and psychosocial intervention; (2) education or psychotherapy even when psychotropic medication prescribed; (3) family and individual involvement and education about side effects; (4) side effects monitoring and "reporting" method; (5) response "reporting" system; and (6) reduction to lowest maintenance dose.
1971	Accreditation Council for Facilities for the Mentally Retarded (ACFMR)	Accreditation	First and original psychotropic medication standard on May 5, 1971 within institutional standards: "Chemical restraint shall not be used excessively, as punishment, for the convenience of staff, as a substitute for program, or in quantities that interfere with a resident's habilitation program." (p. 22)
1972	*Wyatt v. Stickney* [2] (Alabama)	Legal (U.S. District Court)	First and original class-action lawsuit. Incorporated 1971 ACFMR chemical restraint statement, changed "chemical restraint" to "medication," and required recording of drug effect and dose change on behavior.
1973	ACFMR	Accreditation	Incorporated 1971 chemical restraint statement into community facility standards. Changed "chemical restraint" to "medication."
1974	Department of Health, Education and Welfare (DHEW)[3]	Regulatory (federal)	First set of federal regulations. Sole psychotropic medication statement is exact 1971 ACFMR chemical restraint statement.
1974	Food and Drug Administration (FDA) Advisory Panel [4]	Professional	FDA Advisory Panel formed after Mental Health Law Project petitioned FDA to stop the unapproved (indication) use of antipsychotic medication. Recommendations leading to package insert changes included discouraging daily doses greater than 500 mg of chlorpromazine (Thorazine) 400 mg of thioridazine (Mellaril), little evidence of efficacy beyond 6 months, potential learning performance interference, and periodic reduction to ascertain continued need.
1976	*Welsch v. Likins* [2] (Minnesota; also includes 1977 *Welsch v. Dirkswager*)	Legal (U.S. District Court	Class action lawsuit expanding Wyatt. Required specific target behaviors, baseline, data collection method such as time sample or frequency count, data to evaluate efficacy after initiation or dose or drug change, and "drug holidays" to determine continued need.
1977	Accreditation Council for Services for Mentally Retarded and Other Developmentally Disabled Persons (ACMRDD)	Accreditation	Institutional and community standards combined and 1971/1973 psychotropic medication statement expanded to incorporate interdisciplinary team concept, use within overall program plan, target behaviors, specific data methods to judge efficacy, gradual dose reduction, agency oversight committee review, and written informed consent.

Table 9.1. Continued

Year	Source [1]	Type	Comment
1978	Health Care Financing Administration (HCFA)	Regulatory (federal)	Revised 1974 regulations. Little change except in terms of rights: (1) right to refuse treatment, participate in planning own care, and receive full information; and (2) informed consent. Chemical restraint emergency use added and defined as injury to self.
1978	*Wuori v. Zitnay* [2] (Maine)	Legal (U.S. District Court)	Applied standards to any psychotropic medication (most cases had only specified antipsychotics). Required: (1) specific method to assess and monitor side effects; (2) coordinated and monitored annual gradual reduction to determine lowest dose; and (3) psychopharmacology consultant review for situations such as polypharmacy or continued antipsychotic medication use if serious side effects.
1980	*Clites v. Iowa* [2] (Iowa)	Legal (State Court)	First tardive dyskinesia (TD) case tried to verdict with extensive written opinion. $750,000 awarded and upheld on appeal. Required antipsychotic medication monitoring for TD, diagnosis, actions if occurrence to minimize impact, and education as part of informed consent.
1986	Sovner	Professional	Quality assurance items to evaluate psychotropic medication use including proper assessment and diagnosis, target behaviors to monitor efficacy, side effects and TD monitoring, informed consent, inappropriate polypharmacy, frequent changes, and excessive PRN use.
1987	Accreditation Council on Services for People With Developmental Disabilities (ACDD)	Accreditation	Stressed functional analysis of behavior and set limits on the emergency use of psychotropic medication before interdisciplinary team had to meet and address problem.
1988	HCFA	Regulatory (federal)	Major revision of 1978 regulations: (1) incorporated professional, legal, and accreditation standards developed over the previous decade; (2) quarterly psychotropic medication review unless no progress, in which case, meetings as often as necessary; and (3) gradual reduction at least annually coordinated with interdisciplinary team unless documented contraindication.
1990	American Psychiatric Association	Professional	Task force report on psychiatric services in mental retardation. Stressed: (1) proper diagnosis as basis for rational pharmacotherapy, (2) differentiation of psychotropic medication use for behavioral control versus psychiatric condition, and (3) need for psychiatric training to teach the interplay of psychosocial and biomedical factors, working with interdisciplinary teams, and a wide variety of treatment modalities.
1993	Accreditation Council on Services for People With Disabilities (ACD)	Accreditation	Major revision emphasizing outcome measures.
1995	International Consensus Conference on Psychopharmacology [5]	Professional	Specific psychotropic medication guidelines developed based upon 6-year formal consensus process involving leading authorities in the field (1991-1997; published 1998).

Continued next page

Table 9.1. Continued

Year	Source [1]	Type	Comment
1996	HCFA	Regulatory	Development of general and specific psychotropic medication safety precautions incorporating most accreditation, legal, and professional recommendations involving rational diagnostic and empirical monitoring models. Closely parallels 1995 International Consensus Conference guidelines.

[1] Unless otherwise indicated, the source and year is the reference for each entry. Full citations are provided in the reference section.

[2] Litigation is based upon Sprague (1982). In-depth case information may be found there.

[3] The U.S. Department of Health, Education, and Welfare (DHEW) was renamed the Department of Health and Human Services (HHS) in 1977. The Health Care Financing Administration (HCFA) is a HHS subdivision involved in regulation, interpretative guidelines, survey, and funding.

[4] Lehr, Gilbert, Tatel, Foer, & Kahan, 1976; Lipman et al., 1978; Sprague, 1975.

[5] The reference for the full consensus conference publication is Reiss & Aman (1998). The reference for the psychotropic medication guidelines is Kalachnik et al. (1998).

from professional recommendations, litigation, regulation, and accreditation. While it is beyond the scope of this chapter to review these sources in detail, Table 9.1 presents a summary of the major historical events.

Several comments regarding these events are in order. Although presented in linear order for convenience, events interacted in an amorphous manner. It is important to place events within the context of the social and monetary forces in effect at the time, the alternative intervention and learning techniques developed with time, and the attitudinal changes occurring over time. Concepts have also evolved and should not be reviewed out of their historical context. For example, the mid-1970s "annual drug holiday" has been replaced by an in-depth psychotropic medication risk-benefit review conducted at least annually in relation to the underlying condition or hypothesis, treatment stage, risk factors, dose, side effects, index behavior data, quality of life, and concurrent nonpharmacological interventions. If reduction is deemed possible, a gradual reduction plan is developed to determine the lowest maintenance dose, which may be, but is not necessarily, zero medication. It should be remembered that the original drug holiday requirement occurred because in numerous situations psychotropic medication had been used for years in large doses for unknown, vague, or forgotten reasons, and little

or no data, records, or monitoring existed.

What is particularly interesting about this history of events is that despite differences between sources in terms of exact details, there is remarkable consistency as to what constitutes proper psychotropic medication use and monitoring. For example, differences of opinion exist in regard to oral versus written informed consent and the specific circumstances compromising a client's competency to give consent. However, except for emergencies, it is impossible to find a credible source advocating the use of psychotropic medication without informed consent. Additionally, and contrary to public opinion, federal regulations have chronologically followed and incorporated professional, legal, and accreditation findings and recommendations.

Recent Psychotropic Medication Use and Monitoring Guidelines

The most current paradigms for the proper use and monitoring of psychotropic medication with individuals with developmental disabilities are the guidelines developed by the International Consensus Conference on Psychopharmacology (Kalachnik et al., 1998) and the general safety precautions developed by the Health Care Financing Administration (HCFA, 1996). While the exact language differs, the two sources closely parallel each other. Indeed, the introduction to the HCFA document states:

The need for knowledge in this field is the fundamental reason the Nisonger Center convened an International Consensus Conference on Psychopharmacology in June, 1995, at the Ohio State University. The Conference proceedings, an extensive consensus from the best minds in the fields of psychopharmacology and developmental disabilities, discuss general principles of differential diagnosis in persons with developmental disabilities who suffer from mental illness....The "Safety Precautions" in this document focus on surveyor and provider education and the relationship between principles of psychopharmacological [sic] and regulations governing participation of facilities in the Medicaid program. These "Safety Precautions" are compatible with the Nisonger Handbook. The use of both will serve to build practices, skills, and experience that will create a safer and more empowering environment for persons with developmental disabilities. (p. 2)

Table 9.2 presents the 14 International Consensus guidelines in a "do" and "don't" format. Table 9.3 presents the 10 HCFA general safety precautions. It is critical to note that *these tables provide only global summary statements. More detailed information regarding exceptions and the range of clinical variations are contained in the sources.* For example, the International Consensus Conference document provides a *what it means* and *what it does not mean* chart for each guideline. HCFA further details each general safety precaution and provides specific safety precautions for antianxiety, sedative-hypnotic, antiepileptic, antipsychotic, antidepressant, and beta-blocker medications. (Information on obtaining the documents is presented at the foot of the tables.)

Basic Concepts

This section reviews six basic concepts related to proper use and monitoring of psychotropic

medication: (a) the formal definition of a psychotropic medication, (b) the biopsychosocial model, (c) a coordinated multidisciplinary treatment plan, (d) the rational-empirical model, (e) short-term versus long-term psychotropic medication use, and (f) informed consent. These concepts provide the foundation upon which applied methodology is built.

Psychotropic Medication Definition

A psychopharmacologic medication is any drug prescribed to stabilize or improve mood, mental status, or behavior.

This is the definition provided by the International Psychopharmacology Consensus and the federal safety precautions (HCFA, 1996; Kalachnik et al., 1998). The phrase *stabilize or improve* is now used instead of words such as *control, modify,* or *normalize.* Psychopharmacologic medication is not intended to control, modify, or normalize an individual. Like any medication, the purpose of psychopharmacologic medication is to improve or stabilize a condition that is interfering with a person's quality of life.

Table 9.4 lists common psychotropic medications as of 1999. Included are antipsychotic, antianxiety, antidepressant, antimania, stimulant, and sedative-hypnotic classifications (American Psychiatric Association [APA], 1992). A "miscellaneous" category of other medications sometimes used as psychotropic medication is also included.

Defining psychotropic medication is important for several reasons. Although a list like that in Table 9.4 can be constructed, new psychotropic medications will be developed, and older, infrequently used but still available medications may not be included. More important, drugs typically classified as psychotropic may have other indications. For example, the antianxiety agent diazepam (Valium) may be prescribed for spasticity and the stimulant methylphenidate (Ritalin) may be prescribed for narcolepsy. Similarly, drugs not typically classified as psychotropic may have psychiatric indications; for instance, the antiepileptic carbamazepine (Tegretol) may be prescribed for certain affective diagnoses.

TABLE 9.2

International Consensus Conference on Psychopharmacology Guidelines for the Use of Psychotropic Medication With Individuals With Developmental Disabilities [1-4]

Do's	Don'ts
1. Treat any substance prescribed to improve or stabilize mood, mental status, or behavior as a psychotropic medication.	1. Don't use psychotropic drugs excessively, for convenience, as a substitute for meaningful psychosocial services, or in quantities that interfere with quality of life activity.
2. Use psychotropic medication within a coordinated multidisciplinary care plan.	2. Avoid frequent drug and dose changes.
3. Use psychotropic medication based upon a psychiatric diagnosis or a specific behavioral-pharmacologic hypothesis and only after conducting complete diagnostic and functional assessments.	3. Avoid intraclass polypharmacy and minimize interclass polypharmacy to the degree possible in order to decrease the likelihood of patient noncompliance and side effects.
4. Obtain written informed consent from the individual or guardian and establish a therapeutic alliance involving all decisions.	4. Minimize to the degree possible: Long-term PRN orders Use of long-acting sedative-hypnotics (e.g., chloral hydrate [Noctec]) Long-term use of short-acting sedative hypnotics (e.g., temazepam [Restoril]) Long-term use of benzodiazepine anti-anxiety medications (e.g., diazepam [Valium]) High antipsychotic medication doses Long-term use of anticholinergic medication (e.g., benztropine [Cogentin])
5. Track treatment efficacy by defining objective index behaviors and quality of life outcomes and measure them using empirical methods.	
6. Monitor for side effects using standardized assessment instruments.	
7. Monitor for tardive dyskinesia using standardized assessment instruments if antipsychotic or other dopamine blocking medications are prescribed.	
8. Conduct clinical and data reviews on a regular and systematic basis.	
9. Strive to use the lowest "optimal effective dose."	
10. Monitor drug and monitoring practices through a peer or external quality review or improvement group.	

---

[1] The reference for the complete International Consensus Conference publication is Reiss & Aman (1998). The reference for the guidelines document is Kalachnik et al. (1998) which is contained in Reiss & Aman. Full citations are provided in the reference section.

[3] The numbers used here do not match the actual International Consensus guideline number (e.g., "don't" item 1 is actually Guideline 2). The Guidelines Consensus Committee placed the 14 guidelines into a series of "do's" and "don'ts" for purposes of overview convenience.

[3] It is critical to: (a) not take the guidelines out of context and (b) read the entire document for exceptions and the range of clinical situations. For example, "Avoid frequent drug and dose changes" is not meant to apply to a documented titration plan.

[4] *The International Consensus Handbook* may be purchased by contacting: AAMR Publications Distributions Center, P.O. Box 25, Annapolis Junction, MD 20701, (301) 604-1340.

TABLE 9.3

Health Care Financing Administration General Safety Precautions for Psychopharmacological Medications for People With Developmental Disabilities [1-3]

General Safety Precaution	Some of What It States [4]
1. Rule Out Other Causes	Before beginning psychopharmacological medication, the facility has substantial information to demonstrate that it considers and rules out other reasons such as medical, environmental, or psychosocial causes for the behavioral or psychiatric symptom.
2. Collect Baseline Data	Before beginning psychopharmacological medication, the facility has substantial information to demonstrate that it collects baseline data on specific objectively defined target behaviors or psychiatric symptoms for a sufficient time of 2 to 4 weeks. In determining the baseline, the facility should use a recognized data collection method such as frequency count, duration recording, time sample, interval recording, rating scale, or some combination involving these methods.
3. State a Reasonable Hypothesis	The facility has stated a reasonable hypothesis of the underlying cause of the behavioral or psychiatric symptoms. This hypothesis includes the relationship or rationale between the person's symptoms and how the prescribed psychopharmacological medication will treat these symptoms to achieve the desired outcome.
4. Intervene in the Least Intrusive and Most Positive Way	The facility has substantial information to demonstrate that it attempted the least intrusive and most positive interventions to manage behavioral or psychiatric symptoms before it considered using psychopharmacological medication. Initially, the least intrusive and most positive intervention to treat behavioral or psychiatric symptoms may be the use of a psychopharmacological medication. However, nonpharmacological active treatment programs specific to the behavior or psychiatric condition should be started within a reasonable period of time.
5. Monitor for Adverse Drug Reactions (ADRs)	The facility has substantial information to demonstrate that it adequately monitors for adverse drug reactions. If ADRs do occur, the facility has substantial information to show why the ADR is not significantly impairing the person's functional staus or quality of life or why the psychopharmacological medication is not changed, discontinued, or decreased in dose. The term "adequately monitors" includes the periodic assessment of the person with a standardized side effects rating scale or checklist.
6. Collect Outcome Data	The facility has substantial information, including quality of life information, to demonstrate that it determines and supports with objective data that the psychopharmacological medication achieves the desired outcome. Objective data include the use of a recognized data collection method for the person's target behavior(s) or psychiatric symptom(s) and comparison to available baseline data. In determining the outcome, the facility should use a recognized data collection method such as frequency count, duration recording, time sample, interval recording, rating scale, or some combination involving these methods.

Continued next page

Table 9.3. Continued

General Safety Precaution	Some of What It States [4]
7. Start Low and Go Slow	The facility has substantial information to demonstrate that it uses low initial and maintenance doses of psychopharmaological medication commensurate with age, weight, and symptomatology to achieve the desired outcome, minimize adverse drug reactions, and maintain optimal functional status.
8. Periodically Consider Gradual Dose Reduction	The facility has substantial information to demonstrate that unless clinically contraindicated it periodically attempts to gradually reduce the dose of psychopharmacological medication to determine if the person's behavioral or psychiatric symptoms can be treated with a lower dose or whether the psychopharmacological medication can be discontinued altogether. Any attempt to reduce the dose should be coordinated with the interdisciplinary team, in a carefully monitored program.
9. Maintain Active Treatment Objectives	The facility has substantial information supported with objective data to demonstrate that the psychopharmacological medication is not causing the person to regress or to fail to progress in achieving the stated objectives in the individual program plan in comparison with measurements taken before and after psychopharmacological medication is started.
10. Maintain Optimal Functional Status	The facility has substantial information, supported with objective data, to demonstrate that the psychopharmacological medication is not diminishing the person's functional status from his or her baseline functional status measures. Loss of functional status is defined as a measurable loss of a person's previously possessed ability to function in one or more of the following ways: (a) activities of daily living such as locomotion, bathing, dressing, or eating; (b) cognition or thinking especially in memory and orientation; (c) communication; (d) continence, bladder, or bowel; or (e) motivation and interest in preferred activities.

[1] The reference for the safety precautions is the Health Care Financing Administration (1996). The full citation is provided in the reference section.

[2] It is critical to: (a) not take the guidelines out of context, and (b) read the entire document for exceptions and range of clinical situations. For example, "Collect Baseline Data" does not mean an individual already prescribed a psychotropic medication without a baseline must be removed from the psychotropic medication in order to obtain a baseline. In such a case, data would be collected under the current condition against which future drug or dose changes could be compared.

[3] A full copy of the general and specific safety precautions may be obtained by contacting Dr. Sam Kidder, Health Standards, Health Care Financing Administration, U.S. Department of Health and Human Services, 7500 Security Blvd., Baltimore, MD 21244-1850.

[4] While the statements listed are close to the original, some are not exact quotes. Some have been condensed or slightly reworded for ease of presentation.

TABLE 9.4
Examples of Psychotropic Medication as of 1999 [1]

ANTIDEPRESSANT

Generic Name	Trade Name
amitriptyline	Elavil/Endep
amoxapine*	Asendin
bupropion	Wellbutrin
citalopram	Celexa
clomipramine	Anafranil
desipramine	Norpramin
doxepin	Sinequan/Adapin
fluoxetine	Prozac
fluvoxamine	Luvox
imipramine	Tofranil
maprotiline	Ludiomil
mirtazapine	Remeron
nefazodone	Serzone
nortriptyline	Aventyl/Pamelor
paroxetine	Paxil
phenelzine	Nardil
protriptyline	Vivactil
sertraline	Zoloft
tranylcypromine	Parnate
trazodone	Desyrel
trimipramine	Surmontil
venlafaxine	Effexor

ANTIMANIA

lithium carbonate	Lithobid/Eskalith

ANTIPSYCHOTIC

Generic Name	Trade Name
chlorpromazine*	Thorazine
clozapine**	Clozaril
fluphenazine*	Prolixin/Permitil
haloperidol*	Haldol
loxapine*	Loxitane
mesoridazine*	Serentil
molindone*	Moban
olanzapine**	Zyprexa
perphenazine*	Trilafon
pimozide*	Orap
quetiapine**	Seroquel
risperidone**	Risperal
thioridazine*	Mellaril
thiothixene*	Navane
trifluoperazine*	Stelazine

ANTIANXIETY

Generic Name	Trade Name
alprazolam	Xanax
buspirone	BuSpar
chlorazepate diK	Tranxene
chlordiazepoxide	Librium
chlormezanone	Trancopal
diazepam	Valium
halazepam	Paxipam
hydroxyzine	Atarax/Vistaril
lorazepam	Ativan
meprobamate	Equanil/Miltown
oxazepam	Serax
prazepam	Centrax

SEDATIVE/HYPNOTIC

amobarbital	Amytal
chloral hydrate	Noctec
estazolam	ProSom
ethchlorvynol	Placidyl
flurazepam	Dalmane
glutethimide	Doriden
pentobarbital	Nembutal
quazepam	Doral
secobarbital	Seconal
temazepam	Restoril
triazolam	Halcion
zolpidem	Ambien

STIMULANT

amphetamine/d'amphet	Adderall
dextroamphetamine	Dexedrine
methlyphenidate	Ritalin
pemoline	Cylert

MISCELLANEOUS/OTHER

carbamazepine	Tegretol
clonadine	Catapres
clonazepam	Klonopin
naltrexone	Trexan
propranolol	Inderal
valproic acid	Depakene

[1] This is not a comprehensive list. There may be newer, less frequently used, or older drugs not on the list. Some drugs listed may in the future be removed from the market. Other trade names may exist and are not included.

* Associated with tardive dyskinesia (TD).

** "Atypical" antipsychotic medication. May not cause TD or may be associated with TD at a far lower rate than typical antipsychotic medication.

Because medications have different indications, the term psychotropic drug is an operational rather than a chemical definition. The only method to determine if a medication is a psychotropic medication for a specific individual is to ascertain the purpose for which it is prescribed.

The definition also provides a paradigm to more objectively determine if a medication not classified as a psychotropic medication is being used as such to avoid more professional assessment or psychotropic medication monitoring requirements. For example, sedation is a frequent side effect of the antihistamine diphenhydramine (Benedryl). Use of this medication without a formal assessment and a diagnosed condition such as parkinsonism, pruritus (severe itching), the common cold, or allergies for an individual with documented behavior problems would be an indicator to determine if diphenhydramine was in reality being used for behavior problems. Since the use of diphenhydramine to treat mood, mental status, or behavior is not indicated beyond the short-term treatment of insomnia, long-term use without a diagnosed condition would be an indicator to review for use as a chemical restraint.

The Biopsychosocial Model

The biopsychosocial model postulates that biological, psychological, and sociological aspects of care are interdependent, and each must be acknowledged and addressed in order to provide optimal patient care.

The biopsychosocial model was developed in 1977 by the physician George Engel (1977, 1980). Engel contended that traditional biomedicine (the medical model) was in crisis due to its adherence to a model of disease which was no longer adequate for the scientific tasks and social responsibilities of medicine and psychiatry. Reasons included (a) a *reductionistic* premise that complex phenomena are derived from molecular biology and that this ultimately can explain all biological events; (b) *mind-body dualism* or the doctrine that the mental is separate from the physical; and (c) *exclusionism* or the omission of whatever cannot be explained by the underlying reductionistic concept (in this case,

molecular biology). Such a model, Engel contended, resulted in nonhumanistic attitudes toward patients and undesirable, as well as expensive, practices such as unnecessary hospitalization, overuse of drugs, excessive surgery, and inappropriate use of diagnostic tests.

The biopsychosocial model, on the other hand, is based upon general systems theory developed in biology which incorporates natural hierarchy systems on a continuum from the minute such as molecules, cells, and tissues to the complex such as the person and his or her experiences, family, other people, community, and culture surrounding the individual. The basic premise is that the systems are interdependent and that an event at one level potentially affects systems at other levels. In order to provide optimal patient care, biological, psychological, and sociological aspects of care must be acknowledged and addressed. An example is hypertension. Genetic factors may be involved, and the condition may be treated with blood pressure medication. However, stress, diet, and exercise are also important factors. Optimal outcome is based upon a variable combination of medication and lifestyle changes depending on the individual.

The biopsychosocial model is not free of criticism. While endorsing it, Sadler and Hulgas (1992) noted three reasons why it has had limited success in changing prescriber behavior. First, within day-to-day problem solving, the systems hierarchy provides no functional priority of one level over another. Second, methodological limits are placed on the scope of medical inquiry. And third, economics plays a role in decision making. In order to encourage greater use of the biopsychosocial model on the day-to-day clinical level, they proposed the *three faces model* which consists of (1) *the epistemic aspect* (what is the problem?) (2) *the pragmatic aspect* (what actions need to be taken and what will be the consequences?), and (3) *the ethical aspect* (what value implications do my actions have?).

The value of the biopsychosocial (or three faces) model in relation to proper psychotropic medication use is that it avoids the often polemical demarcation of interventions into behavioral versus drug categories. Instead, it recognizes a variety of treatment modalities in relation to the characteristics of the individual and the outcome. On the one hand, it recognizes the value of biochemical interventions (psychotropic medication) for endogenous conditions such as depression, bipolar disorder, and schizophrenia, yet it does not ignore the influence of the environment on such conditions or the fact that psychotropic medication does not in and of itself teach a skill. On the other hand, it recognizes the value of psychosocial interventions (e.g., psychotherapy, behavior modification) for environmentally related problems yet does not ignore the interference of underlying biochemical conditions on learning or the fact that some environmentally related problems may be so pronounced that a psychotropic medication on a short- to intermediate-term basis may be necessary to stabilize the situation before learning can occur.

Overall, the biopsychosocial model is especially important in the care of individuals with developmental disabilities where active treatment has been a driving force for change. As noted by Bishop (1992) in a program outlining the proper use of psychopharmacologic medication:

> The biopsychosocial approach is further enhanced...because at the time that the aberrant behavior is initially identified, there is no immediate need to classify the behavior as either a functional psychiatric syndrome or a behavior dependent on an environmental or operationally conditioned process. All variables that may be maintaining the behavior are examined. Using this model, one is able to move beyond the biologically deterministic standpoint and beyond the stimulus response paradigm to an interactive biopsychosocial model of behavior and treatment. This is not a model designed to test a single theory of etiology, but, rather, a model in which different hypotheses regarding aberrant behavior and its treatment can be examined. (p. 288)

The Rational-Empirical Model

The use of psychotropic medication must be based upon a psychiatric diagnosis or a specific behavioral-pharmacological hypothesis resulting from a full diagnostic and functional assessment. Specific index behaviors and quality of life outcomes must be objectively defined, quantified, and tracked using recognized empirical measurement methods in order to evaluate the efficacy of psychotropic medication.

Since approximately 1990, psychopharmacology with individuals with developmental disabilities has moved to integrate the rational and empirical schools of thought. The *rational* revolves around controlling principles and underlying reasons; in short, diagnosis and psychiatry. The *empirical* revolves around verification through observation or experiment; in short, data and behavioral psychology. This shift has occurred for two reasons.

First, psychopharmacologic intervention based upon the topography of a behavior had not resulted in a consistent response to the same psychotropic medication across individuals with the same behavior because different psychological and neurochemical circumstances can manifest behavior with a similar form (Schaal & Hackenberg, 1994; Sovner & Hurley, 1989; Thompson, Egli, Symons, & Delaney, 1994). For example, aggression could be the result of (a) depression leading to the use of an antidepressant medication (e.g., aggression as a result of irritability or an escape response to demands to eat, get out of bed, or participate in social activities); (b) schizophrenia leading to the use of an antipsychotic medication (e.g., aggression as a result of delusions or hallucinations of danger); (c) obsessive compulsive disorder leading to the use of clomipramine (Anafranil) or fluvoxamine (Luvox) (e.g., aggression as a result of interfering with a ritual or activity); (d) organic personality disorder explosive type or episodic dyscontrol leading to the use of propranolol or Inderal (e.g., aggression as a result of specific stimulus conditions); or (e) environmental factors leading to the use of no medication (e.g., aggression because noise level is excessive combined with impersonal rough grooming assistance by staff).

Second, traditional psychiatric approaches to evaluating drug efficacy had not been successful with individuals with developmental disabilities (Sovner & Hurley, 1987).

A psychiatric diagnosis is generally based upon signs (observable events or behaviors) or symptoms (reports by the individual of feelings or behavior) fitting a standardized classification such as the *Diagnostic and Statistical Manual of Mental Disorders* (*DSM-IV*; American Psychiatric Association [APA], 1994) or the *International Classification of Diseases* (*ICD-10*; World Health Organization, 1992). Given a proper assessment to eliminate other causes, the diagnosis is combined with considerations such as other medical conditions or potential adverse effects which may contraindicate or limit a specific treatment for a specific individual. This leads to the selection of an intervention having the greatest likelihood of success. Empirical measurement is generally based upon the measurement of specific signs or symptoms because a diagnosis per se does not provide information about the intervention's actual effect or the most appropriate dose level (which may change over time) for an individual. Empirical measurement of signs and symptoms may also be of value in determining a diagnosis for individuals with limited verbal skills (Lowry & Sovner, 1992; Sovner, Fox, Lowry, & Lowry, 1993).

A psychiatric diagnosis may be difficult to establish for a number of individuals with developmental disabilities, or pronounced challenging behaviors may not be related to a psychiatric condition. In such cases, an underlying behavioral-pharmacologic hypothesis is established based upon a functional analysis, and an intervention selected based upon the hypothesis. The hypothesis and intervention is empirically tested through the measurement of specific behaviors. Thompson and Symons (Chapter 8, this volume) provide an outstanding in-depth discussion of the issues specific to pharmacological treatment within this type of analysis.

The diagnostic and behavioral-pharmacologic hypothesis models both view maladaptive behavior as a final common pathway reflecting an individual's response to environmental demands, physical discomfort, or disturbances in neurochemical and physiological function. Three general classes of environmental variables have been identified as contributing to maladaptive behavior (Schaal & Hackenberg, 1994). These are *positive reinforcement* such as attention or access to preferred objects, *negative reinforcement* such as escape from unpleasant or demand situations, and *sensory reinforcement* such as feedback arising from self-stimulation. Similarly, a maladaptive behavioral hierarchy has been developed for psychiatric use with individuals with developmental disabilities (Sovner & Hurley, 1989). The hierarchy involves *first order behavior* or primary changes such as mood or affect regulation (e.g., depression-related insomnia); *second order behavior* or increases in long-standing existing behavior following the onset or reoccurrence of a psychiatric condition (e.g., increases in self-injury which has been stabilized at low levels through environmental or psychosocial therapy but which increases such as in the depressive phase of a bipolar disorder); and *third order behavior* or behaviors which develop in response to the onset of a psychiatric condition or family or caregivers' responses to the individual (e.g., attention to tantrums as a result of panic attacks).

An example of the interplay between a psychiatric condition and operant behavioral principles is provided by Lowry (1994) who describes how the onset of a mood disorder such as depression may make normally rewarding activities such as eating and social interaction aversive. An individual who would otherwise enjoy these activities may not want to eat and may wish to be left alone, not participate in social activities, and stay in bed. Upon prompts or demands to comply ("it's time to get out of bed") or participate in such activity ("it's time to eat" or "it's time for the shopping trip to the mall"), the individual may display aggression or self-injurious behavior in order to avoid or escape the activity. This may prevent or terminate the aversive situation which, in turn, negatively reinforces the behavior and thereby increases its strength.

An in-depth assessment is essential because the goal is to see past nonspecific challenging behavior, determine the function of the behavior, and determine whether an underlying environmental-responsive behavior disorder or drug-responsive psychiatric disorder is present (Crabbe, 1989; Sovner & Hurley, 1989). Such an assessment addresses variables such as organic and medical pathology; psychosocial and environmental conditions; health status; current medications; the presence of a psychiatric condition; history, previous intervention, and results; and a functional analysis of behavior. A functional analysis of behavior considers what, if any, antecedents or consequences affect or control a behavior; if behavior represents a deficit, excess, or is situationally inappropriate; whether different patterns occur in different situations; and possible schedule-of-reinforcement effects.

It is important to avoid the following errors when conducting assessments for purposes of formulating a diagnosis or reasonable hypothesis from which to develop a care plan: (a) failure to recognize the contribution of the environment, (b) failure to recognize the presence of a psychiatric condition, (c) overdiagnosing psychosis and schizophrenia, (d) use of behavioral norms more appropriate for people without developmental disabilities, (e) assignment of a psychiatric diagnosis to more easily justify a pharmacologic intervention, and (f) viewing drugs and psychosocial interventions as either/or rather than a flexible combination in a constantly evolving relationship specific to the individual (Bishop, 1992; Crabbe, 1989; Gualtieri & Keppel, 1985; Rogoff, 1984; Werry, 1993).

Coordinated Multidisciplinary Care Plan

Psychotropic medication must be used within a coordinated multidisciplinary care plan designed to improve the individual's quality of life.

Psychotropic medication in and of itself is not a care plan. Behaviors or symptoms may worsen or improve and may do so in different settings. Behavior problems may not be entirely eliminated or may only return to previous

levels (Sovner & Hurley, 1987) meaning that the behavior or condition will still need to be addressed by the individual or others. While the stage is often set for learning to occur or a return to activities of normal daily living, psychotropic medication does not teach new skills or cognitive strategies. Additionally, psychotropic medication does not *prevent* psychiatric relapse, it lowers the *probability* of relapse (Schooler, 1993). A coordinated multidisciplinary care plan is important to address the interactive nature of biochemical, psychological, and sociological aspects of care (see Favell & McGimsey, Chapter 13, this volume).

A number of different professionals or responsible parties may be involved in developing an overall plan to teach skills or provide other therapy, monitor intervention, alter environmental stressors, provide client and family education, or identify prodromal signs or symptoms (behaviors or verbal reports of feelings that precede the challenging behavior of concern; e.g., not sleeping for three nights in a row may precede the manic phase of a bipolar disorder where hypersexuality is the major concern). The people involved may vary from individual to individual and plan to plan. If the prescriber is not responsible for coordinating the multidisciplinary care plan, the responsible party such as a case manager or family member must be clearly identified because care plan members must communicate and not work in isolation. An overall care plan and established coordinator is of particular importance when multiple prescribers are involved or when an individual is treated by a group practice where different physicians may be seen at different times (Davis et al., 1998). Prescribers and all care plan members do not have to attend every review, decision, or conference. Communication may occur via telephone, e-mail, fax, or interactive TV. The key variable is to establish a reciprocal method to exchange and share information in a timely manner.

Multidisciplinary team members, including the prescriber, are not the ones to *approve* the use of psychotropic medication within a multidisciplinary care plan. The individual, if competent, or his or her guardian does. Numerous problems can be avoided if the prescriber does not unilaterally prescribe psychotropic medication in a nonemergency situation without a full assessment outside of the coordinated multidisciplinary care plan approved by the individual or guardian. Similarly, numerous problems can be avoided if other multidisciplinary team members communicate relevant information in an organized manner to the prescriber, so the best decision regarding medication can be made, and do not interfere with medication decisions made by the prescriber within the parameters of the multidisciplinary care plan approved by the individual or guardian. Disagreements between multidisciplinary members regarding the use of psychotropic medication should be presented to the individual or guardian for a decision. If the individual is incompetent and no guardian exists, disagreements should be referred to appropriate peer or external review bodies (Davis et al., 1998). Whatever decision is reached, the strategy selected is monitored within the care plan to determine whether the client is benefiting or if change is required.

A common shortcoming in care plans is the failure to specify parameters of psychotropic medication use and alternatives in the event of nonresponse or side effects. This potentially leads to reactive instead of proactive planning, poor coordination among care team members, and violations of existing informed consent. While every possible situation cannot be anticipated, numerous problems can be avoided by specifying (a) the psychotropic medication dose and dosage range for the individual based upon factors such as the condition, symptomatology, treatment phase, and age; (b) upward ("start low and go slow") or downward ("if continued high, ask why") titration plans; (c) response timelines; (d) expected duration of use; (e) actions in the event of adverse reactions; (f) secondary or tertiary psychotropic medication treatment choices in the event of a nonresponse to the prescribed psychotropic medication; (g) review points to evaluate progress; (h) index behaviors and how data are to be objectively collected and summarized; and (i) outcome indicators.

Outcome indicators establish a benchmark to review expected progress and should include a change in index behavior baseline level and quality of life. Response timelines help to minimize premature conclusions of medication ineffectiveness and help to avoid the continuation of an ineffective medication. Extended periods of time (usually 3–8 weeks, in some cases longer) are required for many psychotropic medications to have their full effect (Crabbe, 1989). Preestablished timelines and review points within the treatment plan help to avoid responding to day-to-day fluctuations of the behavior or condition (Sovner & Hurley, 1987), which can lead to pressure to increase dose, change medication, or add medications.

PRN (*pro ra nata,* a written order to allow use as needed) orders must be included within a treatment plan. While long-term PRN use is generally discouraged except for specific unpredictable events (e.g., extreme anxiety during thunderstorms), PRN use will occur for a limited time in a number of cases. Controversy can be minimized in such cases if five variables are delineated in the treatment care plan: (a) *entry criterion* or specifically defined index behaviors (or specific stimulus situations) indicating PRN use and their frequency or intensity; (b) *pre-implementation criterion* or the alternative interventions or techniques to be considered and implemented if possible before using the PRN; (c) *procedural criteria* or specific actions to occur after the PRN is given such as the times the individual will be checked, the times any necessary nursing assessment procedures will be performed, and required documentation including outcome; (d) *failure criterion* or level of use indicating prescriber review for the possibility that the PRN is excessively used, that further assessment is necessary, or a daily prescription is required (e.g., "more than 10 PRNs for 2 consecutive months or for any 2 months within a 3-month period"); and (e) *exit criterion* or nonuse promoting prescriber review to discontinue the PRN order (e.g., "no use for 6 consecutive months").

Short-Term Versus Long-Term Use

The short-term use of psychotropic medication must be differentiated from the long-term use of psychotropic medication, and acute- or crisis-episode drug and dose levels must be differentiated from maintenance drug and dose levels.

The length of time an individual is prescribed psychotropic medication and the dose level depend on a number of factors such as the diagnosis or condition itself, treatment phase, and relapse history. On the one hand, it is important to remember that the first time an individual is prescribed a psychotropic medication does not necessarily mean that the individual should be prescribed a psychotropic medication for the rest of their life (APA, 1979). On the other hand, it is important to recognize that some individuals, due to the nature of their diagnosis, condition, and history of relapse, may require psychotropic medication on an ongoing basis. The following timelines may assist in reviewing an individual's status (APA, 1979; Depression Guideline Panel, 1993; Marder, Ames, Wirshing, & Van Putten, 1993).

Acute (short-term) use. Acute use is generally 3 to 6 months or less. The key consideration is whether the problem (and resulting diagnosis or hypothesis and treatment plan) is of a short-term nature. In such a situation, psychotropic medication is intended as a short-term aid while adjustment occurs or educational strategies are taught to address a situation. For example, a transition to a new environment such as a group home may be extremely stressful such that an antianxiety medication is required while the person adapts to the new environment. It is important, of course, to assure that the environment itself is not substandard and causing the stress due to factors such as excessive noise, unclean conditions, impersonal care, impolite staff, or poor transition by not incorporating important items or activities from the person's prior life situation (e.g., if the individual enjoys listening to baseball games on the radio each night from April to October in his or her room, the new location ensures this occurs).

Continuation (chronic) use. Chronic use is generally 4 to 24 months depending on the condition. An initial episode of a psychiatric condition such as depression or schizophrenia may require a longer period of treatment in order to lower the probability of relapse. For example, 4 to 9 months of antidepressant medication is recommended to treat first-episode depression. Twelve to 24 months may be required to treat first-episode schizophrenia. In the aforementioned acute use situation, a psychotropic medication discontinuation may result in a return to the original problem or intensity. This may indicate (a) a further need for assessment, reexamination of the hypothesis, and treatment plan, or (b) additional time to teach appropriate skills. In any of these situations, it is important to ensure gradual dose reductions occur and that factors such as withdrawal side effects, the environment, poor active treatment, other medical conditions, or an undiagnosed psychiatric condition are not the reason for deterioration.

Maintenance (extended) use. Maintenance use is generally more than 12 to 24 months with expectation of extended or lifelong treatment. Although exceptions may occur, the individual has generally experienced one or more relapses interfering with quality of life when not prescribed psychotropic medication. In such cases, psychotropic medication is required on an extended or ongoing basis to lower the probability of relapse. For example, a history of three episodes of depression indicates a 90% chance of relapse if antidepressant medication is not continued. Similarly, a treatment-resistant condition or behavior problem may be involved, and numerous psychotropic medications and psychological interventions may have failed. A particular medication or combination may be empirically determined such that tremendous quality of life outcome is achieved ("best he or she has ever been"). While use of the lowest optimal effective dose and least number of psychotropic medications is encouraged, a medication-free status is not in the individual's best interest.

Dose levels. Professional recommendations, especially with more sensitive people such as developmentally disabled individuals, nursing home populations, and children, are to *start low and go slow* in order to minimize side effects and not miss therapeutic benefits achievable at lower dose levels (Marder et al., 1993; Royal College of Psychiatrists' Consensus Panel, 1994). High dose levels, rapid tranquilization, and the use of several medications at once to regain control of a crisis situation are not generally recommended unless a unique case profile or treatment-resistant case is involved, but this is a fact of life in crisis units working under time constraints and managed health care economic pressures. It is not the use of such procedures per se that should be condemned, but rather the indefinite use of a crisis regimen. *It must be remembered that acute crisis doses or regimens are not necessarily maintenance drug and dose regimens. The multidisciplinary team must work together to achieve proper drug and dose levels in the continuation or maintenance use phases once a crisis has remitted and the individual has been stabilized for a sufficiently long period of time.* In short, "if continued high, ask why."

While exceptions occur from individual to individual and drug to drug, when a psychotropic medication is initiated, a period of time is required before full effectiveness is achieved. This is generally 3 to 8 weeks (in some cases longer). If a medication seems not to be working within a couple of days or weeks, all care plan providers must resist the urge to request additional medication or increased dose levels outside of an identified titration plan. Extensive psychosocial support may be required during this time. The reader is urged to consider those times of personal crisis and his or her own support system. The ability to talk to someone, a shoulder to cry on, and perhaps a special friend or family member's concern or extra efforts to check on how one was doing may have made all the difference in terms of weathering an immediate crisis.

Ratcheting. The possibility of *ratcheting* should not be overlooked (Arnold, 1993). This is the insidious increase of dose and number of drugs over time due to factors such as a naturally undulating symptomatic course, the client moving from location to location, change in prescriber, different prescribers within a noncoordinated treatment plan, and relapse despite maintenance medication. Medications are added or doses increased on each occasion (ratcheted up one level like a car jack) such that intraclass or interclass polypharmacy and higher doses occur over time. The rationale for the particular regimen may be forgotten, few wish to rock the boat, and the complex regimen or higher doses is assumed to be permanently needed. Much work and extended time is involved to untangle such a situation to determine exactly what condition is present and the appropriate medications and dose levels. Not only is such a situation economically inefficient, but variables such as ineffective medication, behavioral side effects, other discomforting side effects displayed as behavior change, or drug interactions may be contributing to the problem. Except for situations such as refractory bipolar disorder (generally requiring several medications that should not be altered) or if one psychotropic medication is being substituted for another over a reasonable period of time, the presence of three or more psychotropic medications should serve as an indictor to review for the possibility of ratcheting, especially if another psychotropic medication initiation is being discussed or intraclass polypharmacy is present. Intraclass polypharmacy (also referred to as duplicate therapy) is the prescription of two or more medications from the same class.

Informed Consent

The individual, if competent, or the individual's guardian must provide written informed consent before the nonemergency initiation of any psychotropic medication and must be periodically renewed. Information should be provided orally, in writing, and in an educational manner.

Contemporary models view informed consent as part of a greater ethical duty to establish a therapeutic alliance with the individual or guardian (Appelbaum, Lidz, & Meisel, 1987; Kaplan & Sadock, 1988; Simon, 1987). Involving the individual or guardian in all care decisions on an ongoing basis is a central tenant of this concept which Applebaum et al. (1987) refer to as *process informed consent.* If an individual, if competent, or the individual's guardian refuses consent for the proposed psychotropic medication and the medication is still considered necessary, appropriate procedural and legal due process must be followed (Singh et al., 1992; Sprague & Galliher, 1988).

Concern has been expressed about written informed consent (APA, 1979, 1992), but with the vast majority of individuals with developmental disabilities, it is the guardian and not the individual who provides informed consent. Informed consent forms are useful and provide a structure to the process when they are used and understood to be an adjunct to oral explanation and patient education. The consent form is not a substitute for process informed consent and the continual communication and contact between the multidisciplinary team and guardian on all issues and decisions. Informed consent forms can be easily misdesigned to be excessively vague or complex, and they do not provide legal protection if a patient or guardian does not understand the information or what they are signing. Written patient education material is critical within this process because it is associated with increased professional patient education efforts (Kennedy & Sanborn, 1992). Such efforts and material are respectful of the individual, strengthen the therapeutic alliance, and are *paradoxically reassuring* to the patient or guardian should adverse effects occur because they are not misinterpreted as being part of the underlying psychiatric condition (McElroy, Keck, & Friedman, 1995).

There are a number of different mechanisms to obtain informed consent. In some situations, the prescriber may be in the best position to obtain informed consent. In others, a nurse may be. Yet in others, a social worker or qualified mental retardation professional (QMRP) may coordinate the informed consent process. Any good faith procedure is acceptable if it adheres to the observation by Kaplan and Sadock (1988) that: "Respect for persons incorporates and goes beyond informed consent. It is unfortunate that so much emphasis has been placed on informed consent—its rituals, documentation, and difficulties—at the expense of the higher ethical standard of respect for persons" (p. 121).

Information to be provided to the individual or guardian includes at least: (a) the psychiatric diagnosis or behavioral hypothesis; (b) the specific signs or symptoms which will be changed and how they will be monitored; (c) the proposed treatment, the expected benefits, the probability the proposed treatment will be successful, the length of time it will take for the benefits to occur, and the expected duration the psychotropic medication is to be used; (d) feasible alternatives including the prognosis if the proposed treatment is not undertaken; (e) risks and adverse effects, both expected and unexpected, and the incidence, severity, and significance; (f) specific information about the proposed psychotropic medication including items such as the dose and dosage range appropriate for the individual, the route of administration, the plan if the medication is unsuccessful, and drug, alcohol, and food interactions; (g) an explanation of the right to refuse the proposed psychotropic medication and to change one's mind at any time; (h) an explanation that the consent is time-limited and must be renewed on a periodic basis; and (i) the identity of the professionals involved, how to contact them, and any professional relationships among the individuals treating the patient (APA, 1992; HCFA, 1978, 1988, 1992; Howe, 1984; Kaplan & Sadock, 1988; Simon, 1987; Sovner & Hurley, 1985).

Applied Methods

Space considerations prevent a comprehensive review of all aspects of psychotropic medication monitoring methods. Only the three key elements of psychotropic medication monitoring are discussed. These elements are *index behaviors, side effects,* and *quality of life.* A fourth item, *lowest optimal effective dose* (OED), is also reviewed due to pronounced misunderstanding over the years.

Applied methods are not intended to collect data for data's sake. The goal is to provide organized and longitudinal information to the prescriber and other multidisciplinary team members so as to improve the psychotropic medication risk-benefit analysis. Data itself provides only a first-pass function; that is, it provides only rudimentary information. Data must be reviewed in relation to a myriad of variables such as the psychotropic medication and dose changes; nonmedication active treatment program status; environmental changes; life or stress events; changes in nonpsychotropic medications or dose; recent illness or disease; subjective reports from the client, family, or staff; reports from other areas such as a job; prodromal signs or situations that have high predictability of relapse for the individual; treatment stage; and social, mood, eating, and sleeping patterns.

Index Behaviors

Index behaviors have been historically referred to as *target behaviors,* but the term *index behavior* has recently been recommended in order to reinforce the concept that psychotropic medication use must be based upon a psychiatric diagnosis or specific behavioral-pharmacologic hypothesis (Kalachnik et al., 1998). Such behaviors are indicative of and serve as an observable index of the underlying condition or hypothesis. Specific index behaviors are important to assist the prescriber, other multidisciplinary team members, and the patient or guardian to not only arrive at a diagnosis, but to evaluate progress and psychotropic medication efficacy over time. Index behaviors are not entirely omitted in favor of quality of life measures because quality of life is a molar rather than molecular concept and may not change for a period of time despite index behavior improvement. An analogy is that blood pressure measures are not omitted in favor of quality of life measures when medication for hypertension is prescribed.

Subjective information provided by high-functioning or verbal individuals during face-to-face interviews should not be minimized or overlooked. A number of authorities, however, have concluded that tracking objective index behaviors is important to determine clinical status. Sovner and Hurley (1987) noted, "In our opinion, behavioral monitoring of treatment provides the most effective way of making decisions regarding the response of mentally retarded persons treated with psychotropic medication" (p. 48). Crabbe (1989) observed, "Psychiatrists are adjusting to clinical data collecting from behavioral observations and reports rather than traditional interviewing which has limitations in nonverbal clients" (pp. 19–20).

Index behavior definition. An index behavior is the behavior(s) manifested by or representing the underlying diagnosis, condition, or hypothesis. It is the behavior which should improve as a result of the psychotropic medication (or other intervention). The observable improvement of the index behavior is taken as an indication the psychotropic medication is efficaciously treating the underlying condition.

A critical aspect regarding index behaviors is an unambiguous description and specific examples so that all parties can readily identify and agree on what is to be tracked. For example, the word *agitation* is vague. One observer may classify as *agitated* behaviors such as yelling and jumping up while watching a sporting event on TV or yelling at someone who is attempting to steal her supper portion while another observer may classify these same behaviors as normal. By describing agitation in specific terms such as "waving the arms, pacing back and forth, and repetitive statements such as 'I want to call my mom, I want to call my mom,'" a common set of behaviors is established. Hallucinations, as another example, may be defined for a specific individual as "statements or behaviors not associated with the environment such as 'The pack of wolves is following me' (and repeatedly looking over one's shoulder)." While a term such as agitation or hallucinations might be used as short-hand on data collection sheets and summaries, a full formal definition must be provided in the treatment plan. Index behaviors should be periodically reviewed to prevent observer drift.

An individual may have more than one index behavior. For example, depression may consist of crying episodes, aggression (hitting, kicking, or striking out) due to irritability, and lying in bed or excessive sleeping. While exceptions occur, using three or fewer index behaviors is preferred because it is difficult to synthesize a large number of index behaviors. If more than three index behaviors exist, two questions should be asked. First, can several of the index behaviors be subsumed under one term? For example, kicking, hitting, pinching, and pushing people could all be defined and tracked under the term *aggression to people*. Second, is the index behavior one that can realistically be expected to be treated by a psychotropic medication? Although requiring some form of intervention, "flushing clothes down the toilet," in addition to delusions, rapid speech patterns, and hypersexuality, is not likely to represent the manic phase of a bipolar disorder or an index behavior upon which dosage adjustment can be based. An exception in this case would be if the flushing were the sole behavior and determined to be part of an underlying obsessive-compulsive disorder.

Index behaviors should be defined during the assessment period because a problem has been reported and must be measured. If index behaviors have not been defined (such as when a newly admitted individual has already been prescribed a psychotropic medication), the index behavior is defined post hoc based upon observation and available history. It may be necessary to reexamine or redefine index behaviors in such cases as time passes and changes occur.

Baseline. A baseline is a period of time an index behavior is measured in order to establish the frequency or severity of the index behavior. The most important aspect of a baseline is that it serves as a standard against which the efficacy of subsequent psychotropic medication is evaluated. A baseline is a mandatory part of an assessment.

A baseline prior to psychotropic medication initiation is desirable, but, in reality, many individuals are already prescribed psychotropic medication, and a drug-free baseline is not possible. *Psychotropic medication does not have to be discontinued in order to obtain a baseline.* The technical definition of a baseline is a period of time during which existing conditions or interventions are accepted and not changed. Subsequent changes are compared and evaluated against this period of time and the conditions in place. Thus, if an individual is prescribed 100 mg of sertraline (Zoloft) and no index behavior baseline exists, a baseline would be taken at 100 mg and subsequent change compared against this level.

There are several important points about baselines. First, the length of a baseline can be as long or as short as desired and generally depends upon the severity of the clinical situation and index behavior. At least 2 to 4 weeks is recommended in order to obtain an accurate measure not skewed by a "bad" day or a bad week, to prevent overreaction to a bad day or a bad week, and to consider descending or ascending baseline patterns. A *descending baseline* displays a pattern of lower index behavior occurrences each week. If a psychotropic medication is initiated too quickly, the intervention may be mistakenly assumed to be the controlling variable and continued when in fact the individual was in the process of improving. An *ascending baseline* displays a pattern of higher index behaviors each week. If a psychotropic medication is initiated too quickly (e.g., if severity is such that the intervention must be initiated quickly), the intervention may mistakenly be assumed to be worsening the index behavior when in fact the individual was already in the process of deteriorating. In both of these situations, a well-thought-out treatment plan assists to minimize these events because fail-safe indicators such as expected duration of use, review points, and expected improvement timelines are developed. Second, a major variable may change during a baseline, or the wrong measurement method selected. If this occurs, the baseline must be restarted. And third, a baseline may become outdated over time. In other words, so much time has passed or so many environmental conditions have changed, the original baseline data are no longer valid. A new baseline for comparison purposes may need to be taken.

Methods to measure index behaviors.

Recognized methods to measure index behaviors include frequency count, duration recording, time sampling, interval recording, and rating scales (Aman, Hammer, & Rojahn, 1993; Hall, 1971; Rojahn & Schroeder, 1983; Sovner & Hurley, 1987). These methods can be combined in various ways. For example, a frequency count may incorporate a rating scale code to represent the severity of each incident. Other methods are available such as permanent products, learning performance, and laboratory or instrumental measures, but these are either more research oriented or infrequently used on the applied level.

Each of the methods below has advantages and disadvantages. Additionally, variables such as staffing, the number of individuals pre-scribed psychotropic medication, and the applied setting (e.g., home care, semi-independent apartment, or group home) influence the method selected. A rule of thumb is to do a little less to ensure accurate data rather than too much and risk inaccurate data or staff sabotage.

Frequency count (also called event recording) is the Model T of index behavior measurement. Frequency count measures the number of times an index behavior occurs. Each time an index behavior occurs, it is recorded on a data sheet (or computer if available). A simple tick mark or the time of the index behavior is entered. Frequency counts may be implemented for the entire 24-hour day; a more limited but continuous time period such as 6:00 A.M. to 10:00 P.M.; or selected daily segments such as 7:00–9:00 A.M., 1:00–3:00 P.M., and 7:00–9:00 P.M. The number of index behavior occurrences are totaled for each day. If an index behavior occurs in bursts (e.g., aggression targets several people con-secutively), episodes can be recorded instead of each and every incident.

The advantage of frequency count lies in its simplicity and versatility to a wide range of index behaviors and situations. Several index behaviors are easily tracked. Staff can go about their duties until the index behavior occurs. The disadvantages of frequency count are that very high frequency index behaviors are not easily or accurately measured, and very low frequency but long-lasting index behaviors are not well represented.

During assessment periods, frequency count may be combined with recording of antecedent events that occur before the index behavior and consequent events that occur after the index behavior. Combined with the time of day, this information is valuable in terms of where to focus further inquiry efforts or direct active treatment interventions. However, this variation is labor-intensive and is not recommended beyond the assessment period unless unexplained deterioration occurs or a new assessment must be conducted.

Duration recording measures the length of time an index behavior occurs. The time the index behavior starts and stops is recorded. This can be accomplished with a stopwatch or entering start and stoptimes on a data collec-tion sheet or computer. The time for each index behavior is added to yield a total time per day. The entire 24-hour day or selected periods may be measured.

The advantage of duration recording lies in providing an accurate measure of low frequency but long-lasting index behaviors. The disadvantage is that it is not useful for low frequency behaviors lasting a short time. Duration recording is also inconvenient for high-frequency behaviors because staff must devote considerable efforts to timing the index behaviors. Duration recording is not recom-mended on the applied level except for special cases.

Time sample measures the percent of time an index behavior occurs. Time sample spot checks an individual. Conceptually, it is similar to an opinion poll in that a sample represents the whole. Time sample specifies exact times an individual is checked during the course of a day to determine if the index behavior is occurring (e.g., once every 30 minutes from 6:00 A.M. to 10:00 P.M.: 6:00 A.M., 6:30 A.M., 7:00 A.M., 7:30 A.M., etc.). If the index behavior occurs during the check, a "+" is entered next to the time on the data sheet or computer. If the index behavior does not occur, a "–" is entered. At the end of the day, the total number of checks the index behavior occurred is divided by the total checks to yield a percentage. For example, if an individual is checked for hallucinations 20 times during the day and displays hallucinations on 10 checks, hallucinations occurred 50% of the time. Time sample can vary the time period (e.g., 24-hour day; 8:00 A.M. to 8:00 P.M.; or 8:00–10:00 A.M., 1:00–3:00 P.M., and 7:00–9:00 P.M.), the time between checks (e.g., every 5 minutes, every 15 minutes, or every 30 minutes), and the length of observation at each check (e.g., quick glance, 30 sec observation, or actual interaction such as conversing to determine speech content to judge if the index behavior of hallucinations is present). As a rule of thumb, the shorter the time period checked, the greater number of checks needed. The key variable in time sample is to ensure enough checks are made to provide an accurate representation. Too few checks results in large data variation. Too many checks over too long a time period is labor-intensive for staff.

The advantage of time sample is twofold. First, observers or staff are not required to devote continuous long periods of time to observation. A brief spot check can be made, and the observer can return to other duties or activities until the next spot check. Second, more than one index behavior can be recorded at each check. The major disadvantage of time sample is with low frequency index behavior; the index behavior may not occur during the checks. In other words, the index behavior may be occurring, but is not being measured. Time sample also requires more staff training, especially if several index behaviors are checked.

Interval recording divides the day into equal intervals, and an index behavior is recorded as either occurring or not occurring at any time during each interval. For example, the entire 24-hour day is divided into 30 minute intervals (e.g., 6:00–6:30 A.M., 6:30–7:00 A.M., 7:00–7:30 A.M., etc.). At 6:30 A.M., the observer asks, "Did the index behavior occur at any time from 6:00 to 6:30 A.M.?" If the index behavior occurred, a "+" is entered for that interval on a data sheet or computer. If the index behavior did not occur, a "–" is entered. The number of intervals the index behavior

occurred is either: (a) added to yield a daily total, or (b) divided by the total number of intervals to yield a percentage of intervals displayed. For example, if 8:00 A.M. to 11:00 P.M. is divided into 30-minute intervals, there are a total of 30 intervals for the day (8–8:30, 8:30–9:00, 9:00–9:30, etc.). If aggression occurred during 10 intervals, the index behavior total is 10 intervals for the day or 33% of the intervals. The time period can be varied (e.g., 24-hour day; 8:00 A.M. to 8:00 P.M.; or 8:00–10:00 A.M., 1:00–3:00 P.M., and 7:00–9:00 P.M.) as can the interval length (e.g., 5-min interval, 15-min interval, or 30 min interval). As a rule of thumb, the shorter the time period measured, the shorter the interval length.

The advantage of interval recording is its versatility to a number of situations. It balances frequency and duration and is easy for staff to use. Several index behaviors can be recorded during the interval or a rating scale intensity code can be used instead of a "+" or "–". The disadvantage is that interval recording tends to underreport index behaviors if enough contact does not occur with the individual during the interval. Overall, interval recording is an extremely useful method.

Rating scales present an index behavior question or description, and the observer selects a numerical response representing the index behavior level from a series of defined values such as 0 (not at all), 1 (minimal), 2 (mild), 3 (moderate), or 4 (severe). Rating scales may be applied to long periods of time (e.g., the entire week, 24-hour day, or 8-hour shift) or selected short periods of time (8:00–10:00 A.M. or a specific activity such as meals). Rating scales can range from one to dozens of items. Rating scales can be standardized or developed for individual index behaviors.

The major advantage of rating scales is convenience. Staff can quickly complete rating scale items, and several index behaviors are easily rated. The disadvantage of rating scales are their quasi-objective nature compared to the other methods, observer bias, and, if improperly designed, their tendency toward global measurement and inability to detect change when the index behavior is in fact changing. In terms of standardized scales, great care must be taken to ensure the proper scale is used for the proper population and condition.

Many problems related to individually designed scales can be minimized by defining the index behavior to be rated in great detail; specifying the exact period of time to be rated; providing anchor points for the numerical scoring system (e.g., "2 = mild; 3–5 times during the shift; did not interfere with daily activities or requests; no undue staff time devoted to the index behavior"); rating two or more distinct time periods during the day and either using the average score or totaling the points; and periodically having two or more observers independently complete the rating scale for the same period of time in order to guard against observer bias.

The *Aberrant Behavior Checklist* is recommended for standardized assessment situations (Aman, Singh, Stewart, & Field, 1985). One useful scale for individual index behaviors is the Maladaptive Behavior Scale (MABS) (Thompson, 1988), which is presented in Figure 9.1. As can be seen, a specific numerical value based upon the frequency and intensity of the index behavior is assigned. A numerical grid of 1 to 25 may be useful instead of the 2 to 15 grid for two reasons. First, the scoring system is spread out to better detect change. Second, a determination of the exact number of times a particular frequency-intensity combination occurred during a given period of time is possible.

Summarizing and organizing index behavior data.

In today's economic climate, and given an average of 10 to 15 minutes per client, prescribers do not have the time to review a massive amount of data except in special situations (e.g., assessment phase, treatment-resistant case, or a severe case being closely tracked for a limited period of time). The author has worked with a number of physicians and psychiatrists who are outstanding professionals as well as extremely caring and empathic individuals. One of the most frustrating situations they have expressed is the failure of providers to present index behavior data summarized and organized in a longitudinal manner. As one psychiatrist the author worked with to implement an index behavior reporting system told nurses and staff, "I need some sort of weekly or monthly number about specific behaviors to tell me how things are going. I'll ask you other questions regarding other aspects of the person's life and condition, and I want to hear your other observations."

Following are several basic index behavior summary methods useful on the applied level. Which method to use for a specific case will depend on variables such as the index behavior itself, the severity or complexity of the index behavior and condition, the data collection method, and prescriber and team preference. Other methods also exist.

Daily total. Index behavior data can be summarized by daily totals. Each day is listed on a summary sheet and graph. The total for each day is entered. The advantage is provision of a precise picture. The disadvantage is much "white noise" and daily variability over time that makes it difficult to interpret overall patterns without more complex statistical analysis. Additionally, it is difficult to fit daily totals for an extended period of time, such as a year, on a one-page graph.

Daily total summary is only recommended for short periods of time (e.g., during an assessment period) or for special situations (e.g., a severe case being closely tracked, frequent and numerous changes, a specific program or drug decision using step advancements based upon a 1- to 5-day criterion level being reached, etc.).

Weekly total. Index behavior data can be summarized by weekly totals. The 52 weeks in a year are listed on a summary sheet and graph, and the weekly total is entered. The advantages are the omission of daily variability, easier patterns to interpret over time, and the ability to enter a full year on one graph and summary sheet. The disadvantages are twofold: weekly totals can display great variability, and, if index behavior data are not collected for a day, the weekly total may show a change when in fact no data were collected (i.e., no data equates with zero).

One variation of the weekly total summary is to compute a daily average for the week. The total number of index behavior occurrences for the week is divided by 7 days. For example, 21

MALADAPTIVE BEHAVIOR SCALE (MABS)

FREQUENCY:

Select the letter corresponding to your best estimate of how often the behavior occurred during the previous 8 hours. (*)

0 = Did not occur.

A.   Once.

B.   2 to 3 times.

C.   4 to 6 times.

D.   7 to 12 times.

E.   More than 12 times.

INTENSITY:

Select the letter corresponding to your best estimate of the overall seriousness of the behavior during the previous 8 hours. (*)

F.   Noticeable, but does not interfere with activities of daily living.

G.   Interferes with activities of daily living, but otherwise tolerable and easily ignored.

H.   Disturbing and very difficult to ignore.

I.   Disturbing or repetitive behavior with potential for harm to self, others, or property if continued.

J.   Self-injury, or injury to another person, or property damage.

NONE = 0   **FREQUENCY**

INTENSITY

	A	B	C	D	E
F	2	3	4	5	6
G	4	5	6	7	8
H	6	7	8	9	10
I	9	10	11	12	13
J	11	12	13	14	15

* If the MABS is used for a period of time other than the last eight hour shift (for example, all day), <u>specify exactly</u> what the period of time is.

INSTRUCTIONS

1.   <u>IDENTIFY THE BEHAVIOR(S)</u> to be monitored. Be specific.
2.   <u>DETERMINE WHO WILL ASSIGN THE SCORE.</u> If a staff review at a shift change is involved, the senior person should lead the discussion and assign the score.
3.   <u>SELECT THE SCORE</u> which represents the frequency and intensity of the behavior. If more than one behavior is monitored, assign a score to each behavior. When a staff review is involved and no consensus can be reached, the senior person selects the score based upon the discussion and moves on to the next case.
4.   <u>RECORD THE SCORE</u> onto the Monthly Data Summary Sheet and/or other record keeping mechanisms.
5.   <u>PERIODIC RELIABILITY CHECKS</u> are recommended by having two individuals independently assign scores. Compare.

Figure 9.1. Example of an individual item rating scale.

aggressions for the week divided by 7 days yields an average of three aggressions per day. This method controls for missing days because the missing day is omitted from the denominator (e.g., if 1 day of data is missed, the total is divided by 6 days).

Weekly summary totals are recommended for cases of greater concern or when a number of changes are occurring.

Monthly total. Index behavior data can be summarized by monthly totals. The index behavior total for the month is added. The 12 months in a year are listed on a summary sheet and graph. The monthly total is entered. The advantages are a more global outcome pattern over time, elimination of excessive variability, one calculation and data point per month for staff, and the ability to enter a full year's or more data on one graph and summary sheet. Also, two or three index behaviors are easier to track on the same graph due to the elimination of numerous data entries. The disadvantages include loss of early recognition of developing patterns, and, in cases of numerous changes, inability to determine which change led to the result. Additionally, large weekly variations that may be important to an individual case are lost.

One variation of the monthly total summary is to compute a daily average for the month. The total number of index behavior occurrences for the month is divided by total monthly days. For example, 31 aggressions for the month divided by 31 days yields an average of 1.0 aggression per day for the month. Another variation is to simply list the total number or percentage of days per month the index behavior occurred. For example, if aggression occurred 15 days in a month, it could be expressed as 15 days per month or 50% of the days in the month. The weakness of the latter variation is its global nature. A number of aggressions may be occurring on each of the 15 days. The total number of aggressions may actually be changing, but the days displayed per month may not.

Monthly total summary is recommended for those cases of lower index behavior concern, few changes or numerous changes of a minor nature, long-term stabilization, or established variability over time.

Condition rate. Index behavior data can be summarized by the specific psychotropic medication and dose (and other intervention) conditions. The index behavior total for the entire drug condition is divided by the length of the drug condition to yield an average for the entire condition. This may be a daily average if the total index behaviors is divided by the number of days, a weekly average if divided by the number of weeks, or a monthly average if divided by the number of months. The advantage of this method is a precise average in relation to a specific set of variables. The major disadvantage is variability is overlooked in conditions of great length. Additionally, a final average cannot be computed until a condition is terminated. The procedure is more labor-intensive and confusing to staff. One useful variation for conditions of greater length is to compute monthly rates until the specific condition is over. An overall rate for the entire condition can then be computed.

Condition rate summary should be reserved for research cases or cases involving numerous changes of fairly short duration.

How often should index behavior be collected? There is no absolute answer to this question even for a single individual because both the individual and the environment are dynamic, not static. Acute, chronic, and maintenance treatment phases change as does the environment and the individual. It is not always possible or necessary to collect index behavior data every single day for every single individual for the rest of the person's life. This is especially true for individuals in home health care or semi-independent living situations. However, some form of ongoing, consistent, and periodic data collection is necessary to track and review status. If data are collected periodically, more frequent data collection should occur during the acute treatment phase, and when drug or dose changes are considered.

Daily data collection is recommended during assessment; as baseline; and before and after initiation, addition, or dose change of a psychotropic medication. Daily data collection is also recommended for individuals for whom early indications or data patterns of developing relapse have been established (e.g., 3 days of aggression within any 5-day period serves as an operational definition to signal the start of the depressive phase of a bipolar disorder). If an individual is stabilized with few drug or dose changes and good quality of life, he or she can be spot-checked periodically. For example, a frequency count could be implemented for 1 week per month or 1 week per quarter. This paradigm allows more flexibility, but requires more vigilance as to when to increase or decrease the intensity of the data collection.

Data indicator levels. Given the myriad of duties and clients to care for, it is helpful if the provider and prescriber attempt to develop the following three indicators in relation to index behavior data. These indicators do not mean an action must be taken. They only serve to prompt review of the situation.

First, an *improvement indicator*. This is an index behavior level representing intervention effectiveness. It is developed as part of the treatment plan whenever a psychotropic medication is first initiated or when a new medication added. The improvement level consists of two variables: (a) the actual level of the index behavior to be achieved compared to baseline levels, and (b) a realistic amount of time necessary for this change to occur. The improvement level serves as a red flag for possible change or justification for continued use if not reached. A general rule of thumb is at least a 50% change compared to baseline levels within 2 to 4 months. An example is "physical aggression 5 times or less per month within 3 months" given a baseline level averaging 11 aggressions per month.

Second, a *deterioration indicator*. This is an index behavior level representing possible problems or the need for intervention adjustment. Once an improvement level is reached, it is easy to assume that no further adjustments are necessary. Emerging problems may inadvertently be overlooked. If a deterioration level is reached, it prompts review for adjustments, changes, or justification for continued use. An example is "physical aggression exceeding five times per week for any 2 weeks in a 3-week period." Such a level must obviously take into account normal variability such as a bad month around a holiday. Prodromal

signs or symptoms may also serve as indicators.

Third, a *lowest optimal effective dose (OED) indicator*. It may be easy to overlook individuals who are on maintenance dose medication, especially those for whom prior lowest OEDs have failed. A lowest OED indicator does not mean a dose reduction must occur. Rather, it provides an index behavior level prompt for review. An example is "less than three aggressions per week for 6 consecutive months." Lowest OED methods are reviewed separately later in this chapter.

Summary. One useful systemic activity is to construct a master list of all clients. In the first column, enter the client's name. In the second column, enter whether psychotropic medication is prescribed. If so, list the psychotropic medications and dose. In the third column, enter the diagnosis or behavioral-hypothesis. In the fourth column, enter the specific index behavior(s) representing the diagnosis or hypothesis. In the fifth column, enter the data collection method for the index behavior(s). In the sixth column, enter how the index behavior is summarized longitudinally. If vagueness or gaps exist, efforts can be directed to correcting the problem. A form for an individual client providing this information in more detail may also be helpful.

Side Effects

An old adage states, "There are two effects of every medication: the one we know about and the one we don't know about." Standardized side effect assessments attempt to better obtain information to convert the later into the former so it can be treated.

Various types and degrees of side effects are associated with psychotropic medication. These range from minor transitory side effects such as dizziness from lithium to more serious side effects such as neuroleptic malignant syndrome (NMS) or tardive dyskinesia (TD) associated with typical antipsychotic medication. There are three reasons for the use of standardized side effect assessment instruments: better detection, limited nature of laboratory tests, and the human dimension.

Research suggests adverse drug reactions (ADRs) are detected to a much greater degree when standardized assessment scales are used, as Corso, Pucino, DeLeo, Calis, and Gallelli (1992) succinctly summarized:

> ADRs may go undetected because healthcare providers do not invest the time to question their patients systematically about symptoms that may be related to their medications. In practice, three common methods of detecting ADRs include open-ended questioning, systematic assessment by means of a symptoms checklist, and spontaneous reporting. Studies comparing the first two methods have indicated that ADRs are more frequently detected if a checklist is used. However, the authors of these studies recommend the use of both techniques for optimal assessment. A more recent study suggests that the use of a systematic inquiry method in conjunction with spontaneous reporting of symptoms by patients more than doubles the detection rate of potential ADRs compared with spontaneous reporting alone. (p. 890)

Similarly, the Scandinavian Society of Psychopharmacology (1987) notes:

> Of great importance is...the availability of a reliable way to record and evaluate any possible side effects. Patients do not always report or complain of even important side effects, and there is therefore always a risk the doctor may fail to recognize side effects that ought to be taken into account, if he does not look for them systematically. Even the more obvious side effects, which are easily recognized by both patient and the doctor, may be best followed in their development systematically by use of a standardized procedure... (preface)

Three studies are of particular interest. Bennett and Lipman (1977) compared prospective side effect surveillance versus voluntary reporting. The incidence of ADRs was 0.08% with the voluntary system versus 7.2% with the prospective system. Despite this, the authors concluded that full-time ongoing prospective surveillance is not cost-effective and recommend *periodic* prospective surveillance programs. Herranz, Arteaga, and Armijo (1982) in a study of valproic acid (Depakene) found the frequency of side effects increased from 42.0% to 80.7% when a questionnaire was introduced. They concluded a need exists to perform systematic surveillance for side effects similar to efforts made to assess clinical effectiveness. Rabin, Markowitz, Ocepek-Welikson, and Wager (1992) compared a general inquiry format to a specific inquiry format and found the general inquiry format failed to elicit a significant number (about 40%) of mild to moderate troublesome events that normally would have led to changes in clinical management. While noting that severe events involving safety were detected just as well by general inquiry and cautioning against excessively time-consuming and cost-ineffective specific inquiries, they concluded that some form of more directed inquiry is indicated for side-effect management purposes.

Laboratory test values may suggest or confirm that some side effects exist. However, not all side effects have laboratory tests available. Rather, most side effects are functional in nature and do not have lab tests, and lab tests for nonfunctional side effects are often prompted by functional signs of the biochemical side effects (e.g., fever, pallor, easy bruising which may represent a blood dyscrasia) (Zbinden, 1963). Additionally, sole reliance on laboratory tests does not necessarily lead to fewer reports of patient side effects. In a study of anticonvulsant serum levels, the availability of serum level tests to physicians did not diminish patient reports of side effects (Beardsley, Freeman, & Appel, 1983).

Perhaps the most compelling reason for standardized side effects assessment is the human toll. O'Donnell (1992) notes that a number of deaths can be blamed on side effects each year, approximately 30% of hospitalized patients experience a side effect, and as many as 1.5 million individuals are hospitalized because of side effects annually. Noncompliance with antipsychotic or lithium regimens due to side effects may occur with increased risk of relapse or hospital readmission (Blair, 1990; Gitlin, Cochran, & Jamison, 1989). Psychotropic or antiepilpetic medication side effects may be mistakenly viewed as behavior conditions and inappropriate actions taken that worsen long-term prospects (Hanzel, Kalachnik, & Harder, 1992; Siris, 1985). A German study noted that psychic side effects (i.e., disturbance of consciousness, memory, affect, psychomotor, behavioral manifestations) occurred for 4.5% of 15,264 inpatients treated with psychotropic medication and were the second most common side effect after neurological side effects (Grohmann et al., 1993).

What is a side effect? Feldman and Quenzer (1984) define side effects as secondary effects of a drug that are usually undesirable and different from its therapeutic effect. This is probably the simplest definition to use on the day-to-day level. Side effects, however, are generally referred to as ADRs in the literature. An ADR is defined as any response to a drug that is noxious and unintended and that occurs at doses used in humans for prophylaxis, diagnosis, or therapy, excluding the failure to accomplish the intended purpose (Karch & Lasagna, 1975).

Technically, side effects are one ADR subtype (Linkowich, 1981). ADR classifications are *hypersensitivity* or reactions related to the patient's immunologic response; *idiosyncracy* or reactions manifesting themselves as an inordinate response to a usual dose of a drug (also called intolerance or hyperreactivity); *side effects* or reactions that are unintended and unwanted yet are known pharmacological effects of the drug; *toxic reactions* or reactions that are unintended, unwanted, and are not related to the drug's pharmacologic effects; and *adverse drug interactions* or reactions that are due to the in vivo interaction of two or more drugs.

ADRs are usually listed in standardized pharmacy and nursing references by body areas or systems (*Facts and Comparisons,* 1995; Robinson & George, 1990). While variations

exist, categories include autonomic, cardiovascular, drug interactions, endocrine, gastrointestinal, hematological, hepatic, central nervous system, neurological, ocular, respiratory, dermatologic, and urinary. Neurotransmitter systems involved include acetylcholine (e.g., blurred vision), histamine (e.g., drowsiness), dopamine (e.g., dystonia), norepinephrine (e.g., dizziness) and serotonin (e.g., upset stomach).

Side effect assessment scales. Side effect scales may take one of three tracks, each having its advantages and disadvantages: medication-specific scales, general purpose scales, and side effect specific scales. Table 9.5 lists a number of scales.

Medication specific side effect scales or checklists list the side effects specific to a drug or a drug class. Some standardized scales exist in the literature, such as the Stimulant Drug Side Effects Rating Scale (Barkley, McMurray, Edelbrock, & Robbins, 1990). Alternatively, a checklist can be created from a standard pharmaceutical references such as the *United States Pharmacopeia* (1995), the *American Hospital Formulary Service* (1995), or *Facts and Comparisons* (1995).

The major advantage to a medication-specific scale is that the side effects listed are limited to the psychotropic medication the individual is prescribed. For example, if lithium for bipolar disorder is prescribed, it makes sense to have a scale or checklist specific for lithium or antimania medication. Such a scale is especially advantageous for a clinic or residence that specializes in and primarily serves clients with a specific condition and thus a particular psychotropic medication class is prescribed. The major disadvantage occurs when more than one drug is prescribed, when numerous drug changes occur, or when a variety of medications are prescribed for a variety of clients. Checklists multiply, interactive effects may be overlooked, and staff confusion occurs in switching from checklist to checklist. A second disadvantage is that time must be devoted to constructing a checklist if a scale cannot be found in the literature. Such construction should not be taken lightly

TABLE 9.5

Side Effects Assessment Scales

Scale	Reference	Comment
GENERAL SCALES		
Adverse Drug Reaction Detection Scale (ADRDS)	Corso et al. (1992)	In-depth scale across all medications
Dosage Record and Treatment Emergent Symptom Scale (DOTES)	National Institute of Mental Health (1985)	Useful information such as scoring definitions, but limited items
Interval and Final Rating Sheets on Side Effects	Gofman (1972-1973)	Versions for prescriber, child, and parents
Monitoring of Side Effects Scale (MOSES)	Kalachnik (1985)	Signs and symptoms in layperson's language
Systematic Assessment for Treatment Emergent Effects (SAFTEE)	Levine & Schooler (1986)	Useful inquiry format; psychometrics available
Subjective Treatment for Treatment Emergent Symptoms Scale (STESS)	National Institute of Mental Health (1985)	Open-ended; not recommended
Scandinavian Society of Psychopharmacology Side Effects Rating Scale (UKU)	Scandinavian Society Psychopharmacology (1987)	Psychometrics and full manual available
MEDICATION SPECIFIC		
Antiepileptic Neurotoxicity Scale (ANS)	Cramer et al. (1983)	Psychometrically developed with indicator scores
Stimulant Drug Side Effects Rating Scale	Barkley et al. (1990)	Professionally developed
SIDE-EFFECT SPECIFIC		
Abnormal Involuntary Movement Scale (AIMS)	National Institute of Mental Health (1985)	Well-recognized tardive dyskinesia (TD) scale
Abnormal Involuntary Movement Scale for Recognizing Acute Extrapyramidal System Effects (AIMS-EPS)	Borison (1985)	Extrapyramidal side effects scale (EPSE; akathisia, dystonia, and parkinsonism); items well-defined, but poor scoring system
Akathisia Ratings of Movement Scale (ARMS)	Bodfish et al. (1997)	Akathisia specific; psychometrically developed for mental retardation
Barnes Akathisia Rating Scale (BARS)	Barnes (1989)	Basis for ARMS; items well-defined
Dyskinesia Identification System Condensed User Scale (DISCUS)	Sprague & Kalachnik (1991)	Psychometrically developed TD scale for mental retardation with "indicator score"

Table 9.5. Continued

Scale	Reference	Comment
Neurological Rating Scale (NMS; also called Simpson-Angus)	Simpson & Angus (1970)	EPSE scale; items well-defined with specific scoring system
Tardive Dyskinesia Rating Scale (TDRS)	Simpson et al. (1979)	TD scale; complex scoring system; extensive items well-defined
Texas Research Institute for Mental Sciences Tardive Dyskinesia Rating Scale (TRIMS)	Smith et al. (1983)	TD scale; includes items to differentiate parkinsonism
Withdrawal Emergent Symptoms Checklist (WES)	Engelhardt (1974)	Useful for abrupt withdrawal but limited number of items

because the checklist must ensure professional completeness in a user-friendly format with some type of defined active response (e.g., minimal, mild, severe with each defined).

General purpose side effects scales list side effects for and across numerous drug classes. Most are standardized and have been published. Some have psychometric data involving reliability and validity. These scales usually take one of two forms. The first type lists specific signs and symptoms (e.g., rigidity, eyes rolled up, torticollis, etc.). The second type lists specific side-effect names (e.g., dystonia). These scales may differ in breath of coverage; some are designed to be inclusive of all medications while others are designed for limited areas such as psychotropic medication.

Standardized general purpose scales have a number of advantages. They may be used with a variety of medications and across many clients. Paper is minimized. The publication and professional development adds a semblance of authority and rationale. The major disadvantage is that these scales are sometimes difficult to track down in the literature and are often developed for research rather than for applied clinical use. As a result, many tend to be user unfriendly or require a degree of time to adapt for applied use. Additionally, standardized scales may not address a specific side effect such as tardive dyskinesia (TD) or akathisia in enough detail, or, alternatively, may list too many side effects which do not apply to

the medications prescribed for the individual.

Figure 9.2 provides a copy of the Monitoring of Side Effects Scale (MOSES; Kalachnik, 1988). Another highly recommended general purpose scale is the Adverse Drug Reaction Detection Scale (ADRDS) (Corso et al., 1992). The MOSES is limited to psychotropic and antiepileptic medication. The ADRDS was developed for all medications.

Side effect specific scales address an individual side effect or series of side effects in great detail. While a side effect such as drooling is not complex, others such as extrapyramidal side effects (EPSE) may be composed of various signs and symptoms that can vary from client to client.

The major advantage of side effect specific scales is an in-depth and detailed assessment. These scales tend to be strong in terms of psychometrics, and some provide an indicator score prompting further clinical inquiry. Additionally, these scales provide a method to address side effects of public health concern (e.g., TD) that often are of legal or consumer group interest. Figure 9.3 presents a copy of the Dyskinesia Identification System Condensed User Scale (DISCUS) (Sprague & Kalachnik, 1991).

The disadvantage of these types of scales is that the scale is limited to the specific side effect or clinical situation. The provider is forced to use another side effect scale to check for other side effects. This increases paper.

Monitoring of Side Effect Scale (MOSES)

Rating Date	Client Name
Rater Signature & Title	

Scoring: See other side for details

0: None	2: Mild	4: Severe
1: Minimal	3: Moderate	NA: Not Assessable

Instructions: See other side. Bold items below are primarily observable. Regular print items are primarily client verbalization, staff input, or chart review.

Exam Type (Check one; if "other," specify in rater comments)

☐ Admission   ☐ Baseline   ☐ Dose Increase   ☐ Drug Initiation   ☐ 6-Month   ☐ Other

Ears/Eyes/Head

01. **Blink Rate: Decreased**	0 1 2 3 4 NA
02. **Eyes: Rapid Vert/Horz.**	0 1 2 3 4 NA
03. **Eyes: Rolled Up**	0 1 2 3 4 NA
04. **Face: No Expression/ Masked**	0 1 2 3 4 NA
05. **Tics/Grimace**	0 1 2 3 4 NA
06. blurred/double vision	0 1 2 3 4 NA
07. ear ringing	0 1 2 3 4 NA
08. headache	0 1 2 3 4 NA

Mouth

09. **Drooling/Pooling**	0 1 2 3 4 NA
10. **Dry Mouth**	0 1 2 3 4 NA
11. **Gum Growth**	0 1 2 3 4 NA
12. **Mouth/Tongue Movement**	0 1 2 3 4 NA
13. **Speech: Slurred/ Difficult/Slow**	0 1 2 3 4 NA

Nose/Throat/Chest

14. **Breast: Discharge**	0 1 2 3 4 NA
15. **Breast: Swelling**	0 1 2 3 4 NA
16. **Labored Breathing**	0 1 2 3 4 NA
17. **Nasal Congestion/ Runny Nose**	0 1 2 3 4 NA
18. **Sore Throat/Redness**	0 1 2 3 4 NA
19. **Swallowing: Difficult**	0 1 2 3 4 NA

Gastrointestinal

20. **Vomiting/nausea**	0 1 2 3 4 NA
21. abdominal pain	0 1 2 3 4 NA
22. appetite: decreased	0 1 2 3 4 NA
23. appetite: increased	0 1 2 3 4 NA
24. constipation	0 1 2 3 4 NA
25. diarrhea	0 1 2 3 4 NA
26. flatulence	0 1 2 3 4 NA
27. taste abnormality: metallic, etc.	0 1 2 3 4 NA
28. thirst: increased	0 1 2 3 4 NA

Musculoskeletal/Neurological

29. **Arm Swing: Decreased**	0 1 2 3 4 NA
30. **Contortions/Neck- Back Arching**	0 1 2 3 4 NA
31. **Gait: Imbalance/ Unsteady**	0 1 2 3 4 NA
32. **Gait: Shuffling**	0 1 2 3 4 NA
33. **Limb Jerking/Writhing**	0 1 2 3 4 NA
34. **Movement: Slowed/ Lack Of**	0 1 2 3 4 NA
35. **Pill Rolling**	0 1 2 3 4 NA
36. **Restlessness/Pacing/ Can't Sit Still**	0 1 2 3 4 NA
37. **Rigidity/complaints of muscle pain or aches**	0 1 2 3 4 NA
38. **Tremor/Shakiness**	0 1 2 3 4 NA
39. complaints of jitteriness/ jumpiness	0 1 2 3 4 NA
40. fainting/dizziness/upon standing	0 1 2 3 4 NA
41. seizures: increased	0 1 2 3 4 NA
42. tingling/numbness	0 1 2 3 4 NA
43. weakness/fatigue	0 1 2 3 4 NA

Skin

44. **Acne**	0 1 2 3 4 NA
45. **Bruising: Easy/ Pronounced**	0 1 2 3 4 NA
46. **Color: Blue/Coldness**	0 1 2 3 4 NA
47. **Color: Flushing/Warm To Touch**	0 1 2 3 4 NA
48. **Color: Pale/Pallor**	0 1 2 3 4 NA
49. **Color: Yellow**	0 1 2 3 4 NA
50. **Dry/Itchy**	0 1 2 3 4 NA
51. **Edema**	0 1 2 3 4 NA
52. **Hair: Abnormal Growth**	0 1 2 3 4 NA
53. **Hair: Loss**	0 1 2 3 4 NA
54. **Rash/Hives**	0 1 2 3 4 NA
55. **Sunburns/Redness**	0 1 2 3 4 NA
56. **Sweating: Decreased**	0 1 2 3 4 NA
57. **Sweating: Increased**	0 1 2 3 4 NA
58. chills	0 1 2 3 4 NA

Urinary/Genital

59. menstruation: absent/ irregular	
60. sexual: activity decreased	
61. sexual: activity increased	
62. sexual: continual erection	
63. sexual: erection inability	
64. sexual: orgasm difficult	
65. urinary retention	
66. urination: decreased	
67. urination: difficult/painful	
68. urination: increased	
69. urination: nocturnal/enuresis	

While the side-effects in these two areas are often difficult to determine, please be aware they may occur depending on the specific drug profile. Be certain to inquire about these if the client is verbal.

Psychological

70. **Agitation**	0 1 2 3 4 NA
71. **Confusion**	0 1 2 3 4 NA
72. **Crying/feelings of sadness**	0 1 2 3 4 NA
73. **Drowsiness/Lethargy/ Sedation**	0 1 2 3 4 NA
74. **Irritability**	0 1 2 3 4 NA
75. **Withdrawn**	0 1 2 3 4 NA
76. attention/concentration difficulty	
77. morning "hangover"	
78. nightmares/vivid dreams	
79. perceptual: hallucinations/ delusions	
80. sleep: excessive	
81. sleep: insomnia	

If seen:
• Circle item
• Enter under "Other"
• Assign intensity score

Other

_____
_____
_____
_____
_____
_____
_____
_____
_____
_____

Measures

Blood Pressure: _____   **Pulse:** _____   **Temperature:** _____   **Weight:** _____

Other (specify):

©John E. Kalachnik, 1984. Reprinted with permission. The MOSES may be reproduced for clinical or internal organizational use only.

Figure 9.2. Example of a general side effects assessment scale.

Figure 9.2. Continued

Client Name:

Current Psychotropic, Antiepileptic, Other Drugs of Importance (e.g., anticholinergics, stool softeners, etc), and Total Mg/Day

_____ _____ mg/day   _____ _____ mg/day

_____ _____ mg/day   _____ _____ mg/day

_____ _____ mg/day   _____ _____ mg/day

Rater Comments (cross-reference chart location if more space needed)

Instructions:

1. Observe the client for 5-15 minutes in a quiet area.
2. Perform procedures to ascertain items (e.g., flex arm for rigidity, open mouth to check throat and saliva, watch arm swing while walking, etc). If client is verbal, inquire as to problems on items (e.g., "Are you having trouble seeing what you read? Describe this to me"). If client is verbal, ask at least once an open-ended question (e.g., "How have you been feeling?" or "Is there anything bothering you we need to know about?").
3. Review data such as seizure counts. If possible, talk to and review comments by reliable staff, especially on items which cannot be directly observed during the exam such as eating or sleeping.
4. If a sign or symptom is present, it is scored. This does not mean it is necessarily a side effect. If an item is scored and an explanation exists, describe this in the RATER COMMENTS (e.g., the client displays severe tremor, but is 80 years old and has had severe tremor as part of diagnosed Parkinson's disease).
5. Document in the client's chart that the assessment was conducted. Provide the form to the prescriber for review and signature.
6. The prescriber reviews the assessment, determines and documents appropriate action, and signs the form.
7. The form is filed in client's chart according to facility procedure. Any follow-up actions should be documented in the chart.
8. Refer to the exam and summarize in regularly scheduled quarterly or other medication reviews. Summarize in such reviews the results or status of any follow-up actions.

Is more specialized assessment data required or likely to be needed? (e.g., more specific rating scale, assessment using behavioral measures, etc.)

☐ Yes (describe in comments)   ☐ No

Rater Conclusion:

☐ No immediate action required: Physician review at next visitor quarterly meeting

☐ Action required: Semi-Immediate physician review (≤7 days)

☐ Action required: Immediate physician review (≤72 hours)

Physician Comments (cross-reference chart location if more space needed)

Scoring:
(Bold items are primarily observable. Regular print items are primarily client verbalization, staff input, or chart review)

0: Not Present. The item is not observable or is within the range of normal.

1: Minimal. The item is difficult to detect. It is questionable if the item is in the upper range of normal. The client does not notice or comment on the item. Alternatively, the item may occur a couple of times in a noticeable but short non-intense and non-repetitive manner.

2: Mild. The item is present, but does not hinder the client's normal functioning; i.e., his or her level at pretreatment. While the client is in no extreme discomfort, it is annoyance to the client or may progress to future severity and problems if ignored. Alternatively, the item may be continuously displayed in a non-intense manner or may "come and go" several times in a noticeable but non-intense manner.

3: Moderate. The item is present and produces some degree of impairment to functioning, but is not hazardous to health. Rather, it is uncomfortable and/or embarrassing to the client. Alternatively, the item may be displayed in a semi-intense manner "more often than not."

4: Severe. The item is a definite hazard to well-being. There is significant impairment of functioning or incapacitation. Alternatively, the item may be displayed in an intense and continuous or nearly continuous manner.

NA: The item is not assessable. The client will not cooperate with the item, appropriate data is not available, etc.

Physician Conclusion (check one or more):

☐ No action necessary   ☐ Contra-active/auxiliary drug

☐ Dose reduction   ☐ Drug change

☐ Drug discontinuation   ☐ Increased surveillance

☐ Drug hold   ☐ Lab or other tests/data

Physician Signature   **Date of Review**

This scale is not a complete listing of all possible adverse drug reactions or effects and is not a substitute for other appropriate professional health care responsibilities, assessments, or testing.

NAME	**I.D.**

_____
(facility)

Dyskinesia Identification System: Condensed User Scale (DISCUS)

CURRENT PSYCHOTROPICS/ANTI-CHOLINERGIC AND TOTAL MG/DAY

_____ _____ mg

_____ _____ mg

_____ _____ mg

_____ _____ mg

See Instructions On Other Side

EXAM TYPE (check one)
- ☐ 1. Baseline
- ☐ 2. Annual
- ☐ 3. Semi-Annual
- ☐ 4. D/C — 1 Month
- ☐ 5. D/C — 2 Month
- ☐ 6. D/C — 3 Month
- ☐ 7. Admission
- ☐ 8. Other

COOPERATION (check one)
- ☐ 1. None
- ☐ 2. Partial
- ☐ 3. Full

SCORING

0 — **Not Present** (movements not observed or some movements observed but not considered abnormal)

1 — **Minimal** (abnormal movements are difficult to detect or movements are easy to detect but occur only once or twice in a short non-repetitive manner)

2 — **Mild** (abnormal movements occur infrequently **and** are easy to detect)

3 — **Moderate** (abnormal movements occur frequently **and** are easy to detect)

4 — **Severe** (abnormal movements occur almost continuously **and** are easy to detect)

NA — **Not Assessed** (an assessment for an item is not able to be made)

ASSESSMENT

DISCUS Item and Score (circle one score for each item)

FACE
1. Tics.................................... 0 1 2 3 4 NA
2. Grimaces .... 0 1 2 3 4 NA

EYES
3. Blinking................................ 0 1 2 3 4 NA

ORAL
4. Chewing/Lip Smacking....... 0 1 2 3 4 NA
5. Puckering/Sucking/ Thrusting Lower Lip............ 0 1 2 3 4 NA

LINGUAL
6. Tongue Thrusting/ Tongue in Cheek .... 0 1 2 3 4 NA
7. Tonic Tongue .... 0 1 2 3 4 NA
8. Tongue Tremor .... 0 1 2 3 4 NA
9. Athetoid/Myokymic/ Lateral Tongue .... 0 1 2 3 4 NA

HEAD/NECK/TRUNK
10. Retrocollis/Torticollis .... 0 1 2 3 4 NA
11. Shoulder/Hip Torsion .... 0 1 2 3 4 NA

UPPER LIMB
12. Athetoid/Myokymic Finger-Wrist-Arm .... 0 1 2 3 4 NA
13. Pill Rolling .... 0 1 2 3 4 NA

LOWER LIMB
14. Ankle Flexion/ Foot Tapping .... 0 1 2 3 4 NA
15. Toe Movement .... 0 1 2 3 4 NA

COMMENTS/OTHER
_____
_____
_____
_____
_____

TOTAL SCORE _____
(items 1-15 only)

EVALUATION (see other side)

1. Greater than 90 days neuroleptic exposure? : YES NO

2. Scoring/intensity level met? : YES NO

3. Other diagnostic conditions? : YES NO
   (if yes, specify) _____
   _____
   _____
   _____

4. Last exam date: _____
   Last total score: _____
   Last conclusion: _____

   Preparer signature and title for items 1-4 (if different from physician):

5. Conclusion (circle one):
   - A. No TD (if scoring prerequisite met, list other diagnostic condition or explain in comments)
   - B. Probable TD
   - C. Masked TD
   - D. Withdrawal TD
   - E. Persistent TD
   - F. Remitted TD
   - G. Other (specify in comments)

6. Comments:
   _____
   _____
   _____
   _____
   _____
   _____
   _____

EXAM DATE _____

RATER SIGNATURE AND TITLE	NEXT EXAM DATE	PHYSICIAN SIGNATURE	DATE

Sprague, R.L. & Kalachnik, J.E. (1991). Reliability, validity, and a total score cutoff for the Dyskinesia Identification System: Condensed User Scale (DISCUS) with mentally ill and mentally retarded populations. *Psychopharmacology Bulletin, 27* (1), 51-58.

Figure 9.3. Example of a side effect specific scale for tardive dyskinesia.

Figure 9.3. Continued

Simplified Diagnoses for Tardive Dyskinesia (SD-TD)

PREREQUISITES. — The 3 prerequisites are as follows. Exceptions may occur.

1. A history of at least three months' total cumulative neuroleptic exposure. Include amoxapine and metoclopramide in all categories below as well.

2. **SCORING/INTENSITY LEVEL.** The presence of a **TOTAL SCORE OF FIVE (5) OR ABOVE.** Also be alert for any change from baseline or scores below five which have at least a "moderate" (3) or "severe" (4) movement on any item or at least two "mild" (2) movements on two items located in different body areas.

3. Other conditions are not responsible for the abnormal involuntary movements.

DIAGNOSES. — The diagnosis is based upon the current exam and its relation to the last exam. The diagnosis can shift depending upon: (a) whether movements are present or not, (b) whether movements are present for 3 months or more (6 months if on a semi-annual assessment schedule), and (c) whether neuroleptic dosage changes occur and effect movements.

- **NO TD.** — Movements **are not** present on this exam **or** movements are present, but some other condition is responsible for them. The last diagnosis must be NO TD, PROBABLE TD, or WITHDRAWAL TD.

- **PROBABLE TD.** — Movements **are** present on this exam. This is the first time they are present **or** they have never been present for 3 months or more. The last diagnosis must be NO TD or PROBABLE TD.

- **PERSISTENT TD.** — Movements **are** present on this exam **and** they have been present for 3 months or more with this exam or at some point in the past. The last diagnosis can be any except NO TD.

- **MASKED TD.** — Movements **are not** present on this exam **but** this is due to a neuroleptic dosage increase or reinstitution after a prior exam when movements were present. Also use this conclusion if movements are not present due to the addition of a non-neuroleptic medication to treat TD. The last diagnosis must be PROBABLE TD, PERSISTENT TD, WITHDRAWAL TD, or MASKED TD.

- **REMITTED TD.** — Movements **are not** present on this exam **but** PERSISTENT TD has been diagnosed **and** no neuroleptic dosage increase or reinstitution has occurred. The last diagnosis must be PERSISTENT TD or REMITTED TD. If movements re-emerge, the diagnosis shifts back to PERSISTENT TD.

- **WITHDRAWAL TD.** — Movements **are not seen while** receiving neuroleptics or at the last dosage level **but are seen within** 8 weeks following a neuroleptic reduction or discontinuation. The last diagnosis must be NO TD or WITHDRAWAL TD. If movements continue for 3 months or more after the neuroleptic dosage reduction or discontinuation, the diagnosis shifts to PERSISTENT TD. If movements do not continue for 3 months or more after the reduction or discontinuation, the diagnosis shifts to NO TD.

INSTRUCTIONS

1. The rater completes the Assessment according to the standardized exam procedure. If the rater also completes Evaluation items 1-4, he/she must also sign the preparer box. The form is given to the physician. Alternatively, the physician may perform the assessment.

2. The physician completes the Evaluation section. The physician is responsible for the entire Evaluation section and its accuracy.

3. IT IS RECOMMENDED THAT THE PHYSICIAN EXAMINE ANY INDIVIDUAL WHO MEETS THE 3 PREREQUISITES OR WHO HAS MOVEMENTS NOT EXPLAINED BY OTHER FACTORS. NEUROLOGICAL ASSESSMENTS OR DIFFERENTIAL DIAGNOSTIC TESTS WHICH MAY BE NECESSARY SHOULD BE OBTAINED.

4. File form according to policy or procedure.

OTHER CONDITIONS (partial list)

1. Age
2. Blind
3. Cerebral Palsy
4. Contact Lenses
5. Dentures/No Teeth
6. Down's Syndrome
7. Drug Intoxication (specify)
8. Encephalitis
9. Extrapyramidal Side-Effects(specify)
10. Fahr's Syndrome
11. Heavy Metal Intoxication (specify)
12. Huntington's Chorea
13. Hyperthyroidism
14. Hypoglycemia
15. Hypoparathyroidism
16. Idiopathic Torsion Dystonia
17. Meige Syndrome
18. Parkinson's Disease
19. Stereotypies
20. Syndenham's Chorea
21. Tourette's Syndrome
22. Wilson's Disease
23. Other (specify)

How often should side effect assessments occur? As with index behaviors, the answer to this question depends on a number of factors such as regulations, client risk factors, living setting, treatment phase, and the medication involved. The following general paradigm is adaptable to individual cases.

1. Side effects should be assessed using a general purpose or medication-specific side effects scale at least once every 3 to 6 months. If a new psychotropic medication is initiated or the dose increased, at least one formal assessment should occur within 1 month of the initiation or increase. One model to consider for the initiation of new psychotropic medication is weekly for 1 month. Side-effect assessments upon reduction or discontinuation are not generally required as long as such reductions or discontinuations are gradual. However, more rapid or abrupt reductions should have side effects assessed at least once per week for 1 to 3 weeks since abrupt reduction is more likely to be associated with withdrawal side effects.

2. If an antipsychotic medication, amoxapine (Asendin), or metoclopramide (Reglan) is prescribed, TD assessments using a TD-specific side effects scale should occur at least once every 3 to 6 months. If these medications are discontinued after extended use, TD assessments should occur at least 1 and 2 months after discontinuation to determine the presence of withdrawal dyskinesia.

Summary. The critical variables in monitoring side effects are selecting a standardized assessment device, determining a basic assessment schedule that remains flexible to individual differences, and establishing a communication channel between the people conducting the assessments and the prescriber. Unless a particular condition or set of medications is involved, a general side effect scale is probably most useful. Specific side effect scales are useful to check for side effects of major concern (e.g., TD with antipsychotic medication) or to track for a limited time medication changes in relation to a specific side effect (e.g., to determine if benztropine [Cogentin] is still required to treat EPSE).

In special cases, the index behavior data collection methods previously described may be of value. For example, if a more specific measure of "loss of appetite" is required, a rating scale for mealtimes can be constructed. If a concern such as drooling or drowsiness is present, a 1-week time sample could be used and compared to subsequent weeks after a specific intervention is implemented. These techniques have been especially helpful in assessing behavioral side effects (Kalachnik, Hanzel, Harder, Bauernfeind, & Engstrom, 1995).

Quality of Life

Quality of life is an important consideration in addition to index behavior monitoring and side effects monitoring for two reasons. First, the intended outcome of psychotropic medication (as well as any intervention) is to help the individual live a more productive or fulfilling life. Second, an index behavior may improve (e.g., less aggression), but quality of life may be compromised (e.g., excessive sedation leading to nonparticipation in activities). Balance between index behavior and condition improvement, side effects, and quality of life can often be difficult to achieve. For example, treatment of schizophrenia may lead to improved quality of life because the individual is no longer in acute care and able to work, but development of moderate to severe TD as a result of antipsychotic medication may result in social embarrassment and compromised social activity.

The author is not aware of any convenient numerical device measuring quality of life per se that is applicable to all individuals and situations, nor to the subpopulation of people with severe developmental disabilities. Three suggestions are provided.

First, Hughs, Hwang, Kim, Eisenman, and Killian (1995) provide a comprehensive review of empirical measures in relation to quality of life with individuals with developmental disabilities. A list of 15 dimensions, corresponding components for each dimension, and specific representative measures is outlined. These measures and examples may provide a useful paradigm from which to approach quality of life. One or more of these may be discussed during reviews or, if a numerical tracking measure is needed, a specific index behavior measurement technique such as a rating scale code can be used. The 15 dimensions with examples are social relations and interaction (e.g., affection such as smiling); psychological well-being and personal satisfaction (e.g., self-concept); employment (e.g., job choice and work performance); self-determination, autonomy, and personal choice (e.g., deciding how to spend one's money); recreation and leisure (e.g., going to a movie); personal competence, community adjustment, and independent living skills (e.g., self-care skills such as selecting clothes); residential environment (e.g., living in safe healthy place); community integration (e.g., visiting a religious location or family); normalization (e.g., use of socially appropriate terms); support services received (e.g., perception or satisfaction of services received); individual and social demographic indicators (e.g., age); personal development and fulfillment (e.g., attempting new tasks); social acceptance, social status, and ecological fit (e.g., people's response to the person in public); physical and material well-being (e.g., physical health such as weight and blood pressure); and civic responsibility (e.g., arrests).

Second, HCFA (1996) defines a *loss* of functional status (i.e., quality of life) as a measurable loss of a person's previously possessed ability to function in one or more of the following ways: activities of daily living (e.g., locomotion, bathing, dressing, eating, etc.), cognition or thinking (e.g., memory and orientation), communication, bladder or bowel control, and motivation and interest in preferred activities. Consideration of these areas in a review would provide a paradigm to discuss quality of life.

Third, the author has had success with defining one or more specific activities in relation to the individual's life to be discussed at each psychotropic medication review. Data are not necessarily collected. Rather, the item serves as a reminder to review quality of life or to implement more formal assessment and data collection if problems are reported. For example, the highlight of an elderly woman's life in a nursing home was to watch soap operas each afternoon, gossip, and drink coffee with several of her friends. She was started on a low dose of haloperidol. At one of the reviews, the question was asked, "How is Ms. Doe doing with the soap operas?" Staff became suddenly quiet and then noted, "We haven't seen her down there lately." A 1-week frequency count confirmed this and led to further inquiry that discovered haloperidol was causing a hand tremor which was causing her to spill her coffee. She was embarrassed by this in front of her friends and had begun to stay in her room. A medication reduction and change led to a return to the quality of life activity.

Summary. Assessing quality of life is not as numerically oriented as monitoring index behaviors or side effects. It is often challenging to determine quality of life activities for an individual who is severely compromised by genetics or dementia. Efforts, however, to identify and monitor some positive aspect of the individual's life (or potential aspect if the condition can be stabilized or improved) serve to keep the multidisciplinary team's focus away from treating index behaviors per se and on the underlying condition that is interfering with the individual's life. Perhaps the most valuable aspect of quality of life monitoring is to provide a check against index behavior improvement at the cost of severely compromised quality of life. Thus, it is strongly recommended that at least one quality of life indicator be developed for purposes of discussion at each psychotropic medication review.

Lowest Optimal Effective Dose (OED)

Lowest OED is the least amount of psychotropic medication required to improve or stabilize the index behavior and condition of concern. As a procedure, the phrase *lowest OED plan* refers to a methodology incorporating gradual dose reductions to determine the least amount of psychotropic medication. Similar terms are *minimal effective dose* (MED) and *lowest effective dose* (LED). The 1995 International

Consensus Panel on Psychopharmacology selected the term lowest OED because minimal or lowest effective dose connotes doses that are minimally effective to treat the index behavior and condition of concern (Kalachnik et al., 1998).

Lowest OED is important for several reasons (Bishop, 1992; HCFA, 1992; Schooler, 1993; Sovner & Hurley, 1984). First, there is a greater likelihood of side effects at higher doses. Second, interference with learning may potentially occur at higher doses for some medications, especially antipsychotic, benzodiazepine antianxiety, and sedative-hypnotic medications. Third, a complete remission of a condition may occur, or improvement over time may not be the result of the psychotropic medication or dose level. Fourth, whereas an abrupt reduction may result in relapse and a return to the original or a higher dose level, a lower maintenance dose level without relapse may be possible with gradual reductions. And fifth, as described earlier, ratcheting may occur. All of these considerations also have economic implications.

Lowest OED is not the same as a drug holiday—an outdated 1970s term that refers to abruptly discontinuing psychotropic medication to determine if it is still required. Lowest OED, on the other hand, refers to gradual medication reduction steps over an extended period of time to determine the least number of medications or lowest dose that may be, but is not necessarily, zero medication. Lowest OED procedures are not intended to represent an antimedication position.

Periodic review for lowest OED does not mean a psychotropic medication must be reduced for a specific individual. What is required is a review for the *possibility* at least once each year. The multidisciplinary team must justify, however, why a psychotropic medication and the dose level continues to be required. Some situations contraindicating a lowest OED attempt are that (a) the lowest OED has been established through previous attempts, and the dose is at this level; (b) a psychiatric condition has been diagnosed, a number of relapses have occurred which meet professional recommendations for mainte-

nance medication, and the medication is at the lower end of an established dose range; (c) extreme relapse occurred during the last lowest OED attempt such that an attempt is not in the client's best interests; (d) a refractory condition or a case where the person is "the best they have ever been" which is reflected in quality of life activity; (e) a difficult case where much progress has been made compared to the recent past (e.g., the person was on four psychotropic medications and now is only prescribed one); and (f) major life or environmental changes that have occurred or are about to occur (e.g., living area change, community placement, new job, or death of a close family member).

There are, however, some situations where lowest OED should be considered despite the exceptions noted. These include (a) substantial aging indicating a lower dose due to a change in metabolism; (b) improvement after the start of a new medication which has been added to the previous medication (i.e., the new medication and not the old medication may be the controlling variable); (c) improvement after a new behavior or educational program (i.e., the new program and not the medication may be the controlling variable); (d) outdated analysis or poor previous methodology such as abrupt dose reduction, poor environmental conditions, poor educational programs, or no data collection; (e) minimal medication response and continued problems suggesting nonresponder status or the possibility the medication may be contributing to the problem; (f) an excessive "indicator," such as a dose above FDA recommendations for the age, treatment phase, or condition; intraclass polypharmacy; or interclass polypharmacy without co-morbid conditions and quality of life improvement.

Some clinical situations do not allow or do not require extended gradual dose reductions. These include severe side effects (e.g., NMS, impaction, jaundice, etc.), medical procedures (e.g., surgery), very short-term use, rapidly excreted medication (e.g., lithium or methylphenidate), replacement with another medication from the same class (e.g., fluoxetine [Prozac] is replacing paroxetine [Paxil]), or treatment in a specialized psychiatric inpatient unit under close supervision.

TABLE 9.6

Some Non-OED Reduction Schedules for Avoiding Withdrawal Effects [1]

Psychotropic Drug or Drug Class	Recommended Non-OED Reduction [2]	References
Propranolol (Inderal)	Tapered slowly over 2–3 weeks	Fraser, Ruedrich, Kerr, & Levitas (1998)
Benzodiazepine antianxiety; e.g., diazepam (Valium)	Approximately 25% every 1–4 weeks	Noyes, Garvey, Cook, & Perry (1988)
Tricyclic antidepressant; e.g., amitriptyline (Elavil)	Approximately 25% every 3–4 to 7 days	Garner, Kelly, & Thompson (1993)
Anticholinergic medication; e.g., benztropine (Cogentin)	Over a few weeks	Casey & Gerlach (1984); Pi & Simpson (1986)
Sedative-hypnotic and barbiturate AEDs; e.g., chloral hydrate, phenobarbital	Slow and taking weeks to months	Coulter (1988); Fischbacher (1982)
Antipsychotic medication; e.g., haloperidol (Haldol)	10-25% once every 2–4 weeks	Wilson, Lott, & Tsai (1998)
Fluoxetine (Prozac)	5 mg every 2 weeks until dose is 5 mg; then 2.5 mg every 2 weeks	Skaehill & Welch (1997)
Fluvoxamine (Luvox) Sertraline (Zoloft) Venlafaxine (Effexor)	25 mg every 2 weeks until dose is 25 mg; then 12.5 mg every 2 weeks	Skaehill & Welch (1997)
Paroxetine (Paxil)	10 mg every 2 weeks until dose is 10 mg; then 5 mg every 2 weeks	Skaehill & Welch (1997)

[1] **It is important to note these reductions are for non-OED procedure situations in which the goal is to eliminate a clearly ineffective or no longer needed medication.** The goal is to avoid withdrawal effects.

[2] The text describes lowest OED procedures in detail. Succinctly, typical lowest OED methodology would attempt a longer time period between reductions in order to determine behavioral rates and allow for normal variability because lowest OED methodology is not only concerned with withdrawal effects, but also possible relapse and the lowest maintenance dose (which may be but is not necessarily zero medication). Behavioral or psychiatric relapse may take longer to emerge. Generally speaking and depending on a wide variety of factors such as treatment phase, specific medication and individual history, lowest OED methodology is usually 10% to 25% of the dose once every 1 to 3 months.

One question must always be asked: Is the goal to remove a clearly ineffectual psychotropic medication or to determine the lowest dose to treat the problem of concern? If the goal is to remove a clearly ineffectual medication, gradual reduction is based upon avoidance of withdrawal effects. This usually involves shorter periods of time because comparison of index behavior data is not needed. If, on the other hand, the goal is to achieve the lowest OED, enough time at each dose level is needed to allow meaningful index behavior data comparison. Table 9.6 presents some reduction

recommendations if the goal is to remove a clearly ineffectual psychotropic medication.

Items in a lowest OED plan. There are six items in a lowest OED plan. These can be modified at any time (usually at a monthly or quarterly review). If the index behavior system as described previously is in place, several of these items are easily determined.

1. *Identify the index behavior(s).* This is the objective and measurable behavior tracked to evaluate medication efficacy.

2. *Determine the index behavior(s) rate, list the dates from which the rate is computed, and use a recognized measurement method such as frequency count, time sample, or rating scale.* The rate is generally based upon at least a period of 30 to 90 days before and in close proximity to the medication reduction, but can be longer.

3. *Calculate an index behavior deterioration indicator.* This index behavior level signals that no further medication reductions should occur. As long as the index behavior does not exceed this level, the level reflects normal variability for the individual, and reductions should continue unless other variables are involved. A general rule of thumb is to use a 50% change from the prereduction level (e.g., if 15 episodes of screaming occur per month, the deterioration indicator is 22 episodes per month).

One helpful alternative is to look at weekly or monthly index behavior rates over the past 6 to 12 months, provided no major changes have occurred that would affect rates. These rates represent the range of variability from month to month for the individual. For example, if monthly rates for aggression from January to June are 14, 5, 6, 9, 7, and 8, the highest monthly rate (15 or more) is used as the indicator or a longitudinal pattern is determined (e.g., 10 or more aggressions per month for 2 consecutive months). Another helpful alternative for some cases is to identify prodromal signs that precede full and pronounced behavioral or psychiatric relapse. For example, if poor sleep is a prodromal sign of a developing depressive disorder with subsequent irritability displayed as increased agitation and aggression, the individual would have his sleep pattern formally monitored in addition to agitation and aggression.

4. *Outline a series of gradual reduction steps.* The reduction should generally be a 10% to 25% decrease of the entry dose once every 1 to 3 months depending on the individual. Available dosage forms may require adjustment of the recommended percentage. Within reason, a general rule of thumb is the closer to discontinuation the more gradual the reduction.

5. *Identify potential problems other than the index behavior and possible actions.* Potential problems are determined by the individual's history, especially during any previous reduction attempts. There is nothing worse than to have a previous problem emerge (e.g., pacing at night) and no immediate plan (e.g., efforts to keep person away from other sleeping clients, prompts to sit in a rocking chair every 15 min, soft music, glass of warm milk, and, if needed, a short-term, 21-day course of lorazepam [Ativan] to "buy time" to determine if this is a withdrawal reaction).

6. *Plan for other medication adjustments that may be necessary as a result of the psychotropic medication reduction.* There may be another medication in the treatment plan that needs to be adjusted as a result of the reduction. For example, an anticholinergic medication such as benztropine (Cogentin) may need to be reduced. It should be remembered these other changes may have effects or withdrawal effects of their own, so, if possible, changes should occur as a separate step. Some medications may have to be increased or decreased because of interactions that affect blood levels. Some medications may need to be adjusted because behavioral side effects emerge that were minimized by the medication being reduced. Other medications may need to be prescribed for a short period of time to assist with the reduction. An example of the latter is clonidine (Catapres) to help alleviate adrenergic hyperactivity behavioral withdrawal effects from medications with anticholinergic properties such as thioridazine (Mellaril), chlorpromazine (Thorazine), or mesoridazine (Serentil) (Sovner, 1995).

Reviews and decisions. While the individual is undergoing the lowest OED attempt, reviews should occur at least once a month in order to closely track changes and detect developing relapse. The prescriber does not have to see the individual each month. However, a data review should occur and basic information should be shared with the prescriber (index behavior level, prodromal sign status, quality of life, side or withdrawal effects, indicator level reached, etc.).

There are basically three situations which may occur at a review. In the first situation, the index behavior deterioration indicator is not exceeded, and no other problems emerge. Unless the lowest OED plan calls for more time at the dose level, the dose is usually reduced to the next level. Occasionally, the dose may need to remain at the same level for an extra 1 or 2 months if the client "just doesn't seem to be him- or herself." If zero dose has been reached, monthly reviews continue for 6 months in order to detect developing relapse.

In the second situation, the index behavior deterioration level is exceeded. If the index behavior level cannot be tolerated or if auxiliary interventions implemented are ineffective, the dose is usually increased to the last level. If the index behavior level is tolerable or auxiliary interventions can be implemented, the dose level usually remains the same for the remainder of the reduction step or for an additional specified period of time.

In the third situation, the index behavior deterioration indicator is not exceeded, but other problems or a new problem emerges. If the problem can be tolerated or if auxiliary interventions can be implemented, the dose usually remains the same for the remainder of the reduction step or for an additional period of time. If the problem cannot be tolerated or auxiliary interventions cannot be implemented, the dose is usually returned to the last step. A higher dose may be necessary in some cases, but this should be gradually reduced back to the appropriate nonproblem dose level once the individual has been stabilized for a sufficient period of time.

Lowest OED is determined by one of four possibilities. In the first, zero dose is reached, and the individual does not relapse for 6 months. The lowest OED is zero. In the second, problems occur at the same dose twice. The lowest OED is the dose just prior to the problem dose. In the third, problems occur at different dose levels with the second at a higher level than the first. The lowest OED is just above the second problem dose (e.g., problems occur the first time at thioridazine 100 mg after reducing from 300 to 200 to 100; the dose was returned to 200 mg; problems occurred the second time at 150 mg after reducing from 200 to 175 to 150; the lowest OED is 175 mg). In the fourth, problems occur at a dose level, but the nature or severity of the problem does not allow a second more gradual attempt. The lowest OED is just prior to the problem level dose.

Summary. There is no absolute method to determine who requires psychotropic medication and who does not. There is not a foolproof method to determine the best psychotropic medication dose level for a specific individual. Lowest OED attempts to balance two competing forces: not harming those who truly require psychotropic medication or higher doses and removing or lowering psychotropic medication for those who no longer require psychotropic medication or higher doses. Lowest OED methodology has advanced dramatically over the past 20 years, but problems still occur. Use of the lowest OED methodology, however, lowers the probability of such cases. Most lowest OED studies suggest that approximately 25% of clients will be successfully removed from psychotropic medication, approximately 50% will have lower doses, approximately 20% will remain at the same dose, and approximately 5% will have higher doses (Branford, 1996; Ellenor & Frisk, 1977; Fielding, Murphy, Reagan, & Peterson, 1980; Findholt & Emmett, 1990; Inoue, 1982). Those individuals with a true psychiatric condition are more likely to have lower doses rather than complete discontinuation or are more likely to have inappropriate medication such as antipsychotic medication replaced with more appropriate non-antipsychotic psychotropic medication for the underlying psychiatric condition (Branford, 1996; Luchins, Dojka, & Hanrahan, 1993; Pary, 1995; Spreat, Serafin, Behar, & Leiman, 1993).

Summary

Over the past 25 years, a set of basic psychotropic medication guidelines have been established through a combination of accreditation, professional, legal, and regulatory sources. These guidelines define the expected structures and processes that must be in place to assure quality of care when a psychotropic medication is prescribed for an individual with developmental disabilities.

Psychotropic medication guidelines were driven in 1970s by the conceptual forces of active treatment, multidisciplinary team participation, and informed consent. Guidelines were driven in the 1980s by the need to establish a methodology to track index behaviors, monitor side effects, and establish lowest OED. Guidelines in the 1990s have been driven by the biopsychosocial model, the integration of the rational and empirical schools of thought, and quality of life outcome measures. Guidelines in the future, as they should, will be driven by new conceptual forces. However, no force such as economic pressure or easing of regulations must be allowed to displace the psychotropic medication guidelines established over the past 25 years.

The purpose of this chapter has not been to criticize the community-based model. Rather, it is to sound a warning that unless basic psychotropic medication monitoring occurs, the potential exists for just as many problems in the future as there were in the past. In addition to reviewing basic concepts, methods have been presented for use on the applied level. Succinctly, a standardized process addressing index behaviors, side effects, quality of life, and lowest optimal effective dose must be in place. These procedures, however, must remain flexible to individual situations. The goal of this flexible standardization is to ensure proper psychotropic medication use and monitoring while allowing professionals on the front lines and closest to the situation to determine the exact details appropriate for the individual or situation.

Mark Twain once said about bourbon, "Too much of a good thing is barely enough." Too much of proper psychotropic medication monitoring may be barely enough to prevent a return to the past in light of current economic patterns.

REFERENCES

Accreditation Council for Facilities for the Mentally Retarded. (1971). *Standards for residential facilities for the mentally retarded.* Chicago: Joint Commission on Accreditation of Hospitals.

Accreditation Council for Facilities for the Mentally Retarded. (1973). *Standards for community agencies serving persons with mental retardation and other developmental disabilities.* Chicago: Joint Commission on Accreditation of Hospitals.

Accreditation Council for Services for Mentally Retarded and Other Developmentally Disabled Persons. (1977). *Standards for services for developmentally disabled individuals.* Chicago: Joint Commission on Accreditation of Hospitals.

Accreditation Council on Services for People with Developmental Disabilities. (1987). *Standards for services for people with developmental disabilities.* Boston: Author.

Accreditation Council on Services for People with Disabilities. (1993). *Outcome based performance measures.* Towson, MD: Author.

Ahmed, Z. (1997, January). Effects of reducing anti-psychotic medication in people with learning disabilities. In D. James (Chair), *Consensus document on psychopharmacology and learning disability.* Symposium conducted at the meeting of the Royal College of Psychiatry, Cardiff, Wales, UK.

Aman, M. G. (1984). Drugs and learning in mentally retarded persons. In C. D. Burrows & S. S. Werry (Eds.), Advances in human psychopharmacology (Vol. 3, pp. 121–163). Greenwich, CT: JAI Press.

Aman, M. G., Field, C. J., & Bridgman, G. D. (1985). City-wide survey of drug patterns among non-institutionalized retarded persons. *Applied Research in Mental Retardation, 5,* 159–171.

Aman, M. G., Hammer, D., & Rojahn, J. (1993). Mental retardation. In T. H. Ollendick & M. Hersen (Eds.), *Handbook of child and adolescent assessment* (pp. 321–345). Boston: Allyn & Bacon.

Aman, M. G., Sarphare, G., & Burrow, W. H. (1995). Psychotropic drugs in group homes: Prevalence and relation to demographic/psychiatric variables. *American Journal on Mental Retardation, 99,* 500–509.

Aman, M. G., & Singh, N. N. (1991). Pharmacological intervention. In J. L. Matson & J. A. Mulick (Eds.), *Handbook of mental retardation* (2nd ed., pp. 347–372). New York: Pergamon Press.

Aman, M. G., Singh, N. N., Stewart, A. W., & Field, C. J. (1985). The aberrant behavior checklist. *Psychopharmacology Bulletin, 21,* 845-850.

American Hospital Formulary Service Drug Information. (1995). Bethesda, MD: American Society of Hospital Pharmacists.

American Psychiatric Association. (1979). *Task force report 18. Tardive dyskinesia.* Washington, DC: Author.

American Psychiatric Association. (1990). *Psychiatric services to adult mentally retarded and developmentally disabled persons. Task force report 30.* Washington, DC: Author.

American Psychiatric Association. (1992). *Tardive dyskinesia: A task force report of the American Psychiatric Association.* Washington, DC: Author.

American Psychiatric Association. (1994). *Diagnostic and statistical manual of mental disorders* (4th ed.). Washington, DC: Author.

American Psychiatric Association Committee on Research on Psychiatric Treatments. (1992). Psychopharmacological screening criteria. *Journal of Clinical Psychiatry, 53,* 184–196.

Appelbaum, P. S., Lidz, C. W., & Meisel, A. (1987). *Informed consent. Legal theory and clinical practice.* New York: Oxford University Press.

Arnold, L. E. (1993). Clinical pharmacological issues in treating psychiatric disorders of patients with mental retardation. *Annals of Clinical Psychiatry, 5,* 189–197.

Ayd, F. J. (1991). The early history of modern psychopharmacology. *Neuropsychopharmacology, 5,* 71–84.

Baldessarini, R. J. (1980). Drugs and the treatment of psychiatric disorders. In L. S. Goodman & A. Gilman (Eds.), *The pharmacological basis of therapeutics* (6th ed., pp. 391–447). New York: Macmillan.

Barkley, R. A., McMurray, M. B., Edelbrock, C. S., & Robbins, K. (1990). Side effects of methylphenidate in children with attention deficit hyperactivity disorder: A systematic, placebo-controlled evaluation. *Pediatrics, 86,* 184–192.

Barnes, T. R. E. (1989). A rating scale for drug induced akathisia. *British Journal of Psychiatry, 154,* 672–676.

Beardsley, R. R., Freeman, J. M., & Appel, F. A. (1983). Anticonvulsant serum levels are useful only if the physician appropriately uses them: An assessment of the impact of providing serum level data to physicians. *Epilepsia, 24,* 330–335.

Beatles. (1968, August 30). *Revolution* (R5722). London: Apple Records.

Bennett, B. S., & Lipman, A. G. (1977). Comparative study of prospective and voluntary reporting in determining the incidence of adverse drug reactions. *American Journal of Hospital Pharmacy, 34,* 931–936.

Beyer, H. A. (1988). Litigation and use of psychoactive drugs in developmental disabilities. In M. G. Aman & N. N. Singh (Eds.), *Psychopharmacology of the developmental disabilities* (pp. 29–57). New York: Springer-Verlag.

Bishop, A. C. (1992). Empirical approach to psychopharmacology for institutionalized individuals with severe or profound mental retardation. *Mental Retardation, 30,* 283–288.

Blair, D. T. (1990, March). Risk management for extrapyramidal symptoms. *Quality Review Bulletin,* 116–124.

Bodfish, J. W., Newell, K. M., Sprague, R. L., Harper, V. N., & Lewis, M. H. (1997). Akathisia in adults with mental retardation: Development of the akathisia ratings of movement scale (ARMS). *American Journal of Mental Retardation, 101,* 413–423.

Borison, R. (1985, May). The recognition and management of drug-induced movement disorders (reversible type). Paper presented at the meeting of the American Psychiatric Association, Dallas, TX.

Braddock, D., Fujiura, G., Hemp, R., Mitchell, D., & Bachelder, L. (1991). Current and future trends in state-operated mental retardation institutions in the United States. *American Journal on Mental Retardation, 95,* 451–462.

Branford, D. (1996). Factors associated with the successful or unsuccessful withdrawal of antipsychotic drug therapy prescribed for people with learning disabilities. *Journal of Intellectual Disability Research, 40,* 322–329.

Casey, D. E., & Gerlach, J. (1984). Tardive dyskinesia: Management and new treatment. In H. C. Stancer, P. E. Garfinkel, & V. M. Rafoff (Eds.), *Guidelines for the use of psychotropic medication: A clinical handbook* (pp. 183–203). Jamaica, NY: Spectrum.

Corso, D. M., Pucino, F., DeLeo, J. M., Calis, K. A., & Gallelli, J. F. (1992). Development of a questionnaire for detecting potential adverse drug reactions. *Annals of Pharmacotherapy, 26,* 890–896.

Coulter, D. L. (1988). Withdrawal of sedative anticonvulsant drugs from mentally retarded persons: Development of guidelines. *Journal of Epilepsy, 1,* 67–70.

Crabbe, H. F. (1989). *A guidebook for the use of psychotropic medication in persons with mental illness and mental retardation.* East Hartford: Connecticut Department of Mental Retardation.

Cramer, J. A., Smith, D. B., Mattson, R. H., Delgato Escueta, A. V., Collins, J. F., & the VA Epilepsy Cooperation Study Group. (1983). A method of quantification for the evaluation of antiepileptic drug therapy. *Neurology* (Cleveland), *33*(Suppl.), 26–37.

Cunningham, P. J., & Mueller, C. D. (1991). Individuals with mental retardation in residential facilities: Findings from the 1987 national medical expenditure survey. *American Journal on Mental Retardation, 96,* 109–117.

Davis, S., Wehmeyer, M. L., Board, J. P., Fox, S., Maher, F., & Roberts, B. (1998). Interdisciplinary teams. In S. Reiss & M. G. Aman (Eds.), *Psychotropic medication and developmental disabilities. The international consensus handbook* (pp. 73–85). Columbus: Ohio State University, Nisonger Center.

Department of Health, Education, and Welfare. (1974, January 17). Medical assistance program. Intermediate care facility services. *Federal Register, 39,* 2220–2235.

Depression Guideline Panel. (1993). *Depression in primary care: Vol. 2. Treatment of major depression. Clinical Practice Guideline, Number 5* (AHCPR Publication No. 93-0551). Rockville, MD: U.S. Department of Health and Human Services, Public Health Service, Agency for Health Care Policy and Research.

Ellenor, G. L., & Frisk, A. (1977). Pharmacist impact on drug use in an institution for the mentally retarded. *American Journal of Hospital Pharmacy, 34,* 604–608.

Engel, G. L. (1977). The need for a new medical model: A challenge for biomedicine. *Science, 196,* 129–136.

Engel, G. L. (1980). The clinical application of the biopsychosocial model. *American Journal of Psychiatry, 137,* 535–544.

Engelhardt, D. M. (1974). *Withdrawal emergent symptoms (WES) checklist.* Department of Psychiatry, Downstate Medical Center, State University of New York, Brooklyn.

Facts and Comparisons. (1995). St. Louis, MO: Author.

Feldman, R. R., & Quenzer, L. F. (1984). *Fundamentals of neuropsychopharmacology.* Sunderland, MA: Sinauer.

Fielding, L. T., Murphy, R. J., Reagan, M. W., & Peterson, T. L. (1980). An assessment program to reduce drug use with the mentally retarded. *Hospital and Community Psychiatry, 31,* 771–773.

Findholt, N. E., & Emmett, C. G. (1990). Impact of interdisciplinary team review on psychotropic drug use with persons who have mental retardation. *Mental Retardation, 28,* 41–46.

Fischbacher, E. (1982). Effect of reduction of anticonvulsant on wellbeing. *British Medical Journal, 285,* 423–424.

Fraser, W. I., Ruedrich, S., Kerr, M., & Levitas, A. (1998). Beta-adrenergic blockers. In S. Reiss & M. G. Aman (Eds.), *Psychotropic medications and developmental disabilities: The international consensus handbook* (pp. 271–290). Columbus: Ohio State University, Nisonger Center.

Freeman, R. D. (1970). Use of psychoactive drugs for intellectually handicapped children. In N. R. Bernstein (Ed.), *Diminished people: Problems and care of the mentally retarded* (pp. 277–304). Boston: Little, Brown.

Gadow, K. D., & Poling, A. G. (1988). *Pharmacology and mental retardation.* Boston: College-Hill.

Garner, E. M., Kelly, M. W., & Thompson, D. F. (1993). Tricyclic antidepressant withdrawal syndrome. *Annals of Pharmacotherapy, 27,* 1068–1071.

Gedye, A. (1992). Recognizing obsessive-compulsive disorder in clients with developmental disabilities. *Habilitative Mental Healthcare Newsletter, 11,* 73–77.

Gettings, R. G. (1996). *Recent articles on comparative insitutional and community mortality rates.* (August 5 Memorandum to All State Directors). Alexandria, VA: National Association of State Directors of Developmental Disabilities Services.

Gitlin, M. J., Cochran, S. D., & Jamison, K. R. (1989). Maintenance lithium treatment: Side effects and compliance. *Journal of Clinical Psychiatry, 50,* 127–131.

Gofman, H. (1972–1973). Interval and final rating sheets on side effects. *Psychopharmacology Bulletin, 8-9*(special issue), 182–187.

Greiner, T. (1958). Problems of methodology in research with drugs. *American Journal of Mental Deficiency, 64,* 346–352.

Grohmann, R., Strobel, C., Ruther, E., Dirschedl, P., Helmchen, H., Hippius, H., Miller-Oerlinghausen, B., et al. (1993). Adverse psychic reactions to psychotropic drugs— A report from the AMUP study. *Pharmacopsychiatry, 26,* 84–93.

Gualtieri, C. T., & Keppel, J. M. (1985). Psychopharmacology in the mentally retarded and a few related issues. *Psychopharmacology Bulletin, 21,* 304–309.

Hall, R. V. (1971). *Behavior modification. The measurement of behavior.* Lawrence, KS: H & H Enterprises.

Hanzel, T. E., Kalachnik, J. E., & Harder, S. R. (1992). A case report of phenobarbital exacerbation of a preexisting maladaptive behavior partially suppressed by chlorpromazine and misinterpreted as chlorpromazine efficacy. *Research in Developmental Disabilities, 13,* 381–392.

Harder, S. R., Kalachnik, J. E., Jensen, M. A., & Feltz, J. (1987). Psychotropic drug use with successful and unsuccessful community placed developmentally disabled groups. *Research in Developmental Disabilities, 8,* 191–202.

Harper, D. C., & Wadsworth, J. S. (1993). Behavioral problems and medication utilization. *Mental Retardation, 31,* 97–103.

Harvey, S. C. (1980). Hypnotic and sedatives. In L. S. Goodman & A. Gilman (Eds.), *The pharmacological basis of therapeutics* (6th ed., pp. 339–375). New York: Macmillan.

Health Care Financing Administration. (1978, September 29). Standards for intermediate care facilities for the mentally retarded. *Federal Register, 43,* 45241–45253.

Health Care Financing Administration. (1988, June 3). Medicaid program; Conditions for intermediate care facilities for the mentally retarded. *Federal Register, 53,* 20448–20505.

Health Care Financing Administration. (1992, February 5). Medicare and medicaid programs; Omnibus nursing home requirements. Proposed rule. *Federal Register, 57,* 4516–4534.

Health Care Financing Administration. (1996). *Psychopharmacological medications. Safety precautions for persons with developmental disabilities. A resource for training and education.* Washington, DC: U.S. Department of Health and Human Services.

Herranz, J. L., Arteaga, R., & Armijo, J. A. (1982). Side effects of sodium valproate in monotherapy controlled by plasma levels: A study in 88 pediatric patients. *Epilepsia, 23,* 203–214.

Hill, B. K., Balow, E. A., & Bruinicks, R. M. (1985). A national study of prescribed drugs in institutions and community residential facilities for mentally retarded people. *Psychopharmacology Bulletin, 21,* 279–284.

Holburn, C. S. (1992). Rhetoric and realities in today's ICF/MR: Control out of control. *Mental Retardation, 30,* 133–141.

Howe, E. G. (1984). Legal aspects of psychopharmacology. *Psychiatric Clinics of North America, 7,* 887–900.

Hughs, C., Hwang, B., Kim, J. H., Eisenman, L. T., & Killian, D. J. (1995). Quality of life in applied research: A review and analysis of empirical measures. *American Journal on Mental Retardation, 99,* 623–641.

Inoue, F. (1982). A clinical pharmacy service to reduce psychotropic medication use in an instituiton for mentally handicapped persons. *Mental Retardation, 20,* 70–74.

Jacobson, J. W., & Otis, J. P. (1992). Limitations of regulations as a means of social reform in developmental services. *Mental Retardation, 30,* 163–171.

Kalachnik, J. E. (1985). *Monitoring for side effects system* (MOSES). Unpublished manuscript.

Kalachnik, J. E. (1988). Medication monitoring procedures: Thou shall, here's how. In K. D. Gadow & A. G. Poling (Eds.), *Pharmacotherapy and mental retardation* (pp. 231–268). Boston: Little, Brown.

Kalachnik, J. E., Hanzel, T. E., Harder, S. R., Bauernfeind, J. D., & Engstrom, E. A. (1995). Differential diagnosis of antiepileptic drug behavioral side effects in individuals with mental retardation and the use of behavioral measurement techniques. *Mental Retardation, 33,* 374–382.

Kalachnik, J. E., Leventhal, B. L., James, D. H., Sovner, R., Kastner, T. A., Walsh, K., Weisblatt, S. A., & Klitzke, M. G. (1998). Guidelines for the use of psychotropic medication. In S. Reiss & M. G. Aman (Eds.), *Psychotropic medication and developmental disabilities. The international consensus handbook* (pp. 45–72). Columbus: Ohio State University, Nisonger Center.

Kaplan, H. I., & Sadock, B. J. (1988). *Synopsis of psychiatry. Behavior sciences. Clinical psychiatry* (5th ed.). Baltimore: Williams & Wilkins.

Karch, F. E., & Lasagna, L. (1975). Adverse drug reactions. A critical review. *Journal of the American Medical Association, 234,* 1236–1241.

Kennedy, N. J., & Sanborn, J. S. (1992). Disclosure of tardive dyskinesia: Effect of written policy on risk disclosure. *Psychopharmacology Bulletin, 28,* 93–100.

Lehr, D. J., Gilbert, G. E., Tatel, D. S., Foer, A. A., & Kahan, J. S. (1976). Legal restrictions on the use of phenothiazines in institutions for the mentally retarded. In *Workshop on psychotropic drugs and the mentally retarded* (pp. 150-204) (Contract No. MF 282-75-0417PM). Rockville, MD: National Institute of Mental Health.

Lennard, H. L., Epstein, L. J., Bernstein, A., & Ransom, D. C. (1973). *Mystification and drug use.* London: Jossey-Bass.

Levine, J., & Schooler, N. R. (1986). SAFTEE: A technique for the systematic assessment of side effects in clinical trials. *Psychopharmacology Bulletin, 22,* 343–381.

Lewis, M. H., Bodfish, J. W., Powell, S. B., & Golden, R. N. (1995). Clomipramine treatment for stereotypy and related repetitive movement disorders associated with mental retardation. *American Journal on Mental Retardation, 100,* 299–312.

Linkowich, J. A. (1981). Adverse reaction reviews (ARR). *Hospital Pharmacy, 16,* 549–553.

Lipman, R. S. (1967, May). Results of a survey on psychotropic usage in institutions for the mentally retarded. Paper presented at the meeting of the American Association on Mental Deficiency, Denver, CO.

Lipman, R. S. (1970). The use of psychopharmacological agents in residential facilities for the retarded. In F. J. Menolascino (Ed.), *Psychiatric approaches to mental retardation* (pp. 387–398). New York: Basic.

Lipman, R. S. (1982). Psychotropic drugs in mental retardation: The known and the unknown. In K. D. Gadow & I. Bialer (Eds.), *Advances in learning and behavioral disabilities* (Vol. 1, pp. 261–282). Greenwich, CT: JAI Press.

Lipman, R. S., DiMascio, A., Reatig, N., & Kirson, T. (1978). Psychotropic drugs and mentally retarded children. In M. A. Lipton, A. DiMascio, & K. F. Killam (Eds.), *Psychopharmacology: A generation of progress* (pp. 1437–1447). New York: Raven.

Lowry, M. A. (1994). Functional assessment of problem behaviors associated with mood disorders. *Habilitative Mental Healthcare Newsletter, 13,* 79–84.

Lowry, M. A., & Sovner, R. (1992). Severe behavior problems associated with rapid cycling bipolar disorder in two adults with profound mental retardation. *Journal of Intellectual Disability Research, 36,* 269–281.

Luchins, D. L., Dojka, D. M., & Hanrahan, P. (1993). Factors associated with reduction in antipsychotic medication dosage in adults with mental retardation. *American Journal on Mental Retardation, 98,* 165–172.

MacNamara, R. D. (1994). The Mansfield Training School is closed: The swamp has been finally drained. *Mental Retardation, 32,* 239–242.

Marder, S. R., Ames, D., Wirshing, W. C., & Van Putten, T. (1993). Schizophrenia. *Psychiatric Clinics of North America, 16,* 567–587.

McElroy, S. L., Keck, P. E., & Friedman, L. M. (1995). Minimizing and managing antidepressant side effects. *Journal of Clinical Psychiatry, 56*(Suppl. 2), 49–55.

Minihan, P. M., Dean, D. H., & Lyons, C. M. (1993). Managing the care of patients with mental retardation: A survey of physicians. *Mental Retardation, 31,* 239–246.

Mitchell, D., & Braddock, D. (1993). Compensation and turnover of direct-care staff in developmental disabilities residential facilities in the United States: Part 1: Wages and benefits. *Mental Retardation, 31,* 429–437.

Mitchell, D., & Braddock, D. (1994). Compensation and turnover of direct-care staff in developmental disabilities residential facilities in the United States: Part 2: Turnover. *Mental Retardation, 32,* 34–42.

National Institute of Mental Health. (1985). Rating scales and assessment instruments for use in pediatric psychopharmacology research. *Psychopharmacology Bulletin, 21,* 347–381.

Noyes, R., Garvey, M. J., Cook, B. L., & Perry, P. J. (1988). Benzodiazepine withdrawal: A review of the evidence. *Journal of Clinical Psychiatry, 49,* 382–389.

O'Donnell, J. (1992, August). Understanding adverse drug reactions. *Nursing,* 34–39.

Pary, R. (1993). Psychotropic drugs used with adults and elderly adults who have mental retardation. *American Journal on Mental Retardation, 98,* 121–127.

Pary, R. J. (1995). Discontinuation of neuroleptics in community-dwelling individuals with mental retardation and mental illness. *American Journal on Mental Retardation, 100,* 207–212.

Pi, E. H., & Simpson, G. M. (1986). Prevention of tardive dyskinesia. In N. S. Shah & A. G. Donald (Eds.), *Movement disorders* (pp. 181–193). New York: Plenum Press.

Plotkin, R., & Gill, K. R. (1979). Invisible manacles: Drugging mentally retarded people. *Stanford Law Review, 31,* 637–678.

Rabin, J. G., Markowitz, J. S., Ocepek-Welikson, K., & Wager, S. S. (1992). General versus systematic inquiry about emergent clinical events with SAFTEE: Implications for clinical research. *Journal of Clinical Psychopharmacology, 12,* 3–10.

Reiss, S., & Aman, M. G. (Eds.). (1998). *Psychotropic medications and developmental disabilities. The international consensus handbook.* Columbus: Ohio State University, Nisonger Center.

Rinck, C., Guidry, J., & Calkins, C. F. (1989). Review of states' practices on the use of psychotropic medication. *American Journal on Mental Retardation, 93,* 657–668.

Robinson, D. R., & George, C. F. (1990). Adverse effects and long-term problems of antiparkinsonian therapy. *Adverse Drug Reaction Bulletin, 145,* 544–547.

Rogoff, M. (1984). Psychotropic medications and mentally retarded patients. In J. G. Bernstein (Ed.), *Clinical psychopharmacology* (2nd ed., pp. 211–231). Littleton, MA: John Wright.

Rojahn, J., & Schroeder, S. R. (1983). Behavioral assessment. In J. L. Matson & J. A. Mulick (Eds.), *Handbook of mental retardation* (pp. 227–243). New York: Pergamon.

Royal College of Psychiatrists' Consensus Panel. (1994). The use of high-dose antipsychotic medication. Consensus Statement. *British Journal of Psychiatry, 164,* 448–458.

Sadler, J. Z., & Hulgas, Y. F. (1992). Clinical problem solving and the biopsychosocial model. *American Journal of Psychiatry, 149,* 1315–1323.

Scandinavian Society of Psychopharmacology Committee of Clinical Investigations (UKU). (1987). The UKU side effects rating scale. *Acta Psychiatrica Scandinavica, 76*(334, Suppl.), entire issue.

Schaal, D. W., & Hackenberg, D. W. (1994). Toward a functional analysis of drug treatment for behavior problems of people with developmental disabilities. *American Journal on Mental Retardation, 99,* 123–140.

Scheerenberger, R. C. (1983). *A history of mental retardation.* Baltimore: Brookes.

Schooler, N. R. (1993). Reducing dosage in maintenance treatment of schizophrenia. *British Journal of Psychiatry, 163*(Suppl. 22), 58–65.

Silverman, M., & Lee, P. R. (1974). *Pills, profits, & politics.* Berkeley: University of California Press.

Simon, R. I. (1987). *Clinical psychiatry and the law.* Washington, DC: American Psychiatric Press.

Simpson, G. M., & Angus, J. W. S. (1970). A rating scale for extrapyramidal effects. *Acta Psychiatrica Scandinavica, 212*(Suppl.), 11–19.

Simpson, G. M., Lee, J. H., Zoubok, B., & Gardos, G. (1979). A rating scale for tardive dyskinesia. *Psychopharmacology, 64,* 171–179.

Singh, N. N., Guernsey, T. F., & Ellis, C. R. (1992). Drug therapy for persons with developmental disabilities: Legislation and litigation. *Clinical Psychology Review, 12,* 665–679.

Siris, S. G. (1985). Three cases of akathisia and "acting out". *Journal of Clinical Psychiatry, 46,* 395–397.

Skaehill, P. A., & Welch, E. B. (1997). SSRI withdrawal syndrome. *Consultant Pharmacist, 12,* 1112–1118.

Smith, R. C., Allen, R., Gordon, J., & Wolff, J. (1983). A rating scale for tardive dyskinesia and parkinsonian symptoms. *Psychopharmacology Bulletin, 19,* 266–276.

Sovner, R. (1986). Assessing the quality of a psychotropic drug regimen. In D. Rapoport & J. Parry (Eds.), *The right to refuse antipsychotic medication* (pp. 48–57). Washington, DC: American Bar Association.

Sovner, R. (1995). Thioridazine withdrawal-induced behavioral deterioration treated with clonidine: Two case reports. *Mental Retardation, 33,* 221–225.

Sovner, R., Fox, C. J., Lowry, M. J., & Lowry, M. A. (1993). Fluoxetine treatment of depression and associated self-injury in two adults with mental retardation. *Journal of Intellectual Disability Research, 37,* 301–311.

Sovner, R., & Hurley, A. D. (1984). Discontinuing psychotropic drug therapy: Rationale, guidelines, and side effects. *Psychiatric Aspects of Mental Retardation Reviews, 3,* 41–44.

Sovner, R., & Hurley, A. D. (1985). Assessing the quality of psychotropic drug regimens prescribed for mentally retarded persons. *Psychiatric Aspects of Mental Retardation Reviews, 8/9,* 31–38.

Sovner, R., & Hurley, A. D. (1987). Objective behavioral monitoring of psychotropic drug therapy. *Psychiatric Aspects of Mental Retardation Reviews, 6,* 48–51.

Sovner, R., & Hurley, A. D. (1989). Ten diagnostic principles for recognizing psychiatric disorders in mentally retarded persons. *Psychiatric Aspects of Mental Retardation Reviews, 8,* 9–14.

Sovner, R., & Lowry, M. A. (1990). A behavioral methodology for diagnosing affective disorders in individuals with mental retardation. *Habilitative Mental Healthcare Newsletter, 9,* 55–61.

Sparr, M. P., & Smith, W. (1990). Regulating professional services in ICFs/MR: Remembering the past and looking to the future. *Mental Retardation, 28,* 95–99.

Sprague, R. L. (1975). Research findings and their impact upon the FDA pediatric advisory panel. In *Workshop on psychotropic drugs and the mentally retarded* (pp. 111–132) (Contract No. MF 282-75-0417PM). Rockville, MD: National Institute of Mental Health.

Sprague, R. L. (1982). Litigation, legislation, and regulations. In S. E. Bruening & A. D. Poling (Eds.), *Drugs and mental retardation* (pp. 377–413). Springfield, IL: Charles C. Thomas.

Sprague, R. L., & Galliher, L. (1988). Litigation about psychotropic medication. In K. D. Gadow & A. G. Poling (Eds.), *Pharmacotherapy and mental retardation* (pp. 297–312). Boston: College-Hill.

Sprague, R. L., & Kalachnik, J. E. (1991). Reliability, validity, and a total score cutoff for the Dyskinesia Identification System Condensed User Scale (DISCUS) with mentally ill and mentally retarded populations. *Psychopharmacology Bulletin, 27,* 51–58.

Sprague, R. L., & Werry, J. S. (1971). Methodology of psychopharmacological studies with the retarded. In N. R. Ellis (Ed.), *International Review of Research in Mental Retardation* (Vol. 5, pp. 147–219). New York: Academic Press.

Spreat, S., Serafin, C., Behar, D., Leiman, S. (1993). Tranquilizer reduction trials in a residential program for persons with mental retardation. *Hospital & Community Psychiatry, 44,* 1100–1102.

Strauss, D., & Kastner, T. A. (1996). Comparative mortality of people with mental retardation in institutions and the community. *American Journal on Mental Retardation, 101,* 26–40.

Thompson, T. I. (1988). *Maladaptive behavior scale (MABS).* Unpublished scale, University of Minnesota, Minneapolis.

Thompson, T., Egli, M., Symons, F., & Delaney, D. (1994). Neurobehavioral mechanisms of drug actions in developmental disabilities. In T. Thompson & D. B. Gray (Eds.), *Destructive behavior in developmental disabilities: Diagnosis and treatment* (pp. 133–180). Thousand Oaks, CA: Sage.

Thompson, T., Hackenberg, T. D., & Schaal, D. W. (1991). Pharmacological treatments for behavior problems in developmental disabilities. *Treatment of destructive behaviors in persons with developmental disabilities* (pp. 343–510) (NIH Publication No. 91-2410). Bethesda, MD: National Institutes of Health.

United States Pharmacopeial Convention. (1995). *United States pharmacopeia. Drug information for the patient.* Rockville, MD: Author.

World Health Organization (WHO) (1992). International classification of diseases (10th ed.). Geneva, Switzerland: Author.

Werry, J. S. (1993). Introduction: A guide for practitioners, professionals, and public. In J. S. Werry & M. G. Aman (Eds.), *Practitioner's guide to psychoactive drugs for children and adolescents* (pp. 3–21). New York: Plenum.

Wigal, T., Swanson, J. M., Christian, D., Fulbright, K. K., Wigal, S. B., Spolar, P., Kumanoto, K., & Crinella, F. M. (1994). Admissions to a public residential facility for individuals with developmental disabilities: Change in neuroleptic drug use and tardive dyskinesia. *Journal of Developmental and Physical Disabilities, 6,* 115–124.

Wilson, J. G., Lott, R. S., & Tsai, L. (1998). Side effects: Recognition and management. In S. Reiss & M. G. Aman (Eds.), *Psychotropic medications and developmental disabilities: The international consensus handbook* (pp. 95–114). Columbus: Ohio State University, Nisonger Center.

Zbinden, G. (1963). Experimental and clinical aspects of drug toxicity. In S. Garattini & P. A. Shore (Eds.), *Advances in pharmacology* (Vol. 2, pp. 1–112). New York: Academic Press.

PART THREE

Behavioral Strategies

Treatment for Challenging Behaviors or Mental Health Disorders: A False Dichotomy

Norman A. Wieseler
Eastern Minnesota Community Support Services
Faribault, Minnesota

Ronald H. Hanson
Anoka-Metro Regional Treatment Center
Anoka, Minnesota

Practitioners and service providers exhaustively ponder the origin of behavioral disturbances. A central question is whether problem behaviors are rooted in a mental health disorder. If so, this must be considered in a comprehensive treatment plan. The prevalence of mental health disorders in the developmentally disabled population has been well documented (Bruininks, Hill, & Morreau, 1988; Lewis & MacLean, 1982). Epidemiological studies have discovered that psychiatric disorders occur in persons with developmental disabilities at more than four times the rate observed in the intellectually unimpaired (MacLean, 1993; Rutter, 1971; Rutter, Tizard, Yule, Graham, & Witmore, 1976). Russell (1988) observed that the incidence of psychiatric disorders increases in relation to the severity of retardation. Likewise, Matson and Frame (1986) stated that the full range of psychiatric symptoms is displayed by persons with developmental disabilities. The major psychiatric disorders described in Axis I of the *Diagnostic and Statistical Manual of Mental Disorders* (*DSM-IV*; American Psychiatric Association, 1994) and the personality disturbances described in Axis II have been identified in clients with severe developmental disabilities.

No major psychiatric diagnoses are peculiar to certain levels of intellectual functioning (Rutter, 1971). The array of psychiatric disorders frequently noted in persons with developmental disabilities was presented in Part 1 of this book. These include anxiety disorders, mood disorders, autistic disorders, schizophrenia, obsessive-compulsive disorders, and stereotypic movement disorders such as self-injury. The challenge for practitioners and service providers is to identify when a client has a mental health disorder and make or obtain a diagnosis consistent with the presenting behaviors.

Debilitating mental health disorders are often considered the domain of psychiatrists with behavior management plans serving primarily an adjunctive role. Although the medical model for developmentally disabled persons may be appropriate in some settings, the behavioral model, with its emphasis on psychosocial training, has also proven to be an effective treatment option (Taylor et al., 1982). Many developmental disabilities professionals perceive a dichotomy between psychiatric treatment of mental health disorders and development of comprehensive behavioral support plans. However, upon closer examination, integration of the two approaches of treating challenging behavior in persons with developmental disabilities and a mental health disorder appears the wisest course. The following case example illustrates this integrative approach.

Case Example 1

Ms. Mary Anderson, a 32-year-old woman with severe mental retardation, lives in a community-based group home. She works in a sheltered employment site performing light assembly piecework. Ms. Anderson requires frequent verbal and manual prompts from staff to attend to work. Although staff find Ms. Anderson often distraught and withdrawn, she also displays severe tantrums about three times a week. During these tantrums, she screams, cries, bites her hand, and occasionally strikes her head against the wall or other stationary objects. These tantrums occur at both her residence and work.

In recent times, the severity of Ms. Anderson's tantrums has increased. Her interdisciplinary team believed if immediate effective treatment were not initiated, her community-based placement would be in jeopardy.

A psychiatric evaluation was conducted and Ms. Anderson was diagnosed as having a major mood disorder. Her psychiatrist prescribed a mood stabilizing medication. After a month, when the medication was judged to be at an adequate dose, the severity of her tantrums decreased, and were occurring about twice a week. Although Ms. Anderson did not appear to be as distraught as she was in the past, her interdisciplinary team questioned if additional treatments could be implemented to further decrease her tantrums.

She was then referred to a behavioral psychologist for recommendations on additional treatment strategies. A functional assessment of her challenging behaviors (see Chapter 11, this volume) was completed and it was concluded that Ms. Anderson's tantrums were neither exclusively attention motivated, escape motivated, nor intrinsically rewarding. At home, there were substantially fewer interactions with others than when Ms. Anderson was at work. While there, staff and coworkers interacted frequently with Ms.

Anderson, for both her desirable and undesirable behavior. A written program plan was developed by the psychologist that employed functional communication training that signaled for her, "I want a break from my job" or "I would like some recognition." Functional communication training was conducted in both Ms. Anderson's home and at work (see Chapter 12, this volume).

This communication intervention was effective in further reducing the frequency and severity of her tantrums, which now occurred less than once a month. She generally appeared more productive. Her interdisciplinary team was pleased but now questioned if Ms. Anderson continued to require her mood stabilizing medication.

After consultation with her psychiatrist, the psychotropic medication was discontinued. Approximately 3 weeks after the drug discontinuation, her tantrums began to increase. Her affect became more labile and her productivity declined. Following another psychiatric consultation, the mood stabilizing medication was reinstituted and her behavior improved.

Although the psychiatrist treated Ms. Anderson's behavior primarily as an affective disorder while the psychologist addressed her behavior as primarily under the control of the social environment, both interventions when integrated produced lasting behavioral change. Neither treatment approach alone was as effective as both in combination. The medication prescribed appeared to enhance the positive effects of her behavioral support plan. Ms. Anderson appeared more receptive to an enriched and responsive social environment.

Behavior Analysis Support Plans

The Basics

The scenario of Ms. Anderson incorporated the application of behavioral principles in her treatment plan. A core concept in behavioral psychology is the three-term contingency, that is, (a) the antecedent condition, (b) the behavior, and (c) the consequences (Skinner, 1938, 1969). Since operant behavior occurs in response to internal and external environmental events (Skinner, 1974), psychologists trained in applied behavior analysis attempt to discover the antecedent and consequent conditions that are influencing the client's behavior. The immediate antecedent conditions or situations, referred to as the discriminative stimuli, are those environmental features that are present before and/or during the emission of the target behavior. The consequences, which immediately follow the behavior, may be either positive or negative. These outcomes determine the future probability of the target behavior. The contingent relation among the three components underscores their interdependency. Thus, if a positive environmental event is contingent upon a certain behavior, that event must occur only when following the behavior. To modify the behavior, one or more components of the three-term contingency is altered (Horner & Billingsley, 1988).

Functions of Behavior

Producing behavior change often requires a thorough analysis and understanding of the functional properties of the target behavior (Durand & Crimmins, 1988; Iwata, Dorsey, Slifer, Bauman, & Richman, 1982; O'Neill, Horner, Albin, Storey, & Sprague, 1990; O'Neill et al., 1997). Changing antecedent characteristics or the magnitude of positive consequences may result in dramatic behavioral outcomes (Horner & Billingsley, 1988). Conducting an interview with caregivers concerning the client's disturbed behaviors, directly observing the antecedent and consequent events of the challenging behavior, and recording the behavior frequency produced by environmental manipulation of the antecedent or consequent conditions, either in the actual or simulated environment, are ways of conducting a functional assessment. Defining target behaviors, identifying the conditions under which they occur or do not occur, and generating motivational hypotheses of why the challenging behavior occurs are essential to this assessment (O'Neill et al., 1990, 1997).

Multiple Contingencies

Target behaviors often have transitory functions (Iwata et al., 1982). For example, at times the behavior may be attention motivated. At

other times it may be escape or avoidance motivated. In Ms. Anderson's case, a strong motivation for her at home was attention from peers and staff. Alternatively, a strong motivation for challenging behavior at work was escape/avoidance (i.e., she escaped or avoided work tasks). In addition, some target behaviors do not appear to produce environmental change; thus, they are seen as intrinsically rewarding. These are often considered internally motivated (e.g., sensory stimulating) or automatically reinforcing (Iwata, Vollmer, Zarcone, & Rogers, 1993). Intrinsic motivation is the inferred motivational function when attention or escape motivated relations cannot be directly observed. Often, the challenging behaviors of persons with developmental disabilities experiencing mental illness fall into this category. For example, the aggressive and destructive behaviors of an individual with severe mental retardation and schizophrenia become understood when the individual's delusional beliefs are discovered.

In most environments, concurrent contingencies vie for control over different behaviors. The manner in which they relate can be very complex. A single behavior can be the product of multiple contingencies (Skinner, 1953; Thompson & Lubinski, 1986). This complexity is consternating to the practitioner designing support plans. The shift from a topographical analysis of the target behavior (i.e., the form of the target behavior) toward an analysis of the behavior's motivational function, has broadened the diagnostic formulation to consider fully the influence of antecedent events in addition to those produced by consequences (Bailey & Pyles, 1989). Case Example 2 illustrates the influence of antecedent stimuli over disturbed behavior.

Case Example 2

Mr. Michael Johnson is a 48-year-old man diagnosed with profound mental retardation. Historically, he had severe dangerous assaultiveness, especially when caregivers attempted to interrupt his ingestion of cigarette butts. Treatment of his assaultive episodes relied upon an antipsychotic medication in conjunction with a comprehensive behavior management plan.

In recent times, his dangerous behaviors had diminished and the antipsychotic medication was gradually reduced and eventually discontinued. Mr. Johnson participated in a variety of community-based recreational events. However, at home, he became increasingly teary-eyed and weepy and sobbed for long periods of time. Typically, Mr. Johnson retreated to his bedroom, lay on his bed, avoided contact with his peers, and wept quietly. The consoling attempts of caregivers were ineffective.

Treatment of his depression involved the administration of a selective serotonin reuptake inhibitor (SSRI) antidepressant medication (Hellings, Kelley, Gabrielli, Kilgore, & Shah, 1996). After a 6-week trial, it was evident that little improvement had occurred. A different antidepressant was administered and again there was no appreciable change. Mr. Johnson's psychiatrist examined his history and noted that previously Mr. Johnson had been responsive to an antipsychotic medication. The psychiatrist cautioned the caregivers of the potential adverse long-term side effects that many older typical antipsychotic medications may produce (e.g., tardive dyskinesia).

During the treatment team meeting, a behavioral psychologist suggested data be collected on the frequency of his crying, the times of day when crying was most prevalent, and what activities, if any, were associated with crying or the absence of crying. The resulting scatter plot (Touchette, MacDonald, & Langer, 1985) revealed important information regarding Mr. Johnson's crying episodes. There was a higher frequency of crying at home than at work. When Mr. Johnson engaged in preferred activities, crying rarely occurred; however, during those times when he was not involved in an activity, crying was frequently observed. Overall, Mr. Johnson cried more on weekends than weekdays and did so more frequently after supper than at any other time during the day.

Through close observation and precise record-keeping, it became evident that Mr. Johnson's crying was most likely when he was not involved in an activity. When not engaged in an activity, he often cried. Alternatively, when there were activities Mr. Johnson enjoyed, he became more social and cheerful.

The staff changed Mr. Johnson's daily activity schedule. At work, a staff person was involved with Mr. Johnson during transition times between scheduled activities. At his home, there was usually an out-of-home activity on evenings after work and on the weekends in which he could participate. Staff systematically ignored Mr. Johnson's crying and complimented him when they observed him interacting with his housemates.

Ongoing data collection revealed that Mr. Johnson's crying greatly decreased in frequency with the newly developed procedures that staff employed. The psychiatrist, psychologist, and other members of Mr. Johnson's interdisciplinary team were pleased with the dramatic results achieved without using psychotropic medication.

At first appearance, Mr. Johnson's behavior suggested a major depressive disorder. However, his crying was specific to certain environmental situations and rarely occurred when changes in his daily routine were made.

These procedures produced effective results without using a psychotropic medication. This case is an example of a putative psychiatric disorder being effectively treated with behavioral procedures that identified setting events and antecedent conditions that occasioned the challenging behavior.

Setting Events as Part of Behavior Analysis

The Treatment Environment

The physical environment in which the three-term contingency is embedded becomes especially important for a thorough understanding of the motivational properties of behavior (Bijou & Baer, 1961; Wahler & Fox, 1981). This was very evident in Mr. Johnson's case. Ecological variables are an integral part of the contingency control features of the antecedent and consequent stimuli (Carr, Robinson, & Palumbo, 1990; Favell & McGimsey, 1993). For example, engaging in a nonpreferred task may be more likely in a well-lighted, well-ventilated, pleasant environment with supportive encouragement from a teacher. Without these environmental features, performing a nonpreferred activity is less likely and challenging behaviors are more probable. Assessment of the supportive characteristics of the environment is an essential component when producing a positive valance of the behavioral ecology (Rogers-Warren & Warren, 1977).

Internal Variables

The client's temperament, emotional state, and cognitive abilities are also variables that greatly affect the three-term contingency (Gardner, Cole, Davidson, & Karan, 1986). For example, if a client is unable to sleep at night, the manner in which he or she responds to environmental cues may be greatly altered. Other setting variables related to an individual's internal state include medications (Gadow & Poling, 1988), exercise (Baumeister & MacLean, 1984), ultradian rhythms (Lewis, MacLean, Johnson, & Baumeister, 1981), premenstrual syndrome (Halbreich, Endicott, & Nee, 1983), or an array of other physiological conditions such as eating habits, constipation, allergies, or ulcers (Bailey & Pyles, 1989). Another very important variable for consideration is the mental health of the client.

Mental Health Influencing the Three-Term Contingency

Mental health disorders may alter the controlling efficacy of antecedent stimuli or behavior influenced by consequences. Stimuli to which a client attends may be idiosyncratic due to emotional distress resulting in challenging behavior seemingly unrelated to environmental contingencies. For example, reinforcer value in shaping and maintaining positive behaviors or reducing challenging behaviors may be greatly diminished for the person experiencing emotional distress (Meyer & Evans, 1989). Frequently, positive events may lose their reinforcing potential. Consequently, clients experiencing marked anxiety and displaying tantrum behaviors may be unresponsive to the usual social consequences. Alternatively, at other times the same reward may have a positive effect on the client's behavior.

Mental health may greatly alter the manner in which a client responds to various habilitative training programs. These inconsistent reactions of the client to the treatment strategies often result in the trainers' being unsure of their plan's effectiveness. Staff are then prone to switching to alternative interventions prematurely. If the provoking conditions of the client's anxiety can be identified, the original procedures may be retained and produce the desired outcomes.

In some instances, identifying a mental health disorder may dictate the optimal behavioral support procedures. For example, a client with a rapid-cycling bipolar disorder and IQ below 50 received mood and energy level ratings twice daily by staff working directly with him (Wieseler, Campbell, & Sonis, 1988). As a result of his psychiatric condition, the contingency controlling properties of antecedent and consequent stimuli varied in relation to his mood and energy levels. Hence, program strategies were adjusted to respond to changes in his mood and the reinforcing value of consequences.

Conditions occurring before and after the behavior may alter the future probability of the target behavior in significant ways (Skinner, 1953). Some behaviors displayed by clients experiencing mental health disorders occur without obvious antecedents or consequences. These behaviors appear unpredictable until a greater understanding of the client's delusional beliefs is achieved. For example, one young man with schizophrenia and severe retardation frequently swallowed large, inedible objects. This behavior did not appear attention or escape motivated. Until his delusional beliefs were understood, the behavior seemed bizarre and purposeless. When greater insight into the context of his delusional beliefs was achieved, the behavior became understandable. It is assumed that the extent to which the environmental contingencies are affected by mental health disorders often depends on the severity of the psychiatric disturbance. For example, more influence is likely when a client has a full-blown mania rather than a less severe cyclothymic disorder.

Providing adequate treatment for clients with developmental disabilities must include the adjustment of environmental variables to make habilitative training optimal, and it must consider internal setting events vis-a-vis mental health disorders. In the case example of Ms. Anderson, the services of a psychiatrist and a behavior analyst were necessary to produce effective treatment. The right to effective treatment (Van Houten et al., 1988) requires that all aspects of the individual's needs be addressed to ensure the client prospers in habilitation.

Additional Considerations in Providing Effective Treatment

The label of mental illness poses special concerns for persons with developmental disabilities. Additional diagnoses may further stigmatize the client. However, the recognition that a mental health diagnosis labels the way a client responds to environmental programs rather than merely signifying a chronic illness, unalterable and untreatable, may diminish this potential stigma. The consideration of mental health disorders as setting events affecting the three-term contingency is an additional, often unrecognized perspective necessary for adequately designing support plans.

The task of identifying mental health disorders in clients functioning in the severe/profound range of retardation presents an especially difficult challenge; however, gathering data directly related to the hallmarks of suspected psychiatric disorders often proves beneficial. For example, in addition to data collection on the frequency of aggression to others, self-injury, and property destruction; recording information about sleep patterns, appetite as measured by the amount of food consumed, self-induced isolation, participation in events, incoherent speech, apparent hallucinatory actions, and other behavior sequelae may reveal the possible presence of a mental health disorder.

Providing comprehensive treatment requires a multidisciplinary approach, so that the goals of habilitative programming are realized and all setting variables are considered. It is critical that neither a psychiatric approach nor a behavioral approach to challenging behavior eclipse the importance of the other. The consideration of a client's mental health not only affects the three-term contingency, but also the greater humanistic goals of enhanced freedom, happiness, and emotional stability.

REFERENCES

American Psychiatric Association. (1994). *Diagnostic and statistical manual of mental disorders* (4th ed.). Washington, DC: Author.

Bailey, J. S., & Pyles, D. A. M. (1989). Behavioral diagnostics. In E. Cipani (Ed.), *The treatment of severe behavior disorders: Behavior analysis approaches* (pp. 85–107). Washington, DC: American Association on Mental Retardation.

Baumeister, A. A., & MacLean, W. E. (1984). Deceleration of self-injurious and stereotypic responding by exercise. *Applied Research in Mental Retardation, 5,* 385–393.

Bijou, S. W., & Baer, D. M. (1961). *Child development: Vol. 1. A systematic and empirical theory.* Englewood Cliffs, NJ: Prentice-Hall.

Bruininks, R. H., Hill, B. K., & Morreau, L. E. (1988). Prevalence and implications of maladaptive behaviors and dual diagnosis in residential and other service programs. In J. Stark, F. J. Menolascino, M. H. Albarelli, & V. C. Gray (Eds.), *Mental retardation and mental health* (pp. 3–29). New York: Springer-Verlag.

Carr, E. G., Robinson, S., & Palumbo, L. W. (1990). The wrong issue: Aversive versus nonaversive treatment. The right issue: Functional versus nonfunctional treatment. In A. C. Repp & N. N. Singh (Eds.), *Perspectives on the use of nonaversive and aversive interventions for persons with developmental disabilities* (pp. 361–379). Sycamore, IL: Sycamore.

Durand, V. M., & Crimmins, D. B. (1988). *The motivational assessment scale: An administrative manual.* Unpublished manuscript, State University of New York at Albany.

Favell, J. E., & McGimsey, J. F. (1993). Defining an acceptable treatment environment. In R. Van Houten & S. Axelrod (Eds.), *Behavior analysis and treatment* (pp. 25–45). New York: Plenum Press.

Gadow, K. D., & Poling, A. G. (1988). *Pharmacotherapy and mental retardation.* Boston: College-Hill.

Gardner, W. I., Cole, C. L., Davidson, D. P., & Karan, O. C. (1986). Reducing aggression in individuals with developmental disabilities: An expanded stimulus control, assessment, and intervention model. *Education and Training of the Mentally Retarded, 21,* 3–12.

Halbreich, U., Endicott, J., & Nee, J. (1983). Premenstrual depressive changes. *Archives of General Psychiatry, 40,* 535–542.

Hellings, J. A., Kelley, L. A., Gabrielli, W. F., Kilgore, E., & Shah, P. (1996). Sertraline response in adults with mental retardation and autistic disorder. *Journal of Clinical Psychiatry, 57,* 333–336.

Horner, R. H., & Billingsley, F. F. (1988). The effect of competing behavior on the generalization and maintenance of adaptive behavior in applied settings. In R. H. Horner, G. Dunlap, & R. H. Koegel (Eds.), *Generalization and maintenance: Life-style changes in applied settings* (pp. 197–220). Baltimore: Brookes.

Iwata, B. A., Dorsey, M. F., Slifer, K. J., Bauman, K. E., & Richman, G. S. (1982). *Analysis and Intervention in Developmental Disabilities, 2,* 3–20.

Iwata, B. A., Vollmer, T. R., Zarcone, J. R., & Rodgers, T. A. (1993). Treatment classification and selection based on behavioral function. In R. Van Houten & S. Axelrod (Eds.), *Behavior analysis and treatment* (pp. 101–125). New York: Plenum Press.

Lewis, M., & MacLean, W. (1982). Issues in treating emotional disorders. In J. Matson & R. Barrett (Eds.), *Psychopathology in the mentally retarded* (pp. 1–36). New York: Grune & Stratton.

Lewis, M. H., MacLean, W. E., Johnson, W. L., & Baumeister, A. A. (1981). Ultradian rhythms in stereotyped and self-injurious behavior. *American Journal of Mental Deficiency, 85,* 601–610.

MacLean, W. E. (1993). Overview. In J. Matson & R. Barrett (Eds.), *Psychopathology in the mentally retarded* (2nd ed., pp. 1–16). Boston: Allyn & Bacon.

Matson, J. L., & Frame, C. L. (1986). *Psychopathology among mentally retarded children and adolescents.* Beverly Hills, CA: Sage.

Meyer, L. H., & Evans, I. M. (1989). Strategies to support behavior change. In *Nonaversive intervention for behavior problems: A manual for home and community* (pp. 129–149). Baltimore: Brookes.

O'Neill, R. E., Horner, R. H., Albin, R. W. Sprague, J. R., Storey, K., & Newton, J. S. (1997). *Functional assessment and program development for problem behavior: A practical handbook.* Cincinnati: Brooks/Cole.

O'Neill, R. E., Horner, R .H., Albin, R. W., Storey, K., & Sprague, J. R. (1990). *Functional analysis: A practical assessment guide.* Sycamore, IL: Sycamore.

Rogers-Warren, A., & Warren, S. F. (1977). *Ecological perspectives in behavior analysis.* Baltimore: University Park Press.

Russell, A. T. (1988). The association between mental retardation and psychiatric disorder: Epidemiological issues. In J. Stark, F. J. Menolascino, M. H. Albarelli, & V. C. Gray (Eds.), *Mental retardation and mental health* (pp. 41–49). New York: Springer-Verlag.

Rutter, M. (1971). Psychiatry. In J. Wortis (Ed.), *Mental retardation: An annual review* (Vol. 3, pp. 186–221). New York: Grune & Stratton.

Rutter, M., Tizard, J., Yule, W., Graham, P., & Whitmore, K. (1976). Research report: Isle of Wight Studies, 1964–1974. *Psychological Medicine, 6,* 313–332.

Skinner, B. F. (1938). *The behavior of organisms.* Englewood Cliffs, NJ: Prentice-Hall.

Skinner, B. F. (1953). *Science and human behavior.* New York: Macmillan.

Skinner, B. F. (1969). *Contingencies of reinforcement: A theoretical analysis.* Englewood Cliffs, NJ: Prentice-Hall.

Skinner, B. F. (1974). *About behaviorism.* New York: Alfred A. Knapf.

Taylor, C. B., Liberman, R. P., Agras, W. S., Barlow, D. H., Bigelow, G. E., Gelfand, D. M., Rush, A. J., Sobell, L. C., & Sobell, M. B. (1982). Treatment evaluation and behavior therapy. In J. M. Lewis & G. Usdin (Eds.), *Treatment and planning* (pp. 151–224). Washington DC: American Psychiatric Association.

Thompson, T., & Lubinski, D. (1986). Units of analysis and kinetic structures of behavior repertoires. *Journal of the Experimental Analysis of Behavior, 46,* 219–242.

Touchette, P. E., MacDonald, R. F., & Langer, S. N. (1985). A scatter plot for identifying stimulus control of problem behavior. *Journal of Applied Behavior Analysis, 18,* 343–351.

Van Houten, R., Axelrod, S., Bailey, J. S., Favell, J. E., Foxx, R. M., Iwata, B. A., & Lovaas, O. I. (1988). The right to effective behavioral treatment. *Behavior Analyst, 11,* 111–114.

Wahler, R. G., & Fox, J. J. (1981). Setting events in applied behavior analysis: Toward a conceptual and methodological expansion. *Journal of Applied Behavior Analysis, 14,* 327–338.

Wieseler, N. A., Campbell, G. J., & Sonis, W. (1988). Ongoing use of an affective rating scale in the treatment of a mentally retarded individual with a rapid-cycling bipolar affective disorder. *Research in Developmental Disabilities, 9,* 47–53.

Understanding Problem Behaviors Through Functional Assessment

Raymond G. Miltenberger
North Dakota State University
Fargo, ND

The first step in the treatment of problem behaviors in individuals with mental health disorders and developmental disabilities is to conduct a functional assessment of the behaviors (Iwata, Vollmer, & Zarcone, 1990; Lennox & Miltenberger, 1989). The functional assessment provides information on the antecedents and consequences of the behaviors. Once we understand the antecedents and consequences that are functionally related to the behaviors, we are better able to choose effective interventions to address the problem behaviors (Carr & Carlson, 1993; Iwata, Pace, Cowdery, & Miltenberger, 1994; Kemp & Carr, 1995; Repp, Felce, & Barton, 1988). Consider the following case example.

The Case of Martha

Martha is a 23-year-old woman diagnosed with severe mental retardation and schizophrenia. She resides in a group home for individuals with dual diagnoses (mental illness and mental retardation), goes to a Partial Care program at the local human service center for 3 hours each weekday morning, and works a few hours in the afternoon at a vocational training center for individuals with mental retardation. Although her schizophrenia is treated with antipsychotic medication, she continues to report a delusion in which she believes that worms will come out of her head if she does not wear her scarf at all times. The problem behavior involves frequent discussion of this delusion and insistence on wearing her scarf at all times, indoors and outdoors, regardless of weather conditions. These behaviors were targeted for intervention because they were stigmatizing Martha and interfering with successful integration into her community.

The behavioral consultant first conducted a functional assessment of these problem behaviors to determine the antecedents and consequences that were controlling the behaviors. First, the consultant interviewed staff members who worked with Martha at the group home, the Partial Care program, and the work site. Following the interviews, the consultant instructed staff at each site to conduct direct observation assessments of the antecedents and consequences each time the problem behaviors occurred. Based on information from the interviews and observations, the consultant developed a hypothesis about the function of the problem behaviors and a treatment appropriate to the function.

The assessment results indicated that Martha's talking about the worms coming out of her head and wearing the scarf were positively reinforced by the attention of staff in two of the settings. Staff at the Partial Care program talked with Martha at length about her "delusion" and encouraged her to wear the scarf because it "made her feel more secure." This attention was a reliable consequence at the Partial Care program. As a result, Martha never failed to wear the scarf and frequently talked about her delusion there. She continued to wear the scarf at her vocational site in the afternoon because she already had it on in the morning. Staff reported that they did not discuss the scarf or her delusion with her there. As a result, she talked about the delusions much less at the vocational site. At the group home she mostly wore the scarf and talked about her delusion during the week, but rarely did so on the weekend. Weekday staff responded intermittently with attention to these behaviors while weekend staff never responded with attention. In fact, weekend staff praised her for not wearing the scarf and took her out for ice cream when she ventured into the community without the scarf.

The functional assessment results in this case showed that the problem behaviors were under stimulus control of the settings and people who worked with Martha. Positive reinforcement in the form of attention maintained the behavior in the presence of some people in some settings, while extinction made the behaviors less likely to occur with other people (i.e., the weekend staff) who did not pay attention to the behavior and who reinforced alternative behaviors instead. This information was important for the development of effective interventions for Martha's problem behaviors. Staff at the group home and at the vocational site were taught to use extinction for the problem behaviors and differential reinforcement to strengthen alternative behaviors. As a result, following treatment, Martha rarely wore the scarf or talked about the delusions with them. However, the Partial Care staff believed the problem behaviors were due to her mental illness and refused to participate in the behavioral interventions. As a result, Martha continued to wear her scarf and talk about her delusions at Partial Care.

If a functional assessment had not been conducted, there would have been no clear indication of the environmental variables responsible for the problem behaviors. One consequence is that the behaviors may have been attributed to Martha's mental illness, with the result being an increase or a change in her medication. Without functional assessment information, it would have been difficult to choose appropriate interventions. Therefore, Martha may have had to endure ineffective or more restrictive treatment procedures than those that were based on the knowledge of controlling variables.

Contingencies of Reinforcement for Problem Behaviors and Alternative Behaviors

Martha's problem behaviors, and the problem behaviors of any individual, can be understood in terms of the contingencies of reinforcement for the behavior and for alternative behaviors. A contingency of reinforcement, also called a three-term contingency, involves the antecedents that are present when the behavior occurs, the behavior itself, and the reinforcing consequences that maintain the behavior (Skinner, 1969, 1974). To provide the most effective treatments, one must understand the contingencies of reinforcement. In any situation an individual has a choice of a number of concurrently available behaviors. In the case of a problem behavior, the individual engages in the problem behavior instead of more desirable alternative behaviors. A good functional assessment will identify the contingencies of reinforcement responsible for the problem behaviors and for possible alternative behaviors that may be addressed in treatment (Arndorfer & Miltenberger, 1993). This section briefly discusses the antecedents and consequences of behavior, the problem behavior, and functionally equivalent alternative behaviors as important variables in functional assessment and treatment of problem behaviors.

Antecedents

Antecedents are events occurring before the occurrence of the behavior and may include the situation in which the problem behavior occurs, the people present, specific activities, particular behaviors of another individual (e.g., a comment, a request, physical contact, etc.), or any of a variety of environmental events preceding the behavior (O'Neill, Horner, Albin, Storey, & Sprague, 1990). Antecedents of interest in a functional assessment include discriminative stimuli and establishing operations.

Discriminative stimuli. The immediate antecedent that is present when the problem behavior occurs and is reinforced is called a *discriminative stimulus* (signified by the symbol S^D). There is an increased likelihood that the behavior will occur when this stimulus is present in the future because the behavior has been reinforced in its presence. Alternatively, when the behavior occurs in the presence of some antecedent stimuli and is not reinforced, the behavior will be less likely to occur in the future when these stimuli (called *S-deltas* and signified $S^\triangle$) are present. It is important to assess the antecedents (S^Ds and $S^\triangle$s) to identify when and where the behavior is more likely and less likely to occur. In the case of Martha, the weekend staff at the group home were $S^\triangle$s for the problem behaviors because they never reinforced the behavior with attention. The partial care staff were $S^\triangle$s because in their presence the problem behaviors were reinforced.

Establishing operations. Other important antecedents to the problem behavior may not occur immediately prior to the behavior. These antecedents, which may be more remote in time from the occurrence of the behavior, are called *setting events* (Gardner, Cole, Davidson, & Karan, 1986) or *ecological variables* (O'Neill et al., 1990). Setting events or ecological variables typically serve some motivational function with respect to the problem behavior. They make particular consequences of the behavior more or less potent as reinforcers at a particular time and thus increase the likelihood of the behavior at that time. According to Michael (1982), an antecedent that functions to make a reinforcer more or less potent is called an *establishing operation* (EO). Consider the following examples.

If a client has not eaten in 6 hours, food will be a more potent reinforcer than it would if the client had just finished a large meal. The 6 hours of food deprivation is an EO.

If a client is asked to engage in a difficult or unpleasant task, escape from the task may be a potent reinforcer. The aversiveness of the task is an EO that increases the potency of escape from the task as a reinforcer.

If a client takes lithium as a medication, the client may experience increased thirst. Taking the lithium would be an EO that increases the potency of water as a reinforcer.

If a client is ignored or receives very little attention for long periods of time, the lack of attention may function as an EO that makes staff attention a more potent reinforcer at that time. In the case of Martha, she received little routine attention, especially at Partial Care where she sat by herself doing crafts, thus attention was a more potent reinforcer. On the other hand, weekend staff at the group home frequently interacted with Martha, thus attention was a less potent reinforcer for the problem behavior (Vollmer, Iwata, Zarcone, Smith, & Mazaleski, 1993)

Functional assessment of antecedents is not complete until information is gathered on the discriminative stimuli that occasion the problem behavior and the establishing operations that may increase the probability of the problem behavior.

Consequences

The consequences of interest are the events that immediately follow the occurrence of the problem behavior. We assess the consequences to identify the reinforcers for the problem behavior. Reinforcing consequences may include various types of attention or reactions from other individuals, tangible outcomes, escape or avoidance of tasks or activities, or other socially mediated outcomes. Reinforcing consequences may also include automatic effects of the behavior itself such as the self-stimulation from rocking or other repetitive movements (Iwata, Vollmer, Zarcone, & Rodgers, 1993).

A consequence functions as a reinforcer for a particular behavior when it strengthens the behavior. The effects of the reinforcing consequence on the behavior are situation specific. In other words, the behavior is more likely to occur in situations where that reinforcing consequence has previously been contingent on the occurrence of the behavior. In addition, the consequence will be more likely to function as a reinforcer when there is an establishing operation in effect for that particular consequence. For example, escape from a task is more likely to be a reinforcer for a problem behavior when the task is difficult, effortful, painful, or aversive in some other way. Escape from a task is not likely to be a reinforcer when a task is interesting, easy, or preferred. Likewise, attention is likely to be a reinforcer when an individual has not received attention recently. Attention may be a less potent reinforcer when an individual has just received substantial attention (Vollmer & Iwata, 1991).

There are two categories of reinforcement. In *positive reinforcement,* a stimulus or event is added following the behavior and the behavior is strengthened (more likely to occur in the future). The receipt of attention or tangible reinforcers are two types of consequences involved in positive reinforcement. In addition, the production of sensory stimulation (through stereotypic behavior) may be involved in automatic positive reinforcement (Iwata et al., 1993). In *negative reinforcement,* a stimulus or event is removed following the behavior and the behavior is strengthened. Escape from a task or escape from a social interaction are consequences often involved in negative reinforcement. In addition, escape from aversive internal stimulation (e.g., pain or anxiety) may be involved in automatic negative reinforcement (Iwata et al., 1993).

Both positive and negative reinforcement increase the future probability of the behavior. When a problem behavior is occurring, we know that the problem behavior must serve some function(s) for the individual, which means that the behavior produces a positively reinforcing consequence or a negatively

reinforcing consequence or, in some cases, both (Day, Horner, & O'Neill, 1994). The goal of a functional assessment is to identify the function of the behavior, the specific reinforcing consequences maintaining the behavior. In the case of Martha, the problem behaviors were being maintained in some settings through positive reinforcement as the staff responded to the problem behaviors with attention (see Table 11.1).

Problem Behavior

The problem behavior(s) should be defined objectively in terms of the client's specific actions so that the behaviors can be observed and recorded accurately and so that treatment procedures can be implemented correctly. In a functional assessment, important aspects of the problem behavior to identify include (a) the frequency of reinforcement for the behavior, (b) magnitude of reinforcement for the behavior, (c) immediacy of reinforcement for the behavior, (d) and response effort (O'Neill et al., 1990). This information is important for comparison with the same aspects of desirable alternative behaviors.

Functionally Equivalent Alternative Behaviors

An alternative behavior is one that the individual could engage in instead of the problem behavior. Alternative behaviors and problem behaviors can be viewed as concurrent

TABLE 11.1

Example of a Three-Term (Antecedent-Behavior-Consequence) Contingency of Reinforcement

Antecedent ⟶	Behavior ⟶	Consequence
(S^D) Partial Care staff	Martha discusses her delusions and wears her scarf	Staff attention
($S^\triangle$) Weekend staff	Martha discusses her delusions and wears her scarf	No attention from staff

Outcome: Martha is more likely to engage in the problem behaviors with Partial Care staff and less likely to engage in the behaviors with weekend staff.

operants, two available behaviors each maintained by a particular schedule of reinforcement (Mace & Roberts, 1993). The alternative behavior is functionally equivalent when the alternative behavior would result in the same reinforcing *outcome* as the problem behavior (Carr, 1988). Unfortunately, the individual with a problem behavior is engaging in the problem behavior and not engaging in the desirable alternative behavior. There are various reasons why the problem behavior may be more probable than the alternative behavior (Mace & Roberts, 1993). The problem behavior may have a longer history of reinforcement than the alternative behavior; may currently result in more frequent reinforcement than the alternative behavior; may result in a greater magnitude of reinforcement than the alternative behavior; may result in more immediate reinforcement than the alternative behavior; or may require less response effort than the alternative behavior (Horner & Day, 1991; Horner, Sprague, O'Brien, & Heathfield, 1990). Finally, some individuals with extremely limited repertoires may lack the skills to engage in desirable alternative behaviors.

It is important to assess alternative behaviors in the repertoire of the individual engaging in the problem behavior. Functional assessment should include information on the frequency, magnitude, and immediacy of reinforcement, and on the response effort for alternative behaviors relative to the problem behavior. This information will be valuable in the development of appropriate interventions.

To summarize, the functional assessment of behaviors should examine both problem and alternative behaviors. It should gather the following information on contingencies of reinforcement:

Antecedents:

> *Discriminative stimuli (S^Ds) and S-deltas ($S^\triangle$s)*
>
> *Establishing operations (EOs)*

Consequences:

> *Positive reinforcement*
>
> *Negative reinforcement*

Problem behavior:

> *Frequency, magnitude, and immediacy of reinforcement*
>
> *Response effort*

Functionally equivalent alternative behaviors:

> *Frequency, magnitude, and immediacy of reinforcement*
>
> *Response effort*

Functional Approach to Assessment and Treatment

This section briefly describes the functional approach to assessment and treatment to put functional assessment into its larger context.

Conducting a Functional Assessment

The first step in the functional approach is to conduct a functional assessment of the problem behavior. The variables involved in the contingencies of reinforcement for the problem behavior and alternative behaviors are assessed using methods elaborated later in this chapter in the section on Functional Assessment Methods. The development of effective, functional treatments depends on the results of a thorough functional assessment (Axelrod, 1987; Carr, McConnachie, Levin, & Kemp, 1993; Iwata, Pace, Cowdery, & Miltenberger, 1994; O'Neill et al., 1990; Repp et al., 1988). The outcome of a functional assessment is the development of a hypothesis about the antecedents and consequences controlling the problem behavior (Carr & Carlson, 1993; Kemp & Carr, 1995).

Developing Hypotheses

The functional assessment process produces a large amount of information about environmental events related to the problem behavior. This information is then evaluated to make plausible inferences about how various events function with regard to the occurrence of the problem behavior. The hypothesis will identify (a) the probable function the behavior serves or the reinforcing outcome the behavior produces, (b) the probable S^Ds and EOs that increase the likelihood of the behavior in specific situations, and (c) the probable influence of functionally equivalent alternative behaviors on the occurrence of the problem behavior (Carr & Carlson, 1993; Kemp & Carr, 1995).

The hypothesis about controlling variables is confirmed in a couple of ways (Arndorfer, Miltenberger, Woster, Rortvedt, & Gaffaney, 1994). First, confirmation comes when multiple functional assessment methods produce consistent information about the contingencies of reinforcement. Second, confirmation comes when treatments based on the hypothesis are shown to be effective in decreasing the occurrence of the problem behavior and increasing desirable alternative behaviors.

Selecting and Evaluating Treatments

The treatments that are selected based on functional assessment information will directly address the contingencies of reinforcement controlling the problem behavior. Treatments that address the contingencies of reinforcement for the problem are called functional treatments (Miltenberger, 1997). Functional treatments fall into three categories.

1. *Antecedent manipulation.* The antecedents of the problem behavior are addressed. This may involve (a) manipulation of an EO for the problem behavior or alternative behaviors, (b) manipulation of S^Ds or $S^\triangle$s for the problem behavior or alternative behaviors, and (c) manipulation of response effort for the problem behavior or alternative behaviors (Miltenberger, 1997).

2. *Extinction.* The reinforcer or reinforcers for the problem behavior are eliminated in an extinction procedure (Iwata, Pace, Cowdery, & Miltenberger, 1994) or at least attenuated relative to the reinforcement for the alternative behaviors. If the problem behavior no longer pays off or if the payoff is delayed, less frequent, or of lesser magnitude relative to the payoff for the alternative behavior, the problem behavior will be less likely to occur.

3. *Differential reinforcement of alternative behavior.* Differential reinforcement procedures are implemented to strengthen desirable alternative behaviors to take the place of the problem behaviors. If the alternative behaviors are functionally equivalent (i.e., they will produce the same outcome the problem behavior previously produced), they will make the problem behavior unnecessary (Carr, 1988).

Other procedures may be implemented in addition to these approaches, but these three types of interventions should be at the core of any functional approach to treatment:

- antecedent manipulation;

- extinction;

- differential reinforcement.

Treatments, once implemented, are evaluated to determine their effects on the problem behaviors and alternative behaviors. Data collection should be an ongoing component of the treatment process. If the treatment is not achieving its intended effect, there are two possible explanations. First, the treatment may not have been implemented as planned. If this is determined to be the case, the solution is better staff training and management to assure the fidelity of treatment implementation (Reid & Parsons, 1995). Second, the treatment, or components of the treatment, may not be appropriate for the individual's problem. Further functional assessment is needed in this case to confirm or add to the original functional assessment results, and problem solving is needed to decide upon the best treatments based on the functional assessment results.

Functional Assessment Methods

There are three general methods for gathering functional assessment information. Functional assessments can be conducted using indirect methods, direct observation, and experimental manipulations (Iwata et al., 1990; Lennox & Miltenberger, 1989). In this section, the procedures involved in each of these three functional assessment methods are described.

Indirect Assessment Methods

With indirect methods, information is gathered from informants, such as parents, staff, and teachers, who know the client well. Indirect assessment information can also be gathered from the client directly. Indirect assessment methods involve interviews and rating scales in which information is gathered from retrospective reports of the informants (Iwata et al., 1990; Lennox & Miltenberger, 1989).

Although indirect assessments cannot identify a functional relationship between the problem behavior and antecedents and consequences, indirect assessments can lead to hypotheses that are the basis for treatment selection or the use of further functional assessment procedures. Several interview formats and rating scales are commonly used.

Interviews. A number of behavioral assessment interview formats have been developed to gather information systematically on the contingencies of reinforcement and other variables related to the problem (Iwata, Wong, Riordan, Dorsey, & Lau, 1982; Miltenberger & Fuqua, 1985; Veltum & Miltenberger, 1989). O'Neill et al. (1990) developed an interview format specifically for assessing problem behaviors of individuals with developmental disabilities. Their Functional Analysis Interview Format has questions divided into a number of sections designed to assess the problem behaviors, ecological variables, antecedents, consequences, alternative behaviors, potential reinforcers, and past treatments used with the individual. It is a comprehensive interview format that should produce thorough functional assessment information. The format can be used as an interview guideline or as a questionnaire that staff or other informants complete on their own. Table 11.2 lists the major questions covered in the Functional Analysis Interview Format.

The assessor who conducts the behavioral assessment interview is advised to interview a number of individuals to get information from a number of different perspectives. The assessor should ask each informant to provide objective information in response to questions and to refrain from making inferences and interpretations about events. When information is incomplete or unclear, the assessor should ask follow-up questions until the information is clear and complete. Group interviews are valuable because different staff (parents, teachers, etc.) will provide answers to the same questions and the assessor can question the staff when the information is inconsistent. The goal of the interview process is to get clear and consistent information from a number of informants so that confidence in the accuracy of the information is increased. If the O'Neill et al. (1990) Functional Analysis Interview Format is used as a questionnaire, the assessor should follow up with an interview to clarify the informants' responses to the questions.

The behavioral assessment interview is typically the first step in the functional assessment process. The information from the interviews should allow the assessor to develop hypotheses about the contingencies of reinforcement controlling the problem behavior. The hypotheses may be then strengthened with information from behavioral rating scales.

Rating scales. The use of rating scales is another indirect assessment procedure to identify the antecedents and consequences of problem behaviors. One or more informants answer each question or item on the scale, and the results are then tallied and interpreted by the assessor. Two scales designed to identify the function of problem behaviors are the Motivation Assessment Scale (Durand & Crimmins, 1988) and the Functional Analysis Screening Tool (Iwata & DeLeon, 1995). One scale, the Setting Events Checklist (Gardner et al., 1986), is designed to identify antecedents to the problem behavior.

The Motivation Assessment Scale (MAS) contains 16 questions designed to assess four functions: attention, escape, tangible, and sensory stimulation. There are four questions related to each of the functions, for example:

1. Would this behavior occur continuously if the client was left alone for long periods of time (for example one hour)? *[sensory stimulation]*

6. Does this behavior occur when any request is made of the client? *[escape]*

8. Does the behavior occur when you take away a favorite object, activity, or food? *[tangible]*

TABLE 11.2

Topic Areas and Major Questions From the Functional Analysis Interview Format

A. Describe the problem behaviors

What are the behaviors of concern?

For each, define the topography, frequency, duration, and intensity.

B. Potential ecological events

What medications is the person taking?

What medical complications does the person experience?

Describe the sleep cycles, eating routines, and diet of the individual.

Describe the individual's daily tasks and activities. Are they predictable?

How often and in what areas does the person get to make choices?

How many people are in the setting? What is the nature of interactions with others?

Describe staffing patterns and typical staff interactions.

C. Antecedents

When is the behavior most likely and least likely to occur?

Where is the behavior most likely and least likely to occur?

With whom is the behavior most likely and least likely to occur?

What activities are most likely and least likely to produce the behavior?

D. Consequences

What does the person get by doing the behavior?

What does the person get out of by doing the behavior?

Are the person's behaviors more or less likely if you (a) present a difficult task, (b) interrupt a desired event, (c) deliver a stern request, (d) do not interact with the person for a period of time, or (e) do not let the person have something he wants?

E. Define the efficiency of the undesirable behaviors

What amount of effort is involved in the behavior?

Does the behavior pay off immediately? Every time it occurs?

F. Communication abilities

What expressive communication strategies are used by the person?

Does the person respond to verbal requests? Modeling? Gestural prompts?

G. Identify positive reinforcers

H. What functional alternative behaviors are known by the person?

I. What treatments have been used previously and how have they worked?

Note. Adapted from *Functional Analysis of Problem Behavior: A Practical Guide* (pp. 16-24), by R. E. O'Neill, R. H. Horner, R. W., Albin, K. Storey, and J. R. Sprague, 1990, Sycamore, IL: Sycamore. Copyright 1990 by Sycamore Publishing Company.

15. Does the client seem to be doing this behavior to get you to spend more time with him or her? *[attention]* (Durand, 1990, pp. 176-178)

Each question is rated on a 7-point scale from 0 (never) to 6 (always). The summed scores on the four questions for each function are compared to identify which function was rated highest.

The use of the MAS as part of a functional assessment process has been reported in a number of studies. Durand and Carr (1991, 1992) found that the MAS and a functional analysis of child problem behaviors produced consistent results. However, Arndorfer et al. (1994) found that the MAS results were not consistent with the results of a behavioral interview, direct observation, and functional analysis of problem behaviors exhibited by children in three out of five cases. Some researchers have also investigated the reliability of the MAS. Although Durand and Crimmins (1988) reported good reliability of the MAS, others have found modest reliability results (Arndorfer et al., 1994; Crawford, Brockel, Schauss, & Miltenberger, 1992; Zarcone, Rodgers, Iwata, Rourke, & Dorsey, 1991).

The Functional Analysis Screening Tool (FAST) is designed to identify possible functions of the problem behavior as a starting point for using direct observation assessment procedures (Iwata & DeLeon, 1995). The FAST has 27 items in three sections, with a "yes" or "no" response to each item. In the first section, answers suggest whether or not social reinforcement is maintaining the problem. Answers in the second section point to attention, access to specific activities, or escape as the factors involved in maintaining the problem behavior. Answers in the third section indicate whether automatic reinforcement in the form of sensory stimulation or pain attenuation plays a role in maintaining the behavior. As yet there are no published studies on the use of the FAST, although it appears to be a conceptually solid and useful assessment tool.

The Setting Events Checklist was developed by Gardner et al. (1986) to identify remote antecedents (setting events) that may be related to the occurrence of the problem behavior. The Checklist lists 16 possible setting events. The informant is instructed to identify which of the events occurred in the morning and which occurred in the evening prior to the occurrence of the problem behavior. By identifying setting events that are correlated with the occurrence of the problem behavior, the clinician is better able to predict the future occurrence of the problem and to know which events to manipulate to influence the future occurrence of the problem. Following are examples of items on the Setting Events Checklist:

- [The client] was informed of something unusually disappointing.

- [The client] was refused some requested activity.

- [The client] was hurried or rushed more than usual.

- [The client's] medications were changed/missed.

- [The client] appeared excessively tired/lethargic. (Gardner et al., 1986, p. 7)

Advantages and disadvantages of indirect assessment. Indirect assessments have a number of advantages. Because the assessor does not have to go to the site to observe the client engaging in the problem behavior, indirect methods are more convenient, less time-consuming, and less costly. In addition, information can be gathered from a number of sources to look for consistency in the information. A number of instruments exist that are designed to collect functional assessment information.

Indirect assessments also have limitations. Information is gathered from retrospective reports of informants based on previous, unstructured observations. Therefore, the information may be inaccurate or incomplete due to forgetting, bias, or misinterpretation of assessment items, or because the informant has not had exposure to the relevant variables. In addition, indirect assessment information is only correlational in nature. Further assessments (e.g., direct observation) are typically needed to corroborate the information gathered through indirect methods.

Direct Observation Assessment

Direct observation of the contingency of reinforcement for the problem behavior represents a more rigorous form of assessment because the antecedents and consequences are directly observed and recorded immediately after their occurrence (Arndorfer et al., 1994; Bijou, Peterson, & Ault, 1968). Direct observation and recording of the antecedents, behavior, and consequences, also called A-B-C recording, can be conducted by a consultant or by staff, parents, or teachers in the natural environment where the problem behavior typically takes place.

A-B-C recording needs to be done in a structured and precise manner in order to produce useful information. The antecedents occurring immediately prior to the problem behavior and the consequences occurring immediately after the problem behavior must be described in clear and objective terms without interpretation or inference. It is important to capture the events that occur in close temporal proximity to the problem behavior and to describe the specific environmental events or the actions of other individuals. Toward this end, it is important to provide training to the individuals conducting A-B-C recordings so that their recording is accurate and complete. Individuals must be trained to discriminate each occurrence of the problem behavior occurring in the observation period and to objectively describe temporally related events. The biggest obstacle to overcome with training is the tendency for staff to label events rather than to describe them, to make inferences about intention or other supposed motivations of the client, and to be incomplete in their accounts. Staff must learn to describe events in such a way that other individuals could clearly understand the specific events based on reading the description.

Because A-B-C recording typically occurs in the natural environment where the problem behaviors occur, the observer must choose an observation period in which the behavior is most likely to occur. The observer can choose the A-B-C observation period based on information from the behavioral interview or based on information from a scatter plot analysis.

Scatter plot. Scatter plot recording produces information on the temporal patterns of the problem behavior (Touchette, MacDonald, & Langer, 1985). In scatter plot recording, the staff members, parents, or teachers who are with the client throughout the day record whether or not the behavior has occurred in consecutive half-hour blocks of time. Using a grid similar to the one in Figure 11.1, the observer will record in each half-hour box whether the behavior did not occur, occurred one time, or occurred two or more times. Over the course of a week or two, the scatter plot will show the times of day that the occurrence of the problem behavior is most probable. Although the scatter plot does not provide information about events occurring in relation to the problem behavior, the information on the temporal patterns in the behavior can be used to plan the best times for subsequent A-B-C observations or for more focused behavioral interviewing.

A-B-C recording. Direct observation of the antecedents, problem behavior, and consequences can be carried out in an open-ended or descriptive fashion, by using a checklist of likely antecedents and consequences, or in an interval recording system (Miltenberger, 1997).

In *descriptive A-B-C recording,* the observer writes down a description of the antecedents and consequences each time the problem behavior occurs (Bijou et al., 1968). The observer will typically use a three-column data sheet for recording. All that is required to use this method is an operational definition of the problem behavior so its occurrence can be discriminated, minimal training to record antecedent and consequent events objectively, and a data sheet (or a blank piece of paper) for recording. Descriptive A-B-C recording will result in descriptions of all the events that occurred in close temporal relation to the problem behavior. The assessor can develop hypotheses about probable EOs, S^Ds, and reinforcing consequences when specific antecedents and consequences are identified as occurring with regularity. The hypotheses are then strengthened when the antecedents and consequences identified in the A-B-C recording are the same as those identified in indirect assessments.

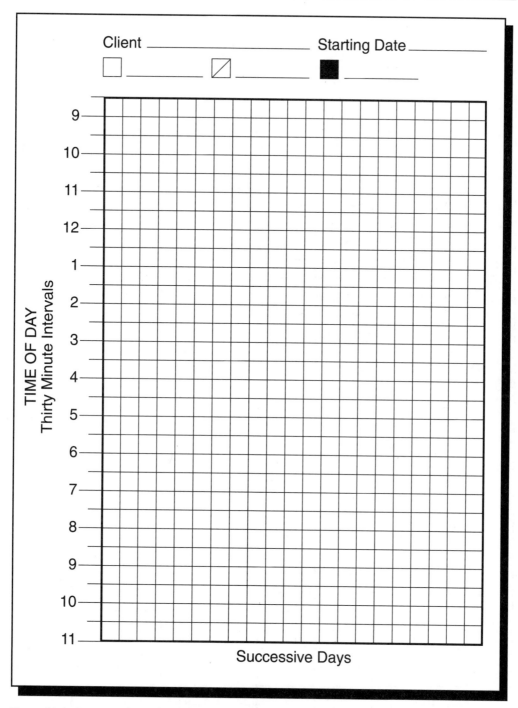

Figure 11.1. A scatter plot grid on which to record the problem behavior each half hour. The square corresponding to a half hour is left blank if the problem behavior did not occur; slashed if it occurred one time; and filled in if it occurred two or more times.

From "A Scatter Plot for Identifying Stimulus Control of Problem Behavior," by P. E. Touchette, R. F. MacDonald, and S. N. Langer, 1985, *Journal of Applied Behavior Analysis, 18*, p. 344. Copyright 1985 by Society for the Experimental Analysis of Behavior. Reprinted by permission.

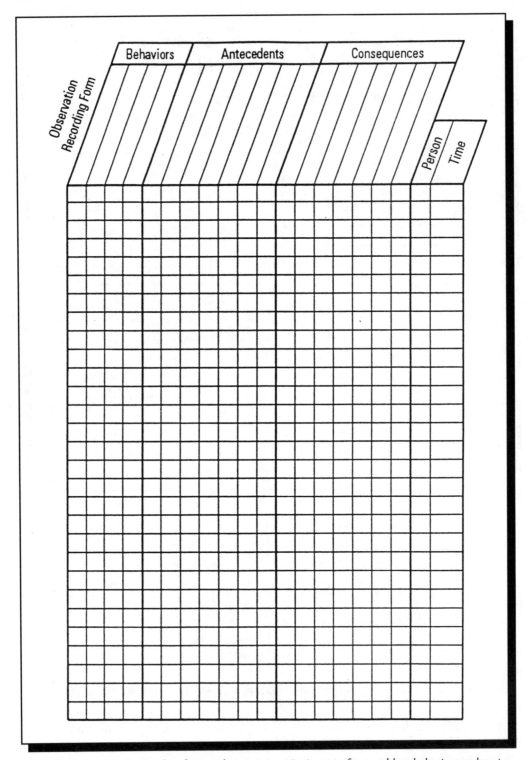

Figure 11.2. An A-B-C recording form with spaces to write in up to four problem behaviors and up to seven antecedents and consequences chosen for observation from other descriptive assessments. Each time the problem behavior occurs, the assessor checks the corresponding column and then checks the columns that correspond to the antecedents and consequences of the problem behavior. The assessor's initials and the time that the problem behavior occurred are also recorded.

In the *checklist method* for conducting A-B-C observations, possible or probable antecedents and consequences are listed on a checklist like the one shown in Figure 11.2, and the observer simply checks the column associated with specific antecedent or consequence events each time the problem behavior occurs (Arndorfer et al., 1994; Miltenberger, 1997; O'Neill et al., 1990). This method is easier and less time-consuming than the descriptive method. However, the possible antecedents and consequences included on the checklist must be identified in advance from previous interviews or descriptive A-B-C recording.

In the *interval A-B-C recording* method, the observer identifies the antecedents and consequences of the problem behavior occurring in consecutive intervals of time (Mace & Lalli, 1991; Rortvedt & Miltenberger, 1994). To conduct interval A-B-C recording, the observer must have previously utilized other indirect or direct assessment methods to identify the antecedents and consequences to be recorded. The observer must also have an interval data sheet and a timing device to cue the recording intervals.

Advantages and disadvantages of direct observation recording. The primary advantage of direct observation assessment is that the assessor directly observes and records the antecedents and consequences as they occur, thus increasing objectivity and, one hopes, accuracy of recording. A disadvantage of A-B-C recording is that it is more time-consuming than indirect methods, although the time commitment can be lessened when a scatter plot is used to identify the best time for A-B-C recording, and when the more efficient checklist or interval methods are used. In addition, more training is required for A-B-C recording to be carried out correctly, especially when the open-ended or descriptive method is used. Finally, the results of A-B-C recording do not demonstrate a functional relationship between the antecedents and consequences and the problem behavior. One must experimentally manipulate these variables to show that they are functionally related to the problem behavior (Iwata et al., 1990, 1993).

Experimental Analysis

Experimental analysis or functional analysis of behavior involves the manipulation of antecedents and/or consequences of the behavior to identify a functional relationship between these variables and the behavior. Although indirect assessment and direct observation of the A-B-Cs in the natural environment can lead to hypotheses about the controlling variables, a functional analysis demonstrates a functional relationship between the controlling variables and the behavior.

At least two features must be present for a successful functional analysis of a problem behavior. First, the problem behavior must increase when a particular antecedent and/or consequence variable is manipulated. Second, the effect must be replicated in an appropriate experimental design such as an alternating treatments design (Iwata, Dorsey, Slifer, Bauman, & Richman, 1982), an A-B-A-B design (Durand & Carr, 1987), or an acceptable variation (Iwata, Pace, Dorsey, et al., 1994; Northup et al., 1991). Since the early 1980s, numerous research articles have been published evaluating functional analysis methodologies for understanding the problem behaviors of individuals with developmental disabilities.

There are two major approaches to the functional analysis of problem behaviors. One involves the manipulation of antecedents and consequences of the behavior (Iwata, Dorsey et al., 1982). The other involves manipulation of only the antecedents of the behavior (Carr & Durand, 1985; Carr, Newsom, & Binkoff, 1980; Durand & Carr, 1987; Weeks & Gaylord-Ross, 1981).

Iwata, Dorsey et al. (1982) described a methodology for analyzing the functions of self-injurious behavior (SIB). They first identified possible reinforcers maintaining SIB—positive reinforcement in the form of attention, negative reinforcement in the form of escape from aversive teaching situations, and self-stimulation (Carr, 1977)—and then systematically manipulated establishing operations and consequences in four different conditions to identify the function of SIB for each individual subject in the study. In the

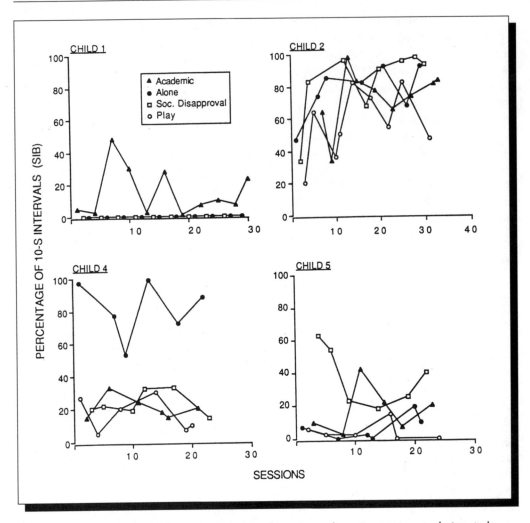

Figure 11.3. Graphed data for four representative subjects in an alternating treatments design study. The level of the child's self-injurious behavior was recorded in each of four experimental conditions: academic demand, social disapproval, alone, and unstructured play.

From "Toward a Functional Analysis of Self-injury," by B. A. Iwata, M. F. Dorsey, K. J. Slifer, K. E. Bauman, and G. S. Richman, 1994, *Journal of Applied Behavior Analysis, 27*, p. 205. Copyright 1994 by Society for the Experimental Analysis of Behavior. Reprinted by permission.

social disapproval condition, the subject was deprived of attention (an EO for SIB maintained by attention) and received attention contingent on SIB. In the academic demand condition, demands were delivered every 30 seconds with physical guidance as needed to assure compliance (an EO for SIB maintained by escape) and the demands were terminated contingent on the occurrence of SIB. In the alone condition, the subject was in a room alone devoid of any stimulation or social interaction (an EO for SIB maintained by self-stimulation). In the unstructured play condi-

tion, the EOs were eliminated—no demands were present, the subject received frequent attention, and a variety of toys were available.

Iwata, Dorsey et al. (1982) evaluated these four conditions in an alternating treatments design and found that attention, escape, and self-stimulation each functioned as a reinforcer for SIB exhibited by different subjects. Figure 11.3 shows the results from four of the subjects in the study by Iwata, Dorsey et al. (1982). For Child 1, the SIB occurred exclusively in the academic demand condition, indicating that the behavior was maintained by escape from tasks. SIB occurred more in the alone condition for Child 4, indicating that self-stimulation maintained the behavior. For Child 5, the SIB was highest in the social disapproval condition, which suggests that attention was maintaining the behavior. Finally, the pattern of data for Child 2 shows high levels of SIB across all conditions, suggesting that SIB served multiple functions or that it was primarily self-stimulatory in nature. The functional analysis strategy developed by Iwata, Dorsey et al. (1982) has been widely used in subsequent research on the analysis and treatment of problem behaviors in people with developmental disabilities (Arndorfer & Miltenberger, 1993; Mace, Lalli, & Lalli, 1991).

Durand and Carr (1987) employed a methodology for conducting a functional analysis in which they manipulated the establishing operations for two possible reinforcers for problem behaviors exhibited by children with autism and developmental disabilities. In one condition, the level of teacher attention was decreased as an EO for problem behavior maintained by attention. In the second condition, the task difficulty was increased as an EO for problem behavior maintained by escape from the task. Durand and Carr evaluated the influence of these two conditions by comparing them to baseline conditions in which the academic task was not difficult and the child received substantial attention. Durand and Carr showed that the problem behaviors of the four students were highest in the increased task difficulty condition but that the level of the behavior was equivalent in the baseline and decreased attention conditions. The results, presented in Figure 11.4, show that increased task difficulty was functionally related to the problem behavior (which suggests that escape from tasks was maintaining the behavior) but that decreased attention was not functionally related to the problem behavior (Durand & Carr, 1987). In subsequent studies, Durand and Carr (1991, 1992) employed a similar functional analysis methodology to identify the reinforcer maintaining problem behaviors in children with developmental disabilities.

In each of the studies described above, the authors manipulated antecedents and/or consequences to evaluate a number of possible functions of the problem behavior. The benefit of this strategy is that it can point to the likely reinforcer maintaining the behavior while ruling out other possible reinforcers. If a problem behavior serves multiple functions, they are likely to be identified using this functional analysis strategy.

One other strategy for conducting a functional analysis links descriptive and experimental analysis to identify the function of the problem behavior (Arndorfer et al., 1994; Belfiore, Browder, & Lin, 1993; Dunlap, Kern-Dunlap, Clarke, & Robbins, 1991; Mace & Lalli, 1991; Sasso et al., 1992). In this strategy, the hypothesis developed from indirect assessments and A-B-C observations is used to develop the functional analysis conditions. The functional analysis is then conducted to confirm the function identified in the descriptive functional assessment procedures. For example, if attention is hypothesized as the reinforcer maintaining a child's problem behavior, the functional analysis might evaluate (a) a condition in which the child is deprived of attention but receives attention contingent on the problem behavior and (b) a condition in which the child receives substantial attention when not engaging in the problem behavior but no attention contingent on the behavior (Arndorfer et al., 1994). In this way, adult attention, the variable hypothesized to be maintaining the problem behavior, is manipulated to determine its affect on the behavior.

Arndorfer et al. (1994) evaluated descriptive and experimental analysis procedures for identifying the functions of aggressive and disruptive behaviors in five children with developmental disabilities. After conducting descriptive assessments using behavioral interviews, they conducted direct observation assessments of the children in their homes and developed hypotheses about the function of the problem behavior for each child. A subsequent functional analysis, in which the hypothesized reinforcer was manipulated, confirmed the hypothesis developed from the interview and

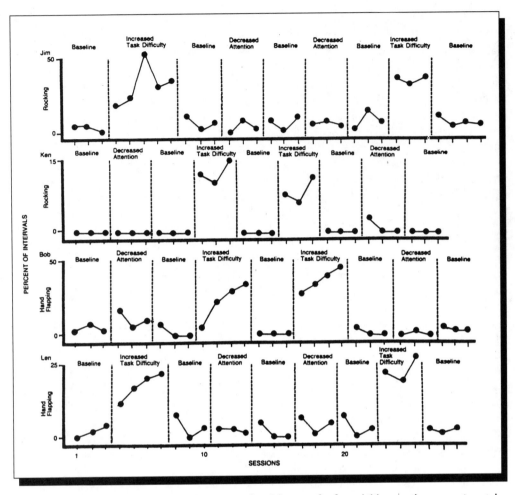

Figure 11.4. Percentage of intervals of rocking or hand flapping for four children as three experimental conditions were implemented: baseline, increased task difficulty, and decreased attention.

From "Social Influences on 'Self-Stimulatory' Behavior: Analysis and Treatment Application," by V. M. Durand and E. G. Carr, 1987, *Journal of Applied Behavior Analysis, 20,* p.124. Copyright 1987 by Society for the Experimental Analysis of Behavior. Reprinted by permission.

direct observation for each child. For three children, problem behaviors were positively reinforced by attention or the receipt of tangible items (toys); for the other two, the behaviors were negatively reinforced by escape from demands. Mace and Lalli (1991) utilized descriptive and experimental analysis techniques to analyze the function of "delusional and hallucinatory" speech exhibited by a man with moderate mental retardation. They first conducted direct observation assessments using interval recording of the A-B-Cs in the group home and hypothesized that the subject's bizarre speech was reinforced by attention in the form of social disapproval and by escape

from instructional demands. Mace and Lalli then conducted functional analysis conditions in which they provided attention and/or escape contingent on the bizarre speech and confirmed the hypotheses from their descriptive assessments. In a similar fashion, other researchers have shown the value of first conducting descriptive functional assessments and then utilizing functional analysis conditions to confirm their results (Belfiore et al., 1993; Dunlap et al., 1991; Repp et al., 1988).

The advantage of the functional analysis strategy, in which only the hypothesized reinforcer(s) is evaluated, is that less time and resources are devoted to the process. The functional analysis results then confirm or disconfirm the hypothesis derived from the previous functional assessment. The potential disadvantage of this strategy is that, because only one or two specific reinforcers are manipulated, the influence of other possible reinforcers may not be identified. The use of descriptive assessment and experimental analysis of a problem behavior is described in the following case example.

Case Example

Willi, a 22-year-old man with Down syndrome, severe mental retardation, and major depressive disorder, was assigned to a room-cleaning crew at a local hotel. One job coach supervised three workers who shared the cleaning responsibilities in each room. Willi's job was to dust the furniture in the room. During training, the job coach used modeling and hand-over-hand guidance to teach Willi to spray furniture polish on the table and to wipe the surface clean. From the start of the job, Willi refused to engage in that task. As a result, the agency referred the case to a behavioral consultant.

The consultant first interviewed the job coach and conducted an A-B-C observation of Willi on the job. The results showed that, as soon as the job coach prompted Willi to engage in the task, Willi dropped to the floor, sat down, and put his head in his lap. The job coach then verbally prompted Willi to get up and dust the table and physically guided him to a standing position. As soon as Willi was standing in front of the table, the job coach prompted him to work again, and again Willi dropped to the floor. The problem behavior was repeated in this manner numerous times each day.

Based on the results of the interview and direct observation assessments, the consultant hypothesized two possible functions of the problem behavior—attention from staff and escape from the task. Both outcomes reliably followed the occurrence of the problem. To determine whether the problem behavior was being maintained by positive reinforcement (attention), negative reinforcement (escape from the task), or both, the consultant designed a functional analysis strategy. He instructed the job coach to respond to Willi in different ways

in different experimental conditions. In the escape condition, when Willi dropped to the floor, the job coach did not respond to the behavior. Therefore, the behavior produced escape from the task, but no attention. In the attention condition, when Willi attempted to drop to the floor, the job coach prevented the behavior and implemented hand-over-hand physical guidance. Therefore the behavior resulted in attention during the guidance but no escape from the task.

The two experimental conditions were replicated a number of times on alternating days and the results showed that Willi's problem behavior was much higher in the escape condition than in the attention condition. The results indicated that escape from the task was reinforcing Willi's problem behavior but that attention played no role in the maintenance of the problem. In this case, the experimental condition involving physical guidance contingent on the behavior was part of the successful treatment. Willi was physically guided whenever he attempted to drop to the floor (extinction of escape-maintained problem behavior), and he received frequent brief breaks for doing his job (negative reinforcement of task-related behavior).

Summary

Understanding the importance of the contingencies of reinforcement for the problem behavior and alternative behaviors is the first step in the process of developing appropriate treatments for problem behaviors exhibited by individuals with mental health disorders and developmental disabilities. The contingencies of reinforcement involve antecedents (S^Ds and EOs), the targeted behavior, and positively or negatively reinforcing consequences of the behavior. The functional approach to the assessment and treatment of problem behaviors involves (a) conducting a functional assessment, (b) developing hypotheses about the contingencies of reinforcement maintaining the problem behavior, and (c) selecting and evaluating treatments based on the hypotheses. There are three general approaches to conducting a functional assessment of a problem behavior. Indirect assessment involves the use of behavioral interviews, questionnaires, or rating scales to generate retrospective reports from informants who know the client well. Direct observation assessments involve observation and recording of the antecedents, behavior, and consequences in the natural environment as the problem behavior occurs. Functional analysis assessments involve the manipulation of antecedents and/or consequences of the problem behavior to document a functional relationship between the controlling variables and the behavior. An adequate functional assessment will include information from multiple sources and will result in hypotheses about the contingencies of reinforcement that can be used to select functional treatments.

REFERENCES

Arndorfer, R. E., & Miltenberger, R. G. (1993). Functional assessment and treatment of challenging behavior: A review with implications for early childhood. *Topics in Early Childhood Special Education, 13,* 82–105.

Arndorfer, R., Miltenberger, R., Woster, S., Rortvedt, A., & Gaffaney, T. (1994). Home based descriptive and experimental analysis of problem behavior in children. *Topics in Early Childhood Special Education, 14,* 64–87.

Axelrod, S. (1987). Functional and structural analyses of behavior: Approaches leading to reduced use of punishment procedures? *Research in Developmental Disabilities, 8,* 165–178.

Belfiore, P. J., Browder, D. M., & Lin, C. H. (1993). Using descriptive and experimental analyses in the treatment of self-injurious behavior. *Education and Training in Mental Retardation, 28,* 57–65.

Bijou, S. W., Peterson, R. F., & Ault, M. H. (1968). A method to integrate descriptive and experimental field studies at the level of data and empirical concepts. *Journal of Applied Behavior Analysis, 1,* 175–191.

Carr, E. G. (1977). The motivation of self-injurious behavior: A review of some hypotheses. *Psychological Bulletin, 84,* 800–816.

Carr, E. G. (1988). Functional equivalence as a mechanism of response generalization. In R. H. Horner, G. Dunlap, & R. L. Koegel (Eds.), *Generalization and maintenance: Lifestyle changes in applied settings* (pp. 221–241). Baltimore: Brookes.

Carr, E. G., & Carlson, J. I. (1993). Reduction of severe behavior problems in the community using a multicomponent treatment approach. *Journal of Applied Behavior Analysis, 26,* 157–172.

Carr, E. G., & Durand, V. M. (1985). Reducing behavior problems through functional communication training. *Journal of Applied Behavior Analysis, 18,* 111–126.

Carr, E. G., McConnachie, G., Levin, L., & Kemp, D. C. (1993). Communication-based treatment of severe behavior problems. In R. Van Houten & S. Axelrod (Eds.), *Behavior analysis and treatment* (pp. 231–267). New York: Plenum Press.

Carr, E. G., Newsom, C., & Binkoff, J. (1980). Escape as a factor in the aggressive behavior of two retarded children. *Journal of Applied Behavior Analysis, 13,* 101–117.

Crawford, J., Brockel, B., Schauss, S., & Miltenberger, R. G. (1992). A comparison of methods for the functional assessment of stereotypic behavior. *Journal of the Association for Persons With Severe Handicaps, 17,* 77–86.

Day, H., Horner, R. H., & O'Neill, R. E. (1994). Multiple functions of problem behaviors: Assessment and intervention. *Journal of Applied Behavior Analysis, 27,* 179–189.

Dunlap, G., Kern-Dunlap, L., Clarke, S., & Robbins, F. R. (1991). Functional assessment, curricular revision, and severe behavior problems. *Journal of Applied Behavior Analysis, 24,* 387–397.

Durand, V. M. (1990). *Severe behavior problems: A functional communication training approach.* New York: Guilford Press.

Durand, V. M., & Carr, E. G. (1987). Social influences on "self-stimulatory" behavior: Analysis and treatment application. *Journal of Applied Behavior Analysis, 20,* 119–132.

Durand, V. M., & Carr, E. G. (1991). Functional communication training to reduce challenging behavior: Maintenance and application in new settings. *Journal of Applied Behavior Analysis, 24,* 251–264.

Durand, V. M., & Carr, E. G. (1992). An analysis of maintenance following functional communication training. *Journal of Applied Behavior Analysis, 25,* 777–794.

Durand, V. M., & Crimmins, D. B. (1988). Identifying the variables maintaining self-injurious behavior. *Journal of Autism and Developmental Disorders, 18,* 99–117.

Gardner, W. I., Cole, C. L., Davidson, D. P., & Karan, O. C. (1986). Reducing aggression in individuals with developmental disabilities: An expanded stimulus control, assessment, and intervention model. *Education and Training in Mental Retardation, 21*, 3–12.

Horner, R. H., & Day, H. M. (1991). The effects of response efficiency on functionally equivalent competing behaviors. *Journal of Applied Behavior Analysis, 24*, 719–732.

Horner, R. H., Sprague, J. R., O'Brien, M., & Heathfield, L. T. (1990). The role of response efficiency in the reduction of problem behavior through functional equivalence training: A case study. *Journal of the Association for Persons With Severe Handicaps, 15*, 91–97.

Iwata, B. A., & DeLeon, I. G. (1995). *The functional analysis screening tool (FAST).* Unpublished manuscript, University of Florida.

Iwata, B. A., Dorsey, M. F., Slifer, K. J., Bauman, K. E., & Richman, G. S. (1982). Toward a functional analysis of self-injury. *Analysis and Intervention in Developmental Disabilities, 2*, 3–20.

Iwata, B. A., Pace, G., Cowdery, G., & Miltenberger, R. G. (1994). What makes extinction work: An analysis of procedural form and function. *Journal of Applied Behavior Analysis, 2*, 131–144.

Iwata, B. A., Pace, G. M., Dorsey, M. F., Zarcone, J. R., Vollmer, T. R., Smith, R. G., Rodgers, T. A., Lerman, D. C., Shore, B. A., Mazaleski, J. L., Goh, H., Cowdery, G. E., Kalsher, M. J., McCosh, K. C., & Willis, K. D. (1994). The functions of self-injurious behavior: An experimental-epidemiological analysis. *Journal of Applied Behavior Analysis, 27*, 215–240.

Iwata, B. A., Vollmer, T. R., & Zarcone, J. R. (1990). The experimental (functional) analysis of behavior disorders: Methodology, applications, and limitations. In A. Repp & N. Singh (Eds.), *Perspectives on the use of nonaversive and aversive interventions for persons with developmental disabilities* (pp. 301–330). Sycamore, IL: Sycamore.

Iwata, B. A., Vollmer, T. R., Zarcone, J. R., & Rodgers, T. A. (1993). Treatment classification and selection based on behavioral function. In R. Van Houten & S. Axelrod (Eds.), *Behavior analysis and treatment* (pp. 101–168). New York: Plenum Press.

Iwata, B. A., Wong, S. E., Riordan, M. M., Dorsey, M. F., & Lau, M. M. (1982). Assessment and training of clinical interviewing skills: Analogue analysis and field replication. *Journal of Applied Behavior Analysis, 15*, 191–204.

Kemp, D. C., & Carr, E. G. (1995). Reduction of severe problem behavior in community employment using an hypothesis driven multicomponent intervention approach. *Journal of the Association for Persons With Severe Handicaps, 20*, 229–247.

Lennox, D. B., & Miltenberger, R. G. (1989). Conducting a functional assessment of problem behavior in applied settings. *Journal of the Association for Persons With Severe Handicaps, 14*, 304–311.

Mace, F. C., & Lalli, J. S. (1991). Linking descriptive and experimental analyses in the treatment of bizarre speech. *Journal of Applied Behavior Analysis, 12*, 553–562.

Mace, F. C., Lalli, J. S., & Lalli, E. P. (1991). Functional analysis and treatment of aberrant behavior. *Research in Developmental Disabilities, 12*, 155–180.

Mace, F. C., & Roberts, M. L. (1993). Factors affecting selection of behavioral treatments. In J. Reichle & D. P. Wacker (Eds.), *Communicative alternatives to challenging behavior: Integrating functional assessment and intervention strategies* (pp. 113–133). Baltimore: Brookes.

Michael, J. L. (1982). Distinguishing between discriminative and motivational functions of stimuli. *Journal of the Experimental Analysis of Behavior, 37,* 149–155.

Miltenberger, R. G. (1997). *Behavior modification: Principles and procedures.* Pacific Grove, CA: Brooks/Cole.

Miltenberger, R. G., & Fuqua, R. W. (1985). Evaluation of a training manual for the acquisition of behavioral assessment interviewing skills. *Journal of Applied Behavior Analysis, 18,* 323–328.

Northup, J., Wacker, D., Sasso, G., Steege, M., Cigrand, K., Cook, J., & DeRaad, A. (1991). A brief functional analysis of aggressive and alternative behavior in an out-clinic setting. *Journal of Applied Behavior Analysis, 24,* 509–522.

O'Neill, R. E., Horner, R. H., Albin, R. W., Storey, K., & Sprague, J. R. (1990). *Functional analysis of problem behavior: A practical guide.* Sycamore, IL: Sycamore.

Reid, D. H., & Parsons, M. B. (1995). *Motivating human service staff: Supervisory strategies for maximizing work effort and work enjoyment.* Morganton, NC: Habilitative Management Consultants.

Repp, A. C., Felce, D., & Barton, L. E. (1988). Basing the treatment of stereotypic and self-injurious behaviors on hypotheses of their causes. *Journal of Applied Behavior Analysis, 21,* 281–289.

Rortvedt, A. K., & Miltenberger, R. G. (1994). Analysis of a high probability instructional sequence and time out in the treatment of child noncompliance. *Journal of Applied Behavior Analysis, 27,* 327–330.

Sasso, G. M., Reimers, T. M., Cooper, L. J., Wacker, D., Berg, W., Steege, M., Kelly, L., & Allaire, A. (1992). Use of descriptive and experimental analyses to identify the functional properties of aberrant behavior in school settings. *Journal of Applied Behavior Analysis, 25,* 809–822.

Skinner, B. F. (1969). *Contingencies of reinforcement: A theoretical analysis.* Englewood Cliffs, NJ: Prentice Hall.

Skinner, B. F. (1974). *About behaviorism.* New York: Vintage Books.

Touchette, P. E., MacDonald, R. F., & Langer, S. N. (1985). A scatter plot for identifying stimulus control of problem behavior. *Journal of Applied Behavior Analysis, 18,* 343–351.

Veltum, L., & Miltenberger, R. G. (1989). Evaluation of a self-instructional program for training initial assessment interviewing skills. *Behavioral Assessment, 11,* 165–177.

Vollmer, T. R., & Iwata, B. A. (1991). Establishing operations and reinforcement effects. *Journal of Applied Behavioral Analysis, 24,* 279–291.

Vollmer, T. R., Iwata, B. A., Zarcone, J. R., Smith, R. C., & Mazaleski, J. L. (1993). The role of attention in the treatment of attention-maintained self-injurious behavior: Noncontingent reinforcement and differential reinforcement of other behavior. *Journal of Applied Behavior Analysis, 26,* 9–21.

Weeks, M., & Gaylord-Ross, R. (1981). Task difficulty and aberrant behavior in severely handicapped students. *Journal of Applied Behavior Analysis, 14,* 449–463.

Zarcone, J. R., Rodgers, T. A., Iwata, B. A., Rourke, D. A., & Dorsey, M. F. (1991). Reliability analysis of the motivation assessment scale: A failure to replicate. *Research in Developmental Disabilities, 12,* 349–360.

Effective Behavioral Support for Socially Maintained Problem Behavior

Joe Reichle
Carol Davis
Rachel Freeman
University of Minnesota, Minneapolis

Robert Horner
University of Oregon, Eugene

Brandenburg, Friedman, and Silver (1990) reported that 14% to 20% of typically developing and at-risk children have behavioral and emotional problems. Retrospective analyses suggest that a significant proportion of individuals with severe behavior problems had onset in early childhood (Green, 1967; Schroeder, Mulick, & Rojahn, 1980). Unfortunately, among many who serve preschoolers who engage in problem behavior, there is a tendency to believe that they may outgrow it. This belief fosters a benign ignoring of low-level repertoires of self-injury, aggression, property destruction, stereotypy, and a host of other socially unacceptable behaviors. Evidence suggests that problem behavior is not outgrown and actually tends to worsen over time (Green, 1967; Smeets, 1971; Walker, Colvin, & Ramsey, 1995). As children grow into adulthood, their problem behavior represents a primary challenge, jeopardizing their success in obtaining and retaining a place in the community for integration and participation (R. C. Lakin, personal communication, 1995).

Authors in previous chapters have alluded to the prevalence of psychopathology in people with severe and profound mental retardation. The influence that mental health disorders have on variables affecting the emission of challenging behavior varies from individual to individual. This chapter focuses solely on behavior challenges in people with severe developmental disabilities and does not discuss the interaction between mental illness and challenging behaviors. Acknowledging mental health disorders in this population is important, but the principles presented in this chapter will apply to people with severe cognitive disabilities with or without mental illness.

In the realm of educational environments, Will (1984) observed that children with behavior problems, to a great extent, do not benefit maximally from their educational placements. In part this may be a result of teachers' and other service providers' propensity to rely more on reactive and suppressive intervention strategies as the frequency and intensity of behavior problems increase (Evans & Meyer, 1985; Guess, 1990; Mace & Shea, 1990). The literature is quite clear that regular educators tend to refrain from reinforcing socially acceptable behavior and to rely on implementation of mild punishment (reprimand) contingent on the emission of socially unacceptable behavior (Lipsey, 1992; Meyer & Evans, 1986; Tolan & Guerra, 1994). Teachers, families, and staff are likely to ignore good behavior and wax and wane between reinforcing and punishing socially unacceptable behavior. These patterns can result in coercive interactions (Patterson, 1982). In a coercive interaction, one member of an interaction engages in socially unacceptable behavior to achieve a desired social function. The other member of the interaction responds with a socially unacceptable reaction. This, in turn, recruits an escalated socially unacceptable response from the originator of the exchange. These exchanges continue to spiral in a game of "social chicken" until one member of the interaction in effect "gives up." When this occurs, both the winner and the loser are reinforced by escaping an aversive situation. Unfortunately, coercive social interactions tend to have devastating consequences for both participants. Individuals who engage in predictable repertoires of problem behavior do so because their socially unacceptable behavior has been reinforced.

A primary component of a successful plan of behavior support requires that an interventionist identify the reinforcing functions served by problem behavior and either (a) rearrange antecedents and consequences to enhance the individual's ability to better self-regulate his decisions that result in problem behavior, or (b) provide a socially acceptable alternative to problem behavior that will result in the delivery of the reinforcer(s) associated with problem behavior. The remainder of this chapter explores (a) the social functions that problem behavior may serve, (b) examples of the range of strategies that may be helpful in developing a comprehensive plan of behavioral support, and (c) some of the challenges that influence the successful implementation of a plan of behavioral support for both children and adults who have developmental disabilities and engage in challenging behavior.

Describing the Relationship Between Problem Behavior and Maintaining Functions That It Serves

O'Neill, Horner, Albin, Sprague, Story, and Newton (1997) articulated six basic functions that problem behavior may serve, and organized these in two broad classes. One class related to the individual's desire to secure or maintain conditions of positive reinforcement. The other class related to a desire to secure negative reinforcement associated with escape and avoidance of aversive events. Each of these two general function classes can be motivated by either social or nonsocial outcomes. When an individual encounters a desirable item that she cannot obtain herself, she may produce problem behavior to influence a social partner in a way that would result in obtaining an item. Alternatively, problem behavior may be produced when a person wishes to secure or maintain the attention of a social partner. Both of the preceding examples presume that desired items and attention serve as positive reinforcers. That is, because they are delivered contingently on the production of problem behavior, the probability increases that problem behavior will be used in the future to obtain these outcomes.

Other situations may arise in which an individual is expected to engage in an activity or interact with an aversive item (e.g., eat vegetables). In these instances, an individual may engage in problem behavior in an attempt to escape from the aversive situation. The outcome of successful efforts to escape and avoid constitute negative reinforcement.

Not all problem behavior is intended for social partners. For example, a person may engage in staring at fluorescent lights while waving his hand back and forth to create a desirable sensory event. Another individual may engage in self-injury that consists of hitting his head with a closed fist in order to obtain a release of endorphins (natural chemicals) that produce a desirable outcome. In each of these instances, positive reinforcement may be operating without the involvement of a social partner. Negative reinforcement can also operate in the absence of a social partner. Consider a child with an active middle ear infection. The child may tug and slap his ear because he believes (whether real or imagined) that this relieves pain. In this instance, the behavior occurs in an effort to obtain the contingent removal of discomfort.

Sometimes behavior that is not originally socially motivated may evolve into socially motivated problem behavior. Pain associated with infected fluid in the middle ear may result in crying and head slapping in an attempt to relieve pain. However, if soothing comfort often results as a consequence for tantruming, the individual may generalize his problem behavior to situations in which he would like comforting attention but does not have an ear infection. Often, socially unacceptable behavior results in a social partner's responsivity when earlier, more socially tolerable idiosyncratic communicative overtures did not glean a response. There is a propensity for typically developing adults to be less responsive to communicative overtures produced by people with more severe developmental disabilities (Linfoot, 1994). The lack of responsivity results in a continuum of long-term effects on people with disabilities. This continuum may range from social styles such as learned helplessness to more assertive styles that involve the emission of problem behavior to more vehemently make wants and needs known. If problem behavior results in those wants and needs being met, positive or negative reinforcement is delivered, and the problem behavior is likely to recur.

In spite of potential limitations in responsiveness to social overtures produced by people with severe disabilities, evidence suggests that the effects of problem behavior predictably influence the future actions of social partners. Taylor and Carr (1993) have found that teachers are apt to deliver increasingly fewer directives to students who engage in escape-motivated problem behavior. Directives given to individuals whose problem behavior is associated with escape are most apt to revolve around tasks that are associated with a history of engagement. Correspondingly, with individuals whose problem behavior serves to obtain attention, social partners are apt to provide substantially greater noncontingent attention than they provide to individuals who refrain from engaging in problem behavior to obtain attention. Partners of individuals who engage in problem behavior alter the context of interactions to minimize problem behavior. Often, the structural modifications of interactions that are made to accommodate the person

who engages in problem behavior result in an unacceptable environment for learning. Consequently, the goal of proactive behavioral support is aimed at designing and implementing comprehensive longitudinal strategies that focus on assimilating the individual with problem behavior into typical social and educational contexts.

In developing a comprehensive plan of behavioral support, parents and professionals are faced with a potentially overwhelming array of strategies. Intervention options selected must directly address the function that the problem behaviors serve. Further, if interventions are to be maintained and appropriately used across a wide range of available opportunities, the interventions must be efficient to implement from the perspective of the interventionist. This means that those who socially interact with the person engaging in problem behavior must be comfortable with the strategies (Albin, Lucyshyn, Horner, & Flannery, 1996). From the perspective of the individual with the challenging behavior, the result of the intervention strategy must also prove as efficient as the effort and outcomes that were in place prior to the implementation of the strategy.

In summary, problem behaviors may begin for many different reasons. However, often they are maintained by their social effect (positive reinforcement; negative reinforcement). Interventions must be guided by the maintaining function of the problem behavior. In the next portion of this chapter, we overview a range of intervention strategies available to parents and professionals that attempt to meet the social needs of both the individuals engaging in problem behavior and their social partners. Subsequently, we discuss the importance of designing behavioral support plans that use a customized combination of intervention strategies that best meet the needs of the individuals and the environments in which they operate. Finally, we discuss the importance of the contextual fit between an intervention plan and its efficiency as perceived by both the individuals and their social partners.

Intervention Strategies That Address Socially Motivated Problem Behavior

Strategies used to address socially motivated problem behavior have changed dramatically in the past 20 years. Traditionally, intervention strategies addressing socially motivated problem behavior have been aimed at suppressing unacceptable forms of responding. The literature is replete with examples of the use of reactive procedures designed to establish consequences to apply for (a) refraining from producing problem behavior (e.g., differential reinforcement of other behavior [DRO]), and (b) engaging in problem behavior (e.g., time-out, overcorrection, response cost). Although a plethora of literature exists describing the efficacy of the exclusive use of reactive procedures, several disadvantages may result from their exclusive use. First, we believe that the greatest success with exclusively reactive procedures rests with individuals who frequently produce problem behavior. Opportunities to implement a procedure that reacts to problem behavior (other than differential reinforcement of acceptable behavior) can occur only when a problem behavior is produced. Consequently, the more frequent the behavior, the greater the density of available intervention opportunities. Secondly, reacting to problem behavior may negatively impact opportunities to provide education in inclusive settings since regular education teachers may be reluctant to have problem behavior modeled for other students. Consequently, there is a tendency for regular educators to want the socially unacceptable behaviors to diminish before inclusive educational activities begin. Reactive procedures (with the exception of differential reinforcement strategies applied to functionally equivalent, socially acceptable alternatives to problem behavior) do little to establish a positive repertoire of alternative behaviors that represent functional alternatives to problem behavior. Without these, reactive consequences may be difficult to fade.

Within the past few years, researchers and practitioners have embraced the position that any plan designed to decrease problem behaviors that are well maintained requires that the intervention be carefully matched to the function(s) associated with the problem behavior. Further, in developing a comprehensive support plan, manipulation of antecedents must be carefully coordinated with the manipulation of consequences for both socially desirable and socially unacceptable behavior. In identifying the range of available behavioral support strategies, interventionists must first determine whether the function served by the problem behavior can be honored unconditionally, can be honored conditionally, or cannot be honored under any circumstances.

Determining Whether the Function of Problem Behavior Can Be Honored

Once events associated with problem behavior have been identified, individuals who comprise the person's educational or habilitation team must make a decision regarding whether (and the conditions under which) the motivation associated with problem behavior can be honored. Within the past 15 years, an assessment technology has emerged that enables the prospective interventionist to systematically utilize both indirect and direct assessment methods to make and verify hypotheses regarding antecedents and consequences that maintain repertoires of problem behavior. Other chapters in this volume provide a clear delineation of the range of assessment strategies that are available. Our discussion assumes that an assessment has resulted in the generation and testing of hypotheses that have led to a delineation of the function(s) and the controlling antecedent conditions associated with problem behavior. Additionally, in accordance with the focus of this chapter, we address social functions associated with problem behavior. Further, in framing intervention options, we focus primarily on problem behavior that has a history of being associated with escaping or avoiding activities or contact with other individuals.

Consider a person who engages in property destruction and aggression to avoid the delivery of certain predictable food items at mealtime. In this situation, interventionists may decide that if the individual used a more socially acceptable behavior to reject the delivery of certain foods, she could be permitted to avoid them. On the other hand, the same individual may have developed a history of using the same problem behaviors to avoid taking seizure control medication. Unfortunately, avoiding medication could create life-threatening medical consequences. In this latter situation, the escape function cannot be honored. Still another possibility is that in some contexts the function of the individual's behavior with respect to an undesired item or event could be honored but in others could not be honored. For example, avoiding a car ride to visit a relative could be honored but avoiding a car ride to a doctor's appointment cannot be avoided. Each of the situations that have been described calls for an individualized intervention strategy. Further, each of the intervention strategies must result in the individual experiencing the events making conditional discriminations about what he should and should not do in particular contexts. Obviously, this is a very challenging task for the interventionist.

Available literature often presumes that a function served by problem behavior can be treated somewhat similarly across social contexts. To this extent, interventionists discuss the degree to which the effects of an intervention strategy will generalize across a variety of situations. We believe that although generalization is important, the conditions under which a particular alternative to problem behavior is utilized are equally important even though they receive relatively limited attention. Consequently, we propose that interventionists must be prepared to embrace multicomponent intervention packages that promote response-efficient strategies that can be matched to the varying conditions encountered in the milieu of an active daily routine.

Effective behavioral support should affect what an individual does on a day-to-day basis: where she goes, whom he spends time with, the type of educational experiences she receives, and the types of recreation available (Horner, O'Neill, & Flannery, 1993). Reduction of problem behavior is now considered insufficient if it is occurring in social or physical isolation or within barren or rigid activity patterns (Horner, 1990; Meyer & Evans, 1989; Turnbull et al., 1986). Behavioral support strategies seek to alter the existing environment in a manner that makes problem behaviors irrelevant, ineffective, and inefficient (Horner et al., 1993). In this section, we discuss a variety of primarily antecedent-based proactive intervention strategies that, when applied in natural contexts, can enhance engagement while at the same time placing the individual in a better position to refrain from problem behavior.

Antecedent-Focused Intervention Strategies That Focus on Altering the Conditions of Social Engagement

Providing Reinforcement Noncontingently

There is an emerging literature (Vollmer, Iwata, Zarcone, Smith, & Mazaleski, 1993; Vollmer, Marcus, & Ringdahl, 1995) suggesting that simply placing the delivery of reinforcers on a random schedule rather than one in which reinforcer delivery is associated with problem behavior serves to decelerate socially motivated problem behavior by interrupting the relationship between problem behavior and the reinforcers that have come to be associated with it.

Establishing Schedules to Order Critical Events Within a Daily Routine

Enhancing predictability is a very important variable in structuring positive environments. Predictability occurs when individuals can foresee events and exert control over their surroundings (Eno-Hieneman & Dunlap, in press). Predictability does not necessarily mean that an individual's environment is rigid and unchanging. Settings that have a lot of variability may still be predictable if the person is able to anticipate the changes (Flannery & Horner, 1994). One approach that enhances predictability and provides opportunities for the individual to exert control over the environment involves creation of daily schedules. Activities in the person's life can be seen as independent variables that have significant effects on behavior and can be manipulated in systematic ways as part of a behavioral support program.

Brown (1991) delineated several critical dimensions that represent a continuum that can be addressed in establishing individualized schedules. First, Brown discusses the *time dimension,* which represents how activities occur across a given time frame. For example, some individuals enjoy knowing that a specific activity will occur in a consistent order or during a specific time of the day. This type of schedule not only promotes independence but, as Brown notes, the completion of one activity may act as a stimulus for initiation of the next activity. At the opposite end of the continuum is the open schedule, in which the person controls the time or sequence of the activities for the day. This type of schedule may or may not reflect consistency.

Content can also be examined and individualized to meet the activities and needs for each person. In this dimension, the continuum ranges from routine content to choice content. Content that is routine refers to specific activities or the form of activities that are expected to occur. An individual's routine activities might include cleaning the bedroom, cleaning the bathroom, and doing outside work. Within any one activity, the form of the activity may be routine. That is, during the bedroom activity the routine form might include making the bed, picking up clothes, and dusting. The content dimension may include choice, in which the individual is given some choice in what activities to complete or the form of the activities.

The third dimension discussed by Brown (1991) is that of *activity sequence.* Activity sequences can range from a single activity to a chain of related activities. For example, getting ready for work may include showering, getting dressed, eating breakfast, and brushing teeth. This is a chain of activities that are related and often should be taught together. Conversely, it may be necessary to teach these activities as a single activity. Brushing teeth is an activity that may be used in more than one chain of events—getting ready for work and getting ready for bed.

Finally, it is necessary to evaluate the effectiveness of the schedule on the reduction of problem behavior and the performance of skills or participation in activities. To do this, it will be necessary to determine which variables would accurately measure change or progress.

Modifying Physical Features of Environment

The physical environment can be engineered to result in a decrease in the frequency and intensity of problem behaviors (Close & Horner, in press). This may be as simple as removing objects that may cause injury to the individual or others in the environment. For example, Archie disliked his morning routine of shaving and brushing his teeth so much he would often stand and throw his chair across the room. By substituting a lighter plastic chair for the heavy wooden chair, the probability that someone would be seriously injured decreased. Pictures can be bolted into the wall and encased in plastic rather than glass, and furniture attached to the floors and walls so that it cannot be easily moved. Curtains can be attached to windows with Velcro™ fasteners so that if they are ripped from walls, no damage will occur. This, in turn, will allow staff to refrain from reactions that provide unnecessary attention to property destruction. The home or school setting for an individual who engages in pica (ingesting objects like paper clips and pen lids) can be cleared of those possible items to decrease available opportunities for that behavior.

Preferred Item or Activity as a Distractor

This strategy uses a preferred item or activity to distract the individual from the variables (i.e., context, events, etc.) that serve to occasion the problem behavior. It involves the use of an object or activity that has a history of functioning as a reinforcer. However, in this application, the reinforcer is delivered noncontingently in an effort to distract the individual from the situation that has come to be associated with problem behavior. This strategy appears to be most effective when an activity associated with problem behavior does not require active participation. For example, consider a child who has tantrums in an effort to escape attending a church service. During future Sunday services, a parent may offer the child a picture book to examine, gum to chew, or crayons for drawing. These activities are designed to distract the child from engaging in escape-motivated problem behavior. In implementing this intervention, the interventionist is willing to sacrifice the child's active participation in the church service.

Prior to implementing this strategy, the interventionist identifies a set of preferred items or activities for the individual. Through the functional assessment process the interventionist will have determined the activities or events that occasion the problem behavior. Prior to engagement in the activity in which problem behavior typically occurs, the interventionist provides the individual with one or more of the preferred items identified.

The preferred-item-as-a-distractor strategy has been implemented in situations in which active participation was not required. Reichle (1995) demonstrated that distracting activities during transportation to and from school dramatically decreased problem behavior associated with the ride to school. Carr and Carlson (1993) found that allowing adults with developmental disabilities to peruse a magazine while waiting to be checked out decreased problem behavior previously associated with waiting.

Choice-Making

A growing number of studies have examined the effects of allowing individuals to make choices as an effective strategy in decreasing problem behaviors (Bambara, Ager, & Koger, 1994; Dunlap et al., 1994; Dyer, Dunlap, & Winterling, 1990; Mithaug & Hanawalt, 1978; Parsons, Reid, Reynolds, & Bumgarner, 1990). Choices can be offered among the positive reinforcers that are available. Additionally, choices among the tasks to be performed (negative stimuli) can also be given. Dyer et al. (1990) compared a multicomponent intervention procedure that provided choice among both reinforcers and tasks that had a history of association with escape-motivated problem

behavior for each of three individuals with severe disabilities. In a within-subject reversal design, the effectiveness of choice and no-choice conditions was compared using dependent measures including problem behavior and engagement. All three participants increased engagement and decreased their emission of problem behavior. As the authors acknowledged, the relative efficacy of offering choices among tasks to be completed and reinforcer choices could not be differentiated. More recent investigations have examined the influence that choice among tasks to complete has on engagement and problem behavior. When choices cannot be given among tasks, choices of materials to complete the task have been associated with deceleration of problem behavior (Dunlap et al., 1994).

Several explanations have been posited for the effectiveness of choice-making as an intervention. Several investigators reported lower levels of problem behavior with preferred activities than with nonpreferred activities (Foster-Johnson, Ferro, & Dunlap, 1994). Given this, it may be likely that when provided with a choice, the individual will choose the more preferred activity and thus engage in substantially less problem behavior. A second hypothesis attributes the effectiveness of choice-making to individual control. That is, by providing a choice of activities in which to participate, materials to use, or reinforcers to be delivered upon completion, the individual gains control of certain aspects of his or her environment. By simply providing the individual with the opportunity to choose, we may be promoting individual independence and decision making, which contribute to an effective comprehensive plan.

Collaboration

Many individuals who engage in escape-motivated problem behavior are also reinforced by social interaction with others. Collaboration is an intervention that can result in the delivery of both positive reinforcement (attention) and negative reinforcement (quicker completion of a less preferred activity). During an episode of collaboration, a second individual works as a team member with the person who engages in escape-motivated problem behavior. Contingent on the individual's task engagement, the work partner will also participate as she also delivers social interaction. For example, Maria has a difficult time learning to match sample food items to picture cards. Using this strategy requires that the interventionist identify the activities and tasks in which problem behavior typically occurs. The interventionist must then divide the responsibilities of the task. The request to participate is then delivered to the individual, indicating that the task will be completed collaboratively. Once a strategy of collaboration has resulted in increased participation and decreased problem behavior, the interventionist can systematically reduce her participation in the task. Once the interventionist's involvement is strictly social, efforts can be made to lesser social engagement during the activity.

Tolerance for Delay in Reinforcement

From time to time, most individuals find themselves in situations from which they wish to escape. For example, after mowing the front lawn for some time, the desire to abandon the lawn-mowing activity increases (habituation). The increasing desire to leave an activity does not always apply only to events that are at least mildly aversive from the outset. For example, you may be attending an extremely interesting meeting. However, knowing that your child needs to be picked up at school creates increasing urgency to leave the meeting. The situations just described cause attention to be diverted from the task as the individual plans escape. In the context of the situation just described, negative reinforcement will be obtained by escape from the meeting.

A tolerance for delay occurs when a warning is given that, contingent on continued good behavior and activity engagement, reinforcement will be delivered. For example, a meeting leader says, "Oh oh, 5 more minutes and we'll be done." In this example, subsequent release from the activity constitutes negative reinforcement. Teaching a tolerance for delay of reinforcement can be implemented around attempts to obtain a requested tangible, activity, or attention. For example, a child can

attempt to obtain the attention of a parent. An occupied parent may say, "Just a second."

Implementing a tolerance for a delay procedure involves implementing a *delay cue* (e.g., "Hang on, we've almost got it made") before the person has engaged in problem behavior. The delay cue signals the individual that reinforcement will be delivered shortly, contingent on desirable behavior. After a brief interval of engagement, a *safety signal* (cue that the individual has obtained negative reinforcement) is offered as he or she is released from the activity. Across opportunities, the length of time or quantity of work required prior to the delivery of the delay cue can be increased systematically. Similarly, the length of time or amount of effort between the delivery of the delay cue and the safety signal can be increased systematically.

Carr and Carlson (1993) implemented a multicomponent intervention that used a form of this procedure. In this study, individuals were participating in a grocery shopping activity. One of the participants began to engage in problem behavior to obtain a preferred food item. When the participant requested the preferred food item, the interventionist asked him to find one of the food items on the grocery list before he could acquire the preferred item. Over subsequent grocery shopping sessions, the participant was required to obtain two and then three items from the list before gaining access to the preferred item. In this example, the process of obtaining other items served as the delay in reinforcement. Several years ago, we increased the amount of work completed by Alex, a 5-year-old who produced escape-motivated behavior during kindergarten activities that included cutting and pasting tasks. At the outset, the amount of work that Alex completed without problem behavior typically involved cutting and gluing two pieces of paper. Once the child had completed two pieces of paper, the interventionist presented one more piece of paper and stated, "We are almost done, one more please." Over time, the interventionist required "two more," "three more," and so on.

The mechanism for the effectiveness of tolerance for delay may involve several important components. First, there is an initial decrement in the instructor's expectation for individual participation. A task that is anticipated to last 20 minutes may initially last only as long as the individual will engage without producing problem behavior. Secondly, the interventionist attempts to pair a delay signal (e.g., "Hang on, we're almost done") with impending release. Across successful opportunities, the delay between task origination and the delivery of the delay cue can be increased systematically. Additionally, the time between the delivery, the delay cue, and the safety signal (cue releasing the individual from the task) can be increased.

It is possible that the critical mechanism in a tolerance for delay is the systematic shift in the criterion of participation prior to release from task. Alternatively, it is possible that the delay cue may generalize to a variety of tasks that were not originally associated with the shifting criterion for participation. If this occurs, a delay cue may have a useful strategy as a cue to assist an individual in self-regulating behavior.

High-Probability Request Sequences

Many individuals engage in problem behavior to escape an activity as a result of the reinforcement history associated with that activity. For example, taking a medication that leaves an unpleasant taste in the mouth may result in inappropriate behavior at the next dose in an attempt to escape it. Three related strategies— embedding, interspersed requests, and high-probability requests—have been demonstrated to be effective across the age range of individuals with varying disabilities. These strategies, similar in procedure, have been effective in increasing successful transitions with elementary-aged students with severe disabilities (Singer, Singer, & Horner, 1987), compliance (Mace & Belfiore, 1990; Mace et al., 1988), task engagement (Horner, Sprague, O'Brien, & Heathfield, 1990), self-medication routines (Harchik & Putzier, 1990), social interactions (Davis, Brady, Hamilton, McEvoy, & Williams, 1994; Davis, Brady, Williams, & Hamilton, 1992; Davis & Reichle, 1996), and communication routines (Davis & Reichle, 1996).

Embedding is a strategy first implemented by Carr, Newsom, and Binkoff (1976) to increase compliance to simple task requests of a 6-year-old child with a psychotic disorder. The strategy consisted of engaging the child in an activity that she enjoyed. During this activity, the interventionist interspersed task requests in which the child was to engage while continuing the preferred activity. *Interspersed requests* is a procedure in which a set of easy requests (three to five) to which the individual is likely to comply is delivered in an interspersed fashion throughout an activity in which the individual is likely to escape. For example, Horner, Day, Sprague, O'Brien, and Heathfield (1991) had identified that an individual would engage in an assembly task for a short period of time before engaging in self-injurious behavior. Before the initial request to engage in the activity was delivered, the interventionist would deliver the set of easy requests. At the point at which the individual began to get agitated but before the problem behavior was emitted, the interventionist delivered another sequence. This continued throughout the activity in an interspersed fashion contingent on the agitation of the individual. Clearly, the majority of the research has focused on a strategy termed *high-probability requests*.

High-probability requests consist of delivering three to five requests that the individual is likely to perform 80% of the time or better immediately prior to asking the individual to perform a task that he or she typically does not perform (40% of the time or less) and that may be associated with a problem behavior. Rather than delivering interspersed requests throughout a task, high-probability requests are delivered prior to asking the learner to engage in an activity identified with problem behavior. Social praise statements or some other positive reinforcement (e.g., tangible food item) are delivered after compliance to each of the high-probability requests and the low-probability requests. Optimizing the effectiveness of high-probability request sequences requires attention to several important procedural variables. First, Mace and his colleagues (1988) found that a low-probability request delivered within 5 seconds of the reinforcement for the last high-probability request was more effective than a low-probability request delivered 20 seconds after reinforcement to the last high-probability request. Second, in a study examining the effects of two different types of high-probability sequences, Davis and Reichle (1996) found that high-probability requests delivered in a variant sequence (i.e., randomized order) were more effective over time than those delivered in an invariant sequence (i.e., same order every time). These investigators hypothesized that when high-probability requests are delivered in the same sequence, the delivery of the associated low-probability request may become more predictable. Consequently, the person may use high-probability requests as part of an extended discriminative stimulus for the low-probability request. When this occurs, the individual may attempt to escape during the delivery of the high-probability requests.

Although high-probability requests can be an effective procedure, there are many unanswered questions regarding their utilization in applied environments. For example, it is unclear how many high-probability requests must be delivered to establish momentum for any given low-probability request. Secondly, it is unclear how the reinforcement value of each high-probability request influences procedural effectiveness. Further, it is unclear whether it is better to deliver high-probability requests after the person has engaged in low-level escape behavior or whether high-probability requests should always be used prior to the delivery of task demands.

In each of the preceding intervention strategies, the assumption has been that the function of the individual's problem behavior cannot be honored. Each of the preceding strategies seeks to make the conditions under which provoking antecedents or consequences occur more palatable. The goal is, however, that over time the individual will engage in socially proactive behavior in the presence of stimulus events that previously provoked problem behavior.

In other instances, the individual may be taught a response that is equivalent but more efficient than his problem behavior and, when used, results in the communicative partners honoring the social function originally associated with problem behavior.

Establishing Socially Acceptable Communicative Alternatives to Problem Behavior

Often, proactively addressing problem behavior involves teaching a socially acceptable alternative response that is functionally equivalent to the problem behavior (Baer, Wolf, & Risley, 1968; Bijou & Baer, 1978; Carr, 1977). Functional equivalence training has proven to be effective in reducing problem behavior (Carr, 1988; Carr & Durand, 1985; Carr, Taylor, Carlson, & Robinson, 1990; Donnellan, LaVigna, Negri-Shoultz, & Fassbender, 1988; Durand & Carr, 1987; Evans & Meyer, 1985; Horner & Budd, 1985; LaVigna & Donnellan, 1986; Meyer & Evans, 1989). It requires that the interventionist conduct a functional assessment to define the events that predict and consequences that maintain a problem behavior and then teach a socially appropriate response under control of the same antecedent events and consequences as the problem behavior (Horner & Day, 1991). The new adaptive behavior then becomes part of the same response class (Johnston & Pennypacker, 1980; Millinson & Leslie, 1979). An advantage of functional equivalence training is that it is proactive rather than reactive, as the focus is on identifying and interrupting the reinforcement contingencies maintaining the problem behavior (Mace, Lalli, Pinter-Lalli, & Shea, 1993). If the rate of reinforcement for the socially appropriate response exceeds that for the aberrant class of behaviors, the more appropriate response will be more likely to occur (Herrnstein, 1970; Herrnstein & Loveland, 1975). Although a seemingly straightforward approach, the range of available communicative functions can make the selection of a specific communicative function challenging. Selecting a communicative function to teach requires a careful consideration of how efficient the function will be in achieving the desired outcome for the individual (compared to the efficiency of the problem emission).

There are at least four variables that affect the efficiency of a response: (a) the physical and cognitive effort involved (actual calories of energy expended), (b) the schedule of reinforcement, (c) the latency between the presentation of a discriminative stimulus and the delivery of reinforcement for the response, and (d) the quality of the reinforcer itself (i.e., strength of preference, appropriate amount) (Horner et al., 1990). For example, a person may find that signing "break" is more efficient than hitting the interventionist. If each sign production is followed by a break, there is a smaller delay between the sign and the delivery of the break. On the other hand, if a longer utterance ("Could I please have help?") must be produced before a break is given, or there are long delays between signing and receiving a break, hitting the interventionist may naturally be the most efficient way of terminating engagement in a task. When a new response can be made more efficient than problem behavior, the new response will tend to be used instead of problem behavior.

Meeting the individual's conditions of response efficiency and at the same time picking a communicative alternative that is likely to result in the most normalized participation in school, home, and community can be very challenging. For example, consider a person who attempts to escape activities. The interventionist could teach a functionally equivalent communicative alternative that consists of a request for a break, a request for assistance, or a rejecting response emitted when the task is offered. If it is not important that the person engage in the activity associated with problem behavior, a rejecting communicative act is a viable alternative. On the other hand, if the individual is perfectly able to complete the task but becomes habituated, a request for a break may be a more viable communicative replacement. Once the individual is requesting a break, the interventionist can address the quality of the work being completed by teaching a request for a work check. In this strategy, the interventionist teaches the use of the request for a break

conditionally upon completing a prespecified amount of work. Finally, it is possible that an individual may attempt to escape an activity that she enjoys because she has reached a difficult step and has been unsuccessful. For example, in assembling a jigsaw puzzle, 10 minutes may have passed without successfully placing a puzzle piece. Consequently, an individual may engage in problem behavior and disengage. An alternative would be to request assistance. Selecting the most efficient communicative alternative to problem behavior represents a challenging task to the interventionist that goes well beyond the simple identification of the general function served by the problem behavior.

Sometimes, it is difficult to make the efficiency of the problem behavior and the new response discriminable to an individual. Another alternative is to enhance discriminability by making the problem behavior a less attractive alternative. For example, Wacker et al. (1990) demonstrated that concurrently placing problem behavior on extinction and teaching a functional communicative alternative to problem behavior was more effective than teaching a communicative alternative in the absence of a contingency delivered for the emission of problem behavior.

In numerous situations the function served by problem behavior should be honored. Many of these situations can be addressed by providing a functionally equivalent, socially acceptable communicative alternative. In other instances, it may not be possible to honor the function served by problem behavior. These situations require a set of intervention strategies that alter antecedents and consequences surrounding events that provoke problem behavior to enhance an individual's self-regulatory skills that minimize problem behavior. A number of efficient strategies have emerged during the past 10 years that have gained a level of social acceptability. We believe that rather than attempting to implement one of these strategies across a wide range of contexts in which problem behavior occurs, interventionists should view each individual strategy as a potential component of a multi-component strategy of behavioral support.

Each of the strategies described here has been demonstrated to be effective in providing positive behavioral support. Unfortunately, in most cases, a combination of concurrently implemented strategies are required to effectively manage problem behavior. Next, we will address the growing trend focusing on multicomponent/multielement intervention plans. Multicomponent plans offer a flexible range of strategies to address the milieu of variables inherent in community environments. We believe that relying on a variety of intervention strategies can maximize intervention efficiency from the perspectives of both the individual and his interventionist.

Designing Multicomponent Intervention Strategies That Address Conditions in Community Environments

Horner & Carr (1997) emphasized that in multicomponent interventions it is important to consider (a) altering antecedent elements of a setting, (b) teaching new skills, (c) manipulating consequences to place problem behavior on extinction, and (d) positively reinforcing socially acceptable behavior. Much of the intervention literature addressing proactive intervention strategies to support individuals who engage in problem behavior has focused on the application of a single intervention strategy across a range of environmental contexts in which the problem behavior occurs. More recently, investigations have begun to focus on the implementation of behavioral support strategies in which a package of intervention strategies is designed to meet a wide range of environmental conditions. In some instances, the package of interventions is designed to address multiple functions associated with problem behavior (e.g., escape and attention). In other instances, a single function (escape) may require a variety of intervention strategies to accommodate aspects of the environment or interventionist teaching styles. Implementing a variety of strategies to address the same social function of a problem behavior may be used to compare the efficiency

of several strategies. Alternatively, implementing a range of strategies to address the same function may make the intervention strategies seem more natural and enable a more covert implementation.

In examining the reasons for implementing a multicomponent approach to intervention, we have attempted to delineate several contexts that might call for the use of multicomponent intervention strategies. These include situations in which (a) there is problem behavior that is associated with a single social function that occurs in a variety of different activities, (b) there is a need to establish the conditional use of a communicative alternative, and (c) different social functions of problem behavior operate within the same activity. Each of these contexts is described, including an example of the implementation of a multicomponent intervention strategy.

Problem Behavior Associated With a Single Social Function Occurs in a Variety of Activities

In some instances we have found individuals who are motivated to escape a variety of activities. For example, several years ago we met Jewell, a 30-year-old woman who was reported to escape any activity that required her to engage in a domestic chore (laundry, cleaning room, weeding garden, dusting, sweeping, etc.). Careful implementation of a functional assessment suggested that this was the case. However, in scrutinizing her preferred activities, we also learned that most of them involved interacting with staff (going to restaurants, shopping at the mall, playing cards and board games with staff). If staff attempted to involve peers in card or board games, Jewell often indicated that she did not want to engage in the activity.

Available data seemed to support an explanation that Jewell's problem behavior was motivated primarily by escape but that she also enjoyed staff's company. Some of the domestic chores that Jewell sought to avoid were ones in which staff could be present. For example, when the dishwasher was loaded, staff were usually putting food away. Other domestic chores like cleaning her room were more difficult to accompany with dense staff attention because Jewell's room was on a lower level out of the main traffic flow of the household. Consequently, several different intervention strategies were implemented concurrently as a function of staff availability and the effect that providing attention would distract Jewell from the task (e.g., independent reading and staff attention were not conducive to task participation).

When Jewell was asked to load the dishwasher, staff approached her, saying, "Let's visit while we load the dishwasher." The staff member and Jewell then visited while she loaded the dishwasher. During this period of "collaboration" (Carr et al., 1994), a period of social attention was delivered during engagement in the targeted activity. At the conclusion of the task, staff sat down at the kitchen table with her and had a 5-minute conversation over coffee. If Jewell's quantity or quality of participation was unacceptable, attention was terminated. Jewell's participation in loading the dishwasher dramatically improved. Over time, a tolerance for delay was paired with the original collaboration to decrease the density of constant attention provided.

Unfortunately, many activities that Jewell refused did not permit the density of staff contact that could occur during dishwashing. One of those tasks was reading independently. Staff members who served Jewell cooperated with school staff to increase her independent reading time. To ensure that she was processing information, staff were directed to ask Jewell questions about what she had read. Although Jewell enjoyed the attention that she got during the period of questions, she strongly disliked the silent reading time. Often she abandoned the task and refused to reengage. Because delivering attention during reading would result in a distraction that was incompatible with reading comprehension, staff devised an intervention strategy different from that used during dishwashing.

Queries directed to Jewell suggested that she liked to read about fashion (clothes, makeup, and women's sports). History also suggested, based on her answers to questions, that she almost always read two pages before

she abandoned the activity. The intervention strategy involved allowing Jewell to select the topic of the reading material. She was then told that as soon as she read a page she should seek out a staff member to, in effect, "request a work check." In Jewell's case, the attention that she received during the question-and-answer session was reasonably reinforcing. If she answered questions correctly, she and the staff member sat down and visited for 5 minutes about a topic of Jewell's choosing. Additionally, when asked to return to silent reading, she was also offered a small snack item to take with her. Across successful days, the length of the passage was increased systematically and the delivery of the snacks upon return to reading was made more intermittent.

In the preceding intervention strategy, attention was constant during the early stages of intervention. In the second strategy, constant attention would have interfered with task engagement. Consequently, we implemented a strategy that systematically increased the work required by establishing a criterion that the individual could monitor (aid contingent on meeting that criterion obtains access to conversational partners).

A Need to Enhance the Conditional Use of a Communicative Alternative to Problem Behavior

Communicative behavior is most efficient and socially appropriate when it is used conditionally. That is, we readily learn when to produce a particular communicative act as well as when to refrain from producing it. For example, when condiments for a hamburger are on the other side of the dining table, an efficient response is to request that they be passed. On the other hand, if they are 6 inches away, it is more efficient to simply reach for them without producing a request to a communicative partner.

Several years ago, we encountered a young man who engaged in massive tantrums whenever he was asked to participate in a reading activity requiring him to read sentences aloud. A series of environmental manipulations confirmed that Tom's problem behavior was escape-motivated. Further, we learned that when unsolicited assistance (spoken models) were presented, Tom's problem behavior diminished and he continued to participate. Subsequently, an intervention procedure was established to teach Tom to request assistance when he encountered a difficult sentence. Quickly, Tom became skilled in requesting assistance. His problem behavior decelerated dramatically with a collateral dramatic increase in participation. Interventionist satisfaction was excellent except for the teaching assistant who served Tom. She concluded that Tom's requesting assistance was promoting learned helplessness. That is, he was producing requests for assistance rather than reading independently (which she was sure that he could do). The challenge was to alter some opportunities so that the efficiency of being independent would be greater than requesting assistance.

We explained to Tom that he had an opportunity to earn a special reinforcer if he could independently read one sentence that would appear in a different color on his reading worksheet. Of course, if he tried and encountered difficulty, he was free to ask for assistance, which, in turn, would speed his release from the task to established reinforcers. As was hypothesized, Tom read the "bonus sentence" independently and received the special reinforcer. Across opportunities, the number of sentences that had to be read independently to obtain the special reinforcer was extended in a changing criterion design. As might be expected, Tom became increasingly more independent in his oral reading. With this independence came fewer opportunities to use his request for assistance. Interventionists were so pleased with Tom's independence that they had become reluctant to add new material to his reading exercise. Consequently, on the first day that additional material was added, his immediate response was to engage in mild problem behavior. The situation was quickly brought under control by more rigorously replicating the original intervention procedure.

We learned valuable lessons from Tom. First, it is clear that learning a communicative alternative to problem behavior is not an end in itself. Individuals operate in a finely tuned ecosystem of response efficiency. When teaching communicative functions such as requesting assistance, interventionists must be diligent to ensure that this utterance is used validly in achieving the social function associated with it. In the preceding instance, the individual's skill acquisition interacted longitudinally with a communicative alternative to problem behavior. Sometimes two concurrently implemented communication strategies can interact in interesting ways.

Several years ago, we met a young woman, Lisa, who attempted to escape most academic tasks. The difficulty of the tasks appeared less provoking than the length of the activity. Consequently, we took steps to implement a strategy designed to teach her to request breaks from an ongoing activity. Lisa used a graphic communication wallet and readily learned to locate and touch a symbol corresponding to the message "I need a break." In an effort to fine-tune her augmentative communication skills, interventionists decided to teach her to differentially use a request for a break and a request for assistance. Requesting a break would be used when she was participating in a task in which her performance was accurate. On the other hand, requests for assistance would be used when she encountered a problem that she could not successfully complete. Teachers were puzzled why Lisa was having so much difficulty learning to use requests for assistance. However, it was apparent that the immediacy of the consequences for each of the two communicative responses was dramatically different. Whenever a request for a break was produced, Lisa was released immediately to a break. Whenever she requested assistance, she was provided with assistance to solve the problem at hand and was then released. Lisa's experience suggested that if she requested a break, she could get released more quickly. Consequently, she chose to use the break symbol instead of a request for assistance, which is not exactly what interventionists had in mind when they designed the intervention strategy.

To address this efficiency issue, interventionists implemented two new procedural components. First, a tolerance for delay was added to requests for a break. Whenever Lisa requested a break, the interventionists acknowledged it and said, "Just a second," and then immediately released her. Across successful opportunities, the latency between her break request and the interventionist's releasing her to a break was increased systematically. Interventionists also added an escape extinction component. If Lisa requested a break and then tried to release herself, her escape was made as inefficient as possible. Additionally, during some occasions when Lisa requested assistance, the interventionists provided a generous amount and then offered her a break as soon as the difficult problem had been solved. These corrections made the relative efficiency between the two communicative utterances less discriminable in terms of their perceived efficiency. Consequently, we believe that Lisa was better able to focus on the social uses of each response. In each of the examples that we have provided, response efficiency from the individual's point of view represented a critical variable that had significant influence on the success of intervention attempts.

Different Social Functions of Problem Behavior Operating Within the Same Activity

Traditionally, intervention research has addressed a single social function associated with problem behavior. However, Carr and Carlson (1993) described multicomponent intervention procedures designed to teach each of three individuals with severe disabilities to participate in a grocery shopping activity. Each person engaged several social motivations associated with problem behavior. Intervention strategies implemented included choice-making, embedding, functional communication training, tolerance for delay in reinforcement, and the introduction of discriminative stimuli for desirable behavior. Results of their investigation demonstrated that individuals' problem behavior decelerated dramatically. Additionally, the time that each of the individuals spent in the store and their proficiency in independently completing task-analyzed steps of a community shopping protocol increased dramatically. An important component of Carr and Carlson's study involved pre and post

ratings by store clerks regarding their dramatically altered perception of the acceptability of individuals' behavior.

In the preceding investigation, the intervention strategies implemented met the individual's criteria of efficiency. That is, participation in grocery shopping was worth the positive and negative reinforcers that were made available. Because the implementation of the intervention strategies maintained over time, it is likely that the intervention strategies selected also met the interventionist's criteria for practicality and usefulness. Interestingly, maintenance is usually evaluated via a dependent measure on individual performance. However, an interventionist's tendency to maintain the implementation of a procedure that has produced helpful reductions in problem behavior may represent an indirect measure of response efficiency from an interventionist's perspective.

Response Efficiency From Interventionist's Perspective

Most intervention research is conducted in situations where the motivations of the interventionists are controlled variables. That is, the assumption is made that the interventionists are highly motivated and very committed to the intervention strategies chosen. Unfortunately, in practice, such may not be the case. There is a growing awareness that effective behavioral support plans must not only be technically accurate, they must be compatible with the interventionists' values, skills, and resources (Albin et al., 1996). In other words, an effective behavior support plan must be a good contextual fit for the interventionist (Albin et al., 1996; Horner, 1994). In any one situation, there are many possible interventions that could result in behavior change (Albin et al., 1996). The key is to find the interventions that can effectively address problem behavior, be implemented by the interventionist, result in generalized effectiveness, and be maintained over time. Although the response efficiency literature has focused primarily on the viewpoint of the individual, the efficiency of instruction from the interventionist's perspective is an important consideration when considering goodness of fit. When given a choice among several equally successful interventions, it seems plausible that the interventionist will choose procedures that require the least amount of effort.

In some situations, a strategy can be implemented that may be reinforcing for an interventionist even though its actual effectiveness is less obvious. Consider two different interventions, one that is more effortful but with highly effective results and one that requires less effort but is not as effective at reducing levels of problem behaviors. It is clear that the concept of contextual fit will become an important variable in providing effective behavior support strategies. Effective technical assistance must jointly consider the needs of the individual as well as the conditions of participation in the assessment and intervention process by those who are charged with the primary responsibility of serving the client. We believe that improving our ability to consider matching assessment and intervention strategies to the interventionist's preferences has important implications for maintenance and generalization.

We suspect that often the individual's definition of response efficiency coincides with the interventionist's expectations for efficiency and also influences directly maintenance and generalization in implementing the procedures. When this occurs, we believe that the probability for a successful intervention increases dramatically. Further, it is reasonable to hypothesize that when a viable intervention is available but does not meet the efficiency expectations of the interventionist, the strategy is less likely to be implemented. For the technical assistance provider, the greatest challenge occurs when there is a narrow range of plausible intervention strategies that fail to meet the interventionist's expectation of efficiency. Unless the interventionist views a recommended strategy as practical, maintenance and generalization in using the strategy are apt to be compromised. The initial task is to consider the range of antecedents and consequences that can be manipulated to increase the efficiency of the available intervention strategy. Briefly, we will examine examples of both antecedent and consequence manipulations aimed at increasing the fit between the individual's needs and the interventionist's expectations for an efficient procedure.

Reichle (1994) examined the task demands placed on the interventionist at the point of instructional program implementation. An interventionist with 2 years' experience serving people with severe developmental disabilities was asked to implement a high-probability request sequence with an adult who engaged in escape-motivated problem behavior. Two specific activities were targeted. In one, the low-probability request occurred when the client was asked to leave a break activity and return to work. During these opportunities, the staff member was responsible for a group of four clients, all of whom had histories of problem behavior. The second opportunity to implement high-probability request sequences involved a low-probability request of engaging in emptying the trash from a kitchen. During this time, the interventionist was one-to-one, with no other teaching responsibilities. Data suggested that in the latter opportunity, the interventionist took advantage of 90% of the available instructional opportunities. During the former activity, she took advantage of 45% of available opportunities to implement the program. Correspondingly, instances of individual problem behavior decreased from occurring during 100% of opportunities during baseline to 10% of opportunities during intervention in the cleaning activity. In the activity associated with more sparse implementation (returning to work after extricating from break), problem behavior decreased from occurrences during 90% of baseline opportunities to 70% during intervention. When asked whether the individual responded well to the intervention strategy, the instructor concluded that the procedure was effective for escape-motivated problem behavior but ineffective for problem behavior being emitted to maintain contact with a desired activity. When asked if her implementation was approximately the same across the two opportunities, she said that she implemented slightly less often during efforts to extricate from break.

During a second phase of our technical assistance, we added a second staff member during the activity associated with fewer implementation opportunities. The second staff member was responsible for other clients in the same household. During the instructional activity in question, the second (new) instructor assumed responsibility. This staffing approximated the one-to-one staff availability that was available in the task that, during phase 1, had been associated with a high probability of program implementation. During a 2-week period, the interventionist implemented high-probability request sequences during approximately 80% of the instructional opportunities. During the cleaning activity, the interventionist implemented high-probability request sequences during 84% of available opportunities compared to implementing during 90% of the opportunities in phase 1. During both activities, the proportion of engagement opportunities associated with problem behavior accounted for fewer than 18% of opportunities. Our tentative conclusion from the preceding data was that response efficiency from the perspective of the interventionist accounted for both the interventionist's and, ultimately, the individual's performance. That is, one staff member found it efficient to implement in both activities while the other staff member found it inefficient.

In the preceding instance, the initial interventionist with whom we collaborated appeared to be highly motivated to implement high-probability request sequences under the favorable circumstances. Had we implemented our procedure only in a condition associated with leaving highly preferred activities, we might have concluded that the interventionist lacked the knowledge to implement. An alternative explanation is that the distractions in one task were too great with respect to the benefits obtained to warrant implementation. Consequently, the original interventionist was not sufficiently motivated to implement the instructional strategy in a necessary range of situations.

Sometimes the efficiency of program implementation can be improved by manipulating consequences for the interventionists who are associated with program implementation. Several years ago, we encountered a paraprofessional, Sally, who served two adults with developmental disabilities in a residential setting. She was the only staff member at the residence during her work hours of 3:00 P.M. to 11:00 P.M. Sally was well liked by the group home administrator but was reported to be somewhat incompetent in systematically implementing instructional procedures designed to teach new skills. Upon further investigation, it became apparent that Sally spent a significant amount of work time on the phone visiting with friends. Together with the administrator, an intervention strategy was designed to increase the probability that Sally would implement instructional programs.

The plan had two components. The first component involved establishing the rule that only emergency personal calls could be made on the residence phone and that all outgoing phone calls would be received monthly in a printout from the phone company. The rationale for this move was to qualify for a less expensive telephone service. At the same time, technical assistance began. The technical assistance provider was on-site twice a week. Between these visits, regular phone meetings were established on each day that there was no on-site business. Phone calls could last for up to 15 minutes. In addition to regularly scheduled phone visits, the staff member was given access to the phone number of the technical assistance provider and was told that she was free to call at any time to discuss instructional progress. When a phone call was received, the technical assistance provider sought to redirect most discussion that was not germane to programmatic issues. If implementation had occurred during the preceding day, the technical assistance provider engaged Sally near the end of the phone call in a 5- to 10-minute visit about a variety of social topics, including television shows, movies, or local sports teams. If the phone call revealed that Sally had not implemented the agreed-upon instructional opportunities, the phone call was terminated politely without specifying the actual reason for the more abbreviated discussion.

Over a 3-month period, Sally's implementation of targeted intervention opportunities improved dramatically. During baseline, she took advantage of approximately 35% of instructional opportunities. After the program was implemented, she took advantage of an average of 71% of instructional opportunities over the 3-month period and 83% of opportunities occurring during the last month of the program. We believe that Sally found social interaction with peers (including the technical assistance provider) to be very reinforcing. We simply tried to minimize her opportunities for those types of interactions that were not related to the performance of her job, but at the same time increase opportunities for social exchanges that could be directly tied to the job. In this example, our explanation of the effect obtained may have been overly simplistic.

Interventionists may fail to maintain the implementation of an instructional program because they need more immediate feedback. In the absence of sufficient expertise to generate needed troubleshooting and in the absence of technical assistance, an interventionist may simply disengage from implementation. Providing staff with immediate means of seeking feedback on the implementation of a program on unexpected individual performance may have a maintaining effect on implementation. In an attempt to obtain a closer look at this issue, we reexamined Sally's performance. During baseline, we examined each point during which more than a single day passed without implementation of targeted instructional objectives. Approximately 82% of the gaps in implementation occurred after a sequence of three or more instructional opportunities in which the client engaged in problem behavior. Subsequently, during intervention, we examined instances in which three or more client failures occurred and whether this influenced Sally's program implementation. During intervention, Sally had gaps of 1 day without implementing during 8% of instructional opportunities. Further, when we examined the pattern of her self-initiated phone contacts, we observed that during 90% of the instances of consecutive errors, Sally called seeking assistance but perhaps also seeking reassuring support.

Taken as a whole, it is unclear whether social reinforcement or directive feedback available on demand improved Sally's performance. Each variable may well have had an impact. What is clear, however, is that a history of dense contact during the early phase of technical assistance was highly successful. Motivation is an important variable. In the course of our work, we often find technical assistance providers complaining about the ineptitude of individuals to whom they provide technical assistance.

The concept of response efficiency must be considered from the individual's and the interventionist's perspective in order to assure the transfer and maintenance of behavioral support strategies. This requires a more sophisticated understanding of the interacting dynamics between the interventionist and individual. Designing interventions which create naturally reinforcing contingencies between the interventionist and individual will contribute to the behavioral support strategy's contextual fit in the targeted environment.

Summary

In this chapter, we have explored a range of components that, when taken together, comprise a plan of positive behavioral support. We believe that in the past, in our zeal to demonstrate clear and consistent relationships between intervention strategies and their effects, we may have overlooked some important considerations in creating an effective package of behavioral support. First, we believe that in the absence of deriving the functions served by problem behavior, it will be more difficult to design a totally acceptable support plan. Second, when functions of problem behavior can be conditionally reinforced (reinforced in some contexts but not in others), we believe that a multicomponent package of strategies will be most effective with the majority of individuals who engage in problem behavior. We have also examined contextual examples that support carefully considering the efficiency of intervention strategy components. We believe that if those providing intervention and technical assistance are to be truly effective, they must carefully consider efficiency from the perspective of both the individual and the staff members who serve him or her. We are not yet proficient in addressing efficiency in applied practice. However, we are beginning to value its importance.

How professionals choose to pursue proactive strategies that can be used to create positive behavioral support plans will have a far-reaching impact on how our service delivery systems develop in the next 10 years. As a society, we are dedicated to serving people with severe disabilities (including those with problem behavior) in inclusive educational, work, and social settings. We believe that this will require an approach that relies far less on reactive strategies to apply once a problem behavior has occurred and far more on strategies that can be implemented before the individual has found it necessary to engage in problem behavior. As we approach the 21st century, we are optimistic that we are far more up to the challenge of serving individuals with problem behavior than we were even a few years ago.

REFERENCES

Albin, R. W., Lucyshyn, J. M., Horner, R. H., & Flannery, K. B. (1996). Contextual fit for behavioral support plans: A model for "goodness of fit." In L. K. Koegel, R. L. Koegel, & G. Dunlap (Eds.), *Positive behavioral support: Including people with difficult behavior in the community* (pp. 81–98). Baltimore: Brookes.

Baer, D. M., Wolf, M. M., & Risley, T. R. (1968). Some current dimensions of applied behavior analysis. *Journal of Applied Behavior Analysis, 1*, 91–97.

Bambara, L. M., Ager, C., & Koger, F. (1994). The effects of choice and task preference on the work performance of adults with severe disabilities. *Journal of Applied Behavior Analysis, 27*, 555–556.

Bijou, S. W., & Baer, D. M. (1978). *Behavior analysis of child development.* Englewood Cliffs, NJ: Prentice-Hall.

Brandenburg, N. A., Friedman, R. M., & Silver, S. E. (1990). The epidemiology of childhood psychiatric disorders: Prevalence findings from recent studies. *Journal of the American Academy of Child & Adolescent Psychiatry, 29*, 76–83.

Brown, F. (1991). Creative daily scheduling: A nonintrusive approach to challenging behaviors in community residences. *Journal of the Association for Persons With Severe Handicaps, 16*, 75–84.

Carr, E. G. (1977). The motivation of self-injurious behavior. A review of some hypotheses. *Psychological Bulletin, 84*, 800–816.

Carr, E. G. (1988). Functional equivalence as a mechanism of response generalization. In R. Horner, G. Dunlap, & R. L. Koegel (Eds.), *Generalization and maintenance: Life style changes in applied settings* (pp. 99–120). Baltimore: Brookes.

Carr, E. G., & Carlson, J. I. (1993). Reduction of severe behavior problems in the community using a multicomponent treatment approach. *Journal of Applied Behavior Analysis, 26*, 157–172.

Carr, E. G., & Durand, V. M. (1985). Reducing behavior problems through functional communication training. *Journal of Applied Behavior Analysis, 18*, 111–126.

Carr, E. G., Levin, L., McConnachie, G., Carlson, J. I., Kemp, D. C., & Smith, C. E. (1994). *Communication-based intervention for problem behavior: A user's guide for producing positive change.* Baltimore: Brookes.

Carr, E. G., Newsom, C. D., & Binkoff, J. A. (1976). Stimulus control of self-destructive behavior in a psychotic child. *Journal of Abnormal Child Psychology, 4*, 139–153.

Carr, E. G., Taylor, J. C., Carlson, J. I., & Robinson, S. (1990). *Positive approaches to the treatment of severe behavior problems.* Seattle, WA: The Association for Persons With Handicaps.

Close, D. W., & Horner, R. H. (in press). Architectural design in positive behavioral support. In J. Scotti & L. Meyer (Eds.), *Behavioral support in community context.*

Davis, C., Brady, M., Hamilton, R., McEvoy, M., & Williams, R. (1994). Effects of high-probability requests on the social interactions of young children with severe disabilities. *Journal of Applied Behavior Analysis, 27*, 619–637.

Davis, C., Brady, M., Williams, R., & Hamilton, R. (1992). Effects of high-probability requests on the acquisition and generalization of responding to requests in young children with behavior disorders. *Journal of Applied Behavior Analysis, 25*, 905–916.

Davis, C. A., & Reichle, J. (1996). Invariant and variant high-probability requests: Increasing appropriate behaviors in children with emotional behavior disorders. *Journal of Applied Behavior Analysis, 29*, 471–482.

Donnellan, A. M., LaVigna, G. W., Negri-Shoultz, N. N., & Fassbender, L. L. (1988). *Progress without punishment: Effective approaches for individuals with behavior problems.* New York: Teachers College Press.

Dunlap, G., de Perczel, M., Clarke, S., Wilson, D., Wright, S., White, R., & Gomez, A. (1994). Choice making to promote adaptive behavior for students with emotional and behavioral challenges. *Journal of Applied Behavior Analysis, 27,* 505–518.

Durand, V. M., & Carr, E. (1987). Social influences on "self stimulator" behavior: Analysis and treatment application. *Journal of Applied Behavior Analysis, 20,* 119–132.

Dyer, K., Dunlap, G., & Winterling, V. (1990). Effects of choice making on the serious problem behaviors of students with severe handicaps. *Journal of Applied Behavior Analysis, 23,* 515–524.

Eno-Hieneman, M., & Dunlap, G. (in press). Some issues and challenges in implementing community-based behavioral support: Two illustrative case studies. In J. R. Scotti & L. H. Meyer (Eds.), *New directions for behavioral intervention: Principles, models, and practices.* Baltimore: Brookes.

Evans, I., & Meyer, L. (1985). *An educative approach to behavior problems.* Baltimore: Brookes.

Flannery, K. B., & Horner, R. H. (1994). The relationship between predictability and problem behavior for students with severe disabilities. *Journal of Behavioral Education, 4,* 157–176.

Foster-Johnson, L., Ferro, J., & Dunlap, G. (1994). Preferred curricular activities and reduced problem behaviors in students with intellectual disabilities. *Journal of Applied Behavior Analysis, 27,* 493–504.

Green, A. H. (1967). Self-mutilation in schizophrenic children. *Archives of General Psychiatry, 17,* 234–244.

Guess, D. (1990). Transmission of behavior management technologies from researchers to practitioners: A need for professional self-evaluation. In A.C. Repp & N.N. Singh (Eds.), *Perspectives on the use of nonaversive and aversive interventions for persons with developmental disabilities* (pp. 157–172). Sycamore, IL: Sycamore.

Harchik, A., & Putzier, V. (1990). The use of high-probability requests to compliance with instructions to take medication. *Journal of the Association for Persons With Severe Handicaps, 15,* 40–43.

Herrnstein, R. J. (1970). On the law of effect. *Journal of the Experimental Analysis of Behavior, 13,* 243–266.

Herrnstein, R. J., & Loveland, D. H. (1975). Maximizing and matching on concurrent ratio schedules. *Journal of the Experimental Analysis of Behavior, 24,* 107–116.

Horner, R. H. (1990). Ideology, technology and typical community settings: The use of severe aversive stimuli. *American Journal on Mental Retardation, 95,* 166–168.

Horner, R. H. (1994). Functional assessment: Contributions and future directions. *Journal of Applied Behavior Analysis, 27,* 401–404.

Horner, R. H., & Budd, C. (1985). Acquisition of manual sign use: Collateral reduction of maladaptive behavior, and factors limiting generalization. *Education and Training of the Mentally Retarded, 20,* 39–47.

Horner, R. H., & Carr, E. G. (1997). Behavioral support for students with severe disabilities: Functional assessment and comprehensive intervention. *Journal of Special Education, 31,* 84–104.

Horner, R. H., & Day, H. M. (1991). The effects of response efficiency on functionally equivalent competing behaviors. *Journal of Applied Behavior Analysis, 24,* 719–732.

Horner, R., Day, M., Sprague, J., O'Brien, M., & Heathfield, L. (1991). Interspersed requests: A nonaversive procedure for reducing aggression and self-injury during instruction. *Journal of Applied Behavior Analysis, 24,* 265–278.

Horner, R. H., O'Neill, R. E., & Flannery, K. B. (1993). Building effective behavior support plans from functional assessment information. In M. Snell (Ed.), *Systematic instruction of persons with severe handicaps* (4th ed., pp. 184–214). Columbus, OH: Merrill.

Horner, R. H., Sprague, J. R., O'Brien, M., & Heathfield, L. T. (1990). The role of response efficiency in the reduction of problem behaviors through functional equivalence training: A case study. *Journal of the Association for Persons with Severe Handicaps, 15,* 91–97.

Johnston, J. M., & Pennypacker, H. S. (1980). *Strategies and tactics of human behavioral research.* Hillsdale, NJ: Erlbaum.

LaVigna, G., & Donnellan, A. (1986). *Alternatives to punishment: Nonaversive strategies for solving behavior problems.* New York: Irvington.

Linfoot, K. (1994). *Communication strategies for people with developmental disabilities: Issues from theory to practice.* Baltimore: Brookes.

Lipsey, M. W. (1992). The effect of treatment on juvenile delinquents: Results from meta-analysis. In F. Losel, D. Bender, & T. Bliesener (Eds.), *Psychology and law: International perspectives* (pp. 131–143). New York: Walter de Gruyter.

Mace, F., & Belfiore, P. (1990). Behavioral momentum in the treatment of escape-motivated stereotypy. *Journal of the Applied Behavior Analysis, 23,* 507–514.

Mace, F., Hock, M., Lalli, J., West, B., Belfiore, P., Pinter, E., & Brown, D. (1988). Behavioral momentum in the treatment of noncompliance. *Journal of Applied Behavior Analysis, 21,* 123–141.

Mace, F. C., Lalli, J. S., Pinter-Lalli, E., & Shea, M. C. (1993). Functional analysis and treatment of aberrant behavior. In R. Van Houten & S. Axelrod (Eds.), *Behavior analysis and treatment* (pp. 75–99). New York: Plenum Press.

Mace, F. C., & Shea, M. C. (1990). New directions in behavior analysis for the treatment of severe behavior disorders. In S. L. Harris & J. S. Handelman (Eds.), *Aversive and nonaversive interventions: Controlling life threatening behavior by the developmentally disabled* (pp. 57–79). New York: Springer.

Meyer, L., & Evans, I. (1986). Modification of excess behavior: An adaptive and functional approach for education and community contexts. In R. Horner, L. Meyer, & H. Fredericks (Eds.), *Education of learners with severe handicaps: Exemplary service strategies* (pp. 315–350). Baltimore: Brookes.

Meyer, L., & Evans, I. (1989). *Nonaversive intervention for behavior problems: A manual for home and community.* Baltimore: Brookes.

Millinson, J. R., & Leslie, J. C. (1979). *Principles of behavioral analysis* (2nd ed.). New York: Macmillan.

Mithaug, D. E., & Hanawalt, D. A. (1978). The validation of procedures to assess prevocational task preferences in retarded adults. *Journal of Applied Behavior Analysis, 11,* 153–162.

O'Neill, R. E., Horner, R. H., Albin, R. W., Sprague, J. R., Storey, K., & Newton, J. S. (1997). *Functional assessment and program development for problem behavior: A practical handbook* (2nd ed.). Pacific Grove, CA: Brooks/Cole.

Parsons, M. B., Reid, D. H., Reynolds J., & Bumgarner, M. (1990). Effects of chosen versus assigned jobs on the work performance of persons with severe handicaps. *Journal of Applied Behavior Analysis, 23,* 253–258.

Patterson, G.R. (1982). *Coercive family process.* Eugene, OR: Castalia.

Reichle, J. (1994). *Response efficiency from an interventionist's perspective.* Unpublished manuscript, University of Minnesota, Minneapolis.

Reichle, J. (1995). *Using preferred items to compete with attention-motivated challenging behavior during bus rides.* Unpublished manuscript, University of Minnesota, Minneapolis.

Schroeder, S. R., Mulick, J. A., & Rojahn, J. (1980). The definition, taxonomy, epidemiology, and ecology of self-injurious behavior. *Journal of Autism and Developmental Disorders, 10,* 417–432.

Singer, G., Singer, J., & Horner, R. (1987). Using pretask requests to increase the probability of compliance for students with severe disabilities. *Journal of the Association for Persons With Severe Handicaps, 12,* 287–291.

Smeets, P. M. (1971). Some characteristics of mental defectives displaying self-mutilative behaviors. *Training School Bulletin, 68,* 131–135.

Taylor, J. C., & Carr, E. G. (1993). Reciprocal social influences in the analysis and intervention of severe challenging behavior. In J. Reichle & D. Wacker (Eds.), *Communicative approaches to the management of challenging behavior* (pp. 63–81). Baltimore: Brookes.

Tolan, P., & Guerra, N. (1994). *What works in reducing adolescent violence: An empirical review of the field.* Boulder: University of Colorado, Center for the Study & Prevention of Violence.

Turnbull, H. R., Guess, D., Backus, L. M., Barber, P. A., Fiedler, C. R., Helmstetter, E., & Sumners, J. A. (1986). A model for analyzing the moral aspects of special education and behavioral interventions: The moral aspects of aversive procedures. In P. R. Dokecki & R. M. Zaner (Eds.), *Ethics of dealing with persons with severe handicaps* (pp. 167–210). Baltimore: Brookes.

Vollmer, T. R., Iwata, B. A., Zarcone, J. R., Smith, R. G., & Mazaleski, J. L. (1993). The role of attention in the treatment of attention-maintained self-injurious behavior: Noncontingent reinforcement and differential reinforcement of other behavior. *Journal of Applied Behavior Analysis, 26,* 9–21.

Vollmer, T. R., Marcus, B. A., & Ringdahl, J. E. (1995). Noncontingent escape as treatment for self-injurious behavior maintained by negative reinforcement. *Journal of Applied Behavior Analysis, 28,* 15–26.

Wacker, D., Steege, M., Northrup, J., Sasso, G., Berg, W., Reimers, T., Cooper, L., Cigrand, K., & Donn, L. (1990). A component analysis of functional communication training across three topographies of severe behavior problems. *Journal of Applied Behavior Analysis, 23,* 417–429.

Walker, H. M., Colvin, G., & Ramsey, E. (1995). *Antisocial behavior in public school: Strategies and best practices.* Pacific Grove, CA: Brookes/Cole.

Will, M. C. (1984). Educating children with learning problems: A shared responsibility. *Exceptional Children, 52,* 411–415.

Author Note

This work was supported in part by Grant No. HO24D40006, A Replication and Dissemination of a Model of Inservice Training and Technical Assistance to Prevent Challenging Behaviors in Young Children, from the U. S. Department of Education; and by Contract No. H133B80048, Research and Training Center on Community Living from the National Institute on Disability and Rehabilitation Research.

Considerations in the Design of Effective Treatment

Judith E. Favell
James F. McGimsey
AdvoServ
Mount Dora, Florida

Challenging behavior has perhaps commanded more resources, research, and rhetoric than any other area in developmental disabilities. Decades of effort have brought problems such as self-injurious behavior out of the psychodynamic mist and into clear perspective as lawful behavior, amenable to change (Favell, 1982). Treatment has evolved from the simplistic, sometimes heavy-handed methods of early efforts to the comprehensive, elegant, and functionally based strategies employed today. In the present era, behaviors such as self-injury, aggression, property destruction, and other topographies of problems no longer loom as mysterious and untreatable barriers that prevent participation in a productive and happy life outside of an institution. However, this time of relative enlightenment should not imply that all is known about these disorders and that all who display them are helped. Instead, much remains to be done. While relatively benign and straightforward problems are increasingly addressed at earlier ages and in more natural ways, other individuals evidencing more complex, puzzling, and dangerous problems percolate up through programs and placements, requiring new models of analysis and treatment.

Individuals who evidence a mental health disorder in addition to a developmental disability are sometimes viewed as requiring a new model of analysis and treatment. The proper, indeed crucial, recognition that the needs of these individuals may differ from those without psychiatric disturbances has led to questions about whether and how their behavioral challenges may differ as well (Nezu, Nezu, & Gill-Weiss, 1992). Is the aggression of an individual with depression and retardation different from the aggression of one who is not depressed? Are the conditions and contingencies that control and maintain that aggression different as a result of depression? For example, are the typical mechanisms of positive reinforcement (e.g., attention) or negative reinforcement (e.g., escape) still applicable if a person shows evidence of mental illness? Does it become essential to introduce intervening and intraorganismic variables to account for the behavior? Very important, are the strategies for treating challenging behavior fundamentally altered by the coexistence of mental illness and a developmental disability?

This chapter explores some of the issues involved with understanding and treating the behavioral challenges of people experiencing both a mental disturbance and a developmental disability. These issues pertain to the full range of mental retardation, including individuals diagnosed in the severe and profound range of disability. Though at this juncture some answers are clear, other questions will only be answered through the same process of systematic research that produced the effective approaches to behavior problems prevalent in developmental disabilities today. Awaiting the definitive results from this continuing research, we highlight in the following pages several fundamental considerations in the development of effective treatment for behavioral challenges in individuals who have a mental illness and varying types and degrees of developmental disabilities.

Starting With the Basics

An initial and major consideration in approaching behavioral challenges in this population is to refrain from unsubstantiated lore about the fundamental differences that may apply. Diagnoses of joint psychopathology and retardation should not immediately imply that all of the rules have changed and an entirely new set of approaches applies. A dual diagnosis is beneficial if it has prescriptive power, for example, in considering the inclusion of psychoactive medication or other appropriate treatment modalities. Such diagnoses are not helpful if they imply the irrelevance of fundamental principles of behavior. Unless compelling objective evidence indicates otherwise, the most parsimonious, the most efficacious approach is one of applying fundamental principles, clarified through decades of research, to each case in which behavioral challenges must be ameliorated. Evidence to this point suggests that variations on the instructional and reinforcement strategies found effective with individuals with mental retardation will be effective with people experiencing psychological disturbances as well. Of course, these methods will be altered to the unique circumstances of the individual; such individualization is at the core of all functional assessment and good behavior-analytic practice. However, such individualization does not imply that basic principles change when a diagnosis of mental illness is introduced. We strongly recommend that rather than assuming the rules are different for individuals with dual diagnoses, clinicians address all challenging behavior through well-understood processes. Rigorous and sensitive evaluation of the efficacy of treatment with each individual will lead to changes in strategies where indicated.

Ensuring a Safe, Engaging, and Orderly Environment

Perhaps the clearest common needs among all individuals with behavioral challenges rest with basic features in their living environments. Thus the design of effective treatment must begin with consideration of basic elements of the adequacy of each individual's social and physical milieu.

A safe, humane environment that encourages the development and use of functional skills and likewise effectively addressees problems is crucial to all individuals in all settings. Such environmental dimensions promote individuals' overall well-being, define basic elements of quality of life, and serve as the foundation for successful amelioration of behavioral challenges. These elements have been described elsewhere in the context of treatment of individuals with developmental disabilities (Favell & McGimsey, 1993), but their applicability to those with mental disturbances deserves equal emphasis.

First, it is essential that environments supporting individuals with challenges are safe for all within them (Hannah, Christian, & Clark, 1981). It is not possible to make rational decisions, to institute proactive therapeutic strategies, or even to maintain a modicum of natural and positive interaction when people are apprehensive and oriented toward crises. Thus, *the first consideration must be safety*, ensuring that the physical environment is not hazardous, that all individuals follow well-specified safety protocols, and that explicit and effective methods are available to handle emergencies, including behavioral outbursts. Such safety considerations are decidedly not confined to larger residential settings; indeed it may be more difficult to reduce risk of harm in smaller, individualized arrangements. Thus, regardless of the setting or circumstance, safety must be considered in developing effective treatment, and a sound risk-management plan instituted as an essential part of overall treatment.

A second fundamental feature of humane and therapeutic environments is *the engagement of individuals in meaningful and enjoy-*

able interactions and activities (Risley, 1990). An engaging environment affords ample opportunity for choice, provides activities and materials that are demonstrably reinforcing and that support individuals' competence and well-being, and features frequent opportunity for interaction with others. A counterpoint to an engaging environment can be seen too frequently in residential and community settings in which individuals have few constructive activities to do, have tasks imposed for their presumed habilitative value but with no consideration for their reinforcing properties, and endure lengthy periods in which they receive little positive social interaction. The degree to which an environment is enriched and responsive, and the degree to which this is confirmed through the actual demonstration of engagement by individuals within it, remains one of the most basic and predictive dimensions of a humane and therapeutic environment (Risley & Favell, 1979). This dimension is not naturally and automatically addressed by movement into more individualized and community-inclusive living arrangements. These environments can be as socially and materially sterile and as devoid of options and activities as the institutional settings they replace. Thus, direct and unbiased observation must serve as the basis of assessing the engagement value of an environment, not a priori assumptions or philosophical beliefs about the inherent virtue of one environment over the other (Risley & Cataldo, 1973).

A third environmental feature on which effective treatment rests is orderliness. Order is subject to wide interpretation, but in our view consists of two basic dimensions: predictability and structure (Favell & Reid, 1988). Predictability refers to the nature and degree of change in an environment, particularly unanticipated change. Adverse reaction to change is relatively common among individuals with developmental disabilities and mental disturbances, and change is regularly implicated in provoking the occurrence of actual behavioral outbursts. Unfortunately, change in caregivers, daily schedules, availability of desired activities, and other events is common in environments serving people with challenges. Instituting a predictable, orderly rhythm of life and social milieu is not necessarily an easy task but is nevertheless essential for quality of life and effective treatment. Though some causes of variability (e.g., caregiver turnover) may be difficult to control, many other sources of unpredictability can be corrected. Careful planning, clear communication, precisely specified protocols, and competency-based staff training are examples of well-known and readily available solutions that can dramatically impact the predictability of services. The absence of these methods of increasing the reliability of supports often points to the lack of a systems approach in the setting, an issue addressed later in this chapter. The point for the present is that for many individuals with behavioral challenges, predictability is a desirable if not essential aspect of their environment, both to ensure consistency in their lives and therapeutic regimes and to remove unnecessary provocation of their behavior problems.

A second aspect of order relates to the degree of structure in the environment. Structure has acquired a relatively negative connotation, invoking scenarios of strictly enforced routines, rigid schedules, lack of choice, and limited opportunity for self-direction. This type of structure characterized many residential programs in the past and epitomized the institutional practices that are devalued in current service settings. Contemporary practice places a premium on more naturalized and relaxed daily rhythms, offering the individual frequent opportunities for choice in the nature and sequence of activities in other aspects of daily life.

The value placed on this greater latitude and independence is assumed to be most appropriate and indeed essential for individuals with more advanced skills and cognitive abilities. Because the skills and abilities of many individuals with a diagnosis of mental illness fall within this spectrum, the assumption may be made that less structure is always reasonable and beneficial. In reality this may or may not be the case. Once again, it is essential to recognize that what constitutes an ideal environment must be decided on an individual basis, determined functionally through direct and systematic observation (Mithaug & Hanawalt, 1978; Parsons, Reid, Reynolds, & Bumgarner, 1990). Just as we cannot presume reinforcers, we similarly cannot predict or pronounce what function other environmental elements will serve until they are empirically tested.

The importance of empirical validation applies even to individuals who can clearly communicate preferences and opinions. Though they clearly can and should contribute in the design of their therapeutic milieu, their preferences and opinions should be matched with actual validation of the functional relation between the individuals' behavior and its environmental context. In short, whatever the individual says about the role or desirability of structure or any other aspect of her environment, all should remain open to information on the actual function these serve when experienced and observed directly. This recommendation certainly does not derive from an assumption of impairments associated with mental illness or developmental disabilities. It is based instead on the well-known lack of correspondence between what people say and what they actually do. Just as tests of correspondence are appropriate for all, they similarly have a place in the development of effective treatment for the individuals who are the focus of discussion here. One may say that he has or will arrive to his job promptly and work productively all day without prompts or support of any kind. However, direct observation may reveal the lack of correspondence between his verbal pronouncements and actual behavior. In such a case, all may agree that additional structure is indicated to avoid his being terminated from the job. Similarly, an individual may indicate that she functions well without medication but nevertheless her behavior may be observed to deteriorate badly when she forgets or refuses her medications. Once again, an increase in structure may be the agreed-upon solution.

In general, development of effective treatment rests upon having in place environmental arrangements that ensure safety, promote constructive engagement, and provide optimal levels and types of order in terms of both predictability and structure. These elements, basic to the well-being of all individuals, must be defined and developed to meet the unique characteristics and needs of each person with challenging behavior.

Promoting Independence and Competence

An additional and crucial aspect of an environment that can support treatment for behavioral challenges relates to the degree to which it supports the development and maintenance of independence and competence. This point appears almost axiomatic in an era when recommended treatment always rests heavily on teaching skills to replace the problem. While this emphasis on skill development is obvious, its actual and proper implementation is far from common. Individuals with challenging behavior can too often be found in environments that do not encourage their growth and development, a fact seen in both the lack of systematic training programs and in few performance requirements being placed on the individuals.

The reasons and rationales for the lack of training, when observed, vary widely. First, it has always been the case that individuals with challenging behavior often effectively negate attempts at training by threats or displays of problems. When such escape-motivated behavior is in evidence, it can be difficult to ensure that caregivers pursue training goals, knowing their demands may provoke problems. Thus, despite all philosophical pronouncements, support plans, and training protocols, actual evidence of training activities and performance expectations may be in very short supply.

Second, an emerging and unfortunate perspective on structured training is becoming apparent. Perhaps in protest to the years of active treatment and forms of habilitation required by standards such as the Title XIX Medicaid Reimbursement Program for Intermediate Care Facilities for the Mentally Retarded (ICF-MR), it is now increasingly common to encounter attitudes that eschew training altogether. One rationale seems to be that in the right environment, individuals will learn needed skills naturally and will no longer require more structured and contrived training. Further, it is proposed that instead of expecting the individual to change his behavior, the environment should be altered to conform to that person's needs. This perspective is reflected in a wide variety of ways that in our view range from reasonable to ridiculous. For example, countless hours of training in shoe tying can be saved by the purchase of loafers, a simple and rational environmental accommodation. Similarly, other training activities can be rethought or deleted altogether with careful assessments of preferences and existing strengths. Individuals need not be subjected to extensive training in meal preparation with the availability of microwaves, arduous training in leisure skills when recreational preferences can be identified, and nonfunctional training in vocational readiness when an actual job can supply the target and context of good work performance. These highly reasonable accommodations can replace unnecessary, futile, and disruptive training activities.

In contrast, other examples of environmental accommodation do not contribute to individuals' independence and competence and instead risk inadvertently supporting dependent and aberrant forms of behavior. The most extreme, but actual, cases can be seen in situations where few if any demands are placed on the individual. Decreasing all requirements to learn or perform appears to derive from an overzealous application of an otherwise legitimate part of treatment: environmental alteration to reduce situations that provoke problems (Carr & Newsom, 1985). It also emanates from a philosophical movement that places a premium on accepting and valuing individuals as they are rather than viewing them as in need of fixing. This philosophy is often contrasted with the traditional emphasis on habilitation in general and a reaction against behavior analysts in particular. Behavior analysts are depicted as obsessed with their own need to control, as oriented principally if not exclusively toward changing individuals, and are never satisfied with their current repertoire. Such a depiction is both unfair to behavior analysis and potentially harmful to people with challenging behavior. Behavior analysis has always included environmental accommodation as a fundamental part of training and treatment and has rejected only one version of acceptance and accommodation: custodial care. It was viewed as intolerable to see an individual fed who could (and later did) learn to feed himself, live in diapers when she could be toilet-trained, remain in restraints due to self-injury when such behavior could be treated. These skill deficits and behavioral excesses and the custodial practices that supported them were indeed intolerable to behavior analysts. The discipline has spent three decades demonstrating that people do not have to live in dependent states, treated in well-intentioned but demeaning ways, nor do they have to suffer the effects of incapacitating drugs, restraints, and other means of controlling their problem behavior. Despite or possibly because of the success of helping people change and grow, behavioral philosophy and methods are now sometimes viewed as too directive and controlling for new approaches termed *person-centered*. Unfortunately, when these new philosophies gravitate to extremes of acceptance over change and accommodation over learning, they risk returning to a thinly veiled, politically correct version of a custodial mentality. Person-centered values are perfectly compatible with the methods of behavior analysis, and the two combined in reasonable and skillful hands can properly foster independence and competence in the individual while avoiding overzealous or ill-conceived approaches to training and treatment.

Analyzing Maintaining Variables

The need for functional and structural assessment and analysis of challenging behavior is as central for designing treatment for this group of individuals as for any other. It is essential that we understand the varying effects of antecedent events on problem and other behavior (structural analysis) and the relative function of differential consequences on those problems and on alternative behavior as well (functional analysis). The principles and methods of these assessments and analyses are addressed in this and other volumes and need not be repeated here (see Vol. 27, No. 2 [1994] of the *Journal of Applied Behavior Analysis)*. However, several points bearing on the successful conduct and use of such analyses bear comment.

First, when individuals have multiple and complex dimensions in their clinical profiles and particularly when these dimensions are articulated in sophisticated ways that invoke difficult-to-observe antecedents and consequences, the concepts and methods of functional and structural assessment may seem inappropriately narrow and primitive. How can these behavioral assessments truly capture the role of, for example, psychosis or depression in the manifestation of a behavior problem? It would seem somehow that the principles and particulars should be different when dimensions of mental illness such as these are in evidence. The point made earlier in this chapter applies here: We must proceed with what we know about fundamental principles underlying behavioral problems and ensure that we understand how environmental and biological factors are influencing the behavior of concern.

The information gleaned through functional and structural assessment can contribute to the design of treatment that can then be implemented and evaluated. If the effects of this treatment are found lacking in terms of meaningful clinical outcomes, other interpretations and treatment modalities may be brought to bear. The essential point is not to overlook the fundamental and known influence of basic principles or to assume that they are not relevant in understanding or treating a particular behavioral disorder. Other interpretations and modalities can be introduced and tested if and when the problem appears to defy the existing array of therapeutic possibilities. Proceeding from known principles and a highly developed literature is a far more defensible strategy than to assume that entirely new rules and principles must be invoked and wholly novel treatment modalities discovered.

Though we argue for parsimony in

analyzing the behavior of individuals with diagnoses of both mental illness and developmental disabilities, it is also suggested that our observational and analytical methods remain open to the rich array of possible variables affecting behavior. The functional and structural assessments in common use today are designed to clarify and quantify the myriad variables operating in an individual's environment and life. These methods have advanced our knowledge of the basic mechanisms and classes of antecedent events, establishing operations and reinforcement systems (O'Neill, Horner, Albin, Storey, & Sprague, 1990; Repp & Singh, 1990). This organization of information for both individual and heuristic purposes has made an invaluable contribution to both the understanding and the treatment of behavior disorders. However, this standardization of information may have the inadvertent effect of limiting our creativity and narrowing our perspective. For example, *demands* are a commonly cited antecedent provoking outbursts, but they are only one of countless events that may control escape or avoidance behavior. Through repeated recitations of the role of demands in setting the occasion for problems, we may either overlook the countless varieties and nuances of what constitutes *demands* or may ignore the operation of many other events as well. What if the demand is issued by an internal voice? What if depression transforms simple requests into monumental tasks? If our standardized observational systems or our narrow definition of demands disallows the inclusion of these variations of antecedent events, crucial mistakes may be made in designing effective treatment. What about other setting events, ones that are more temporally remote and seemingly indirect in their influence and less often cited as the usual suspects in provoking problems? Space must be reserved within our conceptual framework and measurement formats to allow the inclusion of all antecedents that may exert control over the occurrence of behavioral problems. This does not require invoking new philosophies or principles; it simply involves remaining open to the subtle, remote, shifting array of possible examples within our present paradigms. We should not dismiss "voices" as a valid antecedent but instead should attempt to link them to external referents (e.g., an aura) or use the individual's report that these are occurring to assess their relation to subsequent outbursts. A letter received weeks before that saddens or irritates, holiday seasons, premenstrual syndrome, lack of insight about why one's family does not call—all of these may provoke problems and must therefore be included in their analyses.

Similar points apply to the *consequence* side of the analysis. In conducting functional analyses and assessments, it is essential to remain open to widely divergent versions of the basic reinforcement mechanism found to maintain problem behavior. While immediate and obvious attention may not be apparent as the mechanism of reinforcement, more subtle, unusual, and peculiar versions of positive reinforcement may be found to be operational. We have treated life-threatening and intractable forms of self-injury with reinforcers such as gaudy clothing, smelling feet, and physical restraint provided for the display of noninjurious behavior (Favell, McGimsey, & Jones, 1978, 1981). Such individualized, unusual reinforcers may not fit handily into our functional analytic recording methods, but when we do not include them we may miss important elements in the design of effective treatment. If we overlook such potentially powerful yet subtle or unusual reinforcers, the individual and his or her problem may appear to exceed our present understanding, lie beyond known treatment modalities, and therefore call for the need for new principles and technology.

Instead, we recommend that (a) practitioners proceed from a position of parsimony and assume that fundamental principles of learning and environmental control apply to all organisms and (b) use the methods of functional and structural analysis to organize data, but (c) not allow current recording methods and analytic paradigms to blind us to the rich array of variables that can influence behavior. Using this strategy, we can begin to address the needs of individuals that appear beyond our current understanding and analysis and make sense of the seemingly more complex conditions and contingencies that govern their problems.

We approach this task with optimism, remembering that, only two decades ago, the behavior problems of individuals with developmental disabilities were viewed as exceeding the reach of available technology. In a much shorter period, the problems of individuals with multiple challenges are similarly becoming understood and predictable.

Designing and Using Effective Treatment

Treatment of behavioral challenges has advanced over the last decades from singular and simple interventions to a comprehensive and complex array of elements, combined into interlocking and synergistic strategies. These elements are now well known.

1. Diagnoses and treatment for the biological factors and medical conditions that may be contributing to the problem, including the appropriate use of pharmacotherapy for identified psychopathology directly or indirectly associated with the challenging behavior.

2. Assessment and analysis of the environmental conditions and contingencies that are functional in maintaining the challenging behavior, and explicit inclusion of this information in all therapeutic and living arrangements.

3. Alteration of environmental conditions that provoke problems are altered or removed, and circumstances that set the occasion for appropriate alternative behaviors predominate in the person's day and life.

4. Use of instructional methods and reinforcement systems to strengthen behavior that will functionally replace the problems and to strengthen adaptive skills that will allow the individual to function in environments in which the problem will be less likely.

5. Reduction of reinforcement for the problem, specifically decreasing the

magnitude and frequency of reinforcement that the challenging behavior previously produced. This decrease is a relative one, involving the differential shift of reinforcement from problem behavior to alternative elements of the individuals' repertoire that are more benign and adaptive in a conventionally desirable way.

6. Arrangement of specific consequences for the problem itself if the behavior remains dangerous or disruptive despite reasonable attempts to treat it.

7. Systematic programming for generalization and maintenance, ensuring that the arrangements that effectively resulted in improvement in the first place are sufficiently in place in all settings and times to enhance the likelihood that improvement will be pervasive and durable.

These components and the comprehensive strategy that they comprise have been developed and refined over many years of research. They have been validated by countless clinical applications demonstrating the efficacy of these behavioral approaches to many problems with many people in many types of settings.

While these advances are solid, it may be useful to highlight a number of points about our emerging technology. First, it is important to place the components of the comprehensive strategy into their proper synergistic role. Medical treatment for an ear infection, asthma, or flu may effectively resolve a biological condition associated with the behavioral disturbance, but typically will do little to alter the social contingencies that may be reinforcing the problem. Thus, it is often essential to address both the medical and social variables that operate; affecting either alone will likely not be sufficient. Similarly, reducing reinforcement of a problem is often not feasible or sufficient without simultaneously increasing reinforcement for alternative behavior. Viewed this way, *extinction* and *timeout* do not stand alone as interventions, but must coexist with enhanced reinforcement contingencies for alternative behavior to produce significant effects. Conversely, the same is true for reinforcement procedures such as differential

reinforcement of other behavior (DRO) and differential reinforcement of alternative behavior (DRA). It is typically not effective to increase reinforcement for alternative, appropriate behavior without systematically holding the line on reinforcement for the problem itself. Impacting only one part of the differential reinforcement equation is typically not sufficient to truly tip the weight of reinforcement contingencies in a therapeutic direction.

In general, individual elements of the overall treatment strategy should typically not be viewed or employed in isolation from the others. Each contributes an essential and complementary part to the treatment formula, but must be combined with the other components to address all relevant aspects of the problem and achieve meaningful clinical outcomes. Rarely will any single element employed by itself have as striking or significant effects. Thus, in most clinical applications, the entire treatment strategy, with all of its synergistic elements, should be implemented concurrently. These elements should not be viewed as alternative or competing approaches to be plucked from a menu and used in isolation. Research will continue to dissect the relative effects of various procedures and parameters, but the clinical demand remains strong and immediate. Until research informs us otherwise, all of the components listed above should be reflected in any plan designed to address challenging behavior.

One final example of the interdependence of the elements of the comprehensive treatment strategy bears special mention. In the last decade, the role of antecedent events in the maintenance of problems and in their treatment has received increased attention (Pyles & Bailey, 1990). Examples abound of altering or eliminating conditions such as training demands that provoke problems and, conversely, of elaborating conditions that set the occasion for more appropriate behavior and fewer problems. These antecedent arrangements are an efficient and effective element in achieving behavior change. However, they do not stand alone as either a cause of or an intervention for challenging behavior. The function of antecedents lies with the differential contingencies with which they have been paired; their stimulus properties do not exist or endure apart from their associated consequences. Thus alteration of antecedent events may be a part of treatment, but it is not an alternative treatment, serving, as it is sometimes said, as an alternative to contingency management. Altered antecedent events are instead synergistic parts of an overall behavior analytic strategy of treatment and certainly not a substitute for behavior analysis itself.

Another set of issues pertaining to our emerging technology relates to the manner in which we interpret and analyze advances. While it is crucial to remain responsive to and reinforce the development of new methods, it is equally important to critically analyze claims that methods are novel and different. In our zeal to elaborate and refine the technology, there may be tendencies to name or rename phenomena that are in fact well-established in the concepts and practices of treatment. For example, DRA has been a well-understood procedure and a recognized part of comprehensive treatment for many years. Its application to a class of behavior, communication, has contributed greatly to treatment efficacy, providing individuals with alternative communicative means of achieving reinforcers that previously were obtained principally by engaging in problem behavior (Durand, 1990). Though a very enlightening and important application, the teaching and reinforcement of communication belongs as part of well-known principles and methods. It does not stand as a new phenomenon in itself nor a singular cure for all behavior disorders. However, it is difficult to dissuade consumers and inexperienced practitioners from touting it in just those terms. Despite the pressures, it is important that we reference our methods against what is known and properly place our advances in the context of their underlying principles and previously established procedures. Such explicit referencing serves the crucial goal of continuity and advances the systematic accumulation of knowledge. Labels and descriptors that emphasize the novelty of an approach and tend to disassociate it from what has gone before reinforce the image of treatment as a "bag of

tricks" and the field as a meandering search for the Holy Grail. To avoid this misleading and nonproductive course, it is essential that we examine and interpret our advances in their proper technological and conceptual framework.

A third set of issues bears on the development of effective treatment for individuals with both mental illness and developmental disabilities. Our discussion has emphasized the strategies of treatment that derive principally from the field of developmental disabilities. When and what other modalities of treatment may be applicable when diagnoses of mental illness are introduced? Some modes of therapy immediately arise as promising or proven parts of treatment. Pharmacotherapy is the most obvious and well-substantiated clinical intervention for the symptoms of mental illness. It has been empirically shown to directly or indirectly affect a number of challenging behaviors (Wilson, 1989). Problems such as self-injury, aggression, and property destruction may respond directly to judiciously selected medication, or they may be affected by pharmacological treatment of correlated psychiatric symptoms such as psychosis or depression. Other chapters (see Part 2, this volume) detail the positive effects and limitations of pharmacotherapy with these individuals and their problems.

In contrast to this well-substantiated approach to the treatment of problems in this population, other extrapolations may not be as logical or as empirically justified. One example can be seen in the use of various counseling strategies with problems in individuals with pervasive cognitive limitations. For example, the logic seems to be that since psychotherapy has been a common mode of therapy for others with depression, it should be employed with a depressed person with mental retardation as well. It is assumed that if an aspect of mental illness is in evidence, that individual's aggression, property destruction, or self-injury is a more complex phenomenon than its counterpart in individuals with developmental disabilities alone. Being more complex, a different and more complex prescriptive formula is called for.

Such automatic extrapolations have resulted in clinical interventions that are in some cases odd in appearance and highly questionable in effects. Such a perspective ignores the vast body of knowledge regarding effective treatment for a wide range of problems and people. It also risks exposing people to ineffective, even deleterious, clinical strategies.

The standard of appropriate and effective treatment rests on demonstrable improvement in problem behavior, and any therapeutic modality that purports to have relevance with this population should be held to that standard. By this criterion, behavior analysis is not held automatically to be inappropriate, nor are other therapeutic modalities automatically judged to be relevant and useful. Measures of actual behavior change should serve as the basis of selecting or rejecting any clinical strategy.

One final issue regarding the development of effective treatment bears mention. Treatment strategies have evolved and advanced from the use of individual procedures applied in relative isolation to the complex and comprehensive constellation of procedures described in this chapter and volume. This overall strategy is itself evolving, now increasingly applied as less of a contrived set of procedures and more as a set of arrangements that involve lifestyle changes. Within this framework, movement to a more individualized living environment, getting a job that is functional and interesting, and developing friendships within the natural community not only comprise desired outcomes in themselves, but also consist of the means of addressing an individual's challenging behavior. The assumption is that challenging behavior will be ameliorated in the natural milieu, improved by the individualized, meaningful, and enjoyable milieu in which the individual now lives.

Anecdotes and empirical evidence support the beneficial effects of such lifestyle arrangements on challenging behavior. However, two points deserve mention. When and if changes in lifestyle positively impact behavior, the processes at work are not mystical or mysterious but instead reflect the operation of well-known principles of learning and behavior.

These principles, including positive and negative reinforcement, stimulus control, and stimulus and response generalization, operate as surely in these arrangements as they do in more contrived treatment applied in a more controlled clinical sense. If an individual's new home, job, and circle of friends reinforce nonproblematic patterns of behavior relative to aberrant alternatives, if the previous provocations for problems are reduced, if medical conditions exacerbating the problem are resolved, and so on, that person's challenging behavior is likely to be reduced or resolved. If the conditions and contingencies in these new arrangements do not differentially set the occasion for and reinforce desirable alternative behavior over the more problematic patterns, the problems will likely continue.

In short, lifestyle approaches to challenging behavior, while representing the desirable next generation of services, still rest upon basic principles and sound practices. If these are reflected in the individual's life arrangements, positive effects on challenging behavior can be expected. If they are not, it is likely that challenging behavior will reemerge in these circumstances and may figure in the individual's return to living arrangements that are less optimal in other respects.

Supporting Treatment Through Systems Approaches

An additional consideration in the development and conduct of effective treatment for behavioral challenges lies in the soundness of the systems that support treatment. It has been understood for many years that the quality and consistency of all services rest on whether there are systems in place to enable and enforce those services. These systems range from the methods by which staff are trained and supervised to the manner in which schedules and activities are orchestrated to ensure the smooth and proper delivery of quality services. The particulars of these systems have been described by Todd Risley and his living environments group (O'Brien, Porterfield, Herbert-Jackson, & Risley, 1979; Risley & Favell, 1979).

With staff training, for example, the recommended system includes several elements: (a) careful determination of the most functional and important targets for caregiver training (e.g., how to assist with bathing); (b) use of checklists detailing the elements of the required task; (c) training conducted in the actual situation in which the task would ordinarily occur; (d) methods of training consisting of role-playing, practice under decreasing prompts and supervision, performance-based feedback, and training to a level of observed and documented proficiency; and (e) periodic reassessment of the adequacy of staff performance with positive and corrective feedback to reinforce the best and control the rest.

This system contrasts rather sharply with the style with which staff training has been and is typically conducted. Traditional staff training too often includes large amounts of irrelevant and nonfunctional information, lengthy written narratives, and didactic presentations on general principles that do not convey the essentials of actually completing the task; training under simulated and contrived conditions that requires large extrapolations (and often generalizes poorly) to actual situations; training and testing based more on verbal mastery than on actual performance; and the assumption that training is sufficient to ensure good performance and does not require ongoing assessment and feedback.

Years of research and demonstration have supported the efficacy of this competency-based system of staff training over traditional methods, and improvements in staff training became increasingly common in residential settings and staff development departments (Lattimore, Stephens, Favell, & Risley, 1984). However, as community settings took root and individualized living arrangements have begun to sprout, the importance or even need for systems of caregiver training have ironically appeared to wither. The assumption in some quarters appears to be that more natural settings naturally foster good performance, and thus the need for systematic caregiver assessment and training is reduced. This logic is very

unfortunate in light of the ongoing need for skill and proficiency in personnel providing support for individuals with challenges. Dealing with challenging behavior requires technical skill; the recommended interventions may appear to violate common sense and are difficult and arduous to follow in a consistent and high-quality fashion. Because of such factors, systematic training in these interventions is not less relevant or important in smaller, more integrated settings. Any situation purporting or attempting to address an individual's challenging behavior requires functional and efficient training for the people who will supply that support.

Similar points can be made about other areas in which systems are viewed as necessary for institutional settings but of no relevance to more community-based environments. An obvious area is caregiver support and supervision. Consider the poor levels of compliance to prescribed treatment and care regimes reportedly found in institutional settings. The assumption seems to be that these problems disappear when natural motivations and supportive arrangements are in place. Surely, one will not miss a scheduled social outing with a relative, fail to fix a special diet for a person living in one's home, lapse into low rates or negative patterns of interaction with a foster child. Of course, it is now clear that any and all of these undesirable patterns can emerge in any situation. The reality is that to ensure consistent and high-quality service, caregivers in all settings need support. Beyond training, they need the ongoing and direct presence of another, help in solving the problems that interfere with good service, positive reinforcement for providing needed support, and corrective feedback when that support lapses or declines in quality. The need for these systems does not obviate the need for systematic means of supporting the delivery of services. These systems need not appear mechanical or obtrusive, but they must nevertheless be fully functional in teaching caregivers necessary skills and ensuring that essential elements of services are indeed delivered.

271

Measuring Success

A final consideration in the design of effective treatment for challenging behavior in people with developmental disabilities and psychiatric disturbances relates to the aim and measure of success. Early treatment efforts tended to focus on a narrow range of target behaviors as measures of effectiveness. Reductions in measured rates (and sometimes intensities) of a selected target behavior, such as self-injury or aggression, were used as the principal means of judging the efficacy of treatment. Rarely were other measures, such as side effects or outcomes, available in evaluating the success of the therapeutic effort.

In current recommended practice, the aims and measures of effective treatment are greatly expanded and now include a full range of potential direct and indirect effects focusing principally on treatment outcomes. A successful result no longer rests exclusively with a decrease in the challenging behavior but also on whether and how that decrease has resulted in meaningful improvements in the person's life. Treatment efficacy is thus based on the personal outcomes it achieves in terms of enhancing an individual's living arrangements, work, leisure activities, friendships, and roles in the community (Gardner, Nudler, & Chapman, 1996).

The orientation to outcomes as a measure and standard of success represents a significant advancement in the area of challenging behavior. This standard demands that significant and meaningful improvement occur in the challenging behavior, so that individuals can live with success and without stigma as ordinary citizens. Settling for change that is apparent only on a graph, in a session, or under extremely contrived circumstances will no longer suffice. Success cannot be claimed when individuals remain sedated with medication, chronically restrained, or prohibited from participating in a full array of life experiences. All strategies and tactics of treatment should be held to this standard of social validity.

A method's appearances, claims of effectiveness, and political correctness must not be sufficient to endorse and adopt its use. Data on outcomes must continue to lead us in the selection and refinement of our approaches to challenging behaviors.

REFERENCES

Carr, E. G., & Newsom, C. (1985). Demand related tantrums: conceptualization and treatment. *Behavior Modification, 9,* 403–426.

Durand, V. M. (1990) *Severe behavior problems: A functional communication training approach.* New York: Guilford Press.

Favell, J. E. (1982). The treatment of self-injurious behavior. *Behavior Therapy, 13,* 529–554.

Favell, J. E., & McGimsey, J. F. (1993). Defining an acceptable treatment environment. In R. Van Houten & S. Axelrod (Eds.), *Behavior analysis and treatment.* New York: Plenum Press.

Favell, J. E., McGimsey, J. F., & Jones, M. L. (1978). The use of physical restraint in the treatment of self-injury and as positive reinforcement. *Journal of Applied Behavior Analysis, 11,* 225–241.

Favell, J. E., & McGimsey, J. F. & Jones, M. L. (1981). Physical restraint as positve reinforcement. *American Journal of Mental Deficiency, 85* (4), 425–432.

Favell, J. E., & Reid, D. H. (1988). Generalizing and maintaining improvement in problem behavior. In R. H. Horner, G. Dunlap, & R. L. Koegel (Eds.), *Generalization and maintenance: Lifestyle changes in applied settings* (pp. 141–169). Baltimore: Brookes.

Gardner, J. F., Nudler, S., & Chapman, M. S. (1997). Personal outcomes as measures of quality. *Mental Retardation, 35,* 195–221.

Hannah, G. T., Christian, W. P., & Clark, H. B. (Eds.). (1981). *Preservation of client rights: A handbook for practitioners providing therapeutic, educational, and rehabilitative services.* New York: Free Press.

Lattimore, J., Stephens, T. E., Favell, J. E., & Risley, T. R. (1984). Increasing direct care staff compliance to individualized physical therapy body positioning prescriptions: Prescriptive checklists. *Mental Retardation, 22,* 79–84.

Mithaug, D. E., & Hanawalt, D. A. (1978). The validation of procedures to assess prevocational task preferences in retarded adults. *Journal of Applied Behavior Analysis, 11,* 153–162.

Nezu, C. M., Nezu, A. M., & Gill-Weiss, M. J. (1992). *Psychopathology in persons with mental retardation.* Champaign, IL: Research Press.

O'Brien, M., Porterfield, J., Herbert-Jackson, E., & Risley, T. R. (1979). *The toddler center: A practical guide to day care for one- and two-year-olds.* Baltimore: University Park Press.

O'Neill, R. E., Horner, R. H., Albin, R. W., Storey, K., & Sprague, J. R. (1990). *Functional assessment of problem behavior: A practical assessment guide.* Sycamore, IL: Sycamore.

Parsons, M. B., Reid, D. H., Reynolds, J., & Bumgarner, M. (1990). Effects of chosen versus assigned jobs on the work performance of persons with severe handicaps. *Journal of Applied Behavior Analysis, 23,* 253–258.

Pyles, D. A. M., & Bailey, J. S. (1990). Diagnosing severe behavior problems. In A. C. Reff & N. N. Singh (Eds.), *Perspectives on the use of nonaversive and aversive interventions for persons with developmental disabilities* (pp. 381–401). Sycamore, IL: Sycamore.

Repp, A. C., & Singh, N. N. (Eds.). (1990). *Perspectives on the use of nonaversive and aversive interventions for persons with developmental disabilities.* Sycamore, IL: Sycamore.

Risley, T. R. (1990, November). *Treatment of severe behavior problems in persons with developmental disabilities.* Workshop presented at the annual convention of the Association for Advancement of Behavior Therapy, New York, NY.

Risley, T. R., & Cataldo, M. I. (1973). *Planned activity check: Materials for training observers.* Lawrence, KS: Center for Applied Behavior Analysis.

Risley, T. R., & Favell, J. E. (1979). Constructing a living environment in an institution. In L. A. Hamerlynck (Ed.), *Behavioral systems for the developmentally disabled: Vol. II. Institutional, clinic, and community environments* (pp. 3–24). New York: Brunner/Mazel.

Wilson, J. E. (1989). *Pharmacological treatment of the mentally retarded/mentally ill individual.* Special workshop sponsored by the American Association on Mental Retardation, Baltimore.

Discussion

Norman A. Wieseler
Eastern Minnesota Community Support Services
Faribault, Minnesota

Ronald H. Hanson
Anoka-Metro Regional Treatment Center
Anoka, Minnesota

The prevalence of challenging behavior in persons with mental health disorders and severe intellectual disabilities requires responsive and efficacious treatment. This volume espouses an integrative approach using both positive behavioral psychiatric treatment and support based on the principles of behavior analysis.

Part 1 of this book discussed the manner in which mental health disorders are diagnosed and briefly described some of the more prevalent disorders observed in this population. Ferron, Kern, Hanson, and Wieseler provided an overview from the psychiatric, pharmacologic, and behavioral perspectives. They presented some of the other diagnoses observed in this population that did not receive focused attention in the other chapters. Gardner and Willmering described the behavioral features that constitute the major mood disorders and the treatment approaches that have produced positive outcomes. Schreibman, Heyser, and Stahmer explained that the majority of people with autism also have severe mental retardation. The misdiagnosis of this disorder is remedied by more precisely defining the behavioral characteristics associated with it. The authors reviewed treatment options that have been empirically validated. Schroeder, Reese, Hellings, Loupe, and Tessel discussed recent advances in the etiology and maintaining conditions of self-injury. The treatment implications of a biobehavioral approach are factors that practitioners and service providers need to consider in their clinical practices. In the last

chapter of Part 1, Sovner and Hurley identified five commonly held, incorrect beliefs relating to mental illness and developmental disabilities and supplanted these with alternative views.

In Part 2, psychotropic medications and issues surrounding their behavioral effects were discussed. Kern presented summaries of the psychotropic medications, including those recently approved by the U.S. Food and Drug Administration (FDA). Compared to earlier approved psychotropic medications, these medications appear to provide greater clinical effectiveness along with fewer adverse side effects. In his chapter, Gates discussed the high prevalence of epilepsy in this population and the frequent adverse behavioral effects observed from antiepileptic medications, which often produce behaviors resembling psychiatric disturbance. Unfortunately, these clients often receive psychotropic medications and behavior management programs when a simple change to an alternative antiepileptic medication might eliminate these troublesome symptoms. Thompson and Symons introduced a model that integrates behavioral principles with psychotropic medication effects. They suggested that a functional assessment of the target behavior must be conducted to determine the motivational functions of the behavior, the client's reinforcement history, and how a multitude of behavior principles interact with the prescribed psychotropic medications. They concluded that a functional diagnostic approach is an effective model for selecting psychotropic medications for individuals in this population. In the final chapter of Part 2,

Kalachnik discussed the importance of empirically evaluating the behavioral outcomes and side effects of psychotropic medications. This evaluation process was explained in a way that can be readily understood by community service providers. He recommended the use of an empirical index of responsiveness to assist in medication change of dosage titration.

Part 3, the final section of this volume, discussed the treatment of challenging behavior from a behavioral perspective. Wieseler and Hanson provided a transition from a biopsychiatric model to a positive behavioral support approach by presenting an integration of the behavior analytic principles and the two traditionally separate diagnostic and intervention paradigms. In the following chapter, Miltenberger described how to conduct a functional assessment. The purpose of the functional assessment and the utility of the information obtained was clearly illustrated. The chapter by Reichle, Davis, Freeman, and Horner elucidated how the information gleaned from the functional assessment is used in designing effective treatment plans. These authors provided examples that demonstrated the frequent communicative nature of challenging behavior and the practical implementation of behavioral support strategies. Favell and McGimsey discussed the essential elements of an effective treatment environment. Without the environmental features described, it is unlikely that any therapeutic modality will produce lasting effects.

Several important implications for diagnosis and treatment of challenging behaviors have been identified:

1. The presence of psychiatric disorders in the population with developmental disabilities is much higher than it is among the nonhandicapped population. It is inferred that the incidence of mental health disorders is higher among people who have severe developmental disabilities than among individuals functioning in the mild or upper moderate range of mental retardation.

2. Although individuals with severe developmental disabilities may develop the full range of psychiatric disturbances, certain mental health disorders require heightened attention due to their frequent association with challenging behaviors.

3. The presence of mood disorders in people with severe developmental disabilities requires precise measurement of the behavioral characteristics associated with this disorder. Behavioral strategies as well as pharmacologic interventions can be effective in treating the disorder.

4. Autism has characteristics requiring focused consideration. Service providers need to be vigilant to assure this condition is not over- or underdiagnosed. The treatment of autism, employing behavior analysis principles, varies according to the individual client characteristics, the conditions under which strategies are implemented, and the empirically determined treatment results. It is important that multidisciplinary teams consider the array of options before undertaking a specific treatment regimen.

5. Within the past decade, the information concerning organic conditions associated with self-injurious behavior has greatly expanded. This has resulted in an increased variety of treatments available to mental health practitioners to reduce or eliminate the morbid results of self-injury.

6. A number of myths exist concerning the diagnosis of psychopathology in people with severe mental retardation. It is important these incorrect beliefs be dispelled to optimize treatment, especially when challenging behavior is the focus.

7. Within the past few years, there has been a dramatic increase in the number of newly approved psychotropic medications marketed for mental health disorders. These medications are equally or more efficacious than their predecessors and generally have produced fewer side effects. Many more medications are being studied for FDA approval, and their release is on the near horizon. Keeping informed about these new agents is critical for professionals and service providers who work with dually diagnosed clients.

8. The high incidence of epilepsy in individuals with severe mental retardation results in a proportionate usage of antiepileptic medication. In many individuals, these medications have adverse behavioral effects that can mimic psychopathology. Considering these adverse behavioral effects may reduce or prevent the inappropriate and unnecessary use of psychotropic medication and behavioral treatment.

9. Recognizing the interactive effect of psychotropic agents with the principles of behavioral analysis is important. Whether or not a mental health disorder is present, the function of challenging behaviors must be recognized. This variable, combined with a number of behavioral elements, often determines the effectiveness of a psychotropic agent prescribed for a challenging behavior.

10. The behavioral, as well as the physiological, measures of psychotropic effects need to be monitored. The manner in which this can be accomplished is through recording objective data on index behaviors that correlate with mental illness symptoms. It is important that the lowest optimal effective dosage of psychotropic medication be empirically determined.

11. Conducting a functional assessment of the challenging behavior is important whether or not an individual in this population has a diagnosed mental illness. Although the mental health disorder adds an additional challenge, a functional assessment continues to be helpful in the design of a treatment plan.

12. The behavioral support components that assist individuals with severe mental retardation to reduce challenging behaviors are identical whether or not a mental health disorder is present. Therefore, (a) identifying the communicative intent of behavior; (b) examining the environmental features that may contribute to challenging behavior; and (c) creating a treatment plan that alters the setting events, antecedents, or consequences are essential in reducing behavioral challenges.

13. It is essential that people with mental illness and mental retardation live in an effective treatment environment that ensures safety, meaningful and engaging activities, and orderliness in predictability and structure. A desirable treatment environment provides the infrastructure upon which effective treatment rests. Without it, neither positive behavioral support nor pharmacotherapy is likely to produce the desired treatment outcome.

14. It is essential to use what is known about the basic principles that underlie challenging behavior and incorporate the manner in which environmental and biological factors influence these behaviors in each client. An integrative approach between psychiatry and behavioral psychology provides optimal treatment and care for clients, to ensure their highest lifestyle quality.

Historically, the literature on people with developmental disabilities and mental health disorders has focused on individuals functioning in the upper moderate or mild range of retardation. By comparison, only a limited number of publications have focused on the mental health concerns of lower functioning individuals. The treatment of disturbed behavior patterns in people with mental health disorders and severe mental retardation remains a significant challenge for service providers and practitioners responsible for their care and treatment. An integrative approach, drawing from psychiatric and behavioral interventions, is likely to produce optimal effects, especially for those who do not respond to either approach alone.

Although many chapters in this book apply equally to individuals with minimal intellectual impairments, the focus here is on the client with severe developmental disabilities. This challenge is viewed optimistically. Less than three decades ago, treatment of challenging behavior in this population was considered outside the purview of behavioral psychology, and clients were sedated with moderate to heavy doses of phenothiazines. Understanding and addressing the needs of people with mental health disorders and severe developmental disabilities is a recent development and one that requires continued study and methodologically controlled research to assure that clients with dual disabilities receive the very best care and treatment.